BUILDING SOCIALISM

BUILDING SOCIALISM

The Afterlife of East German Architecture in Urban Vietnam

CHRISTINA SCHWENKEL

Duke University Press Durham and London 2020

Designed by Drew Sisk
Typeset in Minion Pro and Eurostile by Westchester Publishing Ser vices

Library of Congress Cataloging-in-Publication Data
Names: Schwenkel, Christina, author.
Title: Building socialism : the afterlife of East German architecture in urban Vietnam / Christina Schwenkel.
Description: Durham : Duke University Press, 2020. | Includes bibliographical references and index.
Identifiers: LCCN 2020016882 (print)
LCCN 2020016883 (ebook)
ISBN 9781478010012 (hardcover)
ISBN 9781478011064 (paperback)
ISBN 9781478012603 (ebook)
Subjects: LCSH: City planning—Vietnam—Vinh—German influences. | Urbanization—Vietnam—Vinh—History—20th century. | Architecture, German—Vietnam—Vinh—History—20th century. | Architecture—Political aspects—Vietnam—Vinh—History—20th century.
Classification: LCC HT169.V5 S394 2020 (print)
LCC HT169.V5 (ebook)
DDC 307.1/21609597/8—dc23
LC record available at https://lccn.loc.gov/2020016882
LC ebook record available at https://lccn.loc.gov/2020016883

Cover art: Façade of block C7 in Quang Trung housing estate, Vinh City, Vietnam, 2011. Photo by Christina Schwenkel.

Duke University Press gratefully acknowledges the University of California, Riverside, which provided funds toward the publication of this book.

CONTENTS

LIST OF FIGURES, PLATES, AND TABLES

FIGURES

PLATES

TABLES

ABBREVIATIONS

BDA	bomb damage assessment
BArch	Bundesarchiv (German Federal Archives)
CIA	Central Intelligence Agency
CACTA	Combat Air Activities
DRV	Democratic Republic of Vietnam
FRG	Federal Republic of Germany
GDR	German Democratic Republic
LOC	lines of communication
NARA	National Archives and Records Administration
NAPA	Nghệ An Provincial Archives
NPL	Nixon Presidential Library
RVN	Republic of Vietnam
SED	Socialist Unity Party (GDR)
SEADAB	Southeast Asia Database
USSR	Soviet Union
SAPMO	Stiftung Archiv der Parteien und Massenorganisationen der DDR (Foundation Archive of Parties and Mass Organizations of the GDR)
CP	Văn Phòng Chính Phủ (Collection of the Office of the Government)
PTT	Văn Phòng Phủ Thủ Tướng (Collection of the Prime Minister's Office)
VIỆT MINH	Việt Nam Độc Lập Đồng Minh (League for the Independence of Vietnam)
VND	Vietnam đồng
VNA	Vietnam National Archives

A NOTE ON TRANSLATION AND TRANSLITERATION

Vietnamese is a tonal language written in an adapted version of the Latin alphabet with additional diacritical marks to signify tones and vowel qualities. Without these diacritics, the meaning of a Vietnamese word is ambiguous. For this reason I have chosen to include diacritical marks in this book to most accurately represent terms, locations, and people's names. However, at the same time, I recognize that diacritics may prove distracting to those unfamiliar with the conventions of the language. Taking into concern both specialists and generalists who may read this book, I opted to keep all Vietnamese diacritical marks except in widely known geographical names such as Vietnam, Hanoi, Ho Chi Minh City, and Saigon. Vietnamese who have migrated to other countries often drop the diacritics from their proper names. I thus refer to individuals according to their own practice and according to their choice in name order (in Vietnam, family names are placed first). While I recognize potential inconsistencies in my own practice here (for example, Ho Chi Minh City versus Hồ Chí Minh Trail), I feel this is the most reliable solution to make the text accessible to all audiences. All translations from German and Vietnamese primary sources are my own, unless otherwise indicated.

ACKNOWLEDGMENTS

My fascination with modernist ruins took me from Buffalo, where I grew up, to Berlin, after the fall of the Wall, to Vinh. Needless to say, it has been a long journey, during which I have incurred enormous social debt. Over the course of this research, I have been the recipient of a humbling amount of goodwill, generosity, and gifts—of time, knowledge, wisdom, friendship, and resources—that I will never be able to fully reciprocate. I owe a tremendous debt of gratitude to the residents of Quang Trung housing complex in Vinh (who will remain anonymous to protect their privacy and confidentiality), who opened their doors and invited me into their remarkable, resilient community. Several people, young and old, who befriended and mentored me have passed since my fieldwork, a testament to the enduring, incapacitating effects of toxic war on their bodies. Their spirit and passion for history, and for sharing knowledge, animate the following pages. It is to their memory that I dedicate this book.

This research would not have been possible without the support of officials in Vinh who provided me with access to the archives at the Provincial People's Committee, especially the director, Nguyễn Thị Hoa, who sat and drank tea with me as we pored over files. The staff at the Municipal People's Committee were extremely generous beyond my expectations, sharing maps and floor plans of Quang Trung. I thank, especially, Nguyễn Đình Cát, for his trust. He opened all doors with his magic red stamp, and I remain profoundly grateful for his support. Hoàng Minh Truyền, director at the Nghệ An Provincial Museum, was most welcoming and gave me access to the photography archives. Nguyễn Minh Sơn, vice director of Vietnam's National Archives No. 3 in Hanoi, who came from the Hà Tĩnh/Nghệ An region, expedited my requests for documents, for which I am most thankful. The principal of the Nghệ An Technical Training School, where I attended classes on architecture, was most gracious to permit my attendance. I also express gratitude to my intrepid research assistant, Bùi Minh Thuận, and the seven students who worked on the survey—Lan Anh, Chính, Thiết, Sáu, Lan Anh, Đức, Chương—all amazing young anthropologists. The nine wardens of Quang Trung went above and beyond; this book would not have been possible without their willingness to answer my questions, share documents, and facilitate my residency in the housing blocks. Tài and Hương, and their children, Đức and Mỹ, have been my family in Vinh for the last two decades; Hương, Jewel, Diễm, and Thùy offered friendship and support. In Hanoi, I thank Linda Mazur for the years of collaboration, as well as mentors Đặng Thái Hoàng and Nguyễn Trực Luyện for conversations and inspiration to examine buildings in Vietnam more closely. Nguyễn Văn Sửu, chair of anthropology at the University of Social Sciences and Humanities, Vietnam National University, Hanoi, welcomed me as a visiting researcher, and Lương Ngọc Vinh prepared endless letters of introduction for me. Chuck Searcy and Phan Văn Hùng at Project RENEW provided bombing data for Nghệ An. Nguyễn Văn Lục (Luki), Nguyễn Sỹ Thúy, and, especially, Ngô Văn Yêm at the Vietnam-Germany chapter of the Nghệ An Union of Friendship Organizations in Vinh made immeasurable contributions to this book and to my general knowledge of Vinh's turbulent architectural history.

In Germany, I am deeply grateful to the men and women from former East Germany who shared their life histories with me—and their love of Vietnam. To maintain their anonymity, I choose not to name them here, but their friendship and trust in me to preserve their archives and document their stories have been profoundly meaningful. I also thank the staff at the German Federal Archives, SODI (Solidarity Service International), and *Neues Deutschland*.

I have been fortunate to work with a brilliant group of scholars across the University of California system. At UC Riverside, the Anthropology and Southeast Asian Studies (SEATRiP) programs have provided an especially supportive community of graduate students and colleagues. In particular, I thank Mariam Lam, Henk Maier, Sally Ness, Deborah Wong, and David Biggs. Conversations with Paul Ryer, my postsocialist comrade, enriched this work greatly. I also thank Karen Xu, Sarah Grant, Shelley Guyton, Chari Hamratanaphon, Bùi Minh Hào, and Phạm Phương Chi for their contributions to this manuscript. The Center for Ideas and Society at UCR provided intellectual and financial support through a three-year Senior Fellowship, for which I thank Georgia Warnke and Katharine Henshaw. I am extremely grateful for the support of the University of California Humanities Research Institute (UC HRI) and the "Urban Ecologies" Residential Research Group that provided a stimulating intellectual environment in which to draft sections of this book. Kavita Philip, Saloni Mathur, and Nancy Kwak offered especially insightful suggestions. A Berlin prize and residential fellowship at the American Academy in Berlin provided the ideal living and working environment for developing ideas with the support of amazing staff, including Carol Scherer and

Johana Gallup, and a cohort of brilliant scholars. For inspiring conversations and hearty laughs over meals, I thank, in particular, Vladimir Kulić, Mary Cappello, Jean Walton, and the much-mourned Moishe Postone.

Several colleagues read and generously commented on chapters of this work. I thank, especially, Erik Harms, Ann Marie Leshkowich, Quinn Slobodian, Diane Fox, and Ken MacLean. Tim Kaiser was a valuable interlocuter in the field. I also thank Zeynep Gürsel, Jen Hosek, Dave Leheny, Đinh Hồng Hải, Kimberley Zarecor, Tema Milstein, David Del Testa, Susan Ossman, Gökçe Günel, Anne Rademacher, Helen Siu, Kirsten Endres, Tom Boellstorff, Bill Maurer, Jane Ferguson, Kriszti Fehérváry, Nikhil Anand, Peter Zinoman, Megan Crowley-Matoka, Max Hirsh, April Eisman, Juliet Feibel, Dominic Boyer, Eli Rubin, Chris Hann, Elizabeth Dunn, and Łukasz Stanek for sharing ideas and extending support and encouragement. I benefited from brainstorming sessions with Liisa Malkki, who continues to be a source of inspiration. Several of the ideas here were presented at workshops and invited presentations, which helped to improve this manuscript immensely. I thank, in particular, Anne Rademacher and K. Sivaramakrishnan (Shivi) for the opportunity to join the Ecologies of Urbanism in Asia II group at the University of Hong Kong; Nguyễn Thị Phương Châm to present ideas to colleagues at the Vietnamese Academy of Social Sciences, Institute of Culture in Hanoi; Tim Bunnell to participate in the Urban Asia Futures workshop in Singapore; Kirsten Endres and Tâm Ngô for opportunities to present works in progress at the Max Planck Institutes for Social Anthropology in Halle and the Study of Religious and Ethnic Diversity in Göttingen, respectively; Johan Lindquist for the invitation to share this work with Asian Studies and Anthropology at Stockholm University; Cole Roskam to join the Socialist Design Institute seminar at the University of Hong Kong; and Martha Lampland, Hunter Bivens, and Victoria Bernal to present chapters of this work at UCSD, UCSC, and UCI. A special thanks to Ines Weizman for the unique opportunity to lecture, together with Vladimir Kulić, at Bauhaus University in Weimar. I also thank Regina Römhild, Minh Nguyen, Andreas Butter, Philipp Misselwitz, Christoph Bernhardt, Steffi Marung, Ursula Rao, and Gertrud Hüwelmeier for invitations to present sections of this work in Berlin, Bielefeld, and Leipzig. I am grateful to Mary Hancock and Smriti Srinivas for their mentorship, and for the opportunity to collaborate on the UC HRI working group on religiosity and urban place making. During the last stages of writing, generative comments from colleagues at Cornell University, as well as colleagues at UC San Diego as part of the Sawyer Seminar on cities, helped to fine-tune my arguments, especially comments from Nancy Kwak and Nancy Postero. Participation in the SSRC's

Inter-Asian Connections IV workshop in Istanbul, led by Erik Harms and John Friedmann, also enriched this manuscript. A School for Advanced Research (SAR) seminar, under the leadership of Nikhil Anand, Hannah Appel, and Akhil Gupta, sharpened my thinking about infrastructure.

Generous grants and fellowships supported both research and writing. I am grateful to Fulbright-Hays, the American Council of Learned Societies, the Deutscher Akademischer Austauschdienst (DAAD), the UC Pacific Rim Research Program, and the National Endowment for the Humanities. A subvention from the College of Humanities, Arts, and Social Sciences at UC Riverside made the color insert possible. A grant from the Graham Foundation for Advanced Studies in the Fine Arts supported production. Some of the ethnographic text in the third section of this book appeared in different form in *American Ethnologist* and *South East Asia Research*. Portions of the latter half of chapter 7 appeared in a different form in "Governing through Garbage: Waste Infrastructure Breakdown and Gendered Apathy in Vietnam" in *The Routledge Handbook of Anthropology and the City*, edited by Setha Low, © 2018 Routledge.

At Duke University Press, I am most grateful to Ken Wissoker for his enthusiastic support of this project, and I also thank Joshua Tranen for his work on the manuscript. The anonymous readers were generous in their close readings of chapters and their insightful suggestions for improvements. With a keen eye, Kristy Leissle carefully edited early drafts of chapters. Her encouragement inspired me to continue writing at moments of uncertainty. A huge thank you to Jutta Turner for her meticulous work on maps and floor plans.

My family and relatives have been a constant source of encouragement and creativity across long distances, especially my siblings and father, who have cheered me on in all my endeavors, and my fearless aunt, my feminist role model, who passed during completion of this book. A special shout-out to my brother for his readiness, often at short notice, to look at drafts of badly written paragraphs. My nieces' and nephews' smiles brought joy and a sense of rejuvenation to my life. Across three continents—North America, Asia, and Europe—my partner has been a pillar of relentless support. The long transnational journey that led to this book began two decades ago in Vinh when we first met. Its completion would not have been possible without his patience, laughter, and love—and his unwavering belief that one day that "*letzter Satz*" would indeed be penned.

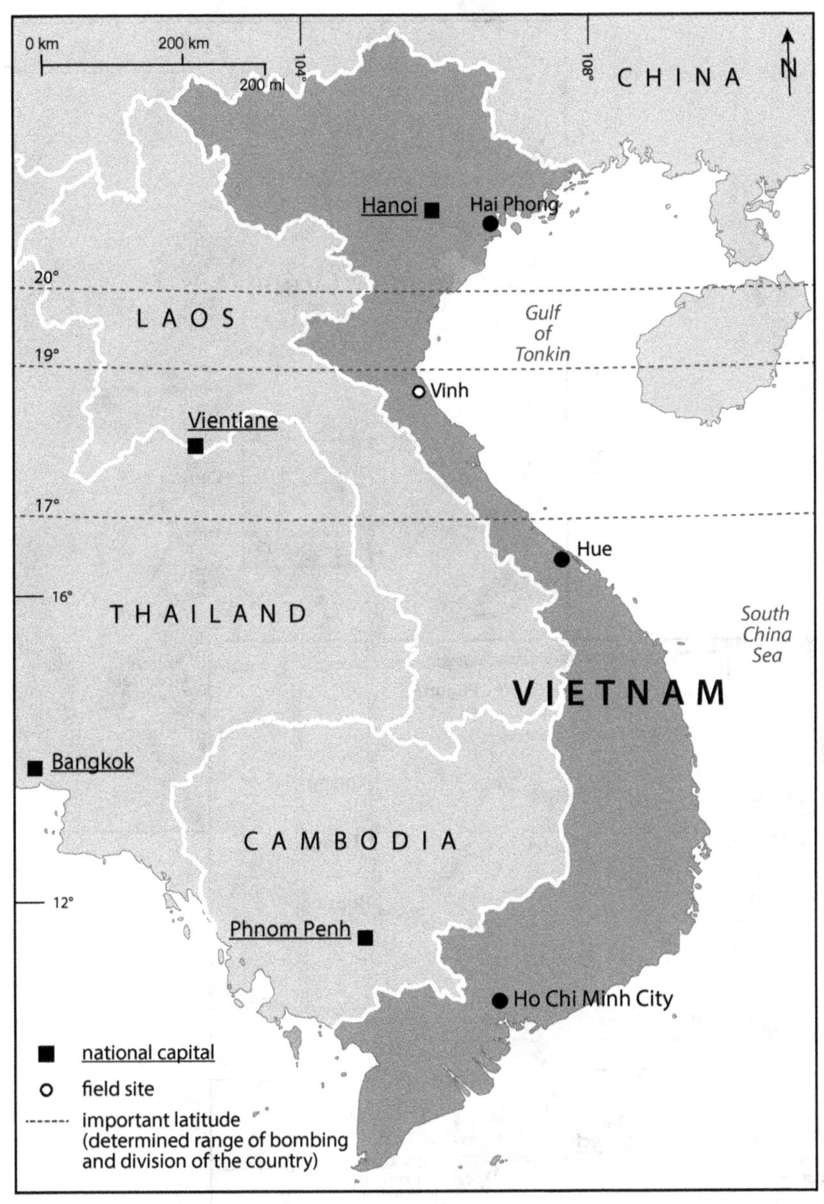

↑ Map of the Socialist Republic of Vietnam with field site. Cartography by Jutta Turner.

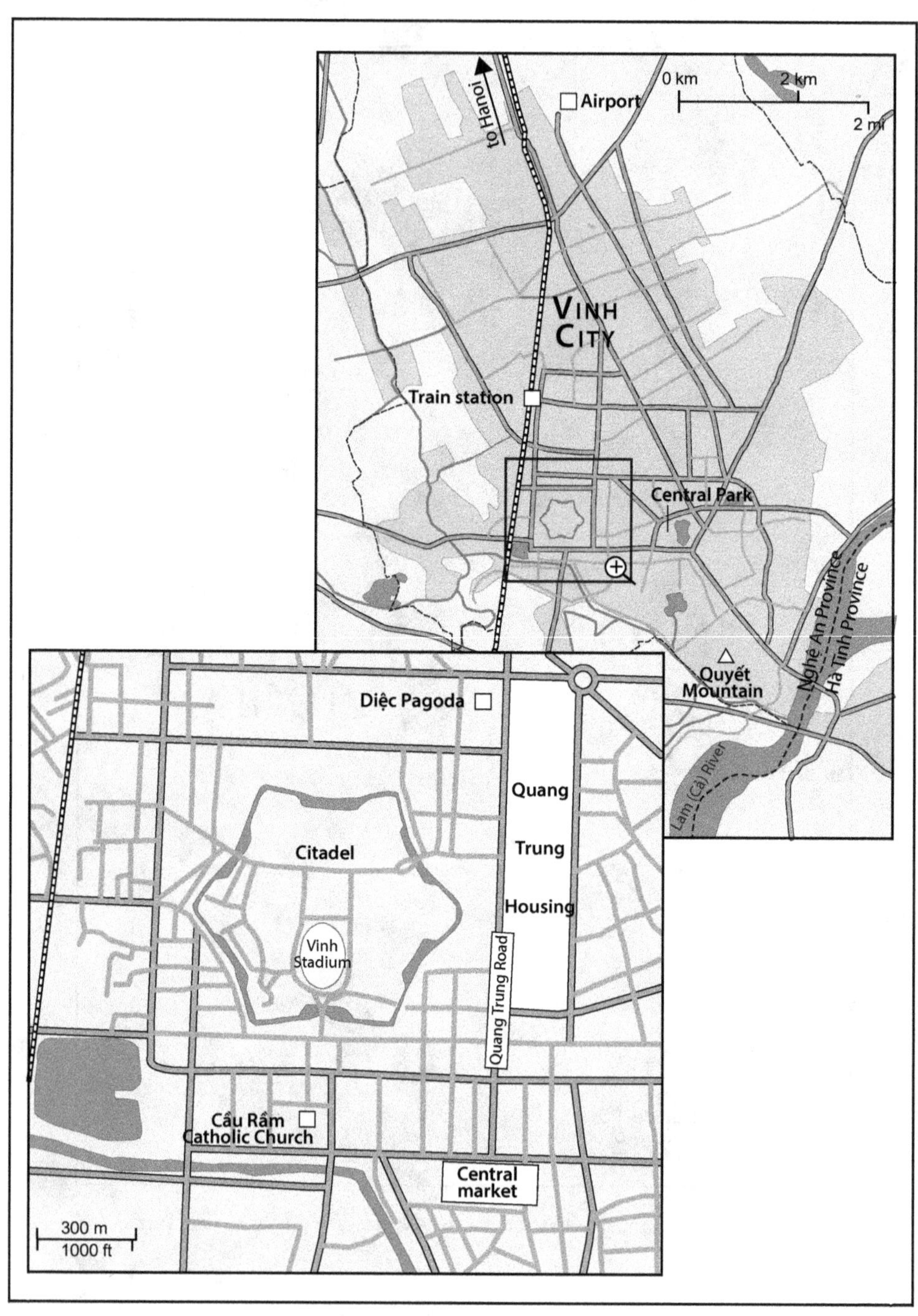

↑ Map of Vinh City, with close up of Quang Trung housing and its environs. Cartography by Jutta Turner.

INTRODUCTION

September 15, 2010, was the first day of my fieldwork in Quang Trung, the sprawling housing estate in the center of Vinh. Designed in collaboration with East German (German Democratic Republic or GDR) architects, and named after the eighteenth-century emperor and founder of the city, the estate's radically different typology signified an entirely novel form of urbanism and way of dwelling that followed the end of aerial assaults in 1973. I had moved into my fourth-floor unit in block C2 a few days earlier and was making the rounds with my research assistant, an anthropology instructor at Vinh University. Nine resident wardens (*khối trưởng*) oversaw the complex's nineteen five-story buildings, and I wanted to introduce myself and the project to each one. Our first stop was ward 1. Residents located the warden with whistles and shouts; he in turn called the ward secretary, a local architect of Quang Trung who would become one of my main interlocutors. Within minutes, we four were in the ward's community center (*nhà văn hóa*, literally "cultural house"), poring over government documents.

"Here, you should make copies of these," the warden urged, handing me a dossier of redevelopment action plans that would require the relocation of residents in the three housing blocks under his jurisdiction. "We [tenants] are not in agreement with these proposals," he announced, pointing to discontent with urban policy that denied their entitlements. With that statement, the warden shifted from government bureaucrat to concerned citizen and offered my first glimpse into how tensions between residents and the state manifested through built forms, especially with impending changes in property rights to the buildings.

Thanking him, I ran to the print shop in the middle of the housing complex, located in the trade center, also GDR-designed, that had been turned into a public library with support from the Gates Foundation and was soon to be demolished to make way for a modern cinema complex. I had spent my mornings there already, meeting the librarians and examining their archival collections. The elderly male residents, some of whom came in to read the daily paper, had told me the utopian origin story of Quang

Trung: how the now decayed blocks had once been idyllic and iconic, offering shelter and infrastructure—and an identity as "modern"—after years of privation and wartime evacuation from the city. After the U.S. air war, the building of Quang Trung marked the dawn of modernity for the ravaged city, and for those individuals fortunate enough to receive user rights to a self-contained unit.

Scholars have recognized the ways in which affects—as collective intensities that manifest through encounter (Thrift 2004, 62)—are entangled with politics and state making, and certainly the sentiments the seniors expressed to me embodied a familiar register of emotion deemed necessary for postwar nation building. As I demonstrate in this book, affects, such as hope in a brighter future of peace and prosperity, were closely tied to transformative materiality: to modern buildings and their plans and construction technologies, which projected future possibilities once unimaginable in the misery of aerial warfare. This affective community was of course fragmented and, like politics, messy (Leheny 2018, 5). Almost as quickly, I learned that not everyone shared the same modernist vision of urban futurity, and that some people had their doubts about the rebuilt environment and the lifestyle it promoted. As I neared the copy shop, a woman who introduced herself as Bích[1]—who, I later discovered, had been among those who built Quang Trung with her hands—approached me and said candidly, "We didn't want to live in these buildings. We were forced to move in" (*bị bắt buộc lên*).

Bích's unexpected counternarrative of involuntary resettlement in *undesirable*, alien buildings, and her detachment from their "cluster of promises" (Berlant 2011, 23), would ultimately transform the direction of my fieldwork on the afterlife of utopian design meant to advance the nation and improve the population through the rebuilt environment. In the late 1970s, Vinh had been an aspiring model socialist city, whose plan for modernist mass housing was bold and unprecedented in its scale and form. Built from the detritus of destruction, the city and its housing assumed a range of conflicting meaning for designers, builders, authorities, and residents, even though framed as progressing toward a common good: socialism. The coexisting affects and temporalities I encountered even during my first days in Quang Trung alerted me to both the positive and negative valences assigned to the buildings as material signs of futures dreamed and denied. These changed over time, space, and scales from global to regional, and even from one area of the complex to another. They also changed with gender and social class within each building, despite claims of egalitarian living conditions.

This book analyzes the heterogeneous meanings and affects attached to the assemblage of buildings and interconnecting spaces that comprise the modernist fantasy of *khu chung cư Quang Trung*, as well as the erosion of that fantasy. Victor Buchli, an anthropologist of architecture, has pointed to the inherently unstable and contested nature of built forms (2013, 67–68). Likewise, I am interested in the temporality of meanings that emerged when different social actors, both Vietnamese and German, envisioned, encountered, and used Vinh's built environment as lived and represented space. These meanings and their affective registers reflected the collective capacity to aspire to emancipation from war and privation on the one hand (Appadurai 2004), and to imagine and build a more just world on the other. At the same time, this form of "transnational urbanism" (Smith 2000, 5) outside the workings of capitalism was steeped in power inequalities and contested spatial practices that disrupt the narrative of seamless global "flows" commonly deployed in literature on networked "global cities."

Quang Trung was a disorienting space of contradictions, caught between global utopian ambitions and local dystopic conditions. For some, the housing estate was a material expression of global connectivity with East Germany and stood as a symbol of its humanitarian beneficence. The buildings were intended to speed up time by overcoming war-induced underdevelopment to establish Vinh at the forefront of Vietnam's urban modernity. As visual evidence of inclusion in the socialist world economy, they affirmed the legitimacy of the Vietnamese state and the Communist Party—as well as that of East Germany—by showing the ability of a caring government to fulfill its obligations to citizens. The estate's unique design enabled authorities to govern daily life more effectively and to discipline subjects through modern infrastructure aimed at improving well-being. At the same time, the radical reorganization of space in ways that departed from previous modes of dwelling afforded tenants new sensory, social, and spatial experiences of the city that were not always desired or welcomed—as Bích informed me outside the copy shop. Like in Brasilia, Brazil (Holston 1989), residents appropriated modernist forms in ways that alarmed authorities, who dreaded a return to backwardness and the loss of national prestige that came from being "more" modern. For some, this new spatial and architectural order assured a hopeful future—of civilization, experimentation, contemporaneity, and material betterment. Many found this urban subjectivity appealing; others like Bích rejected it.

All of this was ephemeral, even though designed to be eternal. While capitalism thrives on obsolescence and the destruction of the old to make way for the new—what scholars identify as "creative destruction," based on

Schumpeter's (1942) postulation—socialism was more invested in durability and displaying the perpetuity of the state through magnificent built forms that would mobilize affect for nation building. Pride and optimism dissolved as the buildings decayed prematurely, however, creating a landscape of inhabited socialist ruins—the material remains of a future yet to come. By the time I arrived, Quang Trung was no longer a grand achievement but a sign of state neglect and failure to deliver on its promises of progress through modern infrastructure. The timelessness of socialist construction, its ability to transmit social and political values into the future through its material legacy, was indeed "timed out"—and affective registers changed accordingly. The hope attached to "utopian materialism" dissipated quickly (Anderson 2006, 700).

This book uses modernist architecture and planning as an entry point into examining socialist nation building in Vietnam as Western utopian fantasy and the attrition of that fantasy, which became "ever *more* fantasmatic" over time, as Lauren Berlant observed of Reagan-era neoliberalism (2011, 11), though her argument resonates with the historical conditions of socialism but with their own material effects and affects. These fantasies of a better urban future, I show, shaped the contours of political worlds (Rose 1996, 79) while forging a collective will to build a new society. As in socialist town planning elsewhere, Vinh's rebuilt environment played an important role in the "transformation of a largely rural population into an urban proletariat" (Fehérváry 2012, 621; Lebow 2013). In Vinh, the state's civilizing project was especially concerned with regulating the urban conduct of rural female migrants, like Bích, who did not display a proper, forward-looking sensibility. Not everyone accepted universalist imaginaries of the good life that traveled from the socialist North to the postcolonial South. Instead, people re-envisioned utopian ideals in an effort to decolonize knowledge and technology. Utopian thought also ran up against harsh material realities that impeded the realization of urban plans.

To better understand the productive tensions between hope and fantasy that coalesced around traveling technologies, this study poses a number of questions about what Bloch has called "creative anticipation" and the horizons of utopian possibility (1986, 202): How did alternative imaginaries of the future city subvert top-down planning and foreign blueprints for urban living? In what ways did the housing estate, as a dramatically different form of spatial organization, redefine political and affective relationships between citizens and the state? To what extent and effect did Vietnamese architects and authorities contest East German standardized design and spatial practices? Quang Trung tenants were not docile subjects, nor were the buildings immutable forms. Rather, tenants remade their social and material worlds according to spatial logics and cultural practices that expressed their own aspirations for urban futurity. Tracing the building of Vietnam's first planned city and what happened to it after the experts left, I argue that underlying the ambivalent and often unpredictable responses to modernist architecture and what I call "unplanned obsolescence" were gendered anxieties about modernity and the future of socialism itself.

MODELING THE FUTURE

The explosion of social scientific research on "global," "world," or "mega" cities in recent years cannot be disentangled from the oft-cited figure that more than half the world's population now lives in urban or urbanizing areas. Indeed, projections of—and anxieties about—rampant urban growth in the global South fuel much of this "metrocentrist" tendency (Bunnell and Maringanti 2010). And yet, as urban theorist John Friedmann (2010) pointed out, smaller, poorer, and less cosmopolitan cities account for most contemporary urban growth around the world. Moreover, scholarship on the production of urban space often takes neoliberalism as axiomatic while disregarding hundreds of socialist-era cities and "new towns" where capital accumulation was *not* the primary mode of social organization. Nonetheless, these other models for organizing society (and achieving industrial productivity) are critical to understanding post–Cold War transformations to urban space, built forms, and daily life. In this book, decentering the logic of capital reveals the "multiplicity of experienced modernities" (Pred and Watts 1992, xiv) and political fantasies at the intersection of universalist and nationalist aspirations to *socialist* modernization as transnational social, material, and affective practice.

This historical ethnography of the aftermath of urban warfare—of Vinh's postwar reconstruction with foreign material and technological assistance—contributes to postcolonial urban scholarship by showing how an "ordinary" city in north central Vietnam entwined with other forms of global connectivity to build a just and emancipated society (Robinson 2006). This particular historical moment and experimental model of Asian urbanism in the service of socialist revolution remains a gap in the literature on the worlding of cities that decenter the West (for example, in the pioneering volume by Roy and Ong [2011]). As with capitalist urbanization, state-led socialist modernization and projected patterns of industrial development shaped urban forms across African, Asian, Eastern European, Soviet, and Latin American countries. Small regional cities, in particular, served as motors of industrial growth. Indeed, city making was an iteration of the "cultural Cold War," as I outline in this book.

It is only recently that scholars have attended to the global circulations of architectural forms and planning practices among socialist countries in the industrialized North and the decolonizing South, or between the "Second" and "Third" Worlds (Stanek 2012). A growing body of architectural history examines these prolific—and often Orientalist—creations as built forms or spatial representation, but not as lived spaces of social practice, a distinction made by Lefebvre (1991) in his theorization of urban space. Moreover, this history has been written largely from the standpoint of the global North, and it often deploys passive metaphors—such as the "export" or "transfer" of knowledge and technology—while denying the agency of beneficiaries. Esra Akcan proposes the more active term "translation" to highlight the dynamic cultural process of "transformation during the *act of transportation*" (2012, 3, emphasis added). While this approach to traveling urban forms is attentive to power asymmetries, it confines the exercise of countervailing power to elite actors involved in transmission and "assimilation." This study expands the scope of Akcan's "translation" of rational built forms to also include the *habitation* and *use* of modernist architecture imbued with affect. As Ash Amin has argued, models of the "good city" intended to improve human welfare "never travel unmodified across space and time" (2006, 1010), nor do they travel devoid of emotional investments.

Vinh's architecture and urban design formed the basis of a celebrated narrative of Vietnam's rebound through collective international effort—until infrastructure broke down and unplanned obsolescence set in. This observation is important for several reasons. The first has to do with urban scale: provincial capitals and regional cities like Vinh have attracted little scholarly attention in Vietnam, compared with the larger and wealthier metropolises of Hanoi and Ho Chi Minh City (but see Endres 2019). Anthropological scholarship itself remains focused more on the fast pace of change in major cities, or on tensions between "tradition" and "modernity" in rural (often ethnic minority) villages, than on so-called secondary cities.[2] Second, scholarship on Vietnam has tended to leap over the subsidy years (*thời bao cấp*) of socialist reconstruction, which entailed crushing poverty and privation for the population. It is as if history involved only "war" until 1975 and then "reforms" after 1986 (known as *Đổi mới*). Some scholars have gone so far as to claim, quite inaccurately, that there was no urban policy or concerted effort at urban planning after the war with the United States until *Đổi mới* (see Smith and Scarpaci 2000). This flawed narrative of urban stagnation reproduces an image of Vietnam as isolated, static, and stuck in time until finally saved by capitalism. The discursive denial of synchronous temporality that was central to racial ontologies (Zeiderman 2016, 181), that is, presenting Vietnamese as living in an earlier historical time, was also a *material* objective of aerial warfare: deny people their modern world by bombing them "back to the Stone Age," as General Curtis E. LeMay warned. Accounts of stagnation also overlook the *global* scope and scale of *multidirectional* circulations of goods, people, finance, technology, and ideas. Socialist mobilities to access labor markets, educational opportunities, technical expertise, and cultural exchanges brought Vietnamese to new corners of the world, as well as new "friends" to Vietnam (Schwenkel 2015d). Collectively, these propelled "socialist transformation" and helped people make sense of their encounters with the world both at home and overseas (Bayly 2008; Schwenkel 2014b).

General neglect of the period of socialist reconstruction has left a gap in our understanding of the human experience of bombing and how people in northern Vietnam collectively rebuilt their social and material worlds after a decade of U.S. air strikes. This book shows how modernist mass housing as a techno-utopian solution to the rapid repopulation of postwar cities profoundly transformed urban landscapes and people's social and sensory encounters with the city. As a technology of governance over the urban environment, this architectural modality was reworked and adapted in Vinh to build the material and ideological foundations of socialism—and to subvert it. Because there exists no sustained ethnographic examination of this form of sociospatial organization, often referred to as *nhà tập thể* or collective housing, and the subjectivities and social practices it generated, this book makes a much-needed contribution to the literature on socialist urbanisms, particularly in the context of Vietnam. Today, this progressively modified built environment faces the same fate as other collapsing dreamworlds: demolition and disappearance from contemporary urban life.

Few people outside Vietnam know either the history of Vinh's annihilation or how a utopian vision for Vietnam's model socialist city arose from its ruins. That Vinh was chosen as the site for urban experimentation and exemplary modernization may seem ironic. Today, guidebooks and Western journalists have branded Vinh the "least attractive city" in Vietnam.[3] Foreigners passing through often smirk at its crumbling "Soviet" façade, unaware of *other* modernizing forces in Vietnam—in this case East Germany, which helped to rebuild the city and provide social and technical infrastructure around the country. Travelers to Vinh also often fail to notice the cement logo "VĐ" (Việt Đức, or Vietnam-Germany) above building entryways within the housing estate.

As a secular stand-in for altars (which residents would add later), VĐ was a good-luck charm, meant to shield inhabitants from harm and bring fortune, like other talismans placed in transitional spaces. Việt Đức and its inverse, Đức Việt, have since become branded icons (the most famous example being domestic-produced sausages), imprinting the history of anti-imperialist solidarity onto desired capitalist commodities.

The ability of an historical object, like a logo or a building, to transmit collective affects across time and space—what Walter Benjamin referred to as "aura" and its afterlife (1969b)—is one critical focal point of this work. The strong auratic effect of the rebuilt city, its transmission of utopian impulses, opened up imaginative possibilities for what the future could be. But when capitalist forces (investors, tourists, development agencies) assigned a negative valence to this material history, the aura declined into a call for demolition (Hansen 2008, 337–38). This negative valence inspired defiance among residents.

The great social experiment that made Vinh a global contact zone was not unknown in East Germany, which was also heavily cloaked in Cold War tropes of isolation and anachronism. A new generation of German studies scholars has challenged the narrative of stagnancy and boundedness by shifting the scholarly gaze away from the capitalist West as the benchmark of modernity.[4] Instead, these authors look toward countries in the postcolonial South, where political fantasies of progress, development, and technological modernity were persuasive though racially and politically fraught. These mostly historical works tend to privilege East German viewpoints, however, or represent postcoloniality through the lens of German archival research. Seldom are these studies methodologically transnational—that is, linguistically and culturally fluent enough to allow for consultation of primary sources and discussions with key informants in the postcolonial countries themselves.[5] Rarely, too, are they ethnographic. Despite subverting dominant epistemologies and expanding the scope of GDR history beyond the boundaries of the nation-state, this growing body of research has not sufficiently afforded subalterns the opportunity to speak.

This scholarship thus lacks analysis of the deeper meanings attached to complex and contested nation-building projects and their lived experiences and legacies. Neglecting their agency too easily configures socialist citizens as docile subjects and construes cooperation schemes as foreign impositions, if not neocolonialism. These scholars are correct to highlight the role of a strong state and the power asymmetries that undergirded "anticolonial solidarity." GDR assistance to Vietnam was not purely altruistic but driven by national interest and a quest for international legitimacy (for both countries). Even so, limiting the framework of solidarity to a state-defined "politics machine" (Weis 2011, 367) overlooks how ideologies of solidarity were *felt* and *lived* as ethical practice and meaningful social action. My approach recognizes the political as affective, and affect as political (Massumi 2015), to understand the seductive appeal and emancipatory potential of East German planning to transcend material ruin and the "residual affects" of war (Navaro-Yashin 2009, 5). Who negotiated and translated utopian, future-oriented design, how, and to what spatial, cultural, and temporal effects are the questions that motivate this ethnographic study of the affects that coalesced around the rapid building and the slow material disintegration of socialism.

THE "RED CITY" AS HISTORICAL FRONTIER

In many ways, Vinh is a frontier city, a seemingly untamed place where the civilizing projects of past empires remained contested and incomplete.[6] Geographically, it lies between the mountains and the sea on the north central coast of Nghệ An, Vietnam's largest province.[7] Historically, this isolated region existed on the margins of power and often served as battlefront between warring forces. After independence from Chinese domination in 938 AD and through the fourteenth century, it was a contested border territory between Đại Việt to the north and Champa to the south (Li 1998, 201–21). During the Trịnh-Nguyễn wars (1627–1672), the Vĩnh Doanh River (now Lam or Cả River) served as a natural defense between feudal clans (Chu 1998, 13–14). A century later, in 1788, this river basin played an important role in the Tây Sơn dynasty. Nguyễn Huệ (Quang Trung) declared this sacred hinterland of benevolent animal spirits—equidistant from Thăng Long (today, Hanoi) and Phú Xuân (today, Huế)—as the new Imperial Phoenix Capital, or Phượng Hoàng Trung Đô (Ninh 2008, 44–45; Dutton 2006, 109–10). Although Quang Trung's grand political center atop Quyết Mountain was never realized (he died soon after proposing the new capital site), his declaration changed the course of Nghệ An's history. In Vietnamese historiography, Quang Trung's vision became Vinh's origin story, ironically foretelling a future of aspirational city building that would face recurring and unforeseen impediments. In this myth, 1788 is the year of the founding of Vinh (then, Vĩnh Doanh), and Emperor Quang Trung is its creator.[8]

While the region enjoys abundant natural resources (Ninh 2003), its remoteness, as an effect of power (Piot 2014, 369), left it economically undeveloped. The teleological notion of underdevelopment has formed the basis of collective impressions about the "character" (*tính cách*) of people who live in Nghệ An (see Chu 2004). In my experience, the province is, more than any other, an object of temporal speculation. In literature and popular imagination, Nghệ An is both ahead of its time and lagging behind, as a paradox of hardship, provincialism, and intellectualism.[9] It is the cradle of the Vietnamese revolution and birthplace of the country's most celebrated scholars and nationalists, including the poet Nguyễn Du and President Hồ Chí Minh. This space of alterity is depicted as a land of suffering (*đất khổ*). Its harsh climate, bouts of warfare, persistent oppression, and natural catastrophes have produced a strong regional identity with distinctive culture traits (*nết văn hóa riêng*), which includes *ví giặm* folk music, with its rhymed satirical couplets. The people are considered dauntless, hardworking, erudite, and rebellious, who live according to their own rule of law. Rumors that feudal lords sent banished rebels and criminals to this wild backwater lend credence to its image as unruly and hostile to outsiders. Guidebooks advise tourists to pass through quickly. The press depicts Vinh as an edgy city prone to violence: mobs lynch dog thieves, and girls film attacks on their schoolmates with their phones to post on social media.[10] The hinterland is thus both object of admiration and source of endless apprehension, triggering both affection and dread in the national imaginary.

Nghệ An's status as borderland changed in 1802, with Vietnam's unification under Nguyễn Phúc Ánh, or Emperor Gia Long. Following the lead of his adversary, Quang Trung, the new emperor sought to establish an administrative center midway between Phú Xuân and Thăng Long, a few kilometers from the not-yet-built Phoenix capital. This brought the renegade frontier under the imperial gaze of the new dynasty. Two years later, construction on the hexagon-shaped citadel (*thành*) began in the Vĩnh Doanh delta, the same year as building began on the imperial city of Huế. Nghệ An was one of the only other sites of planned imperial expansion (other citadels came later),[11] which attests to its strategic importance to the hegemon. The walled fortress established the region as a political center, as Quang Trung had once imagined. This set into motion the slow urbanization of what eventually became the city of Vinh. Citadels require public services and infrastructure, which in turn require labor. The lands outside the royal gates attracted migrants, traders, and craftspeople. No longer solely dependent on a subsistence economy, they formed a small *thành thị*—a term that suggests the synthesis of imperial administration (*thành*) with market trade (*thị*) that gave rise to early Vietnamese "cities" (Ngô 2000, 205). As the population increased, so too did ethnic stratification (Woodside 1971, 32). The arrival of Chinese (and, to a lesser extent, Indian) traders, European businessmen, and, after 1885, French colonists accelerated the frontier's conversion into an international hub of trade and commerce.[12]

Where Gia Long saw political possibility, the French saw economic opportunity. The settler fantasy that Nghệ An was rich in untapped resources further transformed the region through land dispossession and expansion of capitalist modes of production. French officials merged three neighboring townships (*thị xã*) into one colonial municipality, Ville de Vinh–Ben Thuy, which became the largest industrial center in Annam (central Vietnam) but had the lowest standard of living (Nguyễn 2008). The maritime port of Bến Thủy was the focal point of industrial development, with dockyards, a sawmill, a match factory, and a power plant at the base of the planned Phoenix city, while the railway workshop at Trường Thi provided thousands of jobs to an emergent class of landless wage workers (Del Testa 2007). In 1930–1931, these industries became critical sites for the strikes and uprisings that the "Nghệ-Tĩnh Soviets" carried out across the region, earning Vinh the proud moniker "red city" (*thành phố đỏ*).[13] The area around the citadel remained the commercial and administrative center of Ville de Vinh–Ben Thuy, and foreign elites enjoyed the benefits of newly built infrastructure inaccessible to most Vietnamese. As it did in other colonized territories in Southeast Asia, modern infrastructure became a cornerstone of domination that denied full citizenship to indigenous populations (Mrázek 2002). Following Hồ Chí Minh's call to "phá hoại để kháng chiến" (destroy to resist) during the First Indochina War (1946–1954), the VIỆT MINH's scorched-earth policy targeted colonial infrastructure and, along with French (and American) air raids, gutted the built environment, bringing an end to urban capital accumulation.[14]

Emancipation from colonialism and the overthrow of capitalism allowed for a critical reimagining of Vinh as a center of socialist modernization. An emphasis on manufacturing and heavy industry accompanied the "advance to socialism," aided by Soviet and Chinese expertise. By 1961, Vinh boasted sixty state enterprises, including the largest power plant in central Vietnam (Phạm and Bùi 2003, 139) and a new university. That same year, its status changed from township (*thị xã*) to city (*thành phố*), marking its regional ascendancy. Novel built forms populated the landscape, with new infrastructure intended to be universal. Rehabilitation (*khôi phục*) increased both global and national connectivity as workers produced goods for export to socialist bloc countries and Vietnamese students traveled overseas to study in Eastern Europe and the Soviet Union. The completion of repairs to the railway line connecting Vinh with Hanoi in May 1964 affirmed the integration of the hinterland into the national economy. More than five thousand residents turned out, along with officials from Hanoi, to welcome the inaugural train.[15] The train's successful journey to Vinh symbolized growth and progress, not unlike the colonial railway inauguration in 1905 (Del Testa 1999). Even so, Vinh's location as the end station signified its remoteness and disconnection (as well as the division of the country, since the train could not travel farther south). By the start of the U.S. air war (1964–1973), Vinh was poised yet again as a border territory—a frontline to the socialist North and launching pad for incursions into the U.S.-backed South.

American airpower abruptly halted socialist transformation and reversed the course of Vinh's modernization. As a technology to deny shared contemporaneity, U.S. bombing swiftly undid the material achievements of a decade of reconstruction, only two months after that celebrated arrival of the inaugural train. Once the United States began carrying out its threats to return Vietnam to an earlier period of evolutionary time, Vinh found itself once more ruined, empty, and cut off from the rest of the country. Its forced deurbanization required a new savior—a task that fell to East Germany, to the "children of Marx" who aided collective efforts to rebuild the "homeland of Hồ Chí Minh." Technological assistance would not only set Vinh back on the path to progress but also transform the remote frontier city into a global contact zone and showcase of socialist civilization.

FIELDWORK: COLD WAR POSITIONINGS

One cold winter day in 2011, I drove into the spacious grounds of the Nghệ An Provincial Museum on land that once had housed the colonial prison. The guard motioned for me to turn off the engine and walk my motorbike to the parking area. "Where are you from?" he called. "Are you Soviet" (*Liên Xô*)? I smiled and shook my head, accustomed to this socialist-era holdover term for foreigners (akin to *Tây*, or Westerner, used commonly today).[16] "German?" he guessed. "Không phải" (no), I laughed. He thought for a moment, and then asked if I was *Tiệp*, or Czechoslovakian, another obsolete term (now *Séc*, for Czech Republic). His attempt to read my body through Cold War geography suggested a history of *học nghề*, or vocational training in the former Eastern Bloc. I finally gave in and said, cautiously, "Người Mỹ" (American). He snickered. "American? No, I don't believe you" (*Không tin*). As if I would willingly adopt the nationality of a country that had, without remorse, systematically annihilated the very place where we were conversing!

Because I was a white, Vietnamese-speaking, child-free, American woman with a German surname and an absent partner (working elsewhere in Vietnam), my residence in Quang Trung was a conundrum for many people living there. My presence signified many "firsts": the first foreigner to conduct sustained ethnographic research in Vinh and to live in Quang Trung, and the first American (and second foreigner) to gain access to the provincial archives. I was also the first American that most people had met; the few exceptions included those who had apprehended American POWs shot down over Vinh. Local police introduced themselves, shared their version of Vinh's history, and reminded me to register; after that, they left me alone, although they likely continued to keep tabs on me. As we drank coffee together, the police chief briefly expressed concern about my security—a shell-shocked veteran might have a flashback and attack me—before he moved on to other topics, such as his passion for Buddhist temples. It became clear early on that people from all social groups, for different reasons, were eager to speak with a foreigner who, in turn, eagerly listened to their stories. They deployed different tactics, however, to reconcile the fact that I came from the country that had destroyed their homes, families, livelihoods, and city—and then had the gall to return to search for the remains of their own.

Many chose to "forget" that I carried an American passport. Given my German heritage, in-laws, social connections (for example, to the experts who had helped rebuild Vinh), and language fluency, some coded me as *ethnically* German rather than *nationally* American. Others said I was *người Mỹ gốc Đức*, or American with German origins, to which I would respond, jokingly, that I was *Đức kiều*, or overseas German—a play on *Việt kiều*, or overseas Vietnamese, as Vietnamese Americans are commonly called. In Vinh, being German was associated with moral goodness and technological prowess; after all, according to the rescue narrative, the GDR saved Vinh from ruin and underdevelopment. As one might expect, there was considerable ambivalence about the United States, especially among the older generation, but I encountered no palpable, widespread anti-Americanism;[17] indeed, anti-Chinese sentiments were much stronger. In many ways the United States was irrelevant and outside people's *Weltanschauung*, as seen in my interaction with the guard. Youth culture was more oriented to East Asian pop stars (and some European footballers), for instance, than to Western cultural production. There were, of course, exceptions, such as my neighbor, who purchased a U.S. army jeep covered with American flag stickers in Đà Nẵng to use commercially for wedding transportation and photography.[18] As a status symbol, the jeep was less a sign of desire for American things, however, than a triumphant war trophy that translated imperial iconography into expressive, national idioms (Strassler 2010, 80).

My "firsts" in Vinh were only possible because I was not new to the city. I visited Vinh intermittently in 2000 while conducting my dissertation fieldwork on postwar memory (Schwenkel 2009a), and I lived there with my partner, a German aid worker, across from the housing estate during the summer of 2001. There were only a handful of foreign experts and foreign language teachers in the city at the time (and equally few today). International tourists might stop for a night while traveling between Hanoi and Huế and grab a drink at the quirky Zulu Bar. But in contrast to the situation in Hanoi and Ho Chi Minh City, economic reforms were only beginning to strongly affect everyday life in the impoverished city at the turn of the millennium. For example, when Maximart, the city's first "supermarket," opened in late 1999, the large crowds who wanted to visit did not fit inside; it was about as big as a U.S. convenience store.

When I returned to Vinh five years later, there were new buildings and commercial establishments, including new spaces of consumption like indoor cafés.[19] As I walked around Quang Trung with one of its architects, people came out to greet me and tell me the solidarity origin story of their housing. Anthropologists have often noted the role that serendipity plays in fieldwork, and my time in Vinh was no exception. The five-year preparation process—conducting preliminary research in Germany and Vietnam, writing grant applications, securing research permissions, and so on—culminated in an important change in the matrix of my *quan hệ*, or key social relationships based on mutual trust and obligation: the promotion of my partner's former supervisor to chief of staff (*chánh văn phòng*) at the Municipal People's Committee. Within the chain of government command and the Communist Party hierarchy, his stamp of approval on my letters of introduction from Hanoi National University facilitated the permissions I needed to conduct research at all administrative levels in the municipality, from the province (*tỉnh*) to the district (*phường*) and the Quang Trung wards (*khối*). As mediators of bureaucratic efficacy (see Hull 2012, 253), these red-stamped documents enabled other generative processes and relations among bureaucrats, citizens, and anthropologist. They opened doors, secured access to people, institutions, and knowledge, and protected my informants (by affirming they could share information with a foreigner). The red stamp was akin to a talisman that possessed agency, such as the power to accelerate bureaucratic time: documents materialized quickly after its inspection. The red stamps also ensured that I had been vetted accordingly and could be entrusted with government maps, plans, charts, reports, and diagrams. This official paperwork not only constituted my ethnographic authority, but also regulated and circumscribed it: there was no need for officials to comply with requests beyond the scope of my research. For example, one day a young policeman asked if I would like to visit the municipal court with him. But he quickly caught himself and abandoned the idea, saying the courts might not fall under the purview of my research.

My research also involved participant observation in Quang Trung, which expanded and even challenged the official storylines I had gleaned from archival documents by including the unarchived voices of common people like local architects and construction workers. I moved in on a sunny fall morning in September 2010, on a date and time chosen by a local diviner (*thầy bói*) whom my landlord had consulted. The one-bedroom, forty-square-meter apartment on the fourth floor was my home for the next nine months.[20] Along with my research assistant, I introduced myself and my project to each of the nine wardens who administered Quang Trung's nineteen housing blocks across areas A, B, and C. They, in turn, announced my residency on community blackboards (*bảng thông báo*) across the twenty-hectare complex so people would understand what I was doing there—and that my presence was authorized. "An American professor will live among us to conduct research," the notices read. "Please welcome her. Thank you for your cooperation." In the months that followed, I participated in everyday activities, including Women's Day meetings, collective cleaning, poetry readings, holiday events, and funerals. I was not invited to Fatherland Front meetings under the Communist Party, nor did I ask to be included. Along with my neighbors, I hung my flag on national holidays (as instructed on the blackboard) and contributed to maintenance and solidarity funds, which were also recorded on the board: "143 Chị Linh 100,000đ người Hoa Kỳ," or "Room 143, Miss Linh [my Vietnamese name] the American donated 100,000 *đồng*" (VND).[21] Each day, I traversed the complex, moving from café to tea stall to soup stand for meals. I shopped in the outdoor markets, visited with neighbors (at first with my research assistant to establish familiarity, and then by myself), dropped by small shops, went to aerobics, read in the library, played with children, watched sports (such as senior badminton), and talked to as many people as possible in the vibrant, shared outdoor spaces, as well as in the privacy of their homes.

Residents across the housing complex gave me different names, which helped me to place someone quickly when I met them along the paths between buildings, and which gave me insights into their age and social background. In bureaucratic circles, among people I had known for a decade, I was called by my given name, Christina. In the market, traders called me chị Liên Xô, or Miss Soviet, to which I would jokingly reply, "Sụp đổ rồi!" or "Collapsed already!" The wardens and retired female workers in area B called me Linh, based on my middle name, while cultural elites in area C called me Kiều Linh, short for Christina Lyn, which they felt to be more poetic. My gender was also fluid. Several older men in their eighties mentored me. I called them teacher (*thầy*), and they called me *anh*, or brother, given my "male" social role as a mobile professional not embedded in a family structure. My respondents thus "translated the translator" (Williams 1996), continuously shifting aspects of my personhood—name, gender, nationality—to fit the social and moral categories that allowed them to establish cultural intimacy with me.

Because of the scale of Quang Trung, after moving in, I launched a qualitative survey to familiarize myself with the nineteen buildings and the families that inhabited them. I was interested in the spatial organization of the complex and each block's history of design, allocation, and settlement. This information helped me to understand the demographics of the buildings and to gauge residents' sentiments about the privatization of state property, which was underway during my fieldwork. Conducting the survey also made me more visible to residents and allowed me access to their apartments to document changes to interiors. I established connections—including with the designers, planners, and (female) builders of Quang Trung—and set up interviews so that I could better comprehend residents' economic and affective investments in their living spaces. There was also a pedagogical component to this method. My survey team consisted of seven anthropology undergraduates enrolled in a methodology course at Vinh University under the instruction of my research assistant; some had grown up in rural districts hearing about the "tall, yellow, modern buildings" in the center of the city.

According to government statistics, in Quang Trung there were 1,262 households and a total population of 4,439, with an average of 3.5 residents per flat. Our survey found a slightly higher number of households, closer to 1,275, due to shared occupancies. Our strategy was to target 50 percent of apartments in each building for a total sample size of 647 households. The survey took place over a month; questions were both quantitative and qualitative, and they focused on family background and composition, work history, monthly expenses, consumption practices, community activities, and apartment renovations. Open-ended questions also asked about privatization and visions for the future of Quang Trung. Each day, I accompanied a student to a different block to meet the residents. The refusal rate was fairly low, at 2 percent (thirteen households).[22] Most respondents agreed to follow-up interviews and were generally enthusiastic to share their life histories, though I always proceeded with caution and sensitivity to their trauma. There are of course a host of problems with the data that surveys generate. My goal was to get a general picture of Quang Trung's population and its social and economic characteristics rather than create statistically sound facts. Even so, the data did generate useful information that appeared representative of the larger population, as I was able to confirm over the following months of fieldwork. For example, most households, I quickly discovered, were "policy families" (*gia đình chính sách*), who received some form of state support for wartime injuries and losses. Dozens had immediate family members who had fallen (*liệt sĩ*), and even more were registered as wounded veterans (*thương binh*). Fifty families suffered from exposure to Agent Orange, seventeen of which included children of the third generation affected.[23] While little debris was visible in Vinh forty years after U.S. bombings,[24] toxic residues of war continued to manifest in the bodies of my neighbors and their children.

My study of the material and ideological *builders* of socialism took me also to the former East Germany. There, I was as much of a curiosity for my interlocutors as I was in Vinh. As one German architect put it, I was a professor from a capitalist-imperialist country interested in how the labor of socialist solidarity rebuilt what the enemy had destroyed. Ironically, the fact that I was *not* German opened doors in Germany; in Vietnam, by contrast, my presumed embodiment of Germanness was a desirable characteristic. I had begun to build research relationships with East German experts beginning in 2006, only seventeen years after the destruction of the Berlin Wall. Many of these engineers and craftspeople had lost their professional positions after German unification, which some discussed as "colonization" and institutionalized exclusion; for example, as pensioners, they receive lower social security payments than their counterparts in western Bundesländer (states). When I began my research, my contacts felt that scholars from western parts of Germany belittled their history and accomplishments. As an American, I did not see East Germans through the lens of deficiency, as did many of their compatriots in the West (Berdahl 1999). For their part, they saw my research interests as genuine and sympathetic, though not uncritical. Our connections were further supported by the fact that we had mutual acquaintances in Vinh and by my residency in the housing that they had helped to build.

Living and working in danger and austerity in the aftermath of aerial warfare in Vietnam had been deeply formative for these men and women and remained at the core of their subjectivities and social relationships. I came to know a dozen experts whose lives continue to revolve around Vietnam: homes adorned with Vietnamese knickknacks, visits to Vinh, cohort reunions, beer at the Viet Haus in Berlin, *Tết* celebrations, and so on. As Dominic Boyer observed, the sense of loss that accompanied unification was less about the desire for East Germany to continue as a sovereign nation-state than it was sorrow over the end of the fantasy of utopian socialism (2006, 372). This sense of loss deepened with the devaluation of their work to build that utopia, I argue here. Returning to Vietnam, where their achievements were still glorified, revived feelings of accomplishment and self-worth (Schwenkel 2015b). "No one wants to hear about the good things we did," one senior planner told me bluntly about the endurance of Cold War hostility toward former East Germany. "It doesn't fit with the story they've created about the East."[25] He was right. However, the cynicism I encountered in Germany at the start of my research has since begun to wane.[26] There is a resurging interest in socialist modernist architecture (Kulić 2018), and once-maligned forms are now deemed worthy of exhibition or commodification (for example, in coffee table books on the period's "cosmic creativity" and "stunning diversity"), and as objects of ruin-gazing. While this ethnography shows the social and historical significance of modernist buildings for the people who designed, built, and lived in them, my hope is to do so without turning their creation and ruination into spectacle.

MAPPING THE FUTURE CITY

Building Socialism weaves history and ethnography into a multiperspectival account of the affects attached to modernist planning and its afterlife in mass housing. Utopian ideas about how to rebuild and spatially organize postwar society to achieve radical social transformation traveled from countries in the global socialist North to those in the postcolonial South, including Vietnam. Within a Cold War context of deimperialization (Chen 2010), these authoritative ideas underwent significant translation at all stages of design, implementation, and usage. At the center of the narrative is thus a scalar tension between *global* and *national* approaches to socialist reconstruction through *regional* development that aimed to achieve decolonization without lapsing into new dependencies. Competing priorities and socialist worldviews, informed by Western imaginaries of progress through technology, collided in the project to industrialize Vinh and create a global proletariat that transcended race and nation. This twofold project of material and ideological construction—manufacturing cities and the people with appropriate affect displays who inhabited them—captures the double entendre of "building socialism" as a redemptive, urban experiment that was at once a seemingly colonial *and* a decolonizing intervention (Parreñas 2018, 35).

While analogous models across the "socialist global" and the "socialist local" shaped debates about urban planning, this is not a linear national narrative of rebound and recovery through social and technological development. Rather, *Building Socialism* tells of struggles and aspirations to achieve progressive temporality in the aftermath of imperialism. The people of Vinh, busy rebuilding their city according to socialist ideals, wanted no more than to occupy the same historical time as their cosmopolitan contemporaries. Vietnamese authorities thus sought assistance from East German visionaries to help Vinh "catch up" with the rest of the socialist world. Like Benjamin's wreckage of progress, Vinh's history of modernization was nonlinear—it comprised fits and starts, devastation and regeneration, and the desire to advance alongside fear of decline. In the book's three parts, I trace this friction between progressive and cyclical time, which underpinned postcolonial, Marxist-Leninist imaginaries of Vietnamese history advancing toward a prosperous future (Raffin 2008, 338). I illustrate how Vietnamese aspirations to socialist modernity were tinged with temporal anxieties about lagging behind. Interludes in the first two parts contain what I call "urban fragments" to foreground lived spatial and temporal experiences, first of urban devastation and then of postwar urban transformation imbued with utopian promise. In these interludes, pictures, poems, and other cultural expressions offer insights into conflicting timescales of development and the affective relationships that formed between people and the built environment. These expressions included Orientalist tropes of a timelessly resilient Vietnam that were important to Vietnam's political fantasy of Communist Party victory and to East Germany's ambitions to export technological modernity.

The first part of the book, "Ruination," provides historical context for the state-sponsored, nationalist project to transform Vinh into a model socialist city by examining its obliteration by the U.S. military. Highlighting the distinct ways that architecture was used as evidence to make distinctive truth claims (Weizman 2017), each of three chapters offers a different perspective on aerial warfare that left the city empty, flattened, and in need of rescue: the doctrine of U.S. strategic bombing, the lived experience of spatial annihilation, and mobilization of international solidarity.

To date, scholars have paid little attention to America's imperial fantasy of Asian subjugation through its relentless air raids over northern Vietnam. In Vinh, this material and ecological razing left a surreal and uninhabitable landscape poised for utopian possibility. Chapter 1 argues that infrastructural warfare and its modes of seeing, including aerial photography, created an "imaginative geography" of a distant and dangerous place outside history (Said 1978, 57) that made people on the ground invisible. A racialized optics of war that measured "material kills" instead of body counts enabled this erasure of human beings while affirming U.S. claims to technological superiority. Governed by techno-fanaticism, logistical warfare against objects and built forms took an irrational turn as bombers used excessive force to destroy the material and environmental conditions of human life.

Chapter 2 shifts perspective from the air to the ground, from optical mapping to sonic tracking, to highlight the embodied experiences of material devastation and loss that are absent from nationalist histories of the war in Vietnam. This chapter draws on photographs, oral histories, and classified government reports to reveal sensory memories and representations of the war against nonhuman objects that forced people to seek refuge underground. Unlike the metaphors of sight that framed aerial warfare and its knowledge systems for U.S. pilots and military technocrats discussed in chapter 1, here I show how evacuated urban residents apprehended and navigated spatial violence through the senses, particularly through sensorial encounters with the sounds of war.

Chapter 3 moves to the former East Germany, where I develop the idea of solidarity as affective practice, based on German claims to shared victimhood with Vietnamese "kin." These claims reduced Otherness to sameness, denying historical difference, including the history of fascism. Opposition to the air war propelled a state-led apparatus of aid and expertise to assist Vietnam in its struggle against imperialism. A paternalistic sense of responsibility underpinned the sympathetic solidarities that the media produced and sustained among the population. As the GDR asserted its moral superiority as benefactor to the unjustly besieged country, the Cold War between East and West Germany would play out, in part, through Vietnam.

Humanitarian discourses and practices of anti-imperialist solidarity paved the way for East Germany's role in rebuilding Vinh as an "experimental utopia" of new possibilities (Lefebvre 1961). The second part of the book, "Reconstruction," foregrounds the radical visions of socialist modernization that emerged from the devastation of war. International collaborations generated new spatial tools and technologies of state power to liberate the country from the "premodern backwardness" to which it had been bombed.

Chapter 4 analyzes regional industrial development as the driver of postcolonial growth through socialist internationalism. Since the 1950s, participation in modernization efforts in Vietnam allowed weaker socialist countries like East Germany to claim geopolitical legitimacy through large-scale infrastructure projects and the training of Vietnamese experts. Against this backdrop, planning and rebuilding Vinh in the late 1970s became a prestige project rooted in imaginaries of horizontal solidarity. The distinctive labor conditions of postwar reconstruction allowed for new forms of legibility and intimacy between East German experts and Vietnamese nationals that circumvented Soviet imperialism while exacerbating inequalities in both Vietnam and the GDR.

Chapter 5 looks at notions of modernist planning as transferable and transformative, and their limitations. Architectural experiments turned Vinh into an urban laboratory with the goal to scientifically design an optimal socialist city that would increase labor productivity and create a population of enlightened proletarians. The resulting plans expressed conflicting visions and projections of the city's future. They imposed rigid schemes of social and economic order on spaces and people considered disorderly, thus expanding the reach of the state. Technical objects, like maps and blueprints, rendered utopian ideals believable, although in practice they were not always achievable or even desirable. Universalist approaches to planning were framed as benevolent coproduction, which allowed foreign experts to sidestep damaging allegations of neocolonialism.

Chapter 6 shifts the scale from the redesigned city to the more intimate spaces of the family dwelling. It examines standardized housing and its infrastructure as an emblem of socialist modernity that was meant to liberate families from the workplace and women from domestic drudgery. For the Vietnamese state, mass housing was a new technology of social control that extended its power deeper into homes. These architectural forms from the socialist North did not travel to the South unchanged, however. Vietnamese revisions to GDR housing designs revealed conflicting interests, spatial logics, and ideas about socialist urban futurity among officials and residents alike. These tensions notwithstanding, Vinh's new housing complex was positioned to become the design prototype for future building across Vietnam.

The rapid ascendance of Vinh as a model city was followed by its swift descent into deterioration, or what I call "unplanned obsolescence." Utopian ambitions produced dystopian living conditions, the focus of the book's last part, "Obsolescence," which moves from the planned to the unplanned, from designers to dwellers, as collective hope for future betterment turned to mounting despair.

Decay of the housing complex was associated with feminine activity, particularly the conduct of rural migrant women who did not possess an appropriate urban sensibility, the subject of chapter 7. Litter and trash around the housing blocks showed ambivalence about modernization. Female migrant laborers, in particular, were targets of state discipline and ethical discourses about infrastructure. Unruly practices commonly associated with the female sphere of rural domesticity threatened to derail the state's project to build an advanced socialist society inhabited by a modern proletariat. Debates over disorderly conduct in the housing blocks revealed the limitations of utopian design to shape daily practices and exposed hierarchies that undermined socialist commitments to egalitarianism.

So too did breakdowns in infrastructure, the subject of chapter 8. The unplanned use of planned urban space challenged top-down planning and heightened anxieties about failed urbanization and a not-yet-modern population held responsible for the premature aging of the buildings. At the same time, decay and disrepair strengthened residents' solidarities and antipathy toward the state. Crumbling building exteriors and dangerous interiors unsettled future-oriented development, putting residents at risk of architectural catastrophe: the collapse of decrepit buildings. Decay did not disempower residents, however, nor did it affect them equally. As people grew embittered by disrepair and more critical of state neglect, they deployed collective strategies to mitigate risk.

Decay also emboldened those with the means to produce new living environments. In chapter 9, I move from decayed exteriors to renovated interiors to examine how encounters with precarity shaped architecture through the unlawful remodeling of flats. The creative remaking of lived spaces turned residents into designers and architects who challenged the idea that industrialized housing was static, uniform, and beset by poverty. Interior renovations disrupted the temporality of ruins as a linear decline. Aspirational spaces of dwelling redefined residents' relationships with both the state and the dying buildings and became sites for fashioning new middle-class subjectivities and livelihood practices.

The deteriorating city provided fodder for capitalist redevelopment. Chapter 10 examines the politics of value through residents' resignification of "ruins" to contest privatization and the aesthetics of the New Modern. Denationalization of state property was a fraught process, but it also generated political subjectivities that ascribed historical, ecological, technical, and affective values to the crumbling buildings. Anxious about displacement from their homes, residents took collective action to disrupt the cycle of raze and rebuild, which had suspended them in an endless socialist meantime. Ruination thus emerged as a powerful tool in the struggle for control over spatial restructuring and the material conditions of urban life.

PART 1
Ruination

I am a city still, but soon I shan't be—
Where generations used to live and die
Before those deadly birds flew in to haunt me:
One thousand years to build. A fortnight
to destroy.

—BERTOLT BRECHT, *KRIEGSFIBEL* (WAR PRIMER)

↑ Figure P.1.1 Aerial view of Vinh in wartime, n.d. Photo by Hồ Xuân Thành.

1

ANNIHILATION

> "I thought it was a drill . . . until the intercom announced, 'This is no drill. You're going to Vinh.'"
>
> —U.S. COMMANDER HENRY URBAN JR.

In a *New York Times* article from 1968, Commander Henry Urban Jr. recounts the historic first bombing strikes on the Democratic Republic of Vietnam (DRV), also known as North Vietnam. The swift and violent strikes were made in retaliation for the reported torpedo firing on U.S. naval destroyers, known as the Tonkin Gulf Incident (in Vietnamese, *Sự kiện Vịnh Bắc Bộ*), which marked the dawn of a new "yellow peril" for the United States. "Start planning an attack on Vinh," a duty officer informed Urban in the quiet dawn hours of August 5, 1964.[1] Later that morning, Urban would take part in leading a twenty-plane vengeance mission to destroy identified "hostile" targets, including a petroleum storage facility on the outskirts of the city. Many residents of Vinh—some of my research respondents among them—remember the attack as the beginning of ten menacing years of aerial warfare that resulted in mass urban destruction, displacement, and death. For Urban, this distant and very different human landscape of another time and place—outside Western modernity—remained invisible if not irrelevant, and the victims of his acts ungrievable. "I was just in the right place at the right time," he commented callously on the hailed success of his mission. Urban offered no reflection on those ill-fated persons who were, to the contrary, just in the wrong place at the wrong time—the unknown first victims of racial atrocities fueled by irrational anxieties about decolonization as a threat to be subdued.

The invisibilization of human beings, of racial Others who experienced the terror of successive bombardments, was by no means unique to this smug commander. As I argue in this chapter, this systematic denial and erasure of humankind was made possible through visual technologies and ways of seeing the world that Paul Virilio (1989, 1) has called a "logistics of military perception" to identify the strategic importance of vision and the gaze to modern warfare. Propelled by concurrent developments in military science and cinematic techniques, these methods of picturing enemy terrain operated through a "threshold of detectability" that "filtered objects in and out of visibility" (Weizman 2017, 33). For example, they made the annihilation of material and biophysical landscapes hypervisible while obscuring the human toll of that violence. This differs from the usual corporeal politics associated with militarized perception technologies and sighting devices, including contemporary drones that turn abstracted bodies into hostile targets (Wall and Monahan 2011, 239). Here, infrastructural objects were the primary targets, often to the point of obsession, and death or injury to human beings—the "yellow hordes" responsible for spreading Asian communism—became mere collateral damage of U.S. airpower.

There remains an institutionally organized erasure of the scale of trauma inflicted on the Vietnamese people during the U.S.-Vietnam War in the media and in much academic scholarship (Espiritu 2014, 178). Where accounts do exist, they expose the profound physical and emotional suffering of people in the south of Vietnam, who were subjected to routine racialized violence and subjugation. More attention is paid to the South in part because there exists copious visual documentation of atrocities committed on the ground in that part of the country; in the North, the aggrieved bodies of those who were considered not yet fully human remained unseen and unphotographed from the air. Casualties of the air war went uncounted in quantitative terms in the American press (in contrast to the statistical reporting of drone-strike fatalities that appear in the media today), but the victims were also considered uncountable in a humanistic sense. Owing to Cold War notions that communist populations were lesser human beings—fundamentally flawed and without reason or feeling—and that the bombing was a moral imperative, if not a historic responsibility to save Western civilization from the evils of communism (especially the "Oriental" type), the victims' very humanity was categorically denied. As Judith Butler has argued, "An ungrievable life is one that cannot be mourned because it has never lived, that is, it has never counted as a life at all" (2009, 38). For military technocrats, fighter pilots, and bomber crews, being at war with nonhuman objects—trucks, trees, bridges, and smokestacks—meant reducing human lives to unquantifiable abstractions, or nonpersons. Such tactics were exemplary of twentieth-century "terror from the air" that operated by voiding the distinction between violence against people and violence against the very things that made life livable (Sloterdijk 2009, 25).

Despite the unrepresented and uncalculated victims, the American "War of Destruction" (*Chiến tranh phá hoại*), as it is often called in Vietnam, was an intensely scopic war. Aerial warfare relied heavily on enumeration (such as object "kill" statistics) and used image-based practices that accompanied modern weapons of mass harm and destruction to achieve its tactical goals. Like contemporary surveillance by drones, photographic surveillance made the sinister North knowable and penetrable by sophisticated missile technologies through the conversion of raw reconnaissance data into concrete visual targets (Saint-Amour 2003, 370). Whereas in the South, human body counts stood as measures of progress (Appy 1993, 153), in the North, the metric of the air war's success was the tallied destruction of nonhuman objects. Commander Urban's masculine ambition to expand air raids on Vietnam's infrastructure, as conveyed through his panoptic spectatorship of the port of Hải Phòng, reveals a sublime fixation with the annihilation of the material world that unfolds as male Orientalist fantasy. In the last section of the *New York Times* article, subtitled "Wants to Bomb Docks," Urban expressed his impulsive desire to attack and subdue the city's harbor, which he observed as bustling with transportation activity, much to his irritation. The trucks came and went with supplies, the barges moved in and out with their freight. "I'd like to hit that port," he declared, as if the vehicles were pieces on a board game he could control and take out. The city's intact colonial architecture also caught his eye and roused a deep yearning to destroy it as an expression of technical mastery and white male potency. "The desire to bomb a virgin building is terrific," he confided, revealing masculine pleasures attached to the destruction of material forms envisioned as feminine targets of conquest.[2]

Beyond Hải Phòng and Vinh, aerial warfare had a profound effect on Vietnamese urban development. Given the sheer scale of destruction, and the different forms and intensities it took in the North and the South, studies of contemporary urbanization in Vietnam cannot discount this history of American military violence. And yet despite the growth of interest in Vietnamese cities, the long-term effects of the bombing on built environments, economies, and civilian populations remain largely unaddressed. Studies that do explore the impact of war on urban development tend to leave out civilians.[3] Moreover, the lived experience of urban warfare varied greatly across regions and cities. For example, in contrast to the Republic of Vietnam (RVN), in the South, where people fled from rural areas *to* urban centers (Turley 1977),[4] in the North, people escaped *from* cities to the countryside and mountains (see chapter 2). This difference shaped distinct forms of postwar urbanization and geographies of reconstruction: the RVN attempted to depopulate and disperse cities, while the DRV strove to repopulate and consolidate them (Thrift and Forbes 1986).

To understand the magnitude of human and material devastation wrought by ten years of aerial attacks, and how it set the stage for imagining a utopian geography of postwar recovery, this chapter is divided into four sections. In the first, I examine the techno-scopic war on infrastructure in and around the city of Vinh between 1964 and 1973 that was made possible through the rendering of enemy territory first as picture and then as target to "be destroyed as soon as it [could] be made visible," as Rey Chow (2006, 12) has argued of the age of bombing. Here image making would lend itself to formulating a rationalized plan of wholesale destruction, aided by an air technocracy bent on perfecting its strategy and proving its superiority through annihilation of the material development that had taken place over the previous decade of decolonization. Bombing Vietnam out of modern time (and "back to the Stone Age") required mobilization of an immense apparatus of representation and spatial knowledge production through reconnaissance photography to make the cryptic Asian enemy legible and predictable, I show in the second section. In dramatizing distance and difference, this "imaginative geography" justified protracted bombing by drawing a clear moral, racial, and spatial boundary between a "powerful and articulate" Self and a "defeated and distant" Other (Said 1978, 57). U.S. narratives of the hotly disputed war were largely told through visual and statistical data on the "death" of material objects and built forms that were detached from human suffering. This war on nonhuman objects, I argue in the third section, took an irrational turn with the rise of techno-fanaticism (Sherry 1987): an impulsive preoccupation with ever more efficient and sophisticated technologies—weaponry, sighting devices, and guidance systems—and the sense of supreme power and control they appeared to offer, especially for pilots infused with racial hatred. As techno-fanaticism rose among strategists, the air war came to resemble a data-driven, computer-managed operation directed remotely from the other side of the world (Hecht and Edwards 2010, 288). Fascinated with the ability to destroy and to covertly observe hits and misses from afar, pilots used excessive force, often for revenge, to eliminate unyielding targets—an overkill that did not always produce intended results. In the final section, I examine this irrational destruction and its annihilation of Vinh through inflated and incomplete U.S. government records, accompanied by dehumanizing rhetoric, which helped to maintain the façade of American air supremacy and belief in the inevitability of its triumph.

> Certain prestige targets will be restruck repeatedly to demonstrate U.S. resolve. Such attacks will be intended primarily for the psychological effect they will have on the people. . . . Emphasis will be on maintaining a presence night and day to keep the populace continually aware that systematic destruction of the homeland is in progress.
>
> —OPERATION PRIMING CHARGE, DECEMBER 7, 1972

The *New York Times* article on the first Vinh bombing raid in 1964 is noteworthy for a number of reasons. In addition to providing an epistemological framing of war that "fail[ed] to apprehend the lives of others as lost or injured" (Butler 2009, 1), it reminds us that the conditions that made Vietnamese people vulnerable, disposable, uncounted, and uncountable—which included framing the bombing as rational, even ethical—have been largely forgotten in the United States. The average citizen knows little about the extent of Vietnamese casualties and the devastation wrought by the prolonged air war, even though knowledge about "Vietnam" remains inseparable from the war as representation (Schwenkel 2009a). As is often the case with war memory, *American* losses (in this case, pilots who were captured, killed, or unaccounted for) trumped the deaths of others and at the same time turned those innocent victims into enemy perpetrators who aroused little sympathy. In the rare instances that air strikes are remembered, public memory focuses almost entirely on Hanoi—and then only on iconic attacks, such as the 1972 "Christmas bombing." Destruction of smaller provincial cities and industrial centers that sustained the brunt of the violence, such as Vinh, remain neglected places of collective nonmemory, preventing deeper historical understanding of the scale of U.S. violence in Vietnam.[5]

Despite the lingering association of aerial warfare with Hanoi in American public memory, there were extensive references to Vinh in newspaper reports at the time. Much of this referencing relied on maps—visual technologies central to war making that rationalized political space to sustain the idea that two sovereign countries existed side by side: North and South Vietnam.[6] As an important transportation hub in the southern part of the DRV, and a main transfer point for troops and supplies heading south, the provincial capital of Vinh and its surrounds were primary targets of systematic bombing. As the 1972 aeronaval action plan quoted in the epigraph describes, these acts of infrastructural and psychological warfare were intended to produce a "mass shock effect." "Attack maps" that reported military action in the U.S. press typically located Vinh at the critical intersection of Highway 1, which ran north-south to Hanoi, and Highway 7, which ran east-west, connecting the port to Laos. The map of Vietnam at the start of this book shows an example of its strategic location: the lower dotted line represents the former division of the country at the seventeenth parallel. The nineteenth parallel lies fifty kilometers north of Vinh, and the twentieth parallel—above which bombing was halted on April 1, 1968—is just north of Thanh Hóa. Despite its position in a zone of exception, where air assaults could and would be unrelenting, the city presented bombers with an array of visual targeting challenges, including its weather patterns (low cloud ceilings that obscured vision), transport routes that were not mapped by the U.S. military, and the dispersal of industry. Nonetheless, as early as September 13, 1966, the *New York Times* reported that there were more bombs dropped on Vinh than any other area in the North. For example, during Operation Rolling Thunder,[7] which included a record-setting day of 171 attack missions over the DRV, the coastal town of Vinh was reported to have been the "hardest hit area."[8] Six years later, a CIA assessment of the bombing found that 75 percent of air strikes under Operation Linebacker[9] had been carried out in the "panhandle"—the narrow strip of land that extended south from the twentieth parallel to the demilitarized zone, which divided the country into North and South.[10] At the center of the panhandle and Vietnam's Fourth Military Zone (*Quân khu 4*) stood Vinh. The U.S. military divided aerial operations into their own six zones, and Vinh was situated in the "Route Package" or RP 3. Vinh was also commonly referenced in U.S. media for another reason, which helped earn it the moniker *Heldenstadt* ("City of Heroes") in the East German press: U.S. planes were frequently shot down there by antiaircraft artillery.[11]

The *New York Times* article is also noteworthy in highlighting the first air raid in 1964, which foreshadowed a decade of ruthless aerial assaults in and beyond the DRV. By the time of the article's publication more than three years later, a vast air technocracy had emerged, led by elite military experts whose job it was to expand air operations and build cutting-edge systems of military technology. The search for faster, larger, and smarter technologies—more effective weapons and surveillance techniques—meant that air operations became "an exercise in management effectiveness" (Tilford 2009, 117). This efficacy hinged on rational calculations of how to achieve "maximum destruction and greatest impact,"[12] both psychological and economic, at the least financial and human cost to the U.S. military. New military technologies with improved efficiency and capacity were presented as the most humane technical solution to the problem of communist infiltration. In military doctrine, bombing was framed as rational—deliberate and yet restrained—as well as ethical. In the words of General Maxwell Taylor, "The purpose of a rational war is to break the will of the adversary and cause him to adjust his behavior to our purpose" (cited in Thompson and Frizzell 1977, 135). Military technocrats rationalized advances in the technological scale and force of modern firepower as necessary to achieve *peace*—an example of a "harm-making project of pacification" (Feldman 2015, 2) that masks state violence as a form of justice. This goal of peace would be accomplished by persuading adversaries in Hanoi to accept subordination to a superior power and come to the negotiating table, or suffer the punitive consequences. "We wanted Ho [Chi Minh] and his advisors to have time to meditate on the prospects of a demolished homeland," Taylor threatened. Similar to gendered narratives that the U.S. atomic bombing of Japan during World War II had "rescued" that country,[13] airpower promised, paradoxically, to bring about salvation—an end to the war—through the choreographed destruction of the DRV. It is no coincidence that this fantasy of white male omnipotence was reflected in the racist naming practices of iconic bombers that drew on stereotypes of the noble Indian warrior, including the F-105 Thunderchief and the A-4 Skyhawk, making explicit the historical connection between the civilizing doctrines of nineteenth-century manifest destiny and twentieth-century anticommunist policy as the basis of American exceptionalism.

The immense military bureaucracy responsible for aerial warfare in Vietnam paved the way for the first electronic war in history (Virilio 1989, 82), based on the rapid expansion of militarized systems that would showcase U.S. technological capabilities. This newly engineered arsenal included a range of tactical weapons more destructive than ever, such as cluster and laser-guided bombs and defoliants, as well as new modalities of surveillance that deployed advanced sensory devices to track enemy movement. Acoustic and heat-sensitive detectors dropped along the Hồ Chí Minh Trail, for instance, as well as seismic and magnetic sensors spread around the demilitarized zone, relayed intelligence through sequential images and electronic data-feedback mechanisms (Virilio 1989, 82). So sophisticated was this remote intelligence apparatus that it became inconceivable to military analysts that U.S. airpower could not win the "technowar," as James Gibson called it (1986). While computer models claimed to predict the *future* performance of military operations, it was the compilation of statistical data on *past* battlefield activity that substantiated the appearance of progress. The mutual integration of aerial weapons and surveillance systems produced a vast database of knowledge that tracked and documented the air war. This included a set of objectified facts and measurable indicators such as dates and numbers of sorties, types of aircraft flown, bomb load quantities, targets, and—most importantly for the military—bomb damage assessments (BDA) to evaluate physical and functional loss to target areas. Modern visual technologies deployed by fighters and reconnaissance aircraft made swift BDA feedback possible (though not yet in real time). As I detail in the next section, these militarized ways of seeing (and surveying) affected landscapes converted qualitative images into quantifiable data to affirm the technical efficacy of aerial warfare.

BOMB DAMAGE ASSESSMENT: VISUAL TECHNOLOGIES OF AIRPOWER

> To derive a meaningful cost estimate of destruction to bridges in North Vietnam, [analysts] must rely on post strike photography of each bridge attacked.
>
> —CIA BOMB DAMAGE ASSESSMENT REPORT, 1967

In the United States, tactical airpower, often called "strategic bombing," has long been considered the instrument of swift and decisive victory. Since World War II, strategists have surmised that calculated air strikes could have a formidable material and affective impact on enemy populations by destroying capability as well as resolve (Clodfelter 2006, 2). As Vietnam's cities increasingly came under attack, strategic bombing turned civilians and nonmilitary property into routine targets and casualties of war. Against this backdrop, aerial photography, believed to "surpass all other visual forms in . . . accuracy" (Saint-Amour 2003, 355), came to shape military perceptions of aerial operations, over and above even pilot observations. Delinked from humanist aesthetics (Kaplan 2018, 148), aerial photography thus played a key role in the planning and execution of warfare. Through high-resolution surveillance and reconnaissance imagery, abstract landscapes became legible and targetable as objects to be destroyed. Operating as remote perpetrators, navigators and technicians were able to identify built forms and ascertain proximate knowledge of real-time activities on the ground without detection from below. This knowledge could then be used to strike the enemy and, afterward, to provide visual evidence of its demise, ensuring "maximal visibility . . . for the purpose of maximal destruction" (Chow 2006, 31). In rendering the communist world as target, field training manuals on aerial observation emphasized the importance of amassing critical information through scopic and electronic perception technologies, including lasers and radars, as "an inherent part of all Army aviation missions."[14]

During the war in Vietnam, U.S. leaders held tight to the belief that mass bombardment could defeat Hanoi by destroying morale as well as supply systems. The coupling of infrastructural *and* psychological warfare, as discussed above, underpinned the furious assaults aimed at annihilating not human bodies but the material and environmental conditions necessary for life (Sloterdijk 2009, 15).[15] As Priya Satia has argued of the history of aerial warfare, "Air control was intended as an everyday form of violence that worked through daily terrorization as much as bombardment, both depending on the claim to intimate knowledge" of the Other (2014, 12). In Vietnam, an extensive U.S. intelligence apparatus acquired detailed empirical knowledge of routine activities and enemy movements through sequential aerial photography and by intercepting tactical communications. The panoptic presence of airborne surveillance not only played a vital role in amassing geospatial military intelligence (Gregory 2016, 4); it also reminded people on the ground of imminent punishment from above (Satia 2014, 2).

Remote surveillance turned the landscape into a collection of knowable, countable, and perceivable objects that could be "neutralized," even as its ways of seeing were inherently unstable and ambiguous (Kaplan 2018, 4). Industrial infrastructure and "interdiction points"—which, in U.S. military parlance, included roads, docks, railways, bridges, and transportation for troops and supplies—were tracked and hit relentlessly between 1965 and 1968, during Operation Rolling Thunder, and again in 1972, during Operation Linebacker. Petroleum, oil, and lubricants (POL) sites and electric power plants were also targeted repeatedly, with careful study, documentation, and labeling of attack aftermaths. For example, figure 1.1 details damage to the Lang Chi/Thác Bà hydroelectric plant, built with the support of the Soviet Union in the 1960s. Air strikes in the panhandle continued uninterrupted (albeit at a lower intensity after November 1, 1968),[16] owing to different rules of engagement and a policy of "protective reaction" that permitted aircraft on reconnaissance missions to respond in "self-defense" to "hostile acts" by the DRV, such as radar tracking.[17] As a strategy to spread terror, protective reaction had a profound emotional impact on the population in Vinh, who lived in a constant state of heightened fear and vulnerability. It meant that bombing could and would be uninterrupted, carried out by unseen and yet observing fighter jets, making serial evacuation an enduring condition and strategy of survival for urban residents (see chapter 2).

Reconnaissance photographs reflected an optical politics of positioning (Haraway 1988, 586) from a vantage point looking down on the enemy Other. Before-and-after images, in particular, played a pivotal role in U.S. air

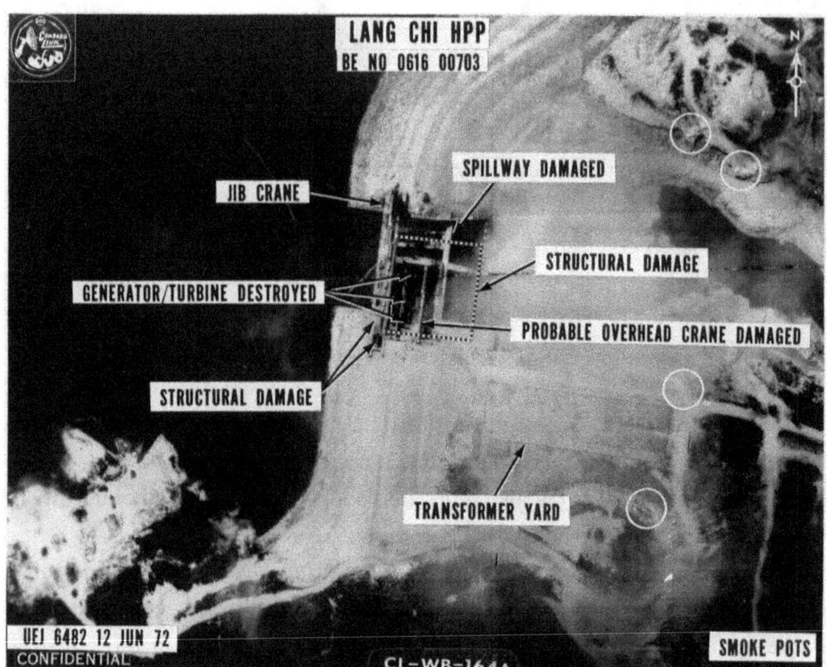

↑ Figure 1.1 Reconnaissance image of the June 1972 destruction of Lang Chi/Thác Bà hydroelectric plant. National Archives and Records Administration.

campaigns, from planning and execution to post-attack appraisement, or BDA. Based on visual and audio intelligence gathered through electronic technologies, government reports offered remarkably comprehensive details of road maintenance and construction, bridge and rail repair, shipments of supplies and equipment (including origin and destination), and numbers of vehicles in use or parked.[18] The collection and interpretation of statistical indicators derived from observed "facts" helped design interventions—a new strike mission, for instance, whose violence was "rationally" framed through material attrition rates of nonhuman objects rather than through human casualties. Both government reports and the media offered up-to-date accountings of infrastructural objects and built structures "taken out" or damaged in air strikes as a quantifiable measure of military efficiency: fifty barges on one mission, sixteen boxcars on another, fifteen military warehouses on another, and so on.[19] These modalities of enumeration, which tended toward anthropomorphism, came to stand as a clear material index of aerial success. Trucks, in particular, occupied a central place in the "cartographic imaginary of war" (Gregory 2016, 26), given their critical role in supporting enemy operations

↑ Figure 1.2 Photographic surveillance of trucks on the Hồ Chí Minh Trail, 1973. National Archives and Records Administration.

in the south (see figure 1.2). "Truck kills" were regularly reported in the press, detached from the operators that brought them to "life." For example, a convoy of fifty trucks south of Vinh—identified as a "rare find"—was "raked" and "pounded" by a sortie of Thunderjets flying armed reconnaissance, reducing the vehicles to smoldering metal carcasses.[20] In the material politics of *non*corporeality that informed U.S. strategy in the North, a sustained war on things—in this case, trucks imbued with nonhuman agency—supplanted the violence done to human bodies that went unrecognized. This refusal to count (and to account for) the human dead—after all, it was the truck and not its driver that was "killed"—shows how entire social worlds were rendered nonexistent by granting agency to objects alone (Latour 2005), an imperialist subterfuge that diverted attention from the real human costs of the war.[21]

Through both aerial photographs and subjective pilot sightings, the U.S. government could track air strike performance and precision over time according to a profit-and-loss model of warfare (Sherry 1987, 235). For example, it could tally truck attrition ratios relative to interdiction efforts: one truck kill for every thirty-four sorties under Operation Rolling Thunder versus one for every twenty-two under Operation Linebacker.[22] BDA images of destroyed infrastructure provided visible evidence of the cumulative achievements of

↑ Figure 1.3 Bomb damage assessment: poststrike photography of railway yards in Vinh, 1972. National Archives and Records Administration.

U.S. airpower, even though the abstract images, frequently engulfed in thick plumes of smoke, hampered detectability, making it difficult to affirm or refute claims of a successful offensive (see figure 1.3). There was also a tension between poststrike photography and supplementary forms of intelligence, particularly pilots' observation reports that overestimated the damage done to infrastructure. The 1967 CIA assessment of bomb damage quoted in the epigraph noted a large discrepancy in truth claims: 121 bridges damaged or destroyed according to image analyses versus 755 sighted by fighter pilots.[23] To counter human error and protect against overly optimistic appearances of progress, the CIA stressed the need to rely on aerial photography, the only trustworthy "witness" that could be converted into reliable intelligence through surface analysis—and which also served as a technology of control of the pilots' performance by their superiors. Miscalculations exposed problems in the underlying rationale for strategic bombing and the knowledge produced about its efficacy. As fascination with technique and achievement—combined with frustration at the rate of failed missions—escalated, military strategy took an irrational turn toward overkill.

IRRATIONAL DESTRUCTION AND TECHNO-FANATICISM

> [The bombing] is something like the repetitive strokes of a jackhammer, if you will. At some point the concrete begins to break up.
>
> —GENERAL HAROLD K. JOHNSON, IN UNITED STATES SENATE, *AIR WAR AGAINST NORTH VIETNAM*, 1967

> True, the aggressors had made careful and comprehensive calculations, banking heavily on the effectiveness of their modern armoury. . . . But reality has completely baffled their plans. The more the U.S. imperialists stepped up their aggressive war, the heavier their failures.
>
> —GENERAL VÕ NGUYÊN GIÁP, *PEOPLE'S WAR AGAINST U.S. AERO-NAVAL WAR*, 1975

The optimism of early pilot sightings and truth claims, with their embellished numbers, gave way to mounting frustration as rational and calculated destruction was shown to be a chaotic and haphazard affair. The strategy was beset by faulty planning, bureaucratic confusion,[24] and unsuccessful missions[25] that revealed a "chasm between fantasy and reality" in conceptions of U.S. airpower (Sherry 1987, 239). This included "friendly loss rates" as high as 5 percent in the Hải Phòng region and 3 percent in the panhandle around Vinh.[26] Despite the reported numbers of "killed" or neutralized target-objects, from early on the U.S. government recognized that the air war was failing to achieve its strategic objectives. Although aerial assaults had seriously disrupted or destroyed much of the DRV's modern infrastructure and industrial capacity, supplies and troops continued to make their way south, particularly through the hardest-hit area of the panhandle near Vinh.

Social evolution theory offered a temporal framework for understanding this ineffectiveness. At issue was not superior American technology but the primitive context for its performance. CIA assessments of Operations Rolling Thunder and Linebacker identified a similar impediment to air strikes: the DRV's "simple" economy, which made the country a poor setting for the execution of strategic bombing. The influential 1942 book *Victory through Air Power* had proposed the social Darwinist idea that the more developed the civilization, the greater its vulnerability to aerial attack.[27] Echoing this thesis, intelligence analysts contrasted the DRV's unsophisticated transportation networks and dispersed, small-scale industry—which contributed little to the war effort, given Hanoi's heavy reliance on imports from China and the Soviet Union—with advanced industrial and infrastructure targets in highly developed countries, which were vital to war-making capabilities.[28] Another study that demonstrated the same logic of temporal othering concluded that the failure of airpower could not be disassociated from the "underdeveloped nature" of the DRV, which offered few valuable targets for bombing.[29] Indeed, its premodern, agrarian society exhibited considerable economic resilience to attacks by modern technology. And yet the fierce strikes continued unabated and even increased as the doctrine of "self-restraint" and "graduated" assault turned into one of relentless "restrike."

The fact that strategic bombing, which had been used effectively to defeat industrialized countries in World War II, was uncritically deployed in Vietnam with little consideration of the country's historical and economic conditions (as well as its different techniques of combat) was but one critique of the air war (Clodfelter 2006). Another involved the restrictive strategies of incremental escalation and controlled, low-intensity attacks (Thompson and Frizzell 1977). And yet military policy unambiguously advocated *minimal* restraint, as shown in General Johnson's call to pound northern Vietnam until the will of the people was broken, their material history rendered nonexistent. This call for unrelenting strikes to lay waste to the country and bring an end to hostilities conjures what Michael S. Sherry has called "technological fanaticism": the nihilistic pursuit of destructive ends through purely technical means (1987, 251–52). In the context of the air war in Vietnam, I truncate this phrase to "techno-fanaticism" to draw attention to the unique cultural, historical, and especially racial dimensions of aerial bombardment as a mechanism to ensure that the enemy remains outside modern history. Though it had deep roots in military science and the development of modern technology, techno-fanaticism achieved a new scale of ferocity during the Cold War, as racial antagonisms increased and as engineers developed more sophisticated weaponry, including "smart" laser-guided bombs, to improve precision and accuracy of target "kill rates." But the logic of these "intelligent" weapons with "predatory capabilities" (De Landa 1991, 43) intended to perfect techniques of war remained unchanged: mass firepower to inflict maximum damage, rather than a strategy to end an unpopular war (Tilford 2009).

For pilots indoctrinated into this Cold War culture of techno-fanaticism, beset by racist imagery of a brutal and indifferent enemy, the quest for technological superiority was closely entwined with the will—and power—to annihilate, as Sherry (1987, 254) has argued was the case during the Pacific

War (World War II). It was also linked to the desire to be a menacing omnipresence in the sky, with total vision (Wall and Monahan 2011, 243). And yet this zeal to destroy, exemplified in Commander Urban's masculine fantasy about crushing virgin buildings, was often foiled by restrictions on targets. For example, the port of Hải Phòng was prohibited, despite Urban's own observations of enemy activity there. It was also limited by technological impediments. A 1967 study on the effectiveness of air attacks on bridges found that only one in forty-seven bombs hit a target and that "an average of six sorties were required to interdict one bridge."[30] Techno-fanaticism can thus be understood as a response to both engagement restrictions and technological limitations that stifled the will to destroy and the ability to see (and take pleasure in) the life-shattering impact of bombardment. In contrast to the "unmanning" of U.S. combat soldiers on the ground, who were "penetrated" by both nature and enemy (Gregory 2016, 26), airpower reaffirmed pilots' masculine domination through the excessive deployment of airborne technology to exterminate rival forces. Less restricted targets, such as bridges and petroleum depots, became objects of obsessive restrike, beyond the rational use of force. This was particularly the case when unruly infrastructure withstood repeated attacks. For example, planes and ships released thousands of explosives on the main power plant in Vinh in hundreds of punishing raids, requiring its repair more than two dozen times.[31] Not one missile, however, brought down the plant's besieged smokestack, which became an emblem of effective urban resistance and American technological incompetence (Schwenkel 2018). Such resilient infrastructures roused masculine anxiety among military technocrats, including pilots, about the inadequacies of their advanced missile technologies to subdue a technologically inferior and feminized enemy.

The lack of inhibition—and technique—in the use of airpower against the smokestack intensified as infrastructural objects refused to "die." The U.S. Air Force had an equally obsessive relationship with the Hàm Rồng (Dragon's Jaw) Bridge in the province of Thanh Hóa, just north of Nghệ An, and became consumed with destroying it. During Operation Rolling Thunder, the bridge had been the target of hundreds of missions that missed or damaged the structure.[32] Owing to the mass mobilization of labor, within days of an attack the bridge would be restored and the passage of vehicles would resume. The sublime power that the bridge held over pilots ultimately came to a head with its demise on May 13, 1972, when dozens of jets pummeled the bridge for its insolence, releasing thousands of pounds of laser-guided bombs that ultimately triggered its collapse. Pilots ritually reenacted its destruction with excessive force long after it had succumbed, as if seeking to kill again that which was already dead. A CIA report ascribed such victories to a wider "freedom" in air operations and improved technologies of firepower deployed during Operation Linebacker: "Targets which often required many strikes to destroy with conventional bombs during Rolling Thunder have in many cases been destroyed by a single strike in the present campaign."[33] And yet for Vietnamese people, both the Hàm Rồng Bridge and the smokestack in Vinh stood as visual proof that modern technological warfare, and its fantasy of conquest, was doomed to fail, as Võ Nguyên Giáp had predicted. Around the world, this irrational destruction—which culminated in the fiercest aerial campaign yet of December 1972—contributed to the growing unpopularity of the air war and aroused intense public criticism, especially of the excessive bombardment of cities like Vinh.

IRRATIONAL DESTRUCTION OF VINH

> In the morning we saw Vinh, or rather what remained of this ancient city. This important industrial center . . . is in ruins. Yet almost every day the news bulletins report new bombings in Vinh. The bombs now fall on the rocks, even the ruins do not remain.
>
> —*UNDER THE SKIES OF VIETNAM*, 1968[34]

The sustained use of excessive force to demolish the power plant is representative of the wider war of irrational destruction that took place against Vinh. It is a tragic irony that a region identified by the U.S. military as having only "low-profile" targets of dispersed and small-scale production facilities was hit so heavily that even the ruins became ruins—pulverized, as a Russian observer remarked in 1968. Vinh would thus emerge as a symbol of the irrationalities and injustices of U.S. government policy, its rubble as material evidence of the crimes of U.S. imperialism. "The bombing was ruthless," a ninety-year-old judge emeritus—one of the first to be appointed in postrevolution Vinh in 1946—described to me one morning.[35] "You can say that the city was annihilated" (*bị hủy diệt*), he stated. "There wasn't one day when bombs didn't fall," a retired architect, assigned to rebuild the damaged power plant, said solemnly. "On average, every thirty meters there was a bomb crater," he recalled.[36] The biophysical impact of this razing—dead persons, flattened structures, slaughtered livestock, downed trees—was a surreal landscape of nothingness, an uninhabited and uninhabitable "anti-landscape" (Nye and Elkin 2014), at times compared with the moon. Through my respondents' eyes it appeared as a "wasteland" (*đất hoang*), where one could "look out over the horizon without anything obstructing your view."

While there is little debate over the scope of the city's destruction—the effects of "deliberate demodernization" as a geopolitical strategy of warfare (Graham 2005)—there are competing figures on the scale of air strikes in and around Vinh. Vietnamese municipal statistics report that the city was subjected to more than forty-seven hundred air strikes between August 1964 and January 1973, during which an estimated 250,555 tons of ordnance were released, averaging 424 tons per square kilometer (Phạm and Bùi 2003, 217), or approximately 3.5 tons of explosives per person, based on preevacuation numbers. At first glance, this tonnage appears high when compared with the figures conventionally cited in Western scholarship, which typically relies on Combat Air Activities (CACTA) files and Southeast Asia Database (SEADAB) records.[37] If these U.S. records are accurate, it would mean that one-quarter of all bombs dropped on the DRV were released over Vinh. Municipal estimates are more aligned with the numbers maintained by the Vietnamese central government, however, which has historically claimed that a greater amount of total bomb tonnage was dropped than the U.S. government reported.[38]

On second glance, this high number of strikes may indeed be plausible. Although CACTA and SEADAB records are replete with missing, redundant, corrupted, or falsified entries (High, Curran, and Robinson 2014, 87), they do offer a sense of the magnitude of strikes and their planned targets. Data show that 24,964 air sorties were flown over the province of Nghệ An between October 1, 1965, and February 19, 1973—the day of the last recorded strike—concentrated along National Routes 1, 7, and 15 (see plate 1). Adjusted to account for missing data—recordkeeping did not commence until seven months into Operation Rolling Thunder, and some months are excluded—this number increases to approximately 32,846 missions.[39] Each mission typically included multiple fighter craft and explosive types; Kocher, Pepinsky, and Kalyvas report that "over 83% of bombing sorties involved more than one aircraft, while the mean number of weapons dropped per sortie was about 14" (2011, 6). The CACTA/SEADAB data show 109,908 aircraft engaged over Nghệ An within this timeframe (an average of eighty-three fighter jets per day during Operation Rolling Thunder), with an estimated total load quantity of 305,228 bombs. Although this number does not distinguish between released and returned ordnance from thwarted attacks (often due to low visibility), it does show intent through the presence of heavy bomb loads on the jets (High, Curran, and Robinson 2014, 96).

The number of air strikes over Vinh recorded in the U.S. database is not far from the Vietnamese municipal government estimate of approximately 4,198 sorties, when adjusted for missing data (not including raids before March 1, 1965). During Operation Rolling Thunder, a monthly average of 135.6 aircraft took part in strikes on the city (or close to 5 fighter jets per day), carrying an average load of twenty-six bombs. These numbers remained fairly consistent during Operation Linebacker in 1972 (averaging 139 sorties monthly), with the last bombs released over the city on January 15, 1973. It is important to note that such figures offer but a partial representation of the attacks that leveled the city more than once. They do, however, help to convey the scale and intensity of attacks in one locality during the longest and most violent campaign of protracted bombing in the history of aerial warfare (McCoy 2012).[40] Although the colossal CACTA/SEADAB archive also includes information about infrastructure targets—sorted into categories such as bridges, railways, vehicles, warehouses, factories, pumping stations, roads, etc.—along with a BDA of each strike, its quantifiable measures obscure the qualitative human toll and sociomaterial losses experienced. The specificity of each human and nonhuman object, along with their aggregate social significance—which bridge, which building, whose house, and whose lives—remained beyond the taxonomic scope of American military technocracy and its (il)logics of total destruction. However, such information *was* documented elsewhere to reveal an opposing set of truth claims. It is to these sensory representations and memories of wartime atrocities that the next chapter turns.

Urban Fragments 1

↑ Figure I.1.1 Man observing a collapsed bomb shelter in Vinh that was struck by American missiles on April 14, 1972. Nghệ An Provincial Museum.

HẦM (THE BUNKER)

Thua đau thì địch cắn càn (Facing a painful defeat, the enemy bites fiercely)
Cắn càn thì cắn đau càng thêm đau[1] (The fiercer it bites, the more painful it gets)
Mấy lời to nhỏ bảo nhau (There are small and big things to remind one another)
Kiểm tra hầm hố nông sâu thế nào? (Check it out, how deep is the shelter?)
Miệng hầm che đậy làm sao? (What is covering the entrance?)
Khách ẩn chỗ nào, chủ nấp chỗ mô? (Where do hosts and guests [evacuees] take cover?)
Nơi công cộng có hầm chưa? (Do public places have bunkers yet?)
Máy móc, tài sản, hồ sơ thế nào? (What about machinery, assets, and records?)

Chống na-pan cháy làm sao? (How to stop the burning of napalm?)
Kế hoạch sơ tán chỗ nào, những chi? (Where is the planned evacuation and what to bring?)
Mấy lời nhắc lại nhắc đi (A few reminders need to be repeated)
Chưa làm thì phải làm đi, chậm rồi. (If not done yet then let's get to work, it's late already.)
Bảo vệ sản xuất, con người (Defend production, protect the people)
Quyết tâm diệt địch, đánh lùi mưu gian (Determined to kill the enemy, defeat its cunning plot)
Ai ơi! Hầm hố sẵn sàng. (Everyone! The shelters are ready.)

—QUỲNH DƯƠNG, 1964[2]

2

EVACUATION

> I remember the first time bombs fell on Vinh in 1964 when I was seven years old. The oil depot out by Hưng Hòa was hit and burned, flooding the city with thick black smoke. The day was August 5th. I was evacuated after that.
>
> —INTERVIEW WITH MS. THỦY, VINH RESIDENT, 2011

> Tôi hát lên với sự quả cảm (With bravery we have sung)
> Nhưng con trai ơi, giờ nay con ở đâu? (But where are you now, my son?)
>
> —JOAN BAEZ, "WHERE ARE YOU NOW, MY SON?," 1973. Lyrics posted in bunker of Hanoi Metropole Hotel, where Baez survived the 1972 "Christmas bombing"

With his squadron of heavily armed warplanes, Commander Urban's first attack on Vinh, which occurred on August 5, 1964, drastically changed the lifeworlds of urban residents. The unexpected assault catapulted the city from a postcolonial "economy of peace," oriented toward socialist transformation after defeat of the French, to one of total war, and consequently deurbanization. According to General Võ Nguyên Giáp's famous dictum, this war with the United States was a people's war, which mobilized an entire society and its resources to defend, in this instance, towns and cities. Cities, he argued, as the harbingers of modernity—with their vital industry, technologies, and lines of transport and communication—were to be protected at all costs (1975, 103).

Across the DRV, sustained aerial bombing set in motion a chain of defensive actions meant to both protect the most vulnerable civilians and maintain urban productivity, as the poem "The Bunker" describes in interlude 1.

Written days after the first air strike that found Commander Urban at the helm, the poem also forecasts the mass deployment of labor that produced an entirely new subterranean reality: a vast network of tunnels and shelters to facilitate mobility out of the city and provide safety underground.[1] More than just a refuge, subterranean architectures were also intended to preserve institutional bureaucracy and protect the means of production ("What about machinery, assets, and records?" the poem asks). Going underground collapsed distinct ontological worlds: the war would be fought simultaneously on, above, and beneath the surface of the earth. Building shelters, Giáp proclaimed, would guarantee continued industry and the ability to wage war from below ground (1975, 108). The results of collective efforts were extraordinary: Clodfelter (1995, 222) reports that up to thirty thousand miles of trenches and twenty-one million bomb shelters were constructed across the country, numbers that were close to Giáp's claim of "tens of millions" of bunkers and tunnels (1975, 44).

This was not excavation for progress or for imagining alternative futures. As Rosalind Williams has argued, subterranean projects in the twentieth century have been motivated by nightmares of defuturing rather than fantastical dreams (2008, 205). In Vinh alone, civil defense teams dug more than twenty-four thousand meters of trenches and sixteen thousand shelters (Phạm and Bùi 2003, 205). "They were everywhere!" (*khắp nơi*), one woman remembered, describing how she was never far from cover when planes approached and sirens sounded.[2] Most residents took part in the obligatory construction of shelters, including children, who dug passages below their beds and desks, and adults, who dug larger underground bunkers, mostly in the dark of night, hidden from the panoptic gaze of reconnaissance planes (see figure 2.1). This type of sensory deprivation—obscuring oneself to defy total vision from above—was a critical survival strategy for urban residents. It also became a strategy of guerilla warfare more broadly, giving rise to the racial imaginary of the "Viet Cong" as the sly and invisible enemy. Not all shelters were created equal, however. Like built forms above ground, subterranean dwellings exposed the uneven distribution of vulnerability in wartime. While rich and famous people, including Jane Fonda and Joan Baez during their antiwar protests in Hanoi, survived the air war in a capacious, concrete-reinforced bunker at an upscale hotel, many "everyday" shelters built of mud, bamboo, and thatch collapsed under the force of explosions, as seen in the image from Vinh in interlude 1. The allocation of resources during the war prioritized not only cities over the countryside but, in this case, Western celebrities over Vietnamese citizens.

For people on the ground who experienced the blasts and their devastating aftermaths firsthand, the air war was anything but "limited" and

↑ Figure 2.1 Youth mobilization: digging tunnels in Vinh, n.d. Nghệ An Provincial Museum.

"restrained," as U.S. military rules of engagement claimed (chapter 1). As the quote by Ms. Thủy in the epigraph reveals, those first explosions were an ominous sign of full-scale war and a decade of mass destruction governed by techno-fanaticism. Like many of my older respondents, Thủy, born in 1957, remembers that pivotal day clearly, along with the vivid corporeal sensations she experienced: her eyes burning from the acrid smoke, the sonic booms that shook the sky, the fear that pierced her body, and, later, the distress from years of displacement and loss of home that came to define her childhood. Such stories of rupture were not uncommon in my fieldwork; a generation of youth experienced powerful sensory encounters with aerial bombardment and prolonged grief from family separation and death. The provincial government would adeptly channel these affective states to train a resolute urban defense force and, later, to advance reconstruction, while demanding that Nixon pay for his "blood debt" (plate 2).

The presumption that there was little of value to bomb in a "backwards" country like Vietnam is perhaps one reason that the air war remains largely forgotten in U.S. public memory. With a few exceptions, it has also been overlooked in academic scholarship, which tends to focus on the grander cityscapes that were reduced to rubble in other wars, such as those of Europe during the Second World War—as if the destruction of "higher" civilizations is somehow more catastrophic than that of "underdeveloped" nations. Vietnam is also given short shrift in much of the recent literature on drones and the war on terror. Where it is discussed (see Gregory 2013), it draws heavily on U.S. military records and leaves out Vietnamese perspectives. This chapter seeks to remedy this critical oversight in the literature—and lack of attention paid to spatial annihilation in urban theory more broadly—by taking a "southern turn" to decenter the United States as the dominant frame of reference, and to write Vietnamese civilians and their traumatic experiences with the deliberate "killing" of their city into the history of aerial warfare.

Lien-Hang T. Nguyen's (2012) work, in particular, reminds us of the deep insights we can glean from the rich and often overlooked materials in Vietnam's harder-to-access archives. Similarly, this chapter draws on rare primary sources from the Nghệ An Provincial Museum and the Nghệ An Provincial Archives (NAPA), both of which are located in Vinh, combined with ethnographic interviews.[3] In the pages that follow, I examine the visual techniques that embedded state photographers used to forensically document the scale of urban annihilation through a focus on the built (and demolished) environment. The architectural remains of everyday urban life they captured in close-up shots contradicted the remote witnessing and truth claims of U.S. pilots. Rather, Vietnamese photographers' insistence on architecture as witness to and evidence of American war crimes helped to validate their own authoritative truth claims (see Weizman 2017). In stark contrast to the invisibilization of Vietnamese people in U.S. reconnaissance imagery and data, here image and fact, expressed through detailed captions, merged to anchor time, place, and subjectivity by making the material consequences of techno-fanaticism central to urban memory. These counterimages humanized the population by inserting victims into specific social and material worlds, including family genealogies, giving meaning to destroyed lives, landscapes, and ecologies. I then turn my attention to the lived sensory experiences of spatial annihilation, often called "urbicide," to encompass deliberate and premeditated attacks on both the built environment and the cultural conditions of urban life (Coward 2008, 14).[4] Through narratives of aerial assault and evacuation, I show how spatial violence was apprehended through the senses (Feldman 1991), especially through rigorous listening, as the panoptical war from above transpired as "sonic warfare" on the ground below (Goodman 2010). For my respondents, sound—alarms, booms, blasts, roars, shouts, sirens, and cries—

more than sight, framed their sensory navigation of bombardment and flight from the city. The last section of this chapter focuses on the coordinated exodus of people and infrastructure from Vinh. The expansion of air raids on the countryside, and the serial evacuations it caused, led to a permanent state of emergency and precarious dwelling, forcing urban residents underground. Their narratives of liminality, of "enforced placelessness" and lives on the move, of listening, predicting and preempting the next attack, reveal the extent to which people's targeted worlds were turned upside down by racial, urbicidal violence (McKittrick 2011, 949). Kenneth Hewitt's discussion of place annihilation during World War II also rings true for Vietnam: as U.S. leaders noted, the poor ability of area bombing to hinder war-making capacities contrasted starkly with its "huge impact on civilian lives, property, and urban culture" (1983, 272).

REHUMANIZATION: VISUALIZING URBAN DEVASTATION

Lack of attention to human and social landscapes in U.S. bomb damage assessments presents a contrast to the photography archive at the Nghệ An Provincial Museum in Vinh. The images in this carefully catalogued collection reveal other truths of war through graphic documentation of the violence of aerial attacks as they unfolded on the ground. The resulting iconography cultivates a shared moral and civil knowledge about urban destruction that remains key to the identity of Vinh and its inhabitants today. Aerial photographs transformed people and concrete structures into abstract forms, offering an ontological distance to those who took and viewed them. The shorter camera-to-subject distance of the in situ photographer, on the other hand, who was at once a reporter and a target of attack, offers a more intimate portrait of the human and material costs of aerial warfare. Unlike combat photographs published in the Western press, often remembered for the celebrity photographers who took them, these photographs never circulated widely. Indeed, most of the images in the Vinh archive have no authorship, unlike the tradition of the photographer "owning" the photo, as in the West. The images thus have moral authority, as Susan Sontag would argue (2003, 57), precisely because they identify with specific sites and people *in front of*, rather than behind, the camera. By inscribing in memory the people and places that mattered in the daily routines of urban life, such images became an important social and political tool to affirm the very humanity and modern temporality of inhabitants that air strikes sought to destroy.

This photographic chronicle shows the extent to which the deliberate targeting of urban lifeworlds was constitutive of modern warfare and its techno-fanaticism. Beyond the destruction of industry, the museum images reveal the immense scale of aerial warfare and the range of structures destroyed, which far exceeded the definition of "strategic infrastructure" in the U.S. military's prescribed rules of engagement. Photographs of architectural ruins offered evidence of the injustices inflicted on the city. The bombing penetrated the most intimate domains of everyday life, rendering civilians vulnerable in both public and private spaces. By zooming in closer on the map of sorties carried out over Nghệ An province (see plate 1), it is possible to see that a number of explosives were dropped on the city's central commercial district, far from any industry, an observation confirmed by images of demolished storefronts in the archive. The official numbers are daunting: according to the District People's Committee, in addition to the decimation of transportation and communication systems and 140 factories and government agencies (not all of which fit the "target" categories), U.S. air strikes demolished thirteen schools, four hospitals, and an estimated 8,663 houses and public buildings (2007, 89). "Only two buildings were left standing," residents repeated in conversations, helping me to envision the barren landscape that had been a growing city.[5] I include these calculations not for mere enumeration—though such figures are alarming for a city with a population of fifty-five thousand at the time—but because, as Diane M. Nelson has stated in language that resonates with that of Butler, to count is to assign accountability, "to have value, to matter" (2015, 39).

Numbers are important, but they are intrinsically unstable and impersonal. As Nelson reminds us (2015, 38), who counts is as important a question as who is being counted. Here, the socialist state did the counting, while U.S. air technocrats *discounted*. In the chaos of mass bombing, statistics are difficult to tally with any degree of certainty. For example, while there is no official death toll, municipal authorities typically estimate less than six hundred casualties—a figure that is low in proportion to the tonnage of explosives released over the city because of forced evacuations that emptied it. Yet even these imperfect numbers continue to matter, more so when substantiated with visual representations. The photographed ruins in the museum archives personalize government numbers by showing sentient life and urban space imbued with affect and sociality. The images did this by emplacing photographed subjects and objects in a particular geography and temporality of the city: the images are named, sited, dated, and/or coded to the extent possible, to trace sequentially the city's progressive "death." The result is not simply a catalogue of material damage to Vinh and its surroundings, but an ontological

↑ Figure 2.2 "Primary and secondary schools destroyed by American bombs on September 8, 1965." Nghệ An Provincial Museum.

representation of life itself as "a set of largely unwilled interdependencies" between human and nonhuman things (Butler 2009, 75).

As I viewed the faded and grainy black-and-white photographs spread out on a small table during one visit to the museum, a narrative timeline began to emerge that gave spatial and visual expression to place annihilation: "Nr. 68, the Polish Hospital destroyed on August 14, 1965"; "Nr. 65, Huỳnh Thúc Kháng High School bombed in the war"; "Nr. 103, Vinh City photo studio in ruins"; "Nr. 147, State canteen devastated by bombs on April 19, 1972"; "National bookstore on Thái Phiên Road demolished"; "University destroyed by American bombs on September 1, 1967"; and so on. There are no signs of human life in these images of rubble and ruin; their absence suggests lives upended rather than uncounted. The use of a straight-on camera angle creates a discomforting archetype of destruction (Azoulay 2012, 155), a recurring spatial pattern in which the gaping holes and debris of collapsing buildings make each ravaged built form surreally similar and yet illegible (126). Seen together, the images convey the sheer magnitude of U.S. airpower and its penetration into the familiar spaces of daily life—places like schools and universities, where the project of future making came to a sudden and violent halt (see figure 2.2).

Attacking architecture and heritage sites imbued with cultural value and national identity has long been a strategy of urban warfare (Bevan 2006;

Coward 2008). As W. G. Sebald once noted, mass bombing is "in perfect sympathy with the innermost principles of every war, which is to aim for as wholesale an annihilation of the enemy with his dwellings, his history, and his natural environment as can possibly be achieved" (1999, 19). In this sense, we might recognize urbicide through carpet bombing as a racialized strategy of temporal othering to cast a population outside modern civilization. In addition to the civic landscape, U.S. air raids demolished the city's valued cultural heritage. Centrally located religious sites, far from industry, faced the brunt of attacks, including Buddhist pagodas (see figure 2.3) and colonial-era churches, such as "Nr. 64, Cầu Rầm Catholic Church that was destroyed on June 12, 1968," as well as historic temples, like "Nr. 42, Yên Trung temple in District 2, hit by American bombs over four years." Nor were historical landmarks exempt from the violence of techno-fanaticism. For instance, five-hundred-pound MK-82 bombs struck the imperial citadel, which had been built in 1804 and was located in the city center, on several occasions: the western gate was hit on March 14, 1967, the southern gate on January 28, 1968, and the eastern gate on May 28, 1972, and again on July 13, 1972. The inner area, once a French military post, was hit on October 10, 1972, destroying the Xô Viết (Soviet) Nghệ Tĩnh Museum of the Revolution, where the colonial prison for revolutionaries had once stood.[6] These urbicidal acts of willful cultural annihilation struck at Vinh residents' strong sense of regional identity, demolishing or seriously damaging sites associated with spiritual and anticolonial activities, including Diệc pagoda, bombed on October 25, 1968. Even the cinema across the street was not spared: it was struck in the same attack. This was not graduated bombing to eliminate targets of military value, but irrational destruction meant to eradicate a way of life. As Katherine McKittrick (2011, 952) argues, the necropolitical consequences of urbicide have not only been the wasting of bodies, built space, and communities deemed disposable but destruction of the very *sense* of place that people inhabited.

These images make explicit the conviction that Vietnamese lives are countable and grievable through the specificity of their content and the methods of cataloguing. Vietnamese state photographers were like ethnographers immersed in their assigned work sites, in contrast to Western journalists (Schwenkel 2009b); as such, their work contrasted with the statistical and optical renderings of the U.S. military. As I argued in chapter 1, U.S. aerial photography accomplished two things: one, it quantified infrastructural objects and gave them human characteristics to the point of treating nonhuman things as enemies (as in "truck kills"); two, it established a visual

↑ Figure 2.3 "Tập Phúc pagoda in Vinh City destroyed by American bombs," n.d. Nghệ An Provincial Museum.

framing of the air war that was detached physically and emotionally from the trauma of bombing below. The "bird's-eye" perspective allowed for ontological and affective distancing that was critical to techno-fanaticism and its excessive, often retaliatory bombing. From the work of photographers on the ground—including East German filmmakers and journalists (see chapter 3)—a more intimate portrait emerges of everyday life under the threat of routine spatial violence. This was particularly the case with photographs of that most intimate of spaces: the home. There is no attack more personal, more invasive, more damaging to people's sense of place and security than air raids on housing. As Ariella Azoulay has argued of Israeli housing demolitions in the Occupied Palestinian Territories, such ruthless acts eliminate the distinction between private and public, outside and inside. Explosives rip open domestic spaces, exposing inner worlds to the outside gaze and rendering inhabitants vulnerable to forces beyond their control (2012, 126). As with the Israeli housing demolitions, aerial bombardment in Vietnam violated the sanctuary of the home, inciting fear and anxiety among the population while conveying that there were few places to hide from the all-seeing enemy in the sky.

Examining these images more than forty years later invites a discomforting proximity that encroaches on the most private of moments: death. As Susie Linfield (2010) has argued in response to Sontag's (2003, 45) critique of the invitation to look, such acts of viewing may be ethically and politically necessary. Indeed, during the war, images of devastation that did circulate helped to forge international solidarity with Vietnam and mobilize the antiwar movement (chapter 3). At the same time, it is hard to dismiss the voyeuristic tendencies involved in "ruin gazing" (Boym 2008): the act of looking inside blasted buildings, especially dwellings, to imagine the vitality of life that once animated them. Worker and student dormitories, for instance, are devoid of the sociability expected of such spaces (see figure 2.4). In a photograph of a bombed monastery, three men stand somberly at the edge of a crater in front of a ruined abbey. The cross at the top of the building is the only trace of the religious activities that once took place inside. Although the photographs afforded Vietnamese authorities evidence of U.S. crimes, they contain little to distinguish housing from other ruined structures; all have been reduced to their base material properties: wood, brick, bamboo, thatch, lime mortar, or cement. Each architectural shell is mapped onto the topography of the city. No area was spared: "Nr. 39, Residential housing on Quang Trung Road destroyed by American bombs in March 1967" shows a collapsing three-story building in the city center set against a row of scorched trees; "Nr. 41, Residential area of one-story housing in District 4 bombed on April 26, 1966" reveals blitzed rows of single-room dwellings for civil servants. When viewed alongside one another, these ruins offer a powerful example of the piling wreckage of modernity, of history as catastrophe, like Benjamin's angel foresaw (1969b).

The photographs of destroyed housing become even more intimate and immediate when the camera lens shifts from communal to individual dwellings. In these images, private residences not only are emplaced in specific localities around the city but are named and linked to individual family histories. This personalizes—and dignifies—the unidentifiable ruin and its occupants: the people who resided, worked, studied, played, and died there. One photograph shows the skeletal frame of a razed structure, still standing but reduced to an aggregate of thatch, bamboo, and wood, its interior exposed to public view (see figure 2.5). There is nothing distinctly familial or domestic about the debris to mark the space as "home," and the absence of any sign of the family leaves one speculating about their fate. The type of house (wood) and its location, directly south of the main market (which was hit several times between January and July 1968), suggest a poorer peasant household on the periphery

↑ Figure 2.4 "Worker housing at the electric plant demolished by American bombs," n.d. Nghệ An Provincial Museum.

of the city, not far from the targeted power plant. In other photographs, captions describe the occupation and social status of the family, for example, "Nr. 151, House of primary school teacher Mr. Nguyễn Sĩ Quang in Vinh Tân district demolished by American bombs, April 8, 1968." In contrast to the debris of wood and thatch depicted in figure 2.5, in the image of the teacher's house the rubble suggests the wreckage of a modest brick home. Its solid walls, still partially standing, evince the family's higher social status (as civil servants) and standard of living.

Up to now, the photographs I have discussed have been largely devoid of human presence. And yet they were not generic images of timeless ruins that might have existed anywhere. Quite the reverse; the photographs showed identifiable places that held great cultural significance for residents—houses, temples, hospitals, churches, museums, shops, and schools—located in precise time and space to accentuate their social biographies, including their moments of "death." One cannot talk about the demise of the city, however, without addressing the loss of sentient life. Here the archive reveals the most intimate and feared moments: that of bodily suffering and untimely death. The immediacy of such

↑ Figure 2.5 "Wreckage of Mr. Nguyễn Văn Định's house in Vinh Tân district, destroyed on April 8, 1968." Nghệ An Provincial Museum.

photographs and their "intolerable realism" bring the viewer closer—too close—to the violence, making the act of looking, even as a witness, unbearable (Sontag 2003, 63). These painful images are a somber reminder of the dire human and animal costs of aerial warfare, beyond material ruination. Images of children with missing limbs, entire families killed in their homes, bodies punctured by shrapnel, buffalo struck dead on the fields (see figure 2.6)—all make explicit the other, also nonhuman, casualties of war, the uncounted "collateral damage" that had no representation in American visual and statistical records.

Contrary to Sontag's provocation, these images do not offer indecent, unnecessary, or "dead information" (Weizman 2017, 37). They do not aestheticize

↑ Figure 2.6 "Buffalo belonging to residents in Hưng Đông commune killed on November 25, 1966." Nghệ An Provincial Museum.

suffering and detach the devastation from the politics of its production. If they had, they might have incited the negligent gazing that some have crassly labeled "ruin porn." What Sontag and others fail to note is that visual exploitation is not inherent in the photograph but is contingent on the context of its production and viewing, and on the nexus of power through which it circulates. Here, that power remains in the hands of the bureaucratic state, more specifically municipal archivists, who identified with the people in the images, as did the photographers who took them.[7] As such, the photographs do not anonymize the victims to create a more comfortable viewing distance, nor do they objectify bodies through graphic representations of pain and suffering. Rather, the faded and curling photographs act as a kind of "surrogate memory" (Edwards 1999, 222), kept dutifully and securely in the museum repository as a solemn witness to the scale of atrocities—visual evidence amassed for future generations. And yet, bearing witness to this traumatic past demands recognition of the casualties not as unidentified bodies but as subjects of history and individual lives with known family genealogies. Like the process of naming and emplacing buildings, the inscription of victims as human beings—their deaths visible and countable—occurred through the archive's classification system. The inclusion of name, lineage, and place of residence, for example, inserted the injured and the dead into families and kinship networks within communities. This technique of humanization is seen in photographs such as "Nr. 83, Mother Trần Thị Quang, 42 years, resident of Vinh City, injured during a B-52 bomb attack." Positioned on a thatched mat, Mother Quang looks away while partially uncovering her body, riddled with open wounds from the shrapnel that penetrated her legs, arms, and back. She is clothed only in black shorts but positioned with a leg pulled close to her chest so as not to expose her breasts. In other photographs, survivors return the camera's gaze, demanding that it recognize their humanity and the violence committed against them—for example, the close-up of a teenager (see figure 2.7), and the image of a toddler girl in "Baby Nguyễn Thị Quế, 37 months, of Vinh Tân district, Vinh City, foot dismembered by American bombs," who stares, wide-eyed, straight into the camera, looking bewildered, perhaps in shock, her hand resting near the missing limb.

In these images, there is a tenderness not often found in representations that traffic in pain, a sensitivity that is at once deeply affective and yet refrains from rendering suffering beautiful (Reinhardt, Edwards, and Duganne 2007). This is also the case with photographs of collective death. Air raids frequently killed groups of people, rather than single persons. In the worst instances, the strikes could reduce whole bodies to parts, an ominous sign in Vietnamese spiritual belief, which values the sanctity of the body intact. Notably, none of the images in the archive exhibited bodies torn apart—to photograph a human being in such a state would be considered an act of irreverence, photographers told me. How afflicted persons were documented on film, however, changed over time to show more cautious representation and care of the dead. For example, in the early days of Operation Rolling Thunder and mass evacuation, a heartrending image shows two young siblings lying supine in what appears to be a small trench, perhaps one they had dug to escape the attacks. Their bodies have been left in the place and position of death, with looks of terror forever etched on their faces. The boys are named and attached to a family, the day and cause of their premature passing marked: "Two brothers, Võ Văn Quý and Võ Văn Hội, children of Mr. Võ Văn Điều of District 2, Vinh City, killed in the bombing on June 7, 1965." In photographs from Operation Linebacker, when more powerful and destructive "smart" munitions were deployed, fatalities are no longer left in situ. Instead, they appear to have been laid out and cared for before the camera, as if to offer a more dignified documentation of death. This style is different from Western photographic practice, which is suspicious of "staged" shots or subject manipulation. One tragic scene shows a mother and her three boys, their

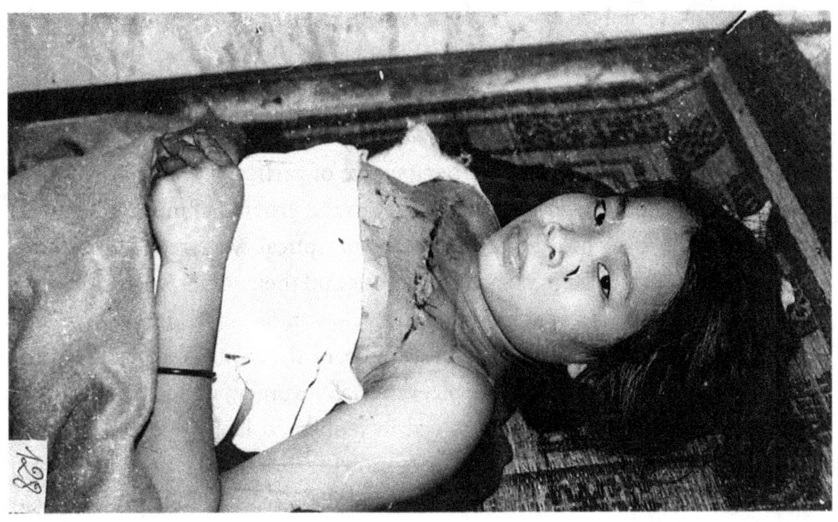

↑ Figure 2.7 "Ms. Nguyễn Thị Lan, 19 years old, of Nghi Phong commune, Vinh City, injured by a B-52 on April 10, 1972." Nghệ An Provincial Museum.

shirts blown off, lying on their backs close to one another in front of a charred branch of bananas, suggesting a rural livelihood: "Nr. 134, Family of Ms. Nguyễn Thị Uyển together with her three children killed in a B-52 attack on Nghi Phong commune on April 10, 1972." That same day and place, another household perished: "Nr. 127, Family of Mr. Nguyễn Ngọc Dũng and Ms. Trần Thị Hậu (three months pregnant) together with their 5 children were killed in a B-52 attack on April 10, 1972, in Nghi Phong commune." Here, the family members have been carefully placed on mats in funerary position, arranged according to age and descent, with the father at the front and the youngest in the rear. The slight bulge of the mother's exposed stomach at the center of the image draws the viewer's eye. These cared-for bodies make visible and undisputable the ineffable suffering of those left uncounted and unobserved by American military technologies, which were more concerned with annihilating space and tallying destroyed things than with the destroyed lives and deaths of human beings.

THE SOUNDS OF WAR: SENSORY EXPERIENCES OF BOMBING

> One day near the port we could hear the planes approaching, but there wasn't enough time to descend into the tunnels. The bombs went off around

us as people scrambled to run away. It was loud and fierce—and swift. Fifteen minutes later it was over. Forty-two people were killed.

—INTERVIEW, VIETNAMESE WAR PHOTOGRAPHER, 2011

In shifting from a distanced aerial perspective of vertical "total vision" to one of intimate, horizontal viewing, the images in the provincial museum subvert the technical (and techno-fanatical) logics of optical warfare (Saint-Amour 2003, 354) that erased the presence of humans and their social worlds. Though I have focused on photographs of material devastation and death, in accordance with the archive's main themes, much of the visual record of war in the DRV presented Vietnamese people, especially women, as social and political agents. Women were often involved in feminized labor deemed productive and heroic, such as digging tunnels, growing rice, tending to family, and defending national territory as part of the Three Responsibilities Movement (*ba đảm đang*), which placed tremendous burdens on them during the war (Turner and Phan 1998). These gendered images were at times staged or reenacted to depict the triumph of a simple, native femininity over a masculine, technologically advanced enemy (Schwenkel 2014a).[8] While such photographs should not be read merely as a chronicle of victimization, neither should they affirm an essentialist narrative of Vietnamese ingenuity and determination. People were resolute and industrious on the one hand, and apprehensive and vulnerable on the other. Such contradictory feelings are difficult to discern from two-dimensional, black-and-white representations with fact-oriented descriptions, but city residents openly expressed them in interviews during my fieldwork.

This section addresses memories of "the time of fierce bombing" (*thời đạn bom ác liệt*) as told to me by civilians who were children, then combatants and workers in factories and government agencies, and who are now retirees. Their narratives provide a context for understanding the profound impact of urban annihilation on both individual subjectivities and the city's identity as a place of fortitude and grit. In the following pages, I focus on references to the sonic dimensions of aerial warfare: in conversations and interviews, commemorative exhibits, literary works, and historical records, sound emerged as a dominant sensory experience of bombing and evacuation. More than anything, survival depended on the ability to hear, if not to *forehear*—to "listen *through* the war" (Daughtry 2015, 35) in order to anticipate approaching attacks through auditory cues when visual signs were absent. It also depended on the capacity of witnesses to become "expert listeners" or diagnosticians (34) who could assess risk levels through their accumulated auditory knowledge of distinctive sounds and vibrational forces—for example, those that accompanied the end of an air raid—especially when sight was obstructed by smoke. Lê Minh Khuê's acclaimed short story "The River" illustrates this sonic assessment of danger: a family listening to "their house explode in flames and the bamboo walls pop and crackle" while trapped in a tunnel beneath it (1997, 226). The sounds of bombardment could also be misleading and temporally dissonant. The war photographer cited above revealed that, by the time the loud vibrations of subsonic jets registered on the ground, explosion was imminent (and the planes long gone). As I show, a number of critical factors mediated the spatial and temporal relationship between noise, speed, risk, and violence in the decade-long struggle to evacuate (for some) and defend (for others) the city.

In contrast to the panoptical war from above, which, after all, began in response to a series of misperceived and fabricated pings, or "noise spooks," as Hillel Schwartz (2011, 26–28) has argued of the Tonkin Gulf incident,[9] people on the ground were forced to navigate raids using sound as acoustic guidance. To be clear: this was not the sonic warfare of World War II, when the screeching of diving bombers was meant to induce terror among civilians. Nor was it like the Israeli sound bombs in the Gaza Strip, which Steve Goodman (2010) describes in his work on the trauma of acoustic violence. And yet, nonlethal sonic weaponry was deployed in the war in Vietnam: Goodman notes the U.S. military's Wandering Soul "audio harassment" campaign that blasted the eerie wails of ghosts into the jungle night to spread panic among Vietnamese guerilla fighters and force their surrender (19–20). While the "cultural weapons" of sonic coercion in the South did not induce flight as planned (guerillas generally stayed put, even if spooked), the sonic effects of aerial assaults in the North did. "When I heard the sound of the planes, I jumped into the tunnels as instructed by the public announcement system," recalled one woman.[10] Here we find scenes where survival depended on listening to concurrent sound sources—to fighter jets and loudspeakers—both of which were closely tied to movement (Daughtry 2015, 35), the instinct to leap to safety, and a directive to do so.

The Wandering Soul campaign points to the nexus of noise and fear, or sound and affect, at the core of sonic violence (Goodman 2010, 12). Similarly, loud overwhelming sounds—including the thunderous roar of B-52s and the earthshaking blasts that followed—kept townspeople in a constant state of dread in Vinh. "I cannot even begin to describe the war, how brutal it was. Many of us youth had to carry the dead or the injured. Some people were blown to pieces, their parts hanging in trees. Just horrendous. When I heard those planes, I was absolutely terrified," Thủy told me bitterly.[11] The sound of the sirens, bells, and drums used to warn residents of an impending attack likewise provoked sheer panic: "I was so scared when I heard the alarm; the bombs were fierce [*ác liệt*] and terrifying [*khủng khiếp*]."[12] In these moments, survival depended on the ability to hear and then to disappear quickly, to make oneself invisible to the watchful eye of the enemy.

Discourses of hypervisibility in U.S. reconnaissance differed from metaphors of void and darkness in Vietnamese narratives. Interviewees remembered the blackouts (*đen ngòm hết*) that bombing produced, the duskiness that set in, even during the day, from the thick and blinding smoke hovering over Vinh. They reflected on the hours spent underground in dark, damp tunnels waiting for the "roar of the bombs" (*ầm ầm tiếng bom*) to subside. Under such conditions, light and lit environments were to be avoided at all costs: if one could see, one could be seen and targeted by the enemy. Under the cover of night, people could avoid detection while partaking in government-mandated activities, such as digging shelters. Evacuations of people and goods usually took place at nighttime. One man recalled how he had made his way from Vinh to China to study politics in 1965. With a group of thirty youths, he set out for Hanoi on foot, walking at night and sleeping during the day, when the bombers were most active. Only after they arrived in Ninh Bình, located above the twentieth parallel, where the air war was limited, could they safely proceed by train.[13] Mandatory blackouts at night also helped to hide dwellings and factories from enemy detection. One woman explained how she worked around this restriction as a pupil: "After the first bomb attack in August 1964, we dug a tunnel under our house. It was there that I continued my studies at night by a small lamp—no light was allowed in the home, or the planes might see us."[14] If light enables the power to see, also photographically, then darkness undoes sight. As such, the absence of light was deployed as a counterstrategy to challenge U.S. visual supremacy as a technique of military domination.

Of course, the "total vision" of the U.S. Air Force was itself impeded by smoke, nightfall, clouds, faulty photo technology, and antiaircraft artillery; American military "sight" was never as omnipresent as the United States liked to believe. Nonetheless, a stark difference in the logistics of perception—seeing versus nonseeing—played out in narratives of spatial violence across enemy lines. For my Vietnamese respondents, lack of sight implied an inability to see (compulsory obscurity) as well as an absent materiality. They described the biophysical devastation of Vinh, for example, through references to negative space and voids: "There was nothing left to see," I was often told—no trees, no houses, no intact buildings, no roads, no people, only emptiness and open cavities (craters). As Gastón Gordillo (2014) has argued of ruined landscapes, such voids make clear the destructive and dislocating effects of the violence of an imperialist modernity. Bombers, too, were often absent from sight. Those that traveled at supersonic speeds had a spectral presence. One might hear, but not see, the aircraft. These ghostly jets presented a problem for people on the ground, due to the dangerous disconnect between the acoustic and the visual. The phantom enemy—including unmanned aerial vehicles or drones (*máy bay không người lái*, or "planes without the driver")—would become the subject of countless puns, poems, and cartoons in Vietnamese popular culture.[15] The soundscapes that bombers produced, captured on tape, have likewise formed an archive of postwar cultural memory. Audio exhibits at tourist sites, such as the War Remnants Museum in Ho Chi Minh City, have created new sonic encounters with Vietnam's war, devoid of fear, violence, and vulnerability. In the bunker excursion at Hanoi's Metropole Hotel, visitors don hard hats to sit in the safety of the darkness underground, with pumped-in air, listening to the sinister explosion of bombs amidst the wailing of sirens that Baez incorporated into her 1973 album, *Where Are You Now, My Son?* (Schwenkel 2017c, 141).

With sight deprivation, sound became the dominant sensory experience. This is not to argue that people never saw bombers—B-52s, for example, were highly visible and provoked feelings of terror—but that the affective and somatic intensities of aerial warfare were framed as predominantly aural (see also Atanasovski 2016). "To witness war," J. Martin Daughtry has argued, "is, in large part, to hear it" (2015, 33), even long after the violence ends, we might add, and sonic looping continues. For instance, in an editorial in the *New York Times*, the author Bảo Ninh described that fateful day of August 5, 1964, through the medium of sound: "From then on, we lived under a sky that was almost always ablaze with the roar of jets, bomb blasts and sirens."[16] The affective intensity of these sonic vibrations has not dissipated over the years for this veteran turned novelist: "I still have nightmares. . . . I still hear the hiss of hundreds of bombs being dropped from B-52s, the roar of artillery barrages and the thrum of the helicopter rotors."

Likewise, my interviewees in Vinh articulated their experiences of bombardment through acoustic metaphors and sonic sensations, describing a jarring soundscape of noise to which they became attuned. The sounds of war became more legible and identifiable over time, though certainly no less fearsome. The U.S. military classified general-purpose bombs by size, measured in weight: 500, 750, or 1000 pounds. In Vinh, people talked about the force of explosions—the sonic waves, booms, and vibrations—and the diameter of the resulting craters. One engineer explained his method of quick assessment: up to ten meters for an average 500-pound bomb, and fifteen meters or more for the louder and more powerful blasts. Over time, bombing became "normalized" (*được bình thường hóa*), in the words of one state planner.[17] The sonic rhythm of daily life, as radically transformed as it was, became structured around the constant threat of attack, requiring people to stay alert with an ear to the ground, listening for the pitch and frequency of those dreaded, approaching sounds.

Survival was coordinated with auditory cues: local officials governed the population through sound, socializing people to respond quickly to impending attacks. Sonic devices, both rudimentary and advanced, were critical to networks of communication and emergency response. An elaborate acoustic apparatus was set in place to keep people informed and forewarned (as well as compliant), including an alarm matrix of sirens, bells, drums, loudspeakers, and gongs. A public address system issued directives, such as instructions to evacuate the city, again showing thc connection between sound and movement. For civilians accustomed to acute listening, loud warnings, like sirens, signaled that they should descend immediately into the nearest shelter. For combatants, including urban self-defense units—what Võ Nguyên Giáp called the "armed forces of the working class and toiling people in the towns" (1975, 141)—they conveyed a message to prepare for imminent battle. Critical to this sound-information assemblage were those forces in charge of "counting bombs" (*đếm bom*). My neighbor in Vinh, a woman who served as head of the bomb detonation team (*tổ trưởng phá bom*), explained how this operation worked: youth volunteer forces (*thanh niên xung phong*), the majority of them women, and air defense units were stationed at the highest points around the city—for example, at the top of Quyết Mountain above the power plant, not far from the port of Bến Thủy. There they sat with binoculars, looking and listening intently. Upon hearing approaching aircraft (that were usually beyond visibility, either too high or too fast), they sounded the gongs, which set off a chain reaction of alarms across the city. They then assumed positions to count both the number of missiles dropped and the ensuing blasts.[18] If there were discrepancies between sight and sound—for example, if they viewed five warheads released but only heard four of them explode—the team would set off to find, and mark with a flag, the dud missile (*bom điếc*): a "deaf" bomb that lacked the power to produce noise (to detonate).[19] A team of engineers, which my neighbor referred to as the "suicide squad" (*đội cảm tử*), and which included herself, would then destroy the unexploded ordnance to "liberate the road" (*giải phóng con đường*). Maintaining the "life" of the road was harrowing, high-risk, *feminized* work that claimed the lives of many female youth, including at the famous Đồng Lộc junction, where my neighbor had been stationed.[20] After bomb clearance was complete, the mostly female team would fill in craters and repair damaged roads or bridges to keep infrastructure "alive" and military traffic and supplies to the South flowing.

Of course, not all undetonated ordnance was "mute," or without sound, as the Vietnamese term implies; many unexploded devices were time bombs (*bom nổ chậm* or slow explosions), intended to trick people into thinking they were duds. These killed and maimed, inflicting serious injury on many, including ruptured eardrums. Acoustic trauma from the pressure of the blasts (*bị sức ép*) was not uncommon among my elderly respondents and produced different degrees of deafness (*tật điếc*). Both my neighbor and her husband, who met on the battlefield, suffered permanent hearing loss as a result of their work on the Hồ Chí Minh Trail. So did another neighbor, a retired worker from the printing press, who told me about a surprise attack that almost killed her. Motioning with her hand for me to speak louder, she explained, "I cannot hear well. A bomb exploded close to me as I was running for shelter with a baby in my arms, and shattered my hearing. I was lucky to survive."[21]

Schwartz's (2011) pioneering study on the history of noise argues for attention to the role that sound, especially unwelcome audio frequencies, has played in the organization of social and ontological worlds across time and space. Likewise, noise (and active, anticipatory listening) emerged as a critical historical force in Vinh, shaping how people experienced the spatial and corporeal violence that decimated their lives and city, and how they remember it today. The thunderous roar of air strikes kept the population in Vinh mobile and alert, always with an ear open to the next attack. This soundscape mobilized people to move quickly to subterranean safety by jumping into trenches, tunnels, bunkers, and one-person shelters. It also inspired people to produce *louder* sounds in response, for example, by "singing to drown the sound of bombs" (*tiếng hát át tiếng bom*). The panic-inducing noise of aerial bombardment, and its catastrophic outcomes, compelled scores of people to leave the city in search of safer ground.

URBAN EXODUS: THE GOVERNANCE OF INSECURITY

With the onset of aerial warfare, the security of the urban population became a central concern of government. Relentless air strikes made it impossible to live in Vinh and forced a mass evacuation to the mountains and countryside, where it was thought to be safer. These sanctuaries for "bare life," in Giorgio Agamben's terms (1998), became absolute spaces of humanitarian emergency born out of a state of exception when ordinary law and life were suspended, including the household registration system (*hộ khẩu*) that restricted mobility. In 1965, as bombers pummeled the city, the municipal government ordered the mandatory evacuation of all nonessential civilians, namely children and the elderly, in a quick (*nhanh chóng*) and orderly (*trật tự*) fashion to protect the security of evacuees, while maintaining state oversight of their movement. Residents were informed of the evacuation order (*lệnh sơ tán*) over the public address system, which was centrally administered by officials at the district and municipal levels in conjunction with leaders in the villages that would provide refuge in compliance with state directives. While a few families sent their children to live with relatives in rural areas, most were evacuated collectively along with their neighborhood, school, or work unit. Dispersal of the population posed a threat to state control, and centralized coordination to direct its flow to certain regions became a technique of governing from afar to regulate movement, maintain public order, and account for people's whereabouts (Foucault 2007, 105). In the memory of one woman, "My family evacuated to Nghĩa Đàn, where another family, under government orders, took us in and provided food and shelter. Our entire district was sent to the same commune. That's how it was organized."[22] Workers at factories and government agencies were likewise split and dispersed to the countryside to maintain basic levels of productivity. Only civil defense units (*dân quân tự vệ*) and people with essential responsibilities in the city—for example, those tasked with repairing industry (mostly men), assisting in emergencies, and growing food (mostly women)—were instructed to remain, in the interest of public security.

This mass depopulation resulted in what people described as a vacant city: "*Sơ tán hết!*" (Everyone was evacuated!) or "*Thành phố không có ai cả*" (Not a soul in the city). This was not entirely accurate. According to municipal statistics from 1966, the prebombing population of Vinh had climbed to roughly fifty-five thousand (28 percent of whom were civil servants and workers, with the remaining 72 percent in agriculture),[23] before dropping to a few hundred residents; it then rose steeply to more than eighty-five thousand, one year after the end of the air war in 1973 (Nguyễn 2005, 229). In any case, as in other Vietnamese cities, the effect of mass evacuation was not only a decade of "zero urban growth" (Thrift and Forbes 1986, 96–97) but ten years of tactical deurbanization. In contrast, rural areas would experience a wave of short-lived development (Turley 1975, 382), as I discuss below. Importantly, this out-migration kept casualty rates moderately low, given the intensity of bombardment: government statistics reported 586 civilian deaths and 964 injured within the city proper (District People's Committee 2007), a death rate of just over 1 percent of the entire prewar urban population.

The scant literature that exists on evacuation procedures tends to focus on Hanoi. Vietnamese filmmakers also privileged Hanoi in wartime features, such as *Em bé Hà Nội* (*Little Girl of Hanoi*, 1974) by director Hải Ninh.[24] Filmed among the rubble and embers of the still-smoldering city in the wake of the "Christmas bombing"—which in Vietnam is called "Điện Biên Phủ trên không" (Điện Biên Phủ in the air) to signify the defeat of Americans, much as the French were defeated in the original battle—the film conveys the scale of urban devastation. It illustrates the profound loss suffered by a young girl who returns from the countryside, to where she had been evacuated, to find her street of Khâm Thiên in ruins. Readers who have spent time in Hanoi will most likely be familiar with stories of evacuation told by middle-aged residents. During my own years in the capital city, I, too, became acquainted with these narratives of sorrowful separation that were eased to some extent by the affective bonds that developed with host families that many former evacuees maintain today. There is a pattern to these stories of forced placelessness and movement between city and countryside. William S. Turley's analysis of urbanization during the air war divides the evacuation into two periods that mirror U.S. categorization of its bombing campaigns: 1965–1968 and 1972, between which people slowly returned to Hanoi only to evacuate again (1975, 380–88). Because Hanoi was located in the zone of limited engagement above the twentieth parallel, and was not destroyed on the same scale as smaller cities, this temporal division perhaps makes sense there. The situation in Vinh, however—and in other towns in the panhandle—was quite different and mandated a paradigm of security governance that transformed the state of exception into a normalized procedure of rule (Agamben 2005, 14).

While Operation Rolling Thunder was winding down over Hanoi in April 1968, the situation was ramping up in Nghệ An. As discussed in chapter 1, strategic bombing was more continuous over other areas of the DRV, including Vinh, which served as a gateway to the South. Vinh was also located in the heavily targeted Fourth Military Zone (*Quân khu 4*), or panhandle, where the partial bombing halt, issued on April 1, did not apply. On the contrary, air attacks intensified. Clodfelter reports that between April 1 and October 1, 1968, 77,081 missions were carried out below the twentieth parallel, compared with 72,095 missions across the entire DRV during the same period in 1967, at the height of Operation Rolling Thunder (2017, 698). Life in Nghệ An—and in neighboring rural districts—became even more difficult after April 1, whereas

Table 2.1. Comparison of Nghệ An before and after the bombing halt above the Twentieth Parallel.

	Prior to April 1, 1968	Four Months after April 1, 1968
Destroyed homes	331	393
Evacuated families	407	1,000
Family members killed	149	177
Employees killed	128	45
Employees injured	151	33

Note: Figures from the Department of Statistics, Nghệ An Province, 1968.

evacuees had begun trickling back into Hanoi, despite the government's discouragement (Turley 1975, 382). A provincial government report from December 1968 on the living conditions of state employees in Nghệ An found that the situation had become critical as a result of much fiercer strikes (*vô cùng ác liệt*).[25] The "limited" air war elsewhere meant that attacks were concentrated on Vinh and rural districts housing evacuees and scattered factories, including Diễn Châu, Yên Thành, Nam Đàn, and Hưng Nguyên. According to the report, the "unprecedented amount of explosives" (*khối lượng bom đạn tàn phá chưa từng thấy*) was deepening a humanitarian crisis, including for the province's eighty thousand civil servants and workers. A study of thirty-seven enterprises in affected areas found that the number of destroyed homes in the four months *following* the partial bombing halt surpassed that of Operation Rolling Thunder and the months leading up to it (see table 2.1). Statistics on family members killed during a bout of intensified attacks showed a fatality increase of almost 20 percent, while the number of families evacuated more than doubled. Only the numbers of employees killed or injured decreased during this period, owing to coordinated relocation.

Under these conditions of increasing instability, the welfare of the population became the target of state efforts to manage, protect, and securitize everyday life. The report concluded that state employees had faced more adversity during the months immediately following "limited bombing" (*bom hạn chế*) than they had since the start of attacks in 1964. Rendering state care moral, officials expressed concern over people's inability to meet their basic needs and the lack of family stability. Material goods were scarce, including such everyday items as soap, sugar, fabric, and salt, especially for evacuees in remote mountainous regions. Economic logics underlay such expressions of concern: production levels had fallen as residents evacuated, and food was in short supply, owing to ruined paddy fields and livestock deaths, which meant trade unions had difficulty providing for workers. Prices on the regulated market had risen, though incomes stayed low. The average state employee earned 57.28 Vietnam *đồng* (VND) per month, of which 34.70 VND went to living costs as workers were forced to supplement meager government provisions.[26] People worked harder, dividing their time between state jobs and cooperative agricultural production, while struggling to stay safe and connected to their families.

In spite (and because) of such dire conditions, evacuees strove to create new opportunities to ensure their survival. For example, it was not uncommon for people to put bomb craters to use: workers at the lumber factory grew swamp spinach (*rau muống*) in the water-filled depressions, my interviewees recounted. They also turned to natural resources for sustenance. A retired physician—one of the first medical school graduates in postcolonial Hanoi—described the life-or-death challenges he faced while stationed at an evacuated hospital on the outskirts of Vinh (see figure 2.8): "We worked as fast as we could to save the lives of bomb victims, especially children. But we lacked everything [*thiếu hết*]; we had very little equipment or medicine. So we gathered materials from nature—herbs, roots, trees, and bamboo. Everything was made from natural resources: the beds, the splints, the bandages, and the medicine. It's all we had—the very cheapest and simplest of supplies. But we were still able to save people. It was humbling work."[27]

Workers and their families were also beset by the instability of serial evacuations and the dispersal of kin as a compulsory security policy meant to protect life. According to the report, 71.1 percent of government employees (civil servants and workers in state factories) were married with children, who had been relocated to the countryside. There, they faced grave shortages, despite support from local families as per government regulations. Thủy recalled the warm welcome she and her siblings received by her fellow compatriots: "Our hosts took care of us. They gave us lodging and shared their cassava. Every day they gave us food. It was a time when people looked after one another."[28] Generosity proved difficult to maintain over the long term. As resources became strained, Thủy worked in the fields and went into the forest to collect snails and edible plants. Her mother, who stayed in Vinh for work, visited with food as often as possible; in fact, many of my interlocuters shared recollections of their mothers risking their lives to move between the city and evacuation areas. According to the provincial report, in 1968 state employees sent a monthly average of 22.48 VND in cash and material goods (close to 40 percent

↑ Figure 2.8 Tunnel evacuation demonstration at a hospital relocated to the countryside, 1968. Nghệ An Provincial Museum.

of their income) to help mitigate scarcity and contribute to the costs of care for their children.[29]

Provincial officials were not only concerned about people's material well-being. They were also anxious about the psychological toll of separation as employees agonized over the safety of their families, and the impact this had on production, morale, and social cohesion. As Gordillo reminds us, destruction disintegrates not only materiality but also sociality (2014, 81). The 1968 study determined that living conditions were even more precarious for evacuees after the partial bombing halt of April 1, owing to a disrupted social fabric. "The lives of family members are not stable," the government warned. Instability had a strong impact on children in particular. One man's recollections of his family's prolonged separation emphasized a typical gendered division of labor:

> My school was evacuated. It was mandatory that we all leave. . . . I walked fifteen kilometers to the evacuation point. My father was required to stay and work in the city so our house was never abandoned, but we lived near Trường Thi [railway works], so it came close to being hit by bombs several times. My mother worked in an agricultural collective [*hợp tác xã*], where her job was to tend to the paddies. She went back and forth to the countryside to visit me. On the weekends I sometimes returned to Vinh to see my parents and to bring food back to my host family.[30]

State concerns about the security of the population meant that mobility, as tied to preemptive listening, was a key experience of aerial warfare. Family members were not only scattered across distant sites, as the government noted with concern; they were also obliged to move to ever more remote locations as the raids came closer to their refuge. An escape from Vinh, evacuees soon learned, was not an escape from violence: as the curator of the photo collection reminded me, some rural districts were subjected to even fiercer attacks. One man recalled the recurrent upheavals and movement across the geography of warfare that shaped his experience as a young teacher after the pedagogical college (now Vinh University) was evacuated in 1965:

> Each department was instructed to move to a different commune. My department [chemistry] first evacuated to Thạch Thành in Thanh Hóa province, then to Thanh Chương, and then Nghi Lộc. Eventually we had to move to Hà Trung. When Hà Trung was bombed, we returned to Thạch Thành. We stayed there for three years before moving to Quỳnh Lưu, and only went back to Vinh when there was finally peace. We completed a full evacuation circle [*đi một vòng sơ tán*] and returned to find nothing left of the city.[31]

A female student, who entered the university in 1969, expressed frustration with serial displacement, and tied abrupt departures to the sonic apprehension of bombing: "We evacuated to so many places! I went right to Quỳnh Lưu when I started university, and then we evacuated to Hà Trung, and after that Thạch Thành and then Nam Đàn. Whenever we heard the bombs, it was time to leave. Even if we were not done building our huts, we had to give up everything and start over in the next place. We also had to carry the [Department] Chair's things! Along the way we would cry. It was constant, extreme misery" [*khổ cực kỳ luôn*].[32]

This state of enduring insecurity, vulnerability, placelessness, and flight wore people down physically and psychologically, especially children and young adults trying to maintain a sense of normalcy in their studies. Recognizing this, the government called on hosts to show solidarity and love of country—and to exemplify a spirit of "nhiễu điều phủ lấy giá gương"[33]—by helping to stabilize the lives of evacuees. Serial evacuation was not only emotionally taxing; it was physically demanding. Thủy recalled the strenuous activity and fatigue associated with successive relocations, similar to the university student's recollections:

> When I was seven, I evacuated with my family in the dark of night to avoid the bombers. My elder brother carried me for a while, and then he would carry my sister. We moved around a lot then; it was grueling. We would walk throughout the night, taking turns to carry our things until we arrived at the next place with food and accommodation that was not under attack. We first went to Hưng Nguyên—I cannot remember for how long. But then we traveled to Thanh Chương. There I went to school for some time, but how long I cannot be sure. The bombs and explosions were always around us; it was so dangerous. The line between life and death was thin [*Sống chết trong gang tấc*].[34]

As the state urged villagers to show generosity toward those whose lives had been turned upside down (*bị đảo lộn*), so too did it urge urban evacuees to work and give back to the rural communities that hosted them. Reciprocal labor served to fold evacuees back into political society as productive members that fit with state efforts toward collectivization. When I asked Thủy what she did during the period of evacuation, her answer mirrored that of my other respondents: "I studied and worked." Depending on the locality, students and pupils refurbished buildings or built thatched huts for their accommodation or classrooms, often under forest canopy to remain undetected. They worked in rice fields, foraged food, and wove straw hats (*mũ rơm*) to protect their heads from shrapnel (see figure 2.9). More than any other labor, they dug foxholes—under their beds and school desks—and trenches in zigzag design for safe, subterranean passage to shelters deeper underground. They also engaged in social projects, such as constructing underground shelters for the elderly and the war wounded. Thủy remembered such collective labor fondly: "We dug our own tunnels first and then we would go and help others in the village. When we were finished, we would dig elsewhere." While Thủy waxed nostalgic for the time when "no one stole paddy and everyone thought only of fighting the enemy," as she phrased it, university students at the time expressed

↑ Figure 2.9 Teacher attaches straw hats to the heads of evacuated children outside tunnels in Diễn Châu (Nghệ An), April 1967. Photo by Phan Thuy. Vietnam News Agency.

frustration with the futile and fatiguing labor of assembly and reassembly that came to define their precarious existence. The experience of serial evacuation was thus one of liminality at the threshold of violence, of life betwixt and between: not yet settled or rested, and ready to flee when the alarms sounded.

Mass evacuation not only emptied Vinh; it also transformed the countryside in line with state developmental priorities. As Turley has argued in the case of Hanoi, the dispersal of people, government agencies, and factories to nonurban areas served to "accelerate rural development" and "narrow the material and cultural gaps between city and country" (1975, 382). Urbanites, in other words, brought "civilization" to peasants and remote ethnic-minority communities through the transfer of knowledge, technology, capital, and goods, however limited. To some extent, evacuation lent itself well to the consolidation of state and party power, and to the goal of socialist transformation, insofar as it broke down social distance and class divisions between rural and urban. In this sense, war was a "great equalizer." Evacuation also helped build regional economies, in compliance with the country's first Five-Year Plan (1961–1965). Architects at the Design Institute in Hanoi, for example, were called upon to exploit the situation to learn more about life in the countryside and to cultivate closer relations among the classes (Nguyễn 1966, 1). Serving the people (*phục vụ nhân dân*) through development, which would mitigate resentment at the compulsory care of evacuees, could be accomplished through the sharing of expertise. "Communal and village planning, roads, the design of civil housing, [People's] Committee headquarters, nursery and primary schools, maternity homes, farmhouses, [and] drying yards" would modernize the countryside (Nguyễn 1966, 2), while strengthening alliances between agriculture and industry to build the technical and material foundations of socialism (Lê Duẩn 1977a, 80).

In Nghệ An, where there were fewer elites and less social distance between town and country, the situation was somewhat different. On the one hand, urban evacuees (many of whom were migrants themselves from the countryside) did contribute to rural development through the transfer of resources, including labor. There was an urgent need for an upgraded rural infrastructure to accommodate people, machines, and equipment. New structures were needed to house the suddenly increased population and to maintain public institutions and industrial output, including schools, warehouses, production facilities, offices, clinics, and lodging. On the other hand, such development was provisional and put undue stress on local populations. Lack of building supplies meant evacuees had to rely on foraged materials such as bamboo, thatch, and wood. Moreover, it had to be possible to quickly disassemble these structures and carry them to the next evacuation point. And unlike the heavier industry around Hanoi and Hải Phòng, many of the smaller factories in Vinh, like brickworks, were not yet fully mechanized and could be quickly relocated, with equipment carried on backs. "How did you manage to move an entire factory?" I asked a woman who had labored during the war to build ferry engines. She explained, "It was extremely strenuous work. The machine factory was divided into clusters [*cụm*] and dispersed [*phân tán*] to different areas: Thanh Chương, Kim Nhan, Diễn Châu, many places! We carried equipment and moved some machinery on large trucks, and hoped we would not be spotted and bombed."[35] Like urban residents, factories and government agencies were subjected to serial evacuations that required the dismantling, transport, and reassembly of operations. There is no evidence therefore that evacuated industry brought lasting development to remote areas, especially as bombers expanded their targets and workers were forced to move again.

Many factories and government agencies returned to Vinh after a bombing halt was declared on November 1, 1968, and preliminary planning for rebuilding the city was underway. The city remained at risk of attack, however, owing to the special rules of engagement discussed in chapter 1.[36] By September 1970, almost two-thirds of the population remained evacuated.[37] In April 1972, after the resumption of strikes, factories and agencies, including the Design Institute, Unification Woodworks, and Nghệ An Food Provisions Company, filed requests for relocation with central authorities; upon confirmation, they evacuated yet again. While most evacuees returned to Vinh only after the definitive end of the air war in 1973, with the signing of the Paris Peace Accords, some enterprises, like the Pharmaceutical Company, remained at their evacuation sites until as late as 1980, due to the lack of housing and infrastructure. All my interviewees expressed to me their shock and disorientation upon returning to the city. "I saw nothing but rubble" (*gạch vụn thôi*), one woman who joined the Design Institute in 1969 described.[38] This indelible image of Vinh in ruins circulated widely among socialist countries, including in the Democratic Republic of Germany (GDR or East Germany), where it fostered empathy and a sense of shared purpose and history, a topic to which the next chapter turns.

→ Figure I.2.1
East German solidarity poster from 1968 on display in the War Remnants Museum in Ho Chi Minh City, 2018.

To the President of America

October 17, 1972

Mr. Nixon!

I demand that you stop this shocking war in Vietnam! I, a pupil in Radebeul, would like to say, "You are leading a senseless war against the Vietnamese, who are a good people."

Ines, Class 4a[1]

Anne Frank Street

VINH LINH BLEIBT IMMER NAHE (VINH [LINH] ALWAYS REMAINS CLOSE)

Wir haben mit Ihnen gelitten (We suffered with you)
als man ihre Hütten verbrannt. (as your huts were burned.)
Wir waren in ihrer Mitten (We were there with you)
und reichten die helfende Hand. (and extended a helping hand.)
Vinh war immer nahe, (Vinh was always close,)
weil ein Bruder zum anderen steht; (because brothers stand together;)
Vinh, Vinh heißt Freiheit—(Vinh, Vinh means freedom—)
heißt Solidarität! (means solidarity!)

Wir haben mit ihnen geschworen (We swore with you)
den Schwur, der uns alle vereint: (the oath that unites us all:)
Glück wird im Kampf nur geboren! (Happiness is only born in struggle!)
Und wir haben den gleichen Feind! (And we have the same enemy!)
Vinh war immer nahe, (Vinh was always close,)
weil ein Bruder zum anderen steht; (because brothers stand together;)
Vinh, Vinh heißt kämpfen—(Vinh, Vinh means struggle—)
heißt Solidarität! (means solidarity!)

—SOLIDARITÄTSLIED (SOLIDARITY SONG), BY WILLI GOLM AND MARTIN HATTWIG, 1973[2]

← Figure I.2.2 GDR lapel pins for sale at a flea market in Berlin, 2018. Photo by the author.

3

SOLIDARITY

> In recent years, the names of Vietnamese cities have been imprinted in our minds—they are connected with the heroic people's struggle against American aggression. And today there is hardly any citizen in our Republic who does not know the name of Vinh.
>
> —GDR SOLIDARITY COMMITTEE, VIETNAM COMMISSION, 1974

Mass bombing not only mobilized the Vietnamese people; it also rallied opposition to the war around the world. Aerial warfare played into the hands of Vietnam's propaganda campaigns by lending support to the notion that the Communist Party was leading its people in a just struggle against an invading enemy, whose goal of neocolonial occupation was evinced in the unambiguous presence of U.S. airpower (Thompson and Frizzell 1977, 127). As I show in this chapter, architectural evidence of such intent—including the obliteration of schools, pagodas, and houses captured on film and circulated to aghast socialist publics—galvanized strong public sentiment against the war in East Germany, driving its own discourse about American and West German (Federal Republic of Germany, or FRG) imperialism. To the chagrin of Western allies, the Vietnam War became a powerful resource for the GDR government to deflect critiques of its policies and unite its population behind a staunch antiwar, anti-imperialist position. Solidarity with Vietnam's struggle for liberation thus emerged as a "key linchpin" in the Cold War rebuke of capitalism (Horten 2013, 558) and helped promote socialist modernization in the decolonizing South, while affording the GDR more international legitimacy. Campaigns that drew on political discourses of *Solidarität* (solidarity) were not only about ideology and politics; premised on a fallacy of historical resemblance, their efficacy also lay in an appeal to sentiment.

State institutions in East Germany used the war in Vietnam, and especially terror bombing, as it was called, to muster solidarity as a form of "affective practice" (Wetherell 2012). Using masculine kinship terms to encourage identification, *Solidaritätsaktionen* (solidarity actions) were framed as a moral imperative—a socialist duty to support struggles for national independence in the decolonizing world and to pass on knowledge, technology, and goods to a fraternal (*brüderlich*) country. Among the older generation especially, gestures of solidarity were motivated by strong feelings of historical affinity between Vietnam and East Germany, given their parallel experiences of partition and destruction. In just a few years, the intersecting histories and shared suffering, to which Hồ Chí Minh referred during his historic first visit to the GDR in 1957, took on new meaning.[1] At the same time, the relentless attacks on Vietnamese cities, just twenty years after the end of the Second World War, instilled a collective sense of urgency in East Germany and compelled citizens to identify emotionally with the victims by evoking their own past trauma. These "sympathetic solidarities," as I call them, were imagined as innate, nonhierarchical, transcendent, and rooted in common interests and experiences of war. They had strong paternalistic undertones, which is one reason why I distinguish them from the more detached "empathic solidarities" as proposed by David Heise (1998). At times, sympathetic solidarities converged with Vietnamese understandings of their relationship with East Germany, especially around aspirations to progressive futurity; at other times, they contrasted with those understandings and came too close to pity. During the war, this moral and ideological positioning allowed for a collective identity among antiwar activists that centered on a common purpose and concrete enemy: imperialism. Solidarity was thus as much a political standpoint as it was a structure of feeling (Muehlebach 2017), a spirit of human connectedness and unity in action captured in the Vietnamese phrase *tình đoàn kết*.[2] While fraught at times, this sentiment recognized the bonds that could form between people involved in the work to manifest solidarity, the affective ties that, in many cases, have outlived the Cold War (Schwenkel 2015a).

In the post-Stalin era, anticolonial solidarity with liberation movements facilitated new cultural and economic encounters between the "Second" and "Third" worlds, constituting an alternative system of socialist globalization and development (Bockman 2015). The forms of internationalism were diverse: resource allocation and scope of aid varied by country and project and depended on the relative wealth and technical expertise of each donor, as well as on national interests (chapter 4). Hungary, for example, typically expressed solidarity by giving loans that needed to be repaid, rather than gifts or grants, to avoid establishing neocolonial patterns of dependency (Mark and Apor 2015). Importantly, and different to the capitalist aid that was used to prevent countries from "going communist" (Ehrenfeld 2004), these exchanges were often multidirectional. They flowed not only from the center of socialist power to the periphery, but also among former colonies, as Christine Hatzky's work on Cuban aid to Angola shows (2012). Vietnam likewise sent thousands of its own experts to train technicians and scientists in Africa (Bayly 2008), even as it received extensive aid packages from Eastern Europe, China, the Soviet Union, and even Cuba. An immense aid apparatus facilitated technical, military, educational, social, and economic assistance, which was touted as "mutually beneficial" and serving bilateral interests. Certainly, there was a seductive appeal to such projects in newly independent countries ravaged by colonialism. As Tobias Rupprecht (2015) has argued of Soviet–Latin American relations, solidarity meant resources and global connectivity for poorer nations seeking international integration. For Vietnam, these relations also translated into diplomatic legitimacy and inclusion in the world community of communist states. Likewise, *brüderliche Hilfe* (fraternal aid) provided a moral platform for East Germany to depict itself as a lawful, rights-affirming country—contrary to Western claims of a fundamental incompatibility between human rights and socialism (Betts 2012, 407). By giving aid to an exploited country like Vietnam, the GDR could show itself as a generous benefactor that played a productive, noninterventionist role in the struggle against neocolonial capitalism. This would stand in contrast to West Germany's destructive support of a genocidal war through its "special alliance" to American imperialism (Horten 2013, 562–63).

The air war changed the kinds of support socialist countries extended to the DRV and intensified commitment to the practice of solidarity. In the GDR, state and organizational initiatives, expressed in humanist terms as "altruistic assistance" (*uneigennützige Hilfe*) increased substantially over the 1960s as bombardment escalated. The Vietnamese government estimates that GDR assistance between 1965 and 1973 amounted to 270 million rubles, of which 150.3 million constituted "free" (nonrepayable) aid. This figure did not include "gifts" of machinery to rebuild industry or citizen donations, which were earmarked for humanitarian projects as part of the spirit of camaraderie, or *tình đoàn kết*.[3]

Sympathetic solidarities and forms of connectivity strengthened with East Germany's prestige project in Vietnam: Vinh's reconstruction, as suggested in the epigraph. Although it was unknown in the United States, Vinh occupied a unique place in socialist memory of the war in East Germany; underpinned by narratives of *co*victimization, however, memory of Vinh also hinged on national forgetting. This chapter addresses the affinities that formed around narratives of "shared" experiences in East Germany and Vietnam, with imperialist partition and devastation on the one hand and the struggle for reunification and socialist reconstruction on the other. My use of the term "affinities" gestures to the related anthropological concept of "affines," which typically describes relationships created through marriage or other union, as distinguished from those based on descent, referred to as "consanguines." As I show, rhetoric that deployed kinship terminology was an important political and humanist device for recognizing and legitimizing membership in the great socialist family. As in any extended family, these relationships depended on the maintenance of boundaries and hierarchies among members. East Germans used the nonhierarchical, albeit masculinist, term *Bruder* (brother) or *Brudervolk* to emphasize *horizontal* kinship with Vietnamese comrades: "Wir wurden als Brüder begrüßt" (We were greeted as brothers), one East German youth delegate to Hanoi reported in 1968.[4] To the contrary, the Vietnamese affirmed *hierarchical* kinship by using the relational term *anh em*, which inferred "big brother" when referring to East Germany and "little sibling" when referring to Vietnam, with the role of senior brother, or *anh cả*, reserved for the Soviet Union. We can also read this as acknowledgment of the asymmetries of socialist assistance that East Germans tended to overlook as they positioned themselves as fellow underdogs: citizens of a small and struggling country up against a larger imperialist enemy (the FRG), not unlike Vietnam. At times, such asymmetries exposed the fault lines of a solidarity derived from Orientalist frameworks as the East German population tried to acquaint themselves with an unfamiliar country and people, even as Vietnam's history of trauma was tactically likened to their own.

I use "affinities" to refer not only to relationships but also to the political fantasy of resemblance across ethnic, cultural, and national difference. Beyond its kinship connotations, the term suggests an intrinsic connection or understanding—in this case, of covictimization at the hands of imperialism. Such correspondences were critical to producing sympathetic solidarities, which were grounded in a discourse of common struggle that erased historical specificity (especially fascism), and set the relationship between Vietnam and East Germany apart from their relationships with other countries. As I show, sympathetic solidarities propelled a robust apparatus of wartime assistance informed by Western notions of progress through technology. This apparatus would culminate in the "gift" of socialist reconstruction to "speed up" historical development. The unknown

↑ Figure 3.1 Branding solidarity: VĐ symbols (Việt Đức, or Vietnam-Germany) adorn housing in Vinh. Photo by the author.

town of Vinh was thus posed to become a metonym for solidarity with Vietnam.[5]

In what follows, I examine the translation of GDR state discourse of Solidarität into an applied practice that extended back to the 1950s and Vietnam's liberation struggle against French colonialism. There is a growing body of German and Anglophone literature that examines the manifold forms of solidarity with Vietnam that transpired in East Germany across time (see, especially, Schleicher 2011, Horten 2013, and Schaefer 2015). My discussion here is thus not meant to be comprehensive; rather, I aim to introduce the role of sentiment into these typically unsentimental conversations. During the U.S.-Vietnam war, solidarity campaigns channeled humanitarian values into concrete action under the banner of *Solidarität hilft Siegen* (solidarity supports victory), resulting in a series of East German encounters with an imagined "Vietnam." The wide range of forms of support gave many antiwar activists—and Vietnamese beneficiaries—something to believe in, hope for, and aspire to, even as such North-South actions were underpinned at times by latent paternalism. Sympathetic solidarities, I show, were not a given; these dispositions needed to be cultivated, sustained, and branded—especially as solidarity fatigue began to set in during the later years of the war. "Who does not recognize the familiar phrase 'Việt Đức' (Vietnam-Germany) that adorns hospitals, schools, and buildings in Vietnam?" asked Tom Peters in the *Neues Deutschland* on August 16, 1984, reminding readers of the positive and productive results their solidarity had achieved to help Vietnam recover and modernize quickly (see figure 3.1).

Though touted as antiracist, this process of cultivating empathy drew on gendered and racialized images, especially of Vietnamese women and children, who signified a pure and innocent humanity in need of rescue and support. Media representations also prompted comparisons between the annihilations of Vinh and Dresden, the focus of the last section in this chapter, as both cities became symbols of the excesses of war. East Germany's experience with urban and industrial reconstruction appealed to the Vietnamese government as it sought postwar assistance and models of recovery. Solidarity with Vietnam—for example, assisting with the rebuilding of Vinh—thus positioned East Germany on the world stage as a progressive, ethical, and benevolent country, in contrast to the FRG, which remained on the wrong side of history. From this view, we see that solidarity was not motivated by altruism or anticolonialism alone, but also by national self-interest and conflict with West Germany as the GDR struggled to establish its political legitimacy. The small industrial city of Vinh would emerge as a key tool in this Cold War rivalry.

SOLIDARITÄT HILFT SIEGEN! MAKING SOLIDARITY EXCEPTIONAL

> The East Germans were the only people who believed in our victory. The Russians didn't believe in us, but the East Germans did. They gave us the material and psychological support we needed to succeed.
>
> —RETIRED GOVERNMENT BUREAUCRAT, HANOI, 2005

The French and American wars in Vietnam (1945–1975) set the stage for a remarkable, but little known, era of internationalism for the newly founded and soon divided postcolonial country. However, this did not happen effortlessly or instantaneously. Despite Lenin's call in 1920 at the Second Congress of the Communist International to attend to the "colonial question" and to aid liberation movements in colonized territories, Vietnam had a difficult time garnering support for its revolution from more advanced socialist countries. Hồ Chí Minh's declaration of independence from France and founding of the Democratic Republic of Vietnam in September 1945 was not met with a warm welcome from the Soviet Union (under the leadership of Joseph Stalin) and the international communist movement, even as the DRV became embroiled in resistance against returning French forces intent on restoring colonial authority in Vietnam the following year. As the historian Christopher Goscha (2006, 64) has argued, Stalin was discernibly leery of the genuineness of Hồ Chí Minh's commitment to communism (and leery of communism taking hold in Asia more broadly). This was in part due to Hồ Chí Minh's public dissolution of the Indochinese Communist Party (ICP) in 1945, a pretense meant to consolidate the power of the VIỆT MINH (League for the Independence of Vietnam) and present a united front against imperialism while the ICP continued to operate in the shadows (60–61).

The DRV remained unrecognized and isolated for several years—notably, through the first half of the war against French recolonization—until it entered into diplomatic relations with the major communist powers in early 1950. As Mari Olsen describes (2006, 16–17), even after diplomatic recognition from Beijing on January 18, Stalin hesitated, if only briefly, to follow suit—perhaps out of fear of alienating France (see also Zhai 2000, 15; Goscha 2006, 64). Clearly, his distrust of Hồ Chí Minh's intentions persisted. More convinced of the capacity for communism in Asia after Mao's victorious rise to power in China in 1949, however, the Soviet Union proceeded to establish relations with the exiled government of Hồ Chí Minh on January 30, 1950. Taking its cue from the USSR, the GDR did the same on February 3. Such recognition was essential to establishing the legitimacy of the DRV, and to obtaining military and technical assistance for its war against France. Stalin, however, was resolute that aid should come primarily from Beijing, a sentiment he conveyed directly to Hồ Chí Minh (Zhai 2000, 17).

This would change after the French defeat at Điện Biên Phủ on May 7, 1954 (and after the death of Stalin in 1953), with the division of the country. The ensuing Economic and Technical Cooperation treaty, ratified one year later on May 18, 1955, made the Soviet Union the largest aid donor to the DRV, surpassing China by the mid-1960s, when the U.S. air war was ramping up (Gaiduk 2003). As argued in chapter 1, the U.S. government saw Soviet assistance as critical to Hanoi's war effort during the years of aerial bombing. As Jon M. Van Dyke wrote in 1970, "One of the main reasons the economy did not collapse was the willingness of socialist countries to give virtually unlimited material aid to the North Vietnamese" (216). And yet, the difficulties in obtaining recognition and support from the Soviet Union in the early years of nation building fostered ambivalence among Vietnamese leaders about Soviet objectives and a perceived lack of belief in their capability, even as Soviet support increased.[6] Douglas Pike has pointed out that Vietnam received consistent "below-the-salt treatment" from the Soviet Union under Khrushchev, Stalin's successor; a lack of interest in Indochina relegated Vietnam to a "position far down the precedence list" (1987, 170). Indeed, as Buu Hoan observed, despite its scale and impact over thirty years, Soviet aid to Vietnam amounted to a mere 7 percent of the assistance it extended to other countries such as Mongolia or Cuba (1991, 374).

Such ambivalence allowed for the less powerful and younger state of East Germany—the third-largest provider of aid (Schaefer 2015), but with far less political significance than the first two—to be perceived as expressing more genuine solidarity.[7] GDR interest in Vietnam stood in stark contrast to Soviet indifference. Where the USSR saw incompetence and weakness (Hoan 1991, 361), the GDR saw capacity and strength. Vietnamese officials noted this positive disposition toward their country, which was a factor in their decision to request assistance from Berlin for the reconstruction of "Hồ Chí Minh's homeland." In their purposeful identification with a weaker, nonthreatening state that was itself struggling for recognition, the DRV looked beyond the communist superpowers of China and the Soviet Union for material support and a model of industrial growth.

This is not to idealize relations between the GDR and DRV, or to suggest that they avoided becoming strained. Indeed, as I argue in this book, some projects were culturally incongruous or overly ambitious given infrastructural constraints in Vietnam at the time, including the development of a precast concrete industry to produce standardized mass housing (see chapter 6). Other endeavors, however, were arguably more successful over the *longue durée*, while Soviet projects, and those involving aligned bloc countries, often stalled or failed, as I discuss in chapter 4. This is one reason why many in the DRV felt that GDR slogans like "Solidarity supports victory" were more than mere political rhetoric, but expressed sincere humanitarian concern. As the retired bureaucrat's quote in the epigraph reveals, some understood GDR support as driven by a certain structure of feeling that inspired "true" (*thực sự*) commitment to Vietnam's anticolonial struggle. For the postcolonial government, the GDR was perceived as a nonthreatening, if not benevolent, friend. An internal report sent to Prime Minister Phạm Văn Đồng in 1973, after a month-long GDR assessment of Vinh, highlighted the sentimentality of East German solidarity, which could be harnessed for future development purposes. Downplaying tensions, the report emphasized the enthusiasm (*nhiệt tình*) and "profound sympathy" (*thông cảm sâu sắc*) of the visitors as they appraised the urban situation: "The delegation worked with a spirit of fraternal camaraderie [*tinh thần đồng chí anh em*] that was not in accordance with usual procedures . . . and was very sympathetic [*rất thông cảm*] to the situation in our homeland."[8] The use of *thông cảm*, literally to feel (*cảm*) across (*thông*), rather than *tình cảm*, to express individual sentiment, is important.[9] GDR solidarity as spirited, if not sentimental, internationalism felt exceptional to Vietnamese authorities, as standing outside the usual political order of things, and was thus perceived as a valuable asset to tap for socialist nation building.

Arguably, this was the case for many East German specialists (*Spezialisten*; in Vietnamese: *chuyên gia*, or "experts") who worked in Vietnam and were involved in this study, especially those who identified closely with anti-imperialism and the greater socialist cause. Their presence in Vietnam *before* the end of the war, one Vietnamese planner explained, and the visibility of their cargo ships with supplies and machinery docked in Hải Phòng, provided material proof of the slogan *Wir glauben an ihren Sieg* (We believe in your victory).[10] This notion of GDR involvement in the war in an enabling rather than leading role circulated in the mass media—for example, in the solidarity song about Vinh quoted in interlude 2, which emphasized the spirit of togetherness: "We were there with you to extend a helping hand." Because Vietnamese respondents interpreted the GDR's commitment to their country in mostly positive and empowering ways, it was not uncommon for them to make embellished remarks along the lines of "We could not have succeeded without their support," like the comment in the epigraph above. This does not deny, however, the ways that solidarity discourse invested the East German population with a sense of paternalistic responsibility to "help" the less fortunate people of Vietnam.

While such actions may be viewed with nostalgia over time, they do reveal how the "stuff" of solidarity gave some people hope for triumph and survival, particularly in moments when optimism was waning. For example, people in Vietnam often encountered tangible and impactful aid in their everyday lives that was more intimate and immediate than the institutional and infrastructural supports extended to the state, including "gifts" (*Geschenke*) of bicycles, blankets, toys, sewing machines, typewriters, clothes, and foodstuffs. Donations of surplus commodities, in crates stamped with "Việt Đức Solidarity," sustained the socialist fantasy of a brighter future of prosperity, literally and metaphorically. Diesel generators, a symbolic gift of light to dispel darkness, compensated for bombed power plants, which had lost up to 73 percent of their national capacity by August 1967 (Van Dyke 1970, 220). Such bestowments were portrayed as *personal* (and personable) donations from like-minded proletarians, as in the "Farmers Helping Farmers" campaign and the Youth

Pioneers' youth-to-youth initiatives, which raised funds for the construction of primary schools.[11] Horten even reports that GDR musicians organized donations of musical instruments for the Hanoi symphony (2013, 570). Musicians also produced a compilation album on "Kämpfendes Vietnam" (Vietnam at War) in 1967, mobilizing sentiment through songs of solidarity. In interviews, Vietnamese citizens appreciatively recalled these meaningful gestures of support, which in their minds had as much to do with boosting morale as with fulfilling their basic needs. Beyond the suggestion of affluence, my Vietnamese interlocutors saw these gifts as a material expression of East Germany's confidence in their ability to defeat an imperial superpower, and a willingness to help them do so, unlike Soviet skepticism and disinterest.

The insistence that East German solidarity was somehow distinctive prompted me, as an anthropologist, to scrutinize such claims. I wanted to gain a deeper understanding of the cultural, moral, and affective logics that nurtured this belief—and continue to sustain it—while locating the point where such exceptionalism broke down. Given the GDR's uneven record with assistance to other postcolonial countries, especially in Africa (Weis 2011), what allowed for solidarity with Vietnam to be construed as more credible and efficacious?

SPENDE FÜR VIETNAM: MORAL ECONOMIES OF GIVING

> You should practice solidarity with peoples fighting for their national liberation and defending their national independence.
>
> —TEN COMMANDMENTS OF SOCIALIST MORALS, 1958[12]

The GDR had long advocated for solidarity with anticolonial revolutions after the end of World War II, as evidenced in the above ethical directive. Today, a new generation of scholars is taking seriously the distinct forms and aims of these aesthetic, economic, and material interventions and their implications for the study of global history.[13] In the process, they are challenging clichéd tropes of isolation while rethinking conventional notions of solidarity (Schwenkel 2014b, 2015a; Rupprecht 2015). Though aid started during the French resistance after recognition of the DRV, the U.S. war in Vietnam marked a change in the scale and scope of support as countries across Eastern Europe ramped up their efforts to build solidarity with their Vietnamese comrades fighting for unification and sovereignty.[14] In the GDR, the mantra of *Solidarität hilft Siegen* (solidarity supports victory) captured the postracial idealism of fraternal equality that informed the rhetoric of socialist internationalism at the time (Slobodian 2015a). Moralizing discourses of a shared history and of socialist humanity inspired peace activists who identified with the subjugated masses attempting to overthrow imperialism. As I show below, these sentiments helped to shape a moral economy of humanitarian giving that formed the bedrock of anti-imperialist alliances with Vietnam.

And yet, despite state-promoted antiracist policies, sympathetic solidarities could not transcend an essentialist belief in racial difference (Chin and Fehrenbach 2009, 127–28). On the one hand, solidarity was premised on the denial of alterity. One man, an artist, described the "natural" affinities between the GDR and decolonizing countries which were similarly "small, weak and poor": "We saw ourselves in unity with *leidenden, kämpfenden Menschen* [suffering, struggling peoples] up against more powerful countries."[15] On the other hand were limits to the fictive kinship constructs, especially with "blood for Vietnam" (*Blut für Vietnam*) campaigns that sought to turn affines into consanguines, a racially unsettling premise for both populations (see below). Indeed, racial Otherness was affirmed through the very inequalities that structured the need for, and ability to provide, aid to the "underdeveloped" South (Hong 2015, 320). These asymmetries exposed the frictions within solidarity efforts by revealing how fraught and unstable even supportive encounters could be, especially those that professed to transgress racial and other social boundaries that remained firmly in place.

Antiracist and anti-imperialist solidarity policies were, moreover, not uncontroversial in Vietnam. Although socialist assistance during the war continues to be widely celebrated—for example, at a museum exhibition titled *The World Supported Vietnam*[16]—this history presented an awkward dilemma for Hanoi. The suggestion that there was an *international* dimension to the U.S. defeat complicates the image of a poor but resilient people—"small and proud"[17]—single-handedly taking on a stronger and better equipped enemy. Recent work by Xiaobing Li (2010), for example, shows that solidarity went beyond material, emotional, and economic support. Li breaks the silence on Russian and Chinese covert operations—which involved logistics officers, instructors, antiaircraft battalions, and military engineers—and offers insights into the *foreign* military machinations behind Vietnam's victory.[18]

Solidarity campaigns in East Germany garnered extensive humanitarian and technical support for Vietnam, the most abundant of any communist country in Europe after the Soviet Union (Horten 2013, 567). Unlike the "moral economy of humanitarianism" in the capitalist West (Fassin 2011, 7), socialist *assistance* was framed as collaborative, enabling, and noninterventionist to distinguish it from capitalist *aid* tied to a neocolonial politics of pity and codependency (Howell 1994). This extensive apparatus was dependent on the ability of the state to channel affect—namely, revulsion at the war—into an ethical politics of action that penetrated social institutions at all levels of society. Solidarity required consent of the masses and their active participation in state-driven initiatives while deflecting criticism *from* unpopular national policies and *toward* American imperialism. In my interviews, people described being moved to act by the horrific violence in Vietnam that they encountered in the media, violence that triggered memories of World War II (see also Wernicke 2003, 318). As a moral imperative, East Germans positioned themselves on the right side of history by participating in solidarity, showing themselves to be good moral citizens and compassionate humanitarians. Most of my middle-class respondents described their support of Vietnam in enthusiastic terms; many spoke of genuine commitment to advancing the causes of peace and human rights: solidarity "aus rechtlichen und moralischen Gründen" (for legal and moral reasons), stated one man, who would go on to work in Vietnam.[19] They stressed that their donations (*Spenden*) were not coerced—"I was excited to support Vietnam and gave willingly," claimed one woman, a retired civil servant[20]—even if facilitated by state institutions, such as trade unions, which recorded donations as *Solimarken* (solidarity stamps) in a worker's membership book (see plate 3). As a moral economy underpinned by notions of justice through the redistribution of wealth, Spende produced its own "*Soli*" vocabulary still in use today.[21] This was made clear to me in an online exchange with a former construction supervisor in Halle who had been recruited to work on a concrete panel factory in Đạo Tú, north of Hanoi, and whose words revealed a tension between free choice, collective action, and political constraint: "The *Solibeitrag* [solidarity contribution] was a voluntary monthly donation. The *Solihöhe* [Soli amount] was agreed upon by the work unit and varied, sometimes .25 marks and other times 1 mark. For me, the humanitarian aspect determined how much *Solispende* [Soli donation] I made to Vietnam."[22]

Collected donations went to the centralized "solidarity account" (*Solidaritätskonto*, also called the *Spendenkonto*) in Berlin that was managed by the GDR Solidarity Committee (formerly the Afro-Asian Solidarity Committee). The Vietnam branch, referred to as the "Vietnam-Ausschuß," coordinated solidarity initiatives across the republic, including those of the Freie Deutsche Jugend (Free German Youth) and other mass organizations. In 1968 alone, donations from GDR citizens were reported to exceed 40 million marks (Wernicke 2003, 316), a two-and-a-half-fold increase in just two years (Horten 2013, 569).

I emphasize that Spende was voluntary without losing sight of the coercive state or the peer pressure to be involved in solidarity efforts. These efforts gave respondents a sense of social membership while belonging to something bigger, a structure of feeling also found in Western charity and voluntarism (Malkki 2015).[23] That said, support for solidarity waxed and waned and was inconsistent across social groups.[24] As Didier Fassin (2011) argues, moral economies of humanitarianism are inherently unstable and marked by contradictions that divide as much as they unite. In the early years of U.S. intervention in Vietnam, for example, there was ambivalence, if not outright disinterest, in solidarity (Horten 2013, 568–69). These sentiments turned into anger and activism, however, as war, and the killing of innocent civilians, escalated.

Donation campaigns were already active during the 1950s, though on a much smaller scale. Funds were raised for the construction of schools, nurseries, and pharmacies, and for the provision of other *Solidaritätsgeschenken* (solidarity gifts).[25] This included a government shipment of medicine in 1952, worth a quarter million marks, to tend to injured civilians and soldiers in the Vietnamese army, including German prisoners of war who had served in the French Foreign Legion (Krüger 1991, 822). Spende also went to the GDR's flagship humanitarian project in Hanoi: the renovation of the colonial Yersin Hospital, starting in 1956.[26] Today, the modern facility, still called Bệnh viện Việt Đức (Vietnam-Germany Hospital), is one of the country's largest and most respected centers for orthopedic surgery.[27]

American airpower would usher in a new era of solidarity in the 1960s that differed from that of the previous decade (Wernicke 2001). As the first bombs fell, the state-controlled media in East Germany called on citizens to strengthen their support of the "sozialistisches Bruderland" (socialist brotherland), adopting kinship terminology to evoke the moral duties of socialist siblinghood. East Germans of all ages, some passionately, others begrudgingly, responded to calls to support the "just struggle" of the "heroic Vietnamese people." Coordinated activities (usually with the prefix "solidarity")—from antiwar demonstrations to protest letters that children sent to the White House (see interlude 2), blood drives, food donations, concerts, fundraisers, information sessions, photo exhibitions, and political meetings with Vietnamese delegations—penetrated daily life and public space, making it difficult *not* to participate in solidarity in some form or another.

The creation of sympathetic solidarities to mobilize the population appeared to be, for all intents and purposes, effective. Horten (2013, 569–70) offers statistics on the steep rise in Spenden during the decade of the U.S. air war: tripling from 16 million marks in 1966 to 48 million by 1973, and then surging to 83 million by the fall of Saigon two years later. The press celebrated high donations—like the 50 marks the worker in Suhl gave to the "small and proud" people—creating competition between work units and mass organizations. And yet beyond this moral economy and the political rituals of social belonging, solidarity was indicative of a disciplinary regime that operated through constant surveillance and assessment of the population (Pfaff 2001). Annual university reports, for example, contained synopses of individual student actions and dispositions toward solidarity, also for international students, including Vietnamese. Collectively, they tracked accounting practices, such as records of donations that student groups amassed over time, to ensure heightened levels of participation and enthusiasm.[28]

The spirit of solidarity would taper off in the mid-1970s with the end of bombing and withdrawal of U.S. troops. It also declined in neighboring socialist countries, even more so as Chile came to displace Vietnam as the "object of revolutionary fascination" (Mark et al. 2015, 462). I refer to this moment of tapering off in the GDR as "solidarity fatigue," drawing on Susan D. Moeller's (1999) analysis of compassion fatigue, where liberal sensitivities are dulled by overexposure to crises and human suffering. With solidarity fatigue, people tired of the pressure to maintain support while their own resources dwindled and goods became scarcer. For some, this led to resentment; according to one filmmaker, who explained the declining sentiment of solidarity over time, "Solange der Krieg ging, war Vietnam beliebt" (As long as the war went on, Vietnam was adored)."[29] Once it was over, the racialized image of small brown people defeating big white enemies—which served as a call to action around the world—no longer provoked the same emotional response. The East German leadership would need fresh campaigns, images, and techniques to maintain identification in the aftermath of war. As fatigue set in, General Secretary of the Socialist Unity Party (SED) Erich Honecker appealed to the population's historical sensibility, and the will to assist subjugated peoples, by calling for solidarity with a devastated Vietnam in need of rebuilding: "Jetzt erst recht!"—Now more than ever! (see figure 3.2).

MANUFACTURING SYMPATHETIC SOLIDARITIES

The cynicism toward solidarity in the early years of the U.S. war reminds us that the sentiment was not innate but had to be produced and sustained over time. Vietnam was a distant and unfamiliar place marked by generic Orientalness;[30] it had to become known and made to matter through a politics of proximity that mediated cultural intimacy. State media played an instrumental

→ Figure 3.2 "Solidarity: now more than ever." A Vietnamese woman pictured among ruins to encourage donations to the solidarity fund.

role in producing an imaginative counter-geography of Vietnam through instruments of modern knowledge and power (Said 1978, 86), which drew on prevailing socialist imagery and terminology to make Vietnam more familiar (but not too close). This was not knowledge for the sake of political or imperial domination, as we saw with the U.S. military's imaginative geography in chapter 1, but knowledge to subvert that domination and the "dramatic boundaries" it had drawn to deny the Vietnamese their humanity (73). Whereas the U.S. imaginative geography dramatized distance and difference (55), the GDR counterimaginary collapsed them. Accordingly, state media broke down and translated racial and cultural difference into palatable images of Vietnam that people in East Germany could empathize with, connect to, and care about, but without creating too much familiarity. It did so by appealing to an abstract universal humanity and by referencing a common history of suffering that

↑ Figure 3.3 Invincible Vietnam: GDR postage stamps from 1966 and 1968.

associated imperialism uniquely with the capitalist West. Orientalist depictions of Vietnamese people as gentle, innocent kin in need of help were meant to incite anger, compassion, and action. These archetypal images and motifs, which were mostly of women and children to suggest innocence and hope for the future (Malkki 2010, 77), circulated in newspapers, television programs, documentaries, posters, postage stamps, *Solimarken*, and other everyday objects (see figure 3.3 and interlude 2). Solidarity in East Germany was thus showcased as the public's moral and political commitment to social justice, decolonization, and a liberating humanist socialism (Witkowski 2015, 76), in contrast to the media's portrayal of the "misanthropic" (*menschenfeindlich*) West German government that sent its "mercenaries" (*Söldner*), in the guise of technicians, to abet American crimes against humanity.[31]

The media paid particular attention to U.S. airpower, at times suggesting parallels between World War II and the war in Vietnam. Its use of the phrase "terror bombing" (*Bombenterror*) had uncanny resonances with national socialism, including linguistic connections with Nazi propaganda; the term had been used in Nazi Germany to describe Allied air attacks. As the press appealed to East German humanitarian sensibilities, the public saw evidence of the destruction of Vietnam in images of ruined buildings and industry placed alongside other provocative terms that triggered anger and empathy, including *Völkermord* (genocide) and *Massenmord* (mass murder). "Everywhere in the GDR: Outrage and Solidarity," read one front-page headline in the *Berliner Zeitung* during the December 1972 "Christmas bombing," linking moral deeds to political affect. "Three times the bomb payload of World War II dropped on the DRV," read a subheading on the next page, whose language was intended to resonate with a generation that had itself experienced intense air strikes. Photographs juxtaposing Hanoi in 1972 with Hiroshima in 1945, an icon of apocalypse that GDR propaganda also linked to Dresden, implied a recurrence of history and a "single thread of imperialist policy" connecting all three countries (Crew 2017, 147). Linguistic analogies conjured German history more candidly and suggested a correspondence between American imperialism and Nazism by disparaging the "Fascist air raids" (*Faschistische Luftangriffe*) on Vietnam carried out by a group of criminal "air-gangsters" (*Luftgangster*), "air-pirates" (*Luftpiraten*), and Hitler-Fascists.[32] Many of my East German respondents held vivid memories of World War II, which shaped their political subjectivities and commitment to peace. For them, these media provocations were a strong, if not effective, call to action against U.S. military intervention in Vietnam.

Vietnamese people were not, however, represented only as victims or objects of pity. As I argued above, pity was derided as a form of liberal humanitarianism or "perversion of compassion," in Hannah Arendt's words, that trafficked in misfortune rather than inspire collective action (2006, 78). One GDR journalist recalled breaking down while meeting a woman whose child had been killed in an air raid. Her Vietnamese translator, disturbed by the spectacle of misery and her overly emotional response, snapped in German, "We need your solidarity, not your pity. Go home if you are here to cry."[33] Socialist solidarity was fashioned instead as a posture of proximate—and restrained—sympathy informed by mutual commitments and a common will to act (Arendt 2006, 79), in contrast to liberalism's self-interested, abject suffering at a distance (Boltanski 1999). East German media highlighted the besieged country's fortitude and agency to convince people that solidarity *was* impactful and could indeed give rise to victory. In the weekly television newscast *Der Augenzeuge* (The eyewitness), for example, long shots of mass destruction were followed by stock images of exploding U.S. bombers. As the balls of fire plunged to earth, viewers were reminded of the susceptibility of the U.S. military and its technology to defeat. Mirroring the practices of the Vietnamese press (see Schwenkel 2009b), East German newspapers tallied the numbers of downed aircraft, affirming progress, much like body counts and truck kills in the U.S. media: "31 strategic U.S. bombers brought down from the sky."[34] Headshots of captured POWs—a topic that piqued public interest—helped persuade avid readers that the enemy had indeed been defeated and rendered powerless.[35]

East German correspondents on the ground in the DRV captured a more intimate portrait of life during war than the statistics supplied by the Vietnam News Agency. Given their location in the North, they frequently took the destruction of cities as their main subject, even as such coverage was mediated and directed because of "security concerns." Vinh, in particular, became a showcase for the crimes of "terror bombing." One journalist explained how the translator, together with a "keeper" or government chaperone, decided the itinerary, took them to the city (bypassing other devastated areas), and arranged interviews. The hazardous journey to Vinh required several days of slow travel on cratered roads and makeshift pontoon bridges. My Vietnamese interlocutors saw such efforts to cover news developments in a conflict area as exemplary of *tình đoàn kết* (solidarity). What else would compel people to risk their lives and leave the safety of home to travel to a foreign war zone?

Being embedded in Vinh (and the wider Nghệ An province) allowed media and film crews to create a rich chronicle of the war, one that drew on conventional documentary practices to personalize the tragedy of mass bombing and confirm its authenticity.[36] This visual and textual record humanized the Vietnamese population for East German readers, turning distant objects of violence into familiar subjects of history. Anna Mudry's reportage in Vinh, for example, traced the life of Hồng, a young woman who experienced a childhood of air raids and evacuation and then complete disorientation upon her return to an unrecognizable city, where she could no longer locate the site where her house had stood.[37] East German documentaries likewise countered the tendency toward "anonymous corporeality" (Malkki 1996, 389). The use of emplaced witness testimony, in the site of trauma, allowed persons with specific family histories to emerge from the pool of generic humanity while conveying the immediacy of events. In *Denkt an mein Land* (Remember my country, 1965), for instance, director Peter Ulbrich introduces Mr. Lâm Ngọc, mayor of a destroyed commune in Nghệ An, and his son, Trung. Standing silently amid the remains of his former house, Mr. Ngọc intends to rebuild his home and hamlet, a narrator explains, and secure a better future for Trung, his only remaining child and family member. Two years later, in the documentary *Ihr fragt, wie wir leben* (You ask, how we live, 1967), Ulbrich pans the wreckage of a simple yet well-equipped primary school before cutting to a shot of a thatched classroom under forest canopy, where pupils have evacuated, a camera technique meant to suggest a reversal in time: the deliberate undoing of socialist progress and a return to a premodern life. As bombers approach, the teacher bangs a drum and children descend quickly into trenches they had dug beneath their desks, much as my respondents had described in chapter 2. The predominant message in this media repertoire was not one of despair, however, but hope for recovery and the resumption of nation building—also with the help of East Germany, as Mudry's report foretold.

Beyond informing—and attempting to rally—the public, this chronicle of everyday experiences of aerial bombing was a way for East Germany to establish itself as a credible actor and regional power. Documentaries that highlighted solidarity aid to Vietnam boasted of the GDR's economic and technological prowess with unmistakable nationalist overtones. Take, for example, the 1966 film by Walter Heynowski and Gerhard Scheumann, *400 c.c.*, on the "Blood for Vietnam" campaign, which depicted blood donations as a form of virtuous labor (Carsten 2019, 73). The clenched fists of donors—a sign of both unity and phlebotomy—showed the intersection of biomedical modernity and revolutionary potentiality, while the charitable gifting of blood symbolized a transcendence of racial difference. Set to an original a cappella score, the narrator suggests that blood donations have the power to transform socialist friends into biological kin: "Wir sind Blutsverwandte geworden" (We became blood relatives). This intimacy was not without resistance, however. Horten (2013, 569) points to racist sentiment in East Germany around the delivery of "white blood" to the "yellow race," but Vietnamese people also had their doubts about becoming "blood brothers." In *Die fernen Freunde nah* (Faraway friends up close, 1979), also by Heynowski and Scheumann, viewers may have been surprised to learn that East German blood donations to the DRV were used to save *U.S.* pilots, not wounded Vietnamese, knowledge that the directors kept from the public so as not to disrupt the goodwill solidarity. Rather than promote postracial unity, the unstable meaning of donated blood paradoxically upended kinship imaginaries by suggesting biological incompatibility to reestablish a clear racial divide.

Tensions over the boundaries between proximity and distance could also be found in the political activities of mass organizations, which also played a critical role in building sympathetic solidarity. Under the banner "Vietnams Kampf ist unser Kampf" (Vietnam's struggle is our struggle), the Free German Youth (Freie Deutsche Jugend, or FDJ) and Youth Pioneers (Jungpioniere) called on young revolutionaries to "strengthen the impulse" for solidarity by attending political rallies and organized social events.[38] This included, for example, the Vietnambasar (Vietnam Bazaar), held in October 1968 in East Berlin to educate young people about the heroism of their Vietnamese contemporaries as well as the "great achievements" of their own country.[39] A multimedia exhibit titled *Solidarität hilft Siegen* introduced visitors to Vietnam: its physical geography, social development, political partition (like their own country's, it was pointed out), and historical struggle for autonomy. Booths sold handicrafts and souvenirs to support humanitarian work in Vietnam, and German (curiously, not Vietnamese) folk dancers performed. Attendees could meet with a representative from the Vietnamese embassy and talk with Vietnamese students and trainees, who were the living proof of the benefits of solidarity. As with news reports and documentaries, events like the Vietnam Bazaar cast solidarity as positive, enabling, and transgressive. Its "safe exoticism" (Desmond 1999, 109) made the mysterious, remote Orient more familiar and known through cultural encounters that, in the context of an unjust war, made the presence of Vietnamese in East Germany nonthreatening.[40] The bazaar's claim to analogous histories of political partition as a strategy to incorporate difference as sameness would reappear in parallels drawn between the catastrophic histories of Vinh and Dresden.

VINH AS DRESDEN: AFFINITIES IN WAR AND RECONSTRUCTION

> In Vietnam, too, the last bit of the legend that the American imperialists had not participated in the bombing of civilian populations in the Second World War for principled humanitarian reasons was lost.
>
> —WALTER WEIDAUER, *INFERNO DRESDEN*, 1966[41]

In 2003, when Germans took to the streets to protest the American-led invasion of Iraq, some of them carried signs that equated the bombing of Baghdad with that of Dresden. While Andreas Huyssen claims that this "sudden" reference to German victimhood was somehow new (2003a, 165), others maintain that the history of selective appropriation of Germany's past by the peace movement extends back to 1991, with the start of the first Gulf War (Heins and Langenohl 2013, 13). Both claims, however, ignore the ways that the bombing of Germany, and especially of Dresden, served as a "memory prompt" in *East* Germany even earlier—for example, in the discourse of *co-suffering* during the war in Korea (Fox 2006, 117). As I argue here, this memory prompt also operated during the war in Vietnam. It is generally held that the air war remained a taboo topic in Germany until W. G. Sebald's *Luftkrieg und Literatur* broke the silence in 1999 (see also Huyssen 2003a, 167). However, this largely West German perspective[42] overlooks the history of Allied bombing as an important Cold War propaganda tool in East Germany, such as Weidauer's book *Inferno Dresden*, cited in the epigraph. Memory of air raids and the obliteration of cities in the GDR highlighted German—and, by extension, communist—victimization by Western imperialism.[43] The 1955 publication of Brecht's *Kriegsfibel* (*War Primer*) in East Germany shows that the air war was not repressed or publicly forgotten—indeed, there was nothing to suppress since the hegemonic *Weltanschauung* at the time placed blame for the war firmly on what the GDR termed the "imperialist fascist West" (Kelly 2010, 138).[44] Instead, the firebombing of German cities was strategically remembered in cultural representations, such as films, and annual commemorations in Dresden (Fox 2006, 114–16)—and to voice opposition to the bombing of Vietnam. For the East, "never again" implied the evil not of Auschwitz, as it did in the FRG, but of Dresden. This socialist politics of memory obfuscated communist culpability for the Holocaust and cast capitalist West Germany squarely in the role of chief perpetrator of crimes carried out under the Nazis (Vees-Gulani 2008, 32).

From the 1950s in the GDR, Dresden had become a powerful symbol of senseless bombing and catastrophic suffering (Heins and Langenohl 2013, 16). More than any other targeted city, Dresden became the emblem of East German victimhood (Fox 2006, 115), displacing from memory the far higher numbers of Nazi victims.[45] For example, the assault of February 13–15, 1945, on the city killed twenty-five thousand people (or more), who are depicted in GDR history as innocent civilians. The government invested this incident with tremendous moral and political significance and leveraged that significance for ideological purposes (Heins and Langenohl 2013, 17). Discourses of victimization shaped public encounters with memories of the firebombing; for example, the plaque that was previously attached to the ruins of Dresden's Frauenkirche condemned the war crimes of "imperialist barbarism." In the press, destruction of German cities by *Luftterror* (air terror) marked the start of the Cold War within the "hot war," World War II. As one 1967 editorial argued, the merciless attacks on towns such as Dresden were, in fact, a "crusade against socialism" (*Kreuzzug gegen den Sozialismus*), not just an attempt to stop fascism.[46] This claim that Dresden was a prelude to the Cold War was aligned with the SED's view that the Allies had firebombed the city to show off their military capabilities as a warning to Stalin (Crew 2017, 146). By snubbing the Allies' perpetrator narrative and positioning communism as the real target of their shelling, the writer of the editorial set up a direct and inevitable link between Germany's past and Vietnam's present: "And from then on, it was a straight road to the officially declared terror attacks on Vietnam."

In tying together the countries' histories of aerial bombardment by zealous American imperialists, it was an easy, if not predictable, leap to connect the total destruction of Dresden and Vinh. Like Dresden, Vinh came to signify excessive bombing and mass civilian suffering. Both were cast as war crimes: "What is going on in Viet Nam today is essentially the same crime perpetrated against Dresden on 13 February 1945—terror, blind-raging destruction and genocide" (Neutzner in Crew 2017, 148). Linguistic correspondences, rooted in Nazi terminology, strengthened such affinities by referencing mutual experiences with "terror bombing" and its criminal obliteration of both cities. While the appropriation of German war memory to frame aerial attacks on the DRV decontextualized two radically different theaters of war, it also functioned to make faraway places in ruin, like Vinh, more familiar.[47]

Yet it took significant political and ideological maneuvering for solidarity to become "especially closely linked" (*besonders eng verknüpft*) to the "heroic city."[48] Despite the claim in this chapter's epigraph that there was hardly a person who did not know the name of Vinh, in fact most people in all likelihood did not. Documentaries about the region's destruction did not circulate widely, and Vietnamese place names and geography could be perplexing, as in the error in the song title quoted in interlude 2 that confused Vĩnh Linh with Vinh. Vietnam was already a distant land, and its small provincial city even more remote and unknown. When solidarity waned at the end of the U.S. air war, it took the media and other political devices, like the Solidarity Committee, to sustain the "spirit of socialist internationalism" (*Geist des sozialistischen Internationalismus*) and interest in rebuilding Vietnam. In the thick of negotiations over the terms of reconstruction, the press published stories about Vinh, deploying Orientalist tropes to describe an exotic, faraway place: a tropical heaven, nestled among green rice fields and swollen rivers. At the same time, it was also a dystopian hell—a land of rubble and ruin that suffered the same fate as readers' own towns just a few decades before.[49]

Recollections of other urban ruins—especially in Dresden—shaped political discourse and reconstruction experiences in Vietnam. For GDR experts who worked in Vinh (see chapter 4), Dresden was a temporal and spatial metaphor for the scale of urban devastation they encountered in the city. As such, it emerged as a recurring theme in interviews. One master planner, for example, who grew up during World War II, strongly identified with pacifism and Vietnam's struggle against American imperialism. He found the reports of abuse, torture, and relentless bombing appalling and claimed they motivated him to become more involved with Vietnam's recovery. He believed that East Germans instinctively identified with the residents of Vinh: "No other country suffered destruction like Germany in the Second World War; no other city suffered destruction like Vinh." It was a natural alliance, in his rationale, based on similitude of suffering and ruin. Later in the interview, he brought out a collection of black-and-white photographs from his first mission to Vinh in

1973, which showed a ravaged landscape of broken walls, empty voids, and scattered debris—a view of modernity violently undone. He recalled the shock he felt upon first seeing the devastation, which conjured images of his youth and a reversal of time: "When I arrived, Vinh was beyond ruins, worse than Dresden at the end of World War II. Just as that American general threatened, they bombed that city back to the Stone Age."[50] Vinh evoked not only another time but another place, or world. Like the character Billy Pilgrim's description of Dresden in *Slaughterhouse-Five*, my research respondents described Vinh as *otherworldly*, as a moonscape, reduced to smoking stones, craters, and ash.[51] "There was nothing left," they said of the land that was utterly foreign and yet strangely familiar, a land in need of catching up.

Vietnamese officials and planning experts also suggested scalar correspondences between Vinh and Dresden. Dresden's spectacular "rise from ashes" into an industrial powerhouse within a few years may have played a role in influencing Hanoi's decision to approach East Germany with a request to lead the reconstruction efforts in Vinh. "Who else in recent history had experience with rebuilding a completely destroyed city?" one Vietnamese architect trained in Weimar asked me rhetorically.[52] When I pointed out that many Soviet Bloc countries actually had the technical means, skills, and experience, he laughed at my naiveté and emphasized the importance of time: "Yes, but only the East Germans knew how to rebuild quickly and efficiently!" This belief in German technological proficiency as an accelerated path to modernity had some historical basis. Archival documents show that Hanoi was cognizant of other infrastructure projects that the GDR carried out overseas, including assisting with the swift reconstruction of Hamhung, North Korea's second largest city and a center of industry.[53] For Vietnamese officials, East Germany had seemingly devised a universal model for rebuilding industrial cities with similar histories of war and partition, a model they deemed suitable for Vinh.

The official written request from Hanoi came on May 19, 1973, though interest had been expressed a few months earlier.[54] On that day, Prime Minister Phạm Văn Đồng sent a letter to the Chairman of the Council of Ministers in East Germany asking for assistance with urban planning in Vinh as part of its efforts to "build socialism and defeat American imperialism."[55] This presented a unique opportunity for the GDR government to bolster its international image—and its claims to moral superiority over the FRG—while influencing the future development of Vietnam. On May 23, the Council of Ministers tentatively approved the request.[56] One week later, Erich Honecker presented the proposal at the Ninth Meeting of the Central Committee, arguing that it expressed the GDR's "spirit of solidarity."[57] A new chapter in Solidarität was to follow: two days later the song "Vinh Always Remains Close" hit the airwaves. Its lyrics, "We suffered with you, as your huts were burned," were intended to prevent solidarity fatigue by reminding the population of their historical kinship with Vietnam (see interlude 2). There was also a renewed campaign for Spenden to replenish the solidarity fund, accompanied by reports in *Neues Deutschland* of "enthusiastic support" for the proposal among the East German population.[58]

Beneath the enthusiasm lurked skepticism, however. Soon after the tentative approval, a delegation of experts from the Ministry of Construction set off for a month-long tour of Vietnam to determine if the task at hand was even possible given the circumstances.[59] This fact-finding mission (which inspired the comments about GDR enthusiasm that I discussed above) was followed by a reciprocal delegation to East Germany after the Council of Ministers approved the DRV's request for assistance on August 23. This was a chance offering for East Germany to showcase its technological modernity: the ten-person task force from Vietnam sought to gain firsthand knowledge of the GDR's touted infrastructure achievements, especially in construction. The first item on the month-long agenda was an examination of urban industry and the rehabilitation of a ruined city as an example of what Vinh *could* become. "They wanted to look at our destroyed cities and see how we rebuilt them," a host to the visitors put it bluntly.[60] The delegation members requested to visit Dresden—their image for Vinh's future—but the schedule was later changed; in the end they were taken to the less controversial town of Dessau and to the new socialist city of Halle-Neustadt.[61] The visit to both rebuilt and new cities in East Germany suggests that GDR recovery offered a persuasive model of progress for Vietnamese planners to apply to the modernization of their homeland and that of Vinh.

Publicity around this symbolic bilateral project was carefully choreographed. As the delegation was wrapping up its visit, Phạm Văn Đồng arrived in Berlin on October 22 to sign the final agreement, titled "Assistance with the design and construction of Vinh City" (*Unterstützung bei der Projektierung und beim Aufbau der Stadt Vinh*; *Việc giúp thiết kế và xây dựng thành phố Vinh*). In a speech one day earlier, Communist Party Secretary Nguyễn Duy Trinh had already declared to the East German people, "Your solidarity is true internationalism," bolstering the notion that GDR support of Vietnam was unique, a sentiment the media then broadcasted around the country.[62] Not without challenges and delays, within several months a team of elite experts with experience in planning and construction, also of ruined cities, would be on the ground, along with a cohort of technicians, engineers, and tradespeople. As a prestige project for East Germany, Vinh was thus poised at the center of a war between the United States and Vietnam, as well as between the two Germanys. Within the Eastern Bloc, the project would allow the GDR to assume a privileged place among the socialist international elite working jointly (but not without competition) to modernize the country, the topic of chapter 4.

PART 2
Reconstruction

↑ Figure P.2.1 Quang Trung housing estate, central Vinh, 1978. Nghệ An Provincial Museum.

4

SPIRITED INTERNATIONALISM

The 1950s offered the GDR a host of opportunities to project a global image as a member of the socialist elite. As Greg Castillo argues, the party leadership chose 1952 as "the year in which East Germany would 'vault into a socialist future'" (2007, 293). This involved frenzied, high-speed building, especially in the capital city of Berlin, to usher in a new urban civilization. But GDR resources, including labor and expertise, would also be mobilized to catapult decolonizing countries, including Vietnam, down the road to socialist modernity (Butter 2017). This was an era when faith in industrialization as the path to development drove advanced socialist countries to build factories around the postcolonial South as part of the "great rush to the future" (Ssorin-Chaikov 2006). Industrial-driven internationalism also intersected with the aims of the antiwar movement and the struggle against imperialism in Vietnam. As argued in chapter 3, support for the DRV, which began in the 1950s during its resistance war against France, was cast as "fraternal" solidarity to imbue initiatives with affect and a sense of common purpose. For both the DRV and the GDR—similarly divided, destroyed, "small, weak, and poor," as one respondent likened both countries[1]—internationalism helped to establish legitimacy, develop national economies, and build global socialism in the process.

Both national interests and global ambitions motivated the GDR's support of Vietnam. The DRV was one of the first countries to receive aid from East Germany (along with North Korea), at a time when its own economy was recovering from the Second World War (Freytag 1998, 47). As with Soviet assistance, GDR aid to Vietnam increased after the ratification of key bilateral agreements, which included treaties on trade, national security, and scientific cooperation, all signed in 1956.[2] In the early years of Vietnam's decolonization, GDR support aimed to modernize the DRV on its course toward socialist construction (*sozialistischer Aufbau*) through technology transfers, as did support from other socialist countries.[3] Assistance with the tools of statecraft, including intelligence training, weapons acquisition, and currency printing, contributed to nation building and the consolidation of power under Hồ Chí Minh's leadership.[4] Per the DRV's first three-year plan (1958–1960), new infrastructure and light industry would propel Vietnam into the future by establishing the material and technical foundations of socialism, which included a cannery in Hanoi (the first of its kind in the North) and a modern glassworks factory in Hải Phòng.[5] Optimistic names, like Progress Printing House (established in 1958), signified the anticipated forward direction of the country. Education and training for selected Vietnamese students in East Germany, in defined areas of technical expertise seen lacking in the DRV and necessary for the growth of industry, were also framed in temporal terms as aid for national development.[6]

Discourse around these early "friendship agreements" emphasized mutual aid and reciprocity (*gegenseitigkeit*) in an effort to flatten hierarchical relations between donor and recipient.[7] And yet reciprocity as envisioned between equals was challenging to achieve: East Germany's unmet request for precious timber in 1957, for example, exposed the infrastructure inequalities that defined early diplomacy between the two countries. A letter from officials in Vinh to Hanoi on September 9 explained the difficulties faced in gathering the requested wood in mountainous regions, owing to weak administration and challenges to transportation.[8] There would be no future returns on solidarity in this instance; rather the socialist gift that was meant to forge bonds of horizontal fraternity would remain unreciprocated, a sign of the deep asymmetries that already structured relations between the newly established countries.

These internationalist projects, undertaken just a few years after the founding of the DRV and the GDR (in 1945 and 1949 respectively), fostered opportunities for self-aggrandizement in East Germany—"Praise for our modern industrial construction," read one newspaper article about the glassworks factory in 1962.[9] Early aid initiatives consolidated East Germany's place as a leading industrial power in the Eastern Bloc and set the stage for playing an even stronger role in rebuilding the DRV after U.S. destruction of the country began two years later. The two countries proved indispensable to one another: Vietnam needed East Germany for socialist nation building as much as East Germany needed Vietnam as it jostled for influence and technological superiority vis-à-vis West Germany, but also the Soviet Union.

From very early on, modernization in the DRV meant the "foreignization" of its infrastructure. Ironically, this was a strategy of decolonization, which involved eradicating the colonial past and its forms of exploitation, to make way for the socialist new as collective mastery (*làm chủ tập thể*), even as this socialist new appeared tinged with colonial undertones. By the onset of war with the United States, internationalism was in full swing. Ambitious promises to build socialism through altruistic transfers of knowledge and technology ensured that Vietnam did not stray from the path of Marxism-Leninism during its postwar years of national reconstruction. This chapter looks at the process and conditions through which this material and technological landscape emerged. I first outline the broader geopolitical context in which competitive socialist countries offered assistance to Vietnam in the aftermath of the U.S. air war. I show how Vinh emerged within this geography of aid both as a symbol of "unbreakable" East German solidarity—a counterpoint to Hanoi, the "indestructible symbol" of Soviet-Vietnamese friendship (Logan 1995, 458)—and as a showcase project that succeeded, albeit incompletely, where others stalled, failed, or were aborted. Among the many distinctive labor conditions that contributed to this perceived success were in situ research, planning, and construction, which required the residency of GDR experts in Vinh. To some extent, the firsthand knowledge of Vietnamese culture and history gleaned through such arrangements arguably made for more effective cooperation than the Soviets and other experts experienced. And yet, while in situ planning produced both fondness and frictions between and among Vietnamese and East Germans, it was predicated on suspicion and competing priorities that mitigated the *Geist*, or spirit of internationalism.

THE GIFT OF INFRASTRUCTURE

While the global Cold War was waged militarily on the battlegrounds of Korea, Vietnam, and other countries fighting for their independence, it played out ideologically in cultural and technological fields that penetrated the most intimate spaces of everyday life.[10] Architecture and urban planning, in particular, emerged as strategic Cold War instruments to hasten the expansion, and depth of penetration, of either capitalism or socialism into the social fabric. In the confrontation between the two emerging superpowers, the United States and the Soviet Union, the built environment—housing, factories, infrastructure, civic buildings, and public facilities—came to stand as material evidence of ideological orientation and wider geopolitical alliances (Stanek 2012, 300). "Gifts" of socialist architecture and planning expertise gave rise to a range of experimental forms and design techniques across the global South. With the growth of modern cities organized around industry, technocrats deployed spatial planning as a new practice of government to manage populations, improve productivity, and enable socialist transformation (Bray 2005).

For the West, decolonization also offered opportunities for benevolent intervention. These "soft power" efforts were made in the name of national development and democracy, as Nancy Kwak (2015) has shown for the export of persuasive ideologies of homeownership to the Philippines through American aid, and as Matthew Hull (2011) has documented for the role of the Ford Foundation in creating a master plan for Delhi at the behest of the Indian government. Socialist interventions in Vietnam were also a form of cultural hegemony that did not overtly threaten its sovereignty. Rather, they signaled a parallel effort to combat the spread of capitalism—just as American support for the European Recovery Program (Marshall Plan) was intended to halt the spread of communism. And yet, as Susan Buck-Morss (2000) reminds us, the visions of utopian futures in both instances were strikingly similar: industrial modernization—through either capitalist or socialist relations of production—would create new kinds of citizens who could overcome scarcity and relish the material pleasures of the good life. In hindsight, the values projected through the built environment—one people oriented, the other capital driven—may look architecturally and spatially similar (D. Smith 1996, 70–71), prompting scholars to ask: what then makes a socialist city distinctly *socialist* (Hirt 2013; Zarecor 2018)?[11] Upon closer examination, however, it becomes possible to see a uniqueness to these individual projects, whether capitalist or socialist, and how they broke with past forms of spatial organization to realize their own dreamworlds of modernity and ideas about "'normalcy' in social life" (Buck-Morss 2000, 238).

As it did in North Korea (see Armstrong 2005), benevolent intervention in Vietnam reflected an ambitious, multilateral initiative. After the signing of the Paris Peace Accords in January 1973, reconstruction (*xây dựng lại*) of Vietnam's ruined infrastructure became a global undertaking to help Vietnam "catch up" with other industrialized nations aligned with Marxism-Leninism. In accordance with the first Five-Year Plan of 1960–1965,[12] the rational development of regional heavy industry was favored over light manufacturing (Vo 1990, 30; Norlund 1984, 94–95). This form of "infrastructural thinking" (Zarecor 2018) guided the scalar parameters of Vietnam's reconstruction.[13] As in postwar socialist Europe, projections about infrastructure development as a scaffold for future growth steered government decisions about national recovery (Zarecor 2018, 99–100). This was a time when "grandiose industrial projects" were the focus of international assistance, especially from the Soviet Union (Hoan 1991, 363), which has received most scholarly attention. These projects were intended to modernize Vietnam while deepening its integration into global networks of socialist production and trade. To soften the asymmetric politics of foreign aid between unequal states, which entangled them in a web of debt and obligation, such aid was often described in altruistic terms—for example, as humanitarian gifts from "the people" of a wealthier allied country. This framing evaded the issue of how gifting socialist infrastructure also indexed strategic realignments of power among competing communist states, such as China and the Soviet Union (Khoo 2011), which sought political influence over Vietnam by controlling access, development, and use of its rich natural resources.

Considering the potential for procedural and structural obstacles from the scale of devastation, the pace of design and approval of these grand infrastructure projects was rather remarkable. Time and speed were of the essence in actualizing socialism: "We must grow quickly in all aspects," Vietnam's prime minister, Phạm Văn Đồng, insisted (1977, 16–18). Both the first and second Five-Year Plans stressed the need for innovative, fast-paced development (*phát triển nhanh chóng*) of heavy industry, especially in the construction sector. As an attribute of modernity, acceleration became a key measure of technological progress (Wajcman 2014): the rapid expansion of material and technical capabilities would quickly advance (*tiến nhanh*) the country out of poverty and backwardness (*từ một nước nghèo nàn, lạc hậu*) (Phạm Văn Đồng 1977, 20). In line with this rush to socialist modernity, by June 1974, just eighteen months after the last aerial attacks, Hanoi had approved more than 359 infrastructure projects, both small and large, from CMEA[14] countries alone, with an estimated investment of 516 million rubles, an amount that would continue to grow sharply over the next years.[15] The list of anticipated projects read like a wish list for modern nation building and included, for example, work on cement plants (Romania), a new concrete factory (Bulgaria), telecommunications expansion (GDR), feed manufacturing (Hungary), railway renovation (Poland), and hydroelectric plants (Soviet Union, and also China), in addition to repair shops, chemical plants, brickworks, mining operations, food-processing facilities (also for export), and so on. Once built, these installations would be visible, material signs of the party-mandated acceleration of time (Ssorin-Chaikov 2006, 360).

Many of these approved infrastructure projects never came to fruition, however. Obstructions slowed the speed of recovery, including a shortage of water, electricity, labor, and construction materials, a government report noted.[16] The fault rested not only with Vietnam, officials were quick to point out. "Promised equipment and materials [from overseas] have yet to arrive," the same report stated critically. Nonetheless, the emphasis on "advancing forward quickly" continued, and by 1979 there were 3,540 foreign experts in country (up from 537 reported in 1974 and 1,800 in 1978). Surprisingly, one-quarter were from nonsocialist countries[17]—a reminder that multilateral assistance did not fall exclusively under the rubric of international socialist solidarity.[18]

Urban design—including the creation of socialist cities meant to serve and grow the working class—took precedence in this frenzied race to reconstruction. Similar to the European Recovery Program, which rebuilt capitalist economies by modernizing infrastructure, this was a coordinated, if not competitive, international effort. In this case, however, it created a distinct topography of socialist fraternity that reflected strategic alignments of power and influence. On May 19, 1973, Prime Minister Phạm Văn Đồng sent a request to Berlin for assistance with creating a master plan for Vinh. That same day, a telegram arrived from the GDR Ambassador to the DRV, Dieter Doering. In it, Doering informed party leadership that Phạm Văn Đồng had contacted a number of other governments on that very day to request similar assistance with the design of cities and townships. The telegram laid out which countries had been requested to design which cities, but not the rationale behind those decisions.[19]

Still, the telegram did reveal how Vietnam's proposed landscape of urban reconstruction, no doubt influenced by Moscow, could be read as a map of its international diplomacy, with countries positioned strategically and carefully, as if on a board game (see figure 4.1). Cities and towns that were tasked for reconstruction by countries of the Soviet Bloc were distanced from those that Asian communist countries would reconstruct. The Soviet Union was entreated to create a master plan for Vietnam's capital, Hanoi, including the government district of Ba Đình and an area referred to as "New Hanoi" (later abandoned), thus securing Moscow's political authority in the heart of the DRV.[20] Far enough away from Hanoi (and from the growing Soviet clout in Vietnam's center of power), China would focus on Thái Nguyên in the north, a decision that illustrated Hanoi's shifting alliances during the Sino-Soviet rift. North Korea would plan the provincial capital of Hà Bắc (Bắc Giang), which lies to the southeast of Thái Nguyên (incorrectly marked on the map in figure 4.1 as north). To the east of Hanoi, Poland was requested to redesign the port city of Hải Phòng, and Hungary the neighboring mining town of Hạ Long (then: Hồng Gai and Bãi Cháy). To the south, Bulgaria was to design the provincial capital of Thái Bình, Romania that of Nam Định, and Czecho-

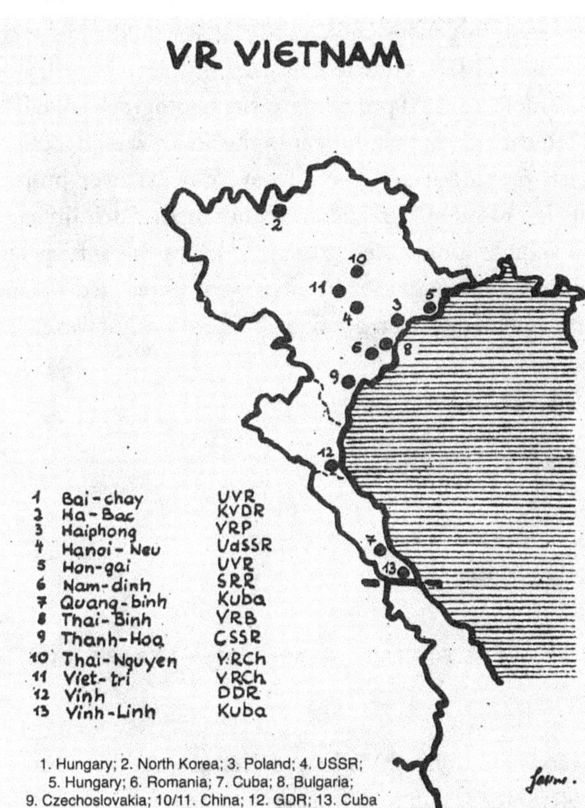

← Figure 4.1 Mapping reconstruction: modernization as international socialist collaboration. BArch DH 1/28526.

slovakia that of Thanh Hóa. And even farther south, in Nghệ An, the revered birthplace of Hồ Chí Minh, the GDR—fittingly, the homeland of Karl Marx, as local newspapers pointed out—was entrusted with the city of Vinh. This was a nod toward the "special" relationship between Hanoi and Berlin.[21]

Across the DRV, experts faced enormous challenges that restricted the flow of "design transfers" to rebuild towns and cities. To start, foreign experts possessed little social scientific knowledge about Vietnam; for example, William S. Logan claims that poor understanding of Hanoi's history and demography led to unrealistic planning by Soviet advisers (1995, 458). Travel on cratered roads and across makeshift bridges was difficult, if not dangerous, with the threat of unexploded ordnance. Equipment and machinery that had to be imported faced delays. As with the other infrastructure projects, water and electricity were lacking, and there was a shortage of skilled labor and local technical expertise. Key documents, including maps and statistics that would assist with planning research, were inaccessible, outdated, or classified. The Ministry of National Defense, for example, resisted providing aerial photographs of cities for reasons of national security, given that the war in the South was ongoing.[22] Power struggles between provincial and central governments over project and planning approvals led to other bureaucratic hindrances. Such difficulties meant that rates of actualization varied greatly. Much of the anticipated design that Hanoi so desperately sought for its cities went unrealized—plans were drawn but not implemented (Logan 2000, 211). There was, however, an exception: the city of Vinh.

CHILDREN OF MARX IN THE LAND OF HỒ CHÍ MINH

> "You are going to North Vietnam? There are communists there!"
>
> "Yes, I am one of them."
>
> —GDR ARCHITECT EN ROUTE TO VINH, TRANSFERRING IN KARACHI, 1974[23]

In many ways, the reconstruction of Vinh was Hanoi's—and Berlin's—paramount prestige project. The vision for Vinh surpassed even the ambitious plans for the expansion of Hanoi, which had not suffered the same level of devastation. Vinh would showcase Vietnam's technological modernity and its inclusion in the family of socialist nations. The making of a model socialist city in the homeland (*quê hương*) of Hồ Chí Minh with the assistance of the "children of the land of Karl Marx" (*người con xứ sở Các-Mác*) captured the attention of much of the country, earning Vinh sister-city status with Karl Marx Stadt, now Chemnitz.[24] Its rational spatial organization and functional design would become a benchmark for socialist planning as well as a celebrated symbol of solidarity cemented by "virtuous action." It was also a project laden with high emotion: "Who is not moved by the sight of our expert friends, sweaty, their faces red, as they toil elbow to elbow with our technicians and workers?" asked the author of one editorial in the Vietnamese press, stirred by the appearance of "technological togetherness" and shared purpose to build a new urban future (Todorov 1995, 48).[25] Where other planning projects fell short, Vinh appeared to succeed on account of social, political, and affective forces that I describe in this chapter. Readers should note the strong feelings of pride that continue to exist among a generation of Vietnamese architects, planners, and builders (and their East German counterparts). As one Vietnamese planner stated bluntly, "The GDR was the only country to follow through with its promises. Other countries signed the agreements but did not produce the results."[26] To be sure, a particular set of conditions and contingencies lent support to this claim and to the reputation of East Germany as a nation that kept its word to help Vietnam spring ahead to become, finally, "modern."

One important political distinction between the work of GDR experts in Vinh and that of socialist foreign experts elsewhere in Vietnam was expansion of the Vinh mission beyond its original purview of town planning and design (*quy hoạch thiết kế*). The GDR's task was much more ambitious in scope to also include comprehensive reconstruction. This meant working collectively on both the creation of a master plan and its realization in built form. This change was evident in the discourse of government documents and reports, which shifted from *Projektierung* (design; *thiết kế*) in the original request of May 19, 1973 to, in the final bilateral agreement, *Projektierung und Aufbau* (design and construction; *thiết kế và xây dựng*), signed five months later, on October 22. Mention of this broader scope was made early in negotiations, already in the GDR's response of June 20: "The Party and Government have decided to assist with and support the design and reconstruction of Vinh City."[27] Surely the first fact-finding mission in July affirmed this need, when GDR delegates witnessed firsthand the extent of destruction and grasped the urgency to rebuild infrastructure.[28] The displaced population was returning in mass numbers, and Vinh was a key industrial center (third after Hanoi and Hải Phòng). Reconstruction had to be comprehensive in order to mobilize labor power and achieve high levels of productivity. As such, GDR experts assumed additional responsibilities, such as developing the construction industry and training its workforce. To sustain and reproduce labor, they were tasked with building public facilities, including a high-density residential area with integrated public amenities, the first of its scale in Vietnam.

In accordance with the vision espoused by the party and government in Vietnam, transfers of knowledge and technology would facilitate decolonization. The goal of comprehensive reconstruction and assistance with socialist city making was to enable "self-reliance" (*tự lực tự cường*) and sustainability over the long term, rather than an "ideology of dependence" (*tư tưởng ỷ lại*) on foreign aid and technological support (Lê T.N. 1977, 26). Technicians and engineers set about building a vast network of modern infrastructure intended to facilitate the production (through skills transfers) and reproduction (through living environments) of a trained, migrant-based workforce that would exemplify the virtues of the New Socialist Man and, at the same time, showcase East German technological expertise.[29]

Vinh is the city most associated with the paternal founder of modern Vietnam (Hồ Chí Minh). Its reconstruction by the descendants of the founding father of socialism (Karl Marx), people who "knew" the country's trauma (chapter 3), carried prestige, which lent itself to labor requirements and affordances that distinguished it from other redesign efforts. First and foremost were the temporal parameters of the project. Government records show that township planning by teams of foreign experts typically took place over the course of two years.[30] The redesign and rebuilding of Vinh, on the other hand, required a much longer project period: apart from two preparatory visits in 1973, the official agreement was for a timeline that ran from January 1, 1974, to December 31, 1978 (five years); this was later extended another two years, through December 1980, at the request of the Vietnamese government, for a total project life of seven uninterrupted years.[31] As in capitalist countries, the coupling of human resources with infrastructure development over the *longue durée* was envisioned as a driver of future growth—in the case of Vinh, to create a "bigger, better, more beautiful city" (see interlude figure 3.1).

Compared with other design projects, the lengthier and more ambitious undertaking in Vinh required a far more diverse set of foreign experts, who were hierarchically ranked. As elsewhere, the state recruited an elite group of planners and architects from government ministries. In the GDR's case, this carefully selected *Arbeitsgruppe* (work unit) included experts with extensive experience rebuilding postwar cities; for example, Dessau, Halle-Neustadt, Dresden, and Hamhung (North Korea). This was intentional; one architect remembered that the Ministry of Construction sought him out because of his experience with designing new towns, which the ministry felt he could adapt to local conditions in Vietnam.[32] Then there were the nonelite cadres, who implemented the plans, comprising the majority of the foreign workforce in Vinh. This group encompassed skilled technicians (*Techniker*) and tradespersons (*Handwerker*), all of whom were male: engineers, carpenters, surveyors, painters, plumbers, welders, pipe fitters, machinists, electricians, crane operators, stone and cement masons, and other professionals, including landscape designers, pedagogues, and doctors. There were palpable tensions between these groups at times: the lay experts, who were generally more distrustful of the state, were suspicious of the more powerful government elite and attempted to keep their distance. For example, one man who was evacuated to Hanoi declined treatment from his embassy's medic, preferring to leave his care in the hands of a Vietnamese physician more competent in tropical diseases, he told me.

Some GDR lay specialists were recruited for their positions in Vietnam, but most had answered ads posted in their workplaces or passed on through word of mouth. All had to undergo strict vetting. Their motivations varied: in interviews with more than a dozen experts (some over the course of several years), almost all expressed humanitarian concerns about an unjust war and the desire to apply their skills to improve the human condition. As I argued in chapter 3, for some, their own traumatic memory of war and experience with urban devastation strengthened their resolve to help and gave them a sense of shared purpose. Their identification with Vietnam was apparent when they spoke to me in interviews and collapsed Vietnam and the GDR into a Cold War construct of "we/us/our side" versus "you/your side" to talk about the war with the United States. But some voiced more self-interested motives owing to constraints of opportunities at home, including hedonistic desires for adventure, travel, money, prestige, or professional development, as well as release from the banality of everyday life. These moral and material inclinations were not necessarily contradictory. In the words of one technician, who talked of anti-imperialism while sharing pictures of himself posing with water buffalo and on sandy beaches, "I was young and wanted to travel. We had been *eingemauert* [walled in] and couldn't leave the GDR. I had started a family, but it wasn't going well, so Vietnam offered an escape from it all."[33] Interviewees had collected photographs of Vietnam's ruin and renewal, a teleology of material progress that mirrored the triumphant story of postwar Germany. But scattered among these images were snapshots of vacation—the socialist good life realized overseas. Visiting experts used work opportunities, annual leave, and their privileged legal status as foreign *chuyên gia* (experts) to travel within Vietnam and see the exotic sights of an ancient land that had survived the decade-long barrage of imperialist bombing (see figure 4.2).[34]

In all, around 220 East German citizens worked on the official reconstruction project in Vinh, 10 percent of whom were women—namely, the wives of specialists who had extended labor contracts with the Vietnam Task Force (*Arbeitsstab Vietnam*) under the Ministry of Construction.[35] Unlike the project in Hamhung, North Korea (Hong 2015, 64), children were not allowed to accompany parents, owing to difficult postwar conditions and anxieties about tropical disease, which influenced some women's decisions not to join the project. One woman, whose husband spent five years in Vinh, cringed at the thought of having to send their children to an elite boarding school in Berlin:

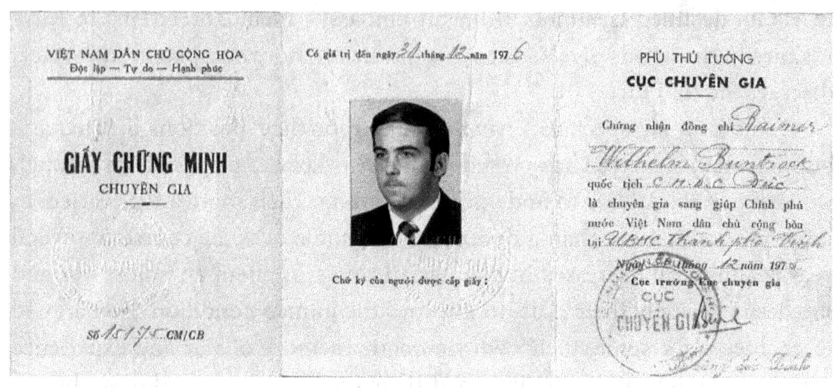

VIỆT NAM DÂN CHỦ CỘNG HÒA
Độc lập — Tự do — Hạnh phúc

GIẤY CHỨNG MINH
CHUYÊN GIA

Số 151/75 CM/CB

Có giá trị đến ngày 31 tháng 12 năm 1976

Chữ ký của người được cấp giấy:

PHỦ THỦ TƯỚNG
CỤC CHUYÊN GIA

Chứng nhận đồng chí Rainer Wilhelm Buntrock
quốc tịch C.H.D.C. Đức
là chuyên gia sang giúp Chính phủ nước Việt Nam dân chủ cộng hòa
tại UBHC Thành phố Vinh
Ngày ... tháng 12 năm 197...
Cục trưởng Cục chuyên gia

↑ Figure 4.2 Expert identification card: evidence that this foreigner was a "certified cadre" who had come to help Vietnam.

"We did not want our kids to grow up around party elites," she stated frankly, expressing discomfort with privilege and disdain for the state.[36] To the best of my knowledge, none of the women who worked in Vinh served in a technical or professional position, though all were required to have an "occupational qualification" (*berufliche Qualifikation*).[37] They were also entitled to the same perks and benefits that came with overseas missions. But despite the premise of gender equality, they took on lower-skilled (and lower-paid) positions in clerical work, nursing, and management of domestic operations, in yet another example of contradictory state policies toward women in socialist regimes (Gal and Kligman 2000, 5). Moreover, their work was not as highly valued as men's: they were not recipients of a certificate of friendship from the Vietnamese government, unlike their husbands, whose labor and expertise were deemed more worthy of state recognition.

IN SITU PLANNING: INTIMACIES AND INEQUALITIES

In situ planning was another critical difference between Vinh and urban design projects elsewhere. Balancing labor proximity with controlled cultural intimacy, in situ planning produced both fondness and frictions *between* foreigners and locals but also *within* these groups. The typical arrangement for international projects was that town planners would come to Vietnam on short-term assignments to make site visits and collect data, staying on average one to three months. The nuts and bolts of planning then took place in their home countries, which made it difficult to get input from or consult with the Vietnamese side, thus failing to embody the spirit of mutual cooperation. Planners might return to Vietnam for brief periods to present their findings, but they had little role in the final execution of their designs. East German experts working on the showcase project in Vinh were, however, an exception to this standard practice. They were permitted to reside in Vietnam "from six months to one or two years, or until construction is completed," according to internal documents.[38] This concession was important for two reasons. First, on-site planning allowed the mission of reconstruction to be framed as *coproduction* within a unified, nonhierarchical community of professional peers working toward the same goal (modernization) and the same socialist future—though, as I argue in chapters 5 and 6, this was not always the case as disagreements formed around conflicting spatial practices and worldviews of socialism. Second, it gave the appearance of self-sacrifice as foreigners took up long-term residency in an annihilated city that lacked basic infrastructure, including potable water, electric power, sanitation, sustainable housing, and adequate provisions of food. East Germans undertook high-risk, demanding work at construction sites with unexploded ordnance in a harsh and unfamiliar climate. These labor conditions injured and sickened many and led to the death of one electrician.[39] The precarious work and living conditions for all sides fostered a sense of shared hardship and purpose: "You know our difficulties," wrote the journalist and poet Lê Duy Phương, in a German-language verse he presented to experts in 1979.[40] Although, in truth, local residents disproportionately bore the suffering and privation, they also recognized the "sacrifices" (*hy sinh*) that their East German visitors made to reside and work there. From the Vietnamese perspective, leaving behind one's family and the material comforts of home to take such risks in an unfamiliar, war-torn country was a clear sign of the genuine *tình cảm* (sentiment) that underpinned their spirited solidarity and the *cảm nghĩ chân thành* (sincere feelings) that existed between the people of both countries.[41]

In addition to the redistribution of risk and vulnerability, collective experiences of critical events in Vietnam's history were important to the creation of *tình cảm* through established patterns of intimate proximity. There were the long-awaited celebrations of the "liberation of Saigon" in the streets of Vinh—with fireworks—on April 30, 1975; the devastating floods of 1978, when experts worked to fortify the dyke and halt rising floodwaters; and the Chinese invasion in 1979 (that experts followed on Radio Manila), which threatened another full-scale war. For the GDR experts I interviewed, facing adversity alongside the residents of Vinh structured their memories of reconstruction as embodied moral practice motivated by common values and interests in building a new and just world through socialism. In their accounts, bodies and affect choreographed solidarity through a politics of proximity and physicality. This ethical subjectivity involved corporeal presence in a moment and place of apprehension or exhilaration ("We were there!") that included manual labor under duress (for example, while digging dykes) or bodily recalcitrance as a means to make a moral and political statement. At the *Befreiungszeit* (moment of liberation), for example, experts were encouraged by their embassy to leave their posts but refused to do so. This collective defiance came up at a group interview I conducted with four experts, including one woman who had managed the kitchen:

> CONSTRUCTION SUPERVISOR: During the final campaign, when the northern troops were moving south, we were told that we might have to evacuate. The Cubans, who were on the front line in Quang Binh, came up to Vinh. We decided as a group not to evacuate to Hanoi but to stay in Nghe An.
> SENIOR ARCHITECT: That's right, we declared, "*Wir bleiben vor Ort!*" (We stay put!)
> CONSTRUCTION SUPERVISOR: Along with the Cubans, we refused to go home.
> SENIOR ARCHITECT [turning to me]: We needed to show the Vietnamese our optimism, that we believed in their victory.
> CONSTRUCTION SUPERVISOR [also turning to me]: Yes, it was our way to support Vietnam, to show our solidarity with them.[42]

"Staying put" was thus a public performance of solidarity grounded in the corporeal practice of "militant optimism" (Bloch 1986, 199). The decision to stay also emerged in experts' recollections of China's incursion into Vietnam in 1979. In the words of a vocational school trainer, "When the Chinese crossed the border, we were given the option to leave. Many teams did, but the GDR work unit decided to remain in solidarity, just like we did in 1975.[43] We said, '*Wir bleiben da!*'" (We're staying!).[44] My Vietnamese respondents expressed being moved emotionally (*cảm động*) by such decisions. From their point of view, the choice of risk over security symbolized a politics of life grounded in notions of collective care (Butler 2004). "Only East Germans and Cubans stayed," several residents told me, signaling the selflessness they felt characterized the relationship.

And yet this was far from a horizontal, integrated community. Rather, the cooperative coexistence between Vietnamese people and foreign experts was structured by notions of radical social, economic, and cultural difference, at times intentionally so. In practical terms, in situ planning and construction were instrumental to realizing the multiyear project, as they cultivated an intimate understanding of people and landscape, albeit one that confronted some impenetrable boundaries. The mission's unique temporal and spatial dynamics allowed visiting experts to become familiar with Vinh, also through their social scientific research (chapters 5 and 6), and to develop deeper social relations and cultural knowledge over time. But they rarely enjoyed unobserved movement or freedom of association. Owing to historical suspicion of the figure of the foreigner-invader, Vietnamese officials regulated intimacy by enforcing physical and cultural boundaries between insiders and outsiders, even those configured as "siblings" or "friends." They discouraged personal relationships, particularly between men and women, even though these occasionally transpired through everyday encounters at work. They monitored friendships that did form, for example, between international experts and their translators—who, with their access to foreigners and their gifts, were themselves ambivalent figures (Babül 2017, 135). Officials did condone sport-derived intimacies, like volleyball games and soccer matches between national teams, as these permitted East Germans and Vietnamese to interact in non-threatening ways that cultivated work spirit while maintaining social divisions that prevented cultural contamination. Cultural encounters—which visiting experts welcomed at the time and now cherish in memory—often reinscribed notions of civilizational difference between "modern" (Occidental) and "not-quite-modern" (Oriental) worlds. We see this, albeit in a playful way, in one expert's story about attending an annual festival, which also infers the need to modernize Vinh: "Every workplace had its own gardens to provide for workers. Where I worked, we had several ponds filled with fish. The ponds were emptied in the fall with a big feast. I later found out that people also used the ponds as a toilet. Well, that was the end of my fish feasts! I had been warned to drink a lot of schnapps when attending those events, and now I know why!"[45]

Incommensurable otherness was also a recurring theme in Vietnamese respondents' memories of foreign experts. Because men were away at war and women dominated construction jobs, in the early years of the project everyday encounters typically took place between German men and Vietnamese women. The former were a source of fascination—and some ridicule—for the latter, as the women turned the Orientalist gaze back onto the white male body. During interviews, retired female workers giggled when they described experts as large, friendly men with long noses, whose clothes exposed their hair-covered bodies. In the words of one woman, "My strongest memory of those experts is big people in short pants riding around the city on little bikes. Everybody knows that image!"[46] German experts also recalled the attention they received: they were laughed at and observed with curiosity, their body hair touched and pulled. These were the lighter, friskier moments of their tenure, when flirtatious exchanges provided a temporary respite from the drudgery of reconstruction. Encounters that became too friendly, however, met with swift discipline. One man remembered a cheerful Vietnamese worker who would stop and greet him regularly, until one day she was gone—relocated to another unit, he presumed.

Beyond racial difference, class inequality and the Germans' privileged access to consumer goods reinforced power asymmetries and foreign-local divisions. Local authorities, suspicious of GDR materialism, sought to contain consumption practices to delimited spaces so as not to pollute the Vietnamese population with "consumer socialism" (Betts 2012, 417). The Vietnamese often went hungry, beholden to postwar scarcity and an insufficient ration system (one engineer remembered women pointing to their stomachs in the morning before work). In contrast, East German experts were well cared for and well fed. They lived and ate separately from local residents. Their German provisions included regular imports of chocolate, beer, sausages, sauerkraut, and other desired foodstuffs. "We got the works!" one engineer exclaimed. Breakfasts and dinner were taken separately at the guesthouse, prepared by a Vietnamese cook under Vietnamese female supervision, and managed by a female East German supervisor. Lunch, however, was another moment of controlled cultural encounter: a modest meal was served daily to workers of all ranks at their respective workplaces.

GDR visiting experts were cognizant of the disparities and of the critical resources that went to their care; for example, one of the only standing buildings after the war underwent expedited renovation for their accommodation (at the time, this was the government guesthouse; it is now the Giao Tế Hotel). I was surprised to find that in retrospect, this did not bother my Vietnamese interviewees, who waved it off as the natural, hierarchical order of things. After all, they surmised, the experts came from a wealthier, modern, and more civilized country. East Germans tried to undo this inequality—and to alleviate their discomfort with it—by redistributing wealth. Both groups of respondents recalled the clandestine circulation of goods, as when GDR experts covertly passed out chocolate, cigarettes, and meat to coworkers and children, away from the prying eyes of local police. These gifts could be instrumental to survival, but they also created inequities among the Vietnamese themselves. One water engineer remembered that the cigarettes he had given as presents were resold to purchase food. Another joked that Vietnamese kitchen staff were the best fed and most envied people in town: visiting experts left their much-desired meat fat for them to put aside to take home to their families in the evening.

Through their invented traditions, the East German work team comprised an elite community unto themselves, with hazing rituals for incomers (who were expected to bring gifts and take the least comfortable rooms) and nightly revelry at a neighborhood beer hall (with Hanoi Beer for a mere one VND). While visiting experts never went hungry, they did report weight loss from both reduced food intake and intestinal diseases and parasites—though they enjoyed another perk that the local population did not, which was a doctor, trained in tropical medicine, who treated the experts on site. They lived simply, having to make do with inadequate amenities and to find creative ways to set up "home" without basic infrastructure like water and electricity. Later cohorts enjoyed these amenities more frequently, which gave rise to a frontier narrative that distinguished the pioneers, who were in Vinh when "there was absolutely nothing," from later groups, who benefited from the infrastructure the former had built. In the words of a planner from the first cohort, "When we arrived on the scene, the city was only craters. Vinh was not yet in the rebuilding phase. And the war was still raging. The experts who came later, especially after 1975, had a completely different experience than we did."[47] The living situation in Vinh also differed from that in other cities, where foreign countries had pressured Hanoi to provide lodging for their experts on par with higher CMEA standards.[48] Still, one cannot overlook the irony that the building of global socialism depended on a two-tiered system that produced the very stratification that the project of egalitarianism intended to do away with.

ACCESSING DESIRABLE GOODS: STRATIFICATION IN THE GDR

Despite the rhetoric of selflessness, visiting experts had material and financial interests that motivated their participation and contributed to socioeconomic inequalities in both Vietnam and East Germany. The 1970s were a time of growth for the East German economy, and prosperity stimulated the desire for more durable and even luxurious consumer goods (Zatlin 2007, 274)—a desire that could be fulfilled by earning hard currency while working overseas. Most experts traveled to Vietnam on one-year labor contracts, though short-term assignments were also possible (depending on the charge). Many stayed for multiple terms, attracted by the task at hand and the fringe benefits—some of which were unexpected, such as a telephone that arrived at a home residence within a week of signing a contract, bypassing a years-long waitlist in East Germany. "Our neighbors thought we were working for the Stasi," a retired machinist joked.[49] His tale, however, revealed how social divisions formed between people who had been ordinary workers in East Germany but who became "GDR specialists" (*DDR-Spezialisten*) with attractive perks by serving in Vietnam, and those East Germans who had less opportunity and remained at home. As per their labor contracts, East German experts continued to receive their regular salaries while in Vietnam, which varied according to rank, as well as a "hardship" bonus of 100 marks per month, tax-free. They also received a one-time payment of 200 marks for travel gear.[50] Over the course of an assignment, money tended to accumulate: one family later used these savings to purchase land, another a cherished color TV, further distinguishing them from resentful neighbors who lacked privileged access to resources and opportunity.

Social differentiation in both Vietnam and East Germany was most pronounced through material culture and the consumption of goods. In Vietnam, foreign experts were given free room and board, paid for by East Germany. They also received a daily allowance of 10 VND for incidental expenses as per their employment contracts.[51] This came to about 300 VND per month, at a time when Vietnamese salaries were on average 60 VND. Allowance money went into an account in Vinh, centrally managed by the Vietnam Task Force. Workers could draw on their accounts to purchase imported daily necessities and desired foodstuffs, like Rostock pilsner, that arrived by ship every few months, transactions that were organized by the task force or through personal arrangement with GDR sea captains. In Hanoi, they could shop at the state-run department store (one specialist proudly showed me a display of French glassware he had gifted his wife) or at the Versorgungsbetrieb Inland-Ausland (VERSINA), which sold East German provisions to overseas workers and diplomats, much like a PX or commissary for American personnel stationed abroad. Funds could also be withdrawn to make purchases in Vinh's local market or while traveling, such as Vietnamese handicrafts or other souvenirs I found displayed in people's homes. Most importantly for the visiting experts and their families back home, this per diem was treated as convertible currency. This meant it could be sent to East Germany as domestic marks converted at an artificially set exchange rate either for deposit into a personal account (less preferred) or for use as more desirable and valuable "GENEX funds." Highly coveted, GENEX funds functioned like virtual currency that could be used to purchase exclusive, luxury consumer goods, manufactured at home or abroad, from the GENEX catalogue.[52] Among my interlocutors, it was not marks in the bank that constituted autonomous subjects with individual desires, as anthropologists of money have argued (Hart and Otriz 2014, 469), but GENEX funds.

"What could you buy from the catalogue?" I asked Petra, the wife of the machinist. "Everything that could not be found in state shops," she replied excitedly; this included high-quality bedding, clothing, tiles, jewelry, furniture, porcelain, electronics, and other hard-to-find household goods. "The glass you are drinking from came from GENEX!" she laughed, pointing to the crystal stemware in front of me.[53] GENEX products inspired envy and helped to create social hierarchies in the GDR by offering the possibility to satisfy consumer dreams (Zatlin 2007, 234). There were also temporal and performative dimensions to GENEX currency that allowed for expressions of new gendered subjectivities. For men, GENEX conferred opportunities for status acceleration that enhanced masculinity—one man had a Wartburg car delivered within two weeks, bypassing the ten-year waiting period. For women, GENEX clothing allowed for the presentation of a chic self that stood out from the ordinary—though not from the other experts' wives. Petra, for instance, told of an occasion when she wore a fashionable leather jacket from GENEX to a gathering of wives whose husbands worked abroad, only to find several other women wearing the same designer coat. Such material signifiers created a club of recognizable elites whose access to desired commodities conferred an identity that set one apart from everyday socialism (Verdery 1996, 29). Despite the stress of separation on families, renewed contracts were often welcomed, not least because they guaranteed opportunities for shopping in East Germany. A postcard that circulated among the experts and their wives made light of this situation (see figure 4.3). A group of senior women gather around to celebrate the news from Vinh: an extended contract—and more consumer goods.[54]

SUSPICION AND DISCIPLINE

In situ planning, as an exception to the norm, was not disconnected from the perception of "true" solidarity. Indeed, the emotional expression of the latter was used to help justify the former. The internal report to Prime Minister Phạm Văn Đồng on the GDR's first fact-finding mission in the summer of 1973, which emphasized the delegates' enthusiasm (chapter 3), also advocated that experts conduct research, draft plans, and manage construction in *Vinh*, "not in Hanoi or Berlin." Despite the risks (to their personal security and in the potential for espionage), the report rationalized the on-site (*tại chỗ*)

POST AUS VINH: „MEIN MANN HAT SCHON WIEDER VERLANGERT!"

↑ Figure 4.3 Mail from Vinh: "My husband extended again!"

immersion of foreign specialists as an "important method" that would benefit the regional economy through rapid industrial development and the transfer of skills to the labor force. As sympathetic comrades, the author and delegation leader, Vũ Đức Thận, noted confidently, East Germans appeared to be in it for the long haul.[55]

This positive assessment was tempered by a guardedness toward foreigners and sometimes outright suspicion, even of those who most appeared to support the cause of anti-imperialism. Suspicion has long accompanied moral economies of compassion and humanitarianism (Fassin 2011), especially those that take place in a state of emergency, as in Vietnam.[56] Socialist solidarity was no different, given the GDR's own notorious surveillance society—the Stasi also monitored East German citizens living abroad—and its training of Vietnamese police. Doubt and uncertainty among East Germans in Vietnam disciplined their behavior and shaped interactions between and among foreigners and locals. Sensitive to Vietnam's history of colonial invasions, experts understood that they were suspect outsiders and that their Vietnamese counterparts were anxious to maintain boundaries, for example, by discouraging East Germans from learning to speak Vietnamese. Visiting experts had ambivalent relationships with some of the Vietnamese translators. Despite developing close ties (which, in certain cases, are still maintained today), GDR experts suspected that they received only select bits of information meant to placate them, or to placate the people with whom they were talking, as translators toned down the Germans' too-direct words. Translation thus involved political and cultural censorship to maintain both classified information and goodwill relations. "They didn't want us to know certain things," one technician surmised about what he felt to be imperfect translations, an assessment I heard from several respondents. "There was a general *Mißtrauen*" (distrust), he continued, and perhaps rightly so. The Stasi had approached this man twice to spy for East Germany, using operatives who posed as a craftsman and a sea captain, and who asked him to photograph installations and collect other kinds of intelligence.[57] Safeguarding linguistic boundaries, along with selective translations that preserved confidential information, maintained social and racial order by preserving the categorical distinctions between trusted loyal insiders and always morally suspect outsiders (Babül 2017, 136).

Socialist "friends" were not only suspected of spying but also of trickery. I was reminded of how deep mistrust of Otherness ran when I learned of the urban legend of the black bronze Buddha, which had gone missing from Diệc pagoda during a previous war. No one could remember which war, but one thing was sure: the Germans had come all the way to Vinh to find and take possession of their cultural property (Schwenkel 2017b). Diệc pagoda was in close proximity to the GDR's flagship project, the construction of mass housing (chapter 6), which provided the perfect cover for such an operation (see figure 4.4). The presence of foreigners carrying suspicious, intelligence-gathering devices like maps and survey instruments fueled apprehension. The halt on construction, followed by the departure of the experts, only confirmed their suspicions. One man recounted the events: "The Germans came here to build high-rises for us in the homeland of Uncle Hồ, but they never completed the plan. Truthfully, they wanted to find the bronze Buddha. You know, they started on block D1, next to the pagoda, and then suddenly stopped. They claimed they ran out of money and materials and needed to return home. But really, when they were digging around, they discovered the statue and left immediately." "That's nonsense!" his wife exclaimed, and corrected some of the details to make Vietnam the victors. "Yes, they wanted to take the Buddha statue, but the [Vietnamese] state found it first! When the Germans realized this, they gave up and went home. We were more clever" (*khôn hơn*).[58] Either way, the allegation was the same: East German experts were not there for purely altruistic reasons of solidarity, but to profit from their plunder.

↑ Figure 4.4 Diệc pagoda across from construction site, 1978. Photo by Raimer Buntrock.

Contrary to the headlines then, solidarity was not unbreakable (*unzerbrechlich*); it was, in fact, a fraught and fragile game that both sides played tactically for certain gains. GDR experts knew that they were also in Vietnam to serve the economic and geopolitical interests of their homeland. As goodwill ambassadors, they treaded carefully, fearful of damaging relations and tarnishing their country's reputation or—even worse—being sent home. There was no room for indiscipline: rumors of a technician who had been sent back to East Germany by the embassy for unknown reasons circulated among later cohorts, reminding them of the ultimate consequence of disobedience. This included showing disrespect toward their Vietnamese counterparts. GDR experts were careful to uphold the antiracist policies of their government and to mitigate against stereotyping or overt racist expression. One of the senior team leaders explained his lack of tolerance for pessimism or signs of racial arrogance: "I did not accept any colonial attitude among the men, walking around thinking that they were better than the Vietnamese. One fellow referred to the locals as 'children.' I had to correct him. I told him, 'These are men; they fought in war.'"[59] Genuine efforts to challenge paternalism often reproduced it: here, postcolonial masculinity was affirmed through enduring Western tropes of soldiering and killing as a male rite of passage into manhood.

Harmful attitudes about Vietnamese people or the project itself were disciplined accordingly and transgressions reported to uphold the moral superiority of antiracist internationalism.[60] One man told the story of a shipmaster who, showing signs of compassion fatigue, complained about the delivery of scarce East German goods which, in his view, Vinh no longer needed. But when he insulted Vietnamese port workers by calling them lazy and uncoordinated, blaming them for broken goods and freight falling into the sea, a group of German experts who witnessed this behavior went to their superior, and the man was not seen in Vinh again. Maintaining the integrity of collaboration meant internal policing of the group (and also by the Stasi: one expert was later "outed" as an informant; he stopped attending reunions), as well as individual self-discipline.[61]

Experts were careful not to offend the sensibilities of their hosts, or worse, not to complete their job—both of which undermined their personal reputation and that of the GDR. Sometimes these twin goals conflicted, for example, when it came to project temporality and work ethics. Even thirty years later, experts avoided direct criticism during interviews; they rationalized theft and waste ("people needed to do what they could to survive") or couched their critique gently to avoid appearing too critical or even paternalistic. Nevertheless, balancing *Bautempo*, or pace of construction, and cultural sensitivity proved challenging at times. For example, GDR experts approached the issue of work habits cautiously, by emphasizing "different understandings of time." There were two calendars, I was told: Vietnamese project time and East German project time; the former was flexible, and the latter was not. They consistently praised women—the majority of the Vietnamese work force—for their hard labor, but one technician, choosing his words carefully, explained that their "work ethic was not quite as high as expected, making it difficult to meet deadlines." "Time pressure was a huge issue," he said, and the prestige of his country was on the line. But rather than push for more productivity—which might subvert the image of horizontal coproduction—the visiting experts worked long hours and weekends to finish projects, such as the pioneer club, to show that they could indeed get the job done while leaving everyone's ego intact.[62]

The Vietnamese not only feared that foreign experts might access their secrets or become too culturally intimate (Herzfeld 2015). There was also anxiety that their East German friends might lose their zeal and not follow through with pledged aid. After the GDR delegation's second fact-finding mission to Vinh (November 22–December 10, 1973), an internal memo raised concerns about Vietnam's disorganization and foot dragging. The memo identified Vietnamese reluctance to provide outsiders with requested documents, and misunderstandings about the volume of support (twenty vehicles for 1974 had become ninety vehicles).[63] Lack of coordination also caused alarm: "There is total confusion on our side [*rất lung tung*] . . . and we are not yet sure if the main actor responsible for managing the design and construction of Vinh City will be the Ministry of Construction or the province of Nghệ An."[64] In addition, lead experts were nervous about bureaucratic delays with imports of equipment and machinery for Vinh, and they raised these concerns with key Vietnamese officials. A personal note to Prime Minister Phạm Văn Đồng and General Party Secretary Đỗ Mười (to whom the memo was addressed), penciled on the side, cautioned that continued poor performance would erode (*làm xói mòn*) the enthusiasm of their comrades or even threaten Vietnam's future place among socialist nations.

But by 1974, the two countries had effectively managed enough of the red tape and organizational difficulties to move forward. By mid-February that year, the first *Arbeitsgruppe* (work unit) of GDR specialists was on site in Vinh, ready to begin the work of reconstruction. The rational planning of a new socialist city—the topic of chapter 5—would proceed.

Urban Fragments 3

↑ Figure I.3.1 "Rebuilding bigger, better, and more beautiful," front page of *Nghệ An News* (Vinh), April 30, 1974, published a day before reconstruction officially began.

EM LÀ THỢ XÂY (I AM A BUILDER)

Em cào gạch vỡ (I rake the shards of brick)
Em lấp hố bom (Fill bomb craters)
Em trồng cây non (Plant young trees)
Lắp nhà ghép mới (Assemble prefab buildings)
Em lợp viên ngói (Install roof tiles)
Chính tay em làm . . . (And do it mostly by hand . . .)

Em xây ước mơ (I build dreams)
Ngôi nhà hạnh phúc . . . (And happy homes . . .)
Anh về em rõ (One day you will return [from the battlefield], I am sure)
—NGÔ TỰU, 1974[1]

↓ Figure I.3.2 The gift of infrastructure: North-South technology transfers to rebuild Vinh, n.d. BArch DH 1/Bild-28564-05-01.

5

RATIONAL PLANNING

> Chúng ta sẽ xây dựng lại đất nước ta đàng hoàng hơn, to đẹp hơn.
>
> —HỒ CHÍ MINH, 1966

It is a well-known story in Vietnam that Hồ Chí Minh, while surveying the destruction of aerial warfare, declared, "We will rebuild our homeland bigger, better, and more beautiful than before." This party slogan (which appears in Vietnamese in the epigraph) would become the spirited mantra that mobilized Vinh's rapid reconstruction and shaped visions of its modernization. The images in interlude 3 of cheerful workers engaged in this utopian project speak to the ideological and material processes of building socialism (*xây dựng chủ nghĩa xã hội*) to make modern, vibrant cities inhabited by happy, cultured people. Scholars remind us that under socialism cities were sites for the "full-scale makeover of the state, society, material culture, and citizens alike" (Pence and Betts 2008, 8). In postwar Vinh, the redesign of urban space to create an entirely new living environment was no less a civilizing project. There, radical spatial interventions would engineer a socialist humanity, reforming social relations and urban practices to serve the state's goal of increased labor productivity. As I argue in this chapter, the landscape of ruins and rubble provided fertile ground for utopian experiments to design the optimal socialist city, and with it, a flourishing population of enlightened proletarians.

I use the term "utopia" with caution, given the dire conditions that threatened people's lives and well-being long after the bombing ended. Though tinged with paradisiacal airs, my use of the term follows the Vietnamese translation of this foreign idea as *điều không tưởng*, or "that which is unimaginable," which intersects with Lefebvre's idea of utopian urbanism as aspirational and dialectical, the making of the impossible *possible*, if not real (Pinder 2015, 34). This disjuncture between the actual, shaped by historical conditions of possibility, and the imaginable, as anticipatory future making, is evident in a premature claim by the Chairman of the State Planning Committee, Nguyễn Duy Trinh, made before the start of aerial warfare: that socialism was no longer a utopian imaginary but an everyday reality.[1] The future *was* now—and then the bombs fell, rendering utopia as a "fundamentally unreal space," as Foucault observed (1986, 24).

Urban planner and theorist John Friedmann (2000, 463) once argued that utopian thought redrew the boundaries of innovation and creativity in modernist planning, which saw space as key to progressive social transformation. Friedmann's temporal understanding of utopia as processual and future oriented is similar to that of Nguyễn Duy Trinh. Indeed, Friedmann maintains that utopian invention encompasses the very ability "to imagine a future that departs significantly from what we know to be a general condition in the present" (462). It was perhaps in moments of gravest despair—of deprivation and ruin, as in Vinh—that utopian planning became a seductive tool for the state to enact its authority through the *fantasy* of the possibility of a different future (Rose 1996, 9). While visionary in its revolutionary potential to transform bleak wasteland (*đất hoang*) into vibrant lived space, utopian planning had an outcome that was far from fantastical or predictable. Rather, efforts to transform fantasy into rational planning (Pile 2005) exposed the incompatibility of universalizing models of urban futuring.

Gendered images and discourses that fit with the Vietnamese state's civilizing agenda communicated these forward-looking and socially transformative values. This persuasive iconography of hope brought the narrative of imperialist victimization to a close by showing modernization as desirable and in full swing. In posters and photographs, images of cranes, smokestacks, and high-rise buildings conveyed a prosperous, technological futurity within reach of the population. In particular, these images used the bodies of working women to convey a hopeful affect coalescing around reconstruction. One such figure was the cheerful female bricklayer who builds both dreams and happy homes; she appears in the poem "I Am a Builder" and the graphic image in interlude 3 (see also figure 5.8), and shows how affects like happiness were deployed for the purposes of collective world making (Ahmed 2010, 2). These overwhelmingly optimistic representations provide insight into the kinds of idealized labor women performed to rebuild the city through material objects, like bricks, that generated proper affective dispositions for nation building (Schwenkel 2013). In fact, training female workers in new technologies was central to constructing a modern socialist future. As Sara Friedman has argued of Maoism in southeastern China, state campaigns frequently identified women as exemplars of "civilizational inadequacy," whose feudal practices stood in the way of realizing a new socialist society (2006, 6). In Vinh, women were likewise the targets of "civilizing interventions" (11), through such means as mechanization, to liberate them from backwardness and guide them toward socialist enlightenment as an emancipated proletariat. The photograph of skills transfer from foreign male experts to Vietnamese female workers in interlude 3 shows the gendered and racialized dimensions to this technological, civilizing mission. Despite claims of fraternal equality, such paternalist displays underscored the vast global disparities in wealth, power, knowledge, and technology that were constitutive of international solidarity and its regimes of expertise.

These constructions, along with Hồ Chí Minh's declaration, touch on the key themes of this chapter on the modernist rational planning of postwar Vinh and its challenges. The first theme is *scale* (bigger, or *to hơn*). The desire was to rebuild Vinh as a larger and more densely populated industrial city that would undo spatial inequality by contributing to regional development and serve as a model of socialist planning for the rest of the country. The second theme is orientation toward the *future* (will, or *sẽ*) and an emergent modernity tethered to a regime of technical expertise. This included developing a set of knowledge practices that could be applied to studying the city to predict—and control—urban growth. The third theme concerns *aesthetics* (beauty, or *đẹp*). Structured by the imperative to bring urban order and stability to postwar chaos, these aesthetics involved the straight symmetrical lines, sharp angles, and mono-use zones that characterized modernist design at the time.[2] The fourth theme is *improvement* of the population (betterment, or *đàng hoàng hơn*). Improvement happened culturally and ideologically through the construction of a new way of life (*nếp sống mới*). In accordance with functional planning, sociospatial harmony would create a more healthful and prosperous city, while subjecting inhabitants to new spatial technologies of urban governance. The final theme is *collectivity* (we, or *chúng ta*), which masked the social hierarchies and racial inequalities intrinsic to the international division of labor to build socialism in the global South. Vinh was thus poised to come back to life, emerging from the rubble—"aus den Trümmern," in the words of a planner—greater and more industrious than before. As national fantasy, it would be Vietnam's model socialist city, and the rest of the country would emulate its rational, orderly planning as a prototype for urban industrial development.

In the sections that follow, I move between the historical and the experiential, starting with narratives of return and the disorientation that evacuees described upon seeing the surreal city-in-ruins. I then address Vinh's redesign as a "blueprint utopia" (Holston 1989), where planning, as political imagination, spatial practice, and domain-specific expertise, produced conflicting visions and projections of the city's future. Through maps, models, and sketches, Vietnamese and East German planners approached the demolished city as an ecological and social scientific problem to be solved collectively through large-scale spatial and technological interventions. Framing the process as "coproduction," they attempted to create a spatial order that contrasted with the previous, more spontaneous iteration of urbanization but was detached from existing material conditions of possibility. In the last section, I address how rational planning endeavored to produce a disciplined international proletariat through spatial logics of the socialist city as an integrated functional system.

THE DISORDERLY CITY: RETURN TO RUBBLE

> Có thành phố nào như thành phố này không
> Chưa thấy nhà cao đã chói lọi sắc hồng
> Đã thấy sắc hồng cười trong gạch vụn?
>
> —THẠCH QUỲ, "GẠCH VỤN THÀNH VINH," 1966[3]

A decade of fierce and relentless bombing took a heavy toll on the built environment and its human and nonhuman populations, leaving a surreal landscape of vast nothingness. "Sập hết"—everything collapsed. Urban evacuees, who slowly began to trickle back to Vinh after the end of bombardment in 1973, were shocked by what they encountered: a ravaged city (*tàn phá nặng nề*) littered with ash and debris, much as Thạch Quỳ described in the poem "The Rubble of Vinh." For returnees, Vinh seemed uninhabitable, with few salvageable buildings, no industry or infrastructure, cratered roads, and barren fields. The erasure of material and ecological objects that had once functioned as landmarks left people disoriented; their urban frames of reference had simply disappeared. "Gạch vụn thôi"—only crushed brick. Reunited families faced tremendous difficulties, including lack of housing, schools, food security, health services, clean water, and electricity. Hunger plagued returnees; in some cases, children died of malnourishment, I was told quietly—an unknown and unfathomable toll of war that continued long after the air raids had stopped.

Repatriation from the countryside was marked by confusion about land repossession. The months after the Paris Peace Accords saw frenzied settlement and haphazard building on "abandoned" land, sometimes by new arrivals to Vinh, including migrant workers with no legal permission, or *hộ khẩu*, to reside in the city. As evacuated enterprises and government agencies returned, Vinh's population grew to an astounding eighty-five thousand by 1974, quickly surpassing preassault numbers (Nguyễn 2005, 229). The more fortunate families, mostly those with relatives obliged to stay in the city for work during the air war, returned to the small parcel of land they had received during agrarian reform in the 1950s. But even those families did not find much left on their plots. According to one woman's recollection (and note the sonic memory), "In 1972, the bombing started again, this time even fiercer with B-52s. Oh, those jets rumbled above us all the time. Our house was smashed then, the buffalo killed. . . . We still had our land after the war, but no materials to rebuild."[4]

Families that were able to reclaim their landholding set about building simple thatch shelters (*nhà tranh*), recycling what they could from the rubble. The less fortunate lost their land to new settlers or new construction. The government tolerated such land grabbing at this tumultuous moment, before formal processes of planning and reallocation could begin. Those who found their land occupied by other returnees or seized for public works were entitled to apply for a new parcel, a bureaucratic process referred to as *xin đất*. This was the case for Mr. Long, a son of factory workers, who grew up in the city and evacuated to Thanh Chương in 1964. When his family returned to Vinh in 1973, they found squatters had taken possession of their small piece of state-allocated land. Their luck soon turned, however: after they appealed to the city, the municipal government granted the family user rights to an even larger parcel, measuring three hundred square meters.

State enterprises, which were responsible for housing employees, secured large tracts of land to relocate production and build communal living quarters, much like the *danwei* system in China. My respondents loathed this provisional *nhà tập thể*, or collective housing. Made of thatch and bamboo, these overcrowded, rudimentary facilities offered no amenities and provided little protection from adverse weather conditions. People with more resources, such as supervisors, claimed adjacent plots and built their own makeshift shelters. The result of these spontaneous forms of resettlement was what appeared to be an uncoordinated and disorderly (*lung tung*) city in urgent need of rational planning to better manage and govern a repatriating population.

There was no lack of trying to produce a spatial order that would allow the state to reassert social control. As early as 1970, during the relative lull of the alleged bombing halt (chapter 1), the provincial government had drafted a preliminary plan for reconstruction to advance the Central Politburo's Resolution from 1961 to transform the small township (*thị trấn*) of Vinh into a regional "industrial socialist city" (*thành phố công nghiệp xã hội chủ nghĩa*), third only to Hanoi and Hải Phòng. This plan included construction of high-density residential housing (*khu tập kết*) in the city center, on the site of the former colonial railway station, which had been moved to the edge of town in the early 1960s (chapter 6). State architects drafted this large-scale project, which was slated for construction in 1971 in anticipation of an end to the war and the mass influx of evacuees back to Vinh.[5] It was to remain as "paper architecture," however, for two key reasons. First, the provincial government was leery about the unparalleled scale of planning, and it requested additional research to assess the ambitious goal to build a socialist city. Second, full-scale bombing resumed in 1972, forcing grand urban plans into an indefinite hold. The fierceness of the B-52 attacks meant another cycle of mass destruction, this time of the modest rebuilding that had taken place between 1969 and 1971. Following the peace treaty of 1973, when refugees began to stream back into Vinh, the proposal was redrafted as a three-year plan for rehabilitation (1973–1975) with the stated objectives to develop the economy, increase productivity, and improve people's material and cultural standards of living.[6] Soon after, the first fact-finding mission from East Germany would enter the scene. Urban planning would become a coordinated effort to produce a new master design that would bring radical spatial order to the devastated and spontaneously resettled city.

Upon their arrival in Vinh, East German specialists encountered an apocalyptic world of fissures, voids, and recesses that prompted comparisons with the decimation of Dresden (chapter 3). Vinh presented entirely different sociohistorical circumstances from Dresden, however, that made its rescue from devastation even more uncertain. On their two fact-finding missions in 1973, GDR experts contemplated how to set Vinh back on the path to modernity while recognizing the difficulty of transferring the East German model and scale of urban recovery—which included massive state investments in infrastructure to rehabilitate industry—to Vietnam.[7] One planner recalled the enormity of the task: "We were not sure how to proceed at first, or if the task at hand was even possible. There was no infrastructure, no construction industry. Nothing! We asked ourselves: how could we bring this city back from ruin?"[8] The extent of annihilation seemed to make full recovery dubious. And yet, ruination also afforded opportunities for urban experimentation. Not unlike other spaces considered unruly and beyond the reaches of civilization, from colonial frontiers (Rabinow 1989) to war-damaged cities (Qualls 2009), Vinh's total destruction enabled a reimagining of the horizons of urban possibility with novel built forms and spatial practices to organize (and order) society, while making the population more amenable to urban governance.

For creation of this new urban world to even begin, Vinh had to be made rebuildable. Voids needed to be filled, land graded, and crevices sealed, one stone at a time. This hard manual labor fell mostly to women. Although women's labor-intensive contributions to the war have long been recognized in scholarship (see Turner and Phan 1998), their role in postwar reconstruction has received much less attention. Women were largely responsible for both the physical and affective labor of reconstruction (Schwenkel 2013). They were, so to speak, Vietnam's *Trümmerfrauen*, or heroic "women of the ruins" (see figure 3.2). In chapter 2, I introduced the women who maintained roads and counted (and detonated) bombs during aerial assaults. Some of the same volunteer forces then reconstituted that destroyed landscape, building the foundations for a future socialist city. Teams of female workers broke up and removed debris, salvaging what they could for their own dwellings. Adopting hand-irrigation methods used in rice fields, they worked in choreographed synchrony to bail out stagnant water from craters and fill them with rubble mixed with gravel and sand from nearby rivers, one gaping pit after the next.[9]

These tedious acts made women's bodies the icons of Vietnam's indestructible spirit, catching the attention of East German journalists and specialists, arguably more than they did that of the Vietnamese (see figure 5.1). The images the GDR photographers produced, of selfless women toiling with their bare hands to birth a better future, mirrored the hopeful iconography of *Trümmerfrauen* in postwar Germany, which conveyed a similar sentiment of the heroic feminine (Crew 2017, 163). For example, in one image an architect shared with me, a young woman pauses in the act of clearing rubble to smile for the camera. The image reinforced the romantic notion of Vinh as a poor but resilient city, victimized yet invincible, on the cusp of a radical new beginning. The city was not dead, one planner commented to me, but brimming with affect and possibility. Crushed brick—the traces of red in the rubble of Thạch Quỳ's poem—was recycled as bedrock for the prosperous, egalitarian society imagined in visionary planning. At the same time, rational planning was redrawing the very gender hierarchy that socialism had promised to dissolve:

↑ Figure 5.1 Women as heroic figures clearing rubble, 1972. Published in *Vinh: Report on a Vietnamese Heroic City*, Solidaritätskomitee der DDR.

while women performed the hard work of land grading, men engaged in the technical labor of mapping to make urban space—and the population—more legible.

VISIONARY PLANNING: MAPPING UTOPIA

As a technology of rule and a science of prediction, socialist planning offered a rational solution to the mounting problem of postwar disorder. Foucault identified this as the problem of population in relation to "the urban question" (1980, 148; see also Rabinow 1989). The transfer of planning knowledge from experts, who had applied their skills to rebuilding East Germany and North Korea and also to town planning in Zanzibar (Wimmelbücker 2012), offered a utopian possibility to save Vietnam from "Stone Age" conditions and generate modern subjectivities in the process. In contrast to the unchecked growth and underregulated planning in capitalist cities, which served the wealthiest citizens,[10] socialist planning aspired to a revolutionary consciousness and a future-oriented, urban sensibility among citizen-workers. The reform of urban space would restructure the material and social relations of production (Castells 1977, 71), while eliminating exploitation and stratification both within the city and between town and country (Fischer 1962, 252)—ambitions that fit with Vietnam's five-year plans for rapid socialist development.

At its core, socialist planning was a utopian science and a fantastical art of projection that often crossed into the realm of the unreal and the unrealistic. Its distinct visual register was as virtual as it was performative and proposed a visionary world radically different from that which existed, as Anthony Vidler (2000, 6) has observed of the representational power of diagrams. In this section, I focus on two kinds of diagrams, or planning visualizations: figurative drawing as a form of virtual scale making, and abstract blueprints as a performative tool to mediate the transfer of technical knowledge. These technological devices rendered utopian ideas about the future city believable, although not always achievable. Maps emerged at the center of debates over what built form—and corresponding ideology—the socialist city might take.

In her book *Dreaming the Rational City*, M. Christine Boyer argues that planning documents, as abstract representations of desired social and spatial orders, offer normative solutions for achieving urban aspirations that rarely take into account structural barriers (1983, 68). Boyer is primarily concerned with spatial rationalities that advance the interests of capitalism in pursuit of economic efficiency. But her emphasis on diagrams as presenting the *illusion* of compatibility (for example, between design and development) is also useful for thinking through how visual renderings of rationalized spatiality sought to increase *socialist* productivity—that is, to serve workers, rather than capital. Maps, urban blueprints, and architectural drawings are by their very nature illusory: they normalize spatial divisions, reference anticipated futures, collapse time, eviscerate culture, distort social form, and obscure inequality to suggest a generic, harmonious order (Boyer 1983, 68). Lefebvre was critical of this abstraction of lived space: in the reduction of the world to shaded, geometric shapes, urban life itself was alienated and rendered merely as image, he argued (1991, 361). Vidler reminds us that these geometric projections do not constitute a universal language or shared ontological understanding of space and spatiality. Rather, they reflect a hermetic visual code whose interpretation requires familiarity with particular "traditions of spatial culture" and insider expertise (2000, 7). Attention to indigenous spatialities and spatial knowledge systems, for example, can reveal radically different renderings of landscapes, as I also observed in evacuation plans proposed by state enterprises.[11] Insofar as blueprints for postwar Vinh embodied a European approach to geospatial mapping that required some degree of technical knowledge to "translate" abstraction, they risked masking urban inequalities and power disparities between foreign and local experts who conceptualized, arranged, used, and regulated space in different ways. Blueprints and drawings, in other words, made concrete the hierarchies of planning expertise while presenting desirable (though largely unattainable) visions of socialist futurity as universal. This is perhaps socialism's rendition of the "agonizing phantasmagoria" of urban capitalism's built environment, which is at once hopeful and illusory in its promise of human security, flourishing, and liberation (Benjamin 1999, 15, 22).

BLUEPRINTS: VISIONS OF COPRODUCTION

Both East German and Vietnamese teams framed urban planning as "coproduction" and "mutual cooperation" (*Zusammenarbeit*,[12] *sự hợp tác*), which downplayed the very global inequalities that structured the need for socialist assistance in the first place. A persuasive and nonthreatening ideology of fraternal solidarity underpinned this horizontal worlding: the benevolent transfer of planning knowledge and technical skills would leave Vinh's future in the hands of competent Vietnamese experts. Such framing allowed both the GDR and Vietnam to sidestep an awkward history of foreign domination, in which architectural fantasies helped to create a colonial order (Norindr 1996). Vietnamese and East German experts I interviewed consistently drew on a discourse of mutuality, interdependence, embeddedness, and semblance to level power asymmetries. Ideas, and their materialization in blueprints and maps, were codeveloped, shared, and negotiated. These claims often exhibited a strong element of romanticism. For example, one East German architect described the collaboration as a symphony in which each expert, regardless of nationality, played a vital role in the finished composition.[13] Such a harmonious sonata made me somewhat skeptical; I had already read about instances of friction in archival documents. However, I recognized the stakes for my Vietnamese respondents, whose claims to equal partnership affirmed their sense of belonging to something greater and global, without loss of dignity or sovereignty. In the written words of one local architect, each task—from research to planning—was carried out in the "spirit of equality" (*tinh thần bình đẳng*) rather than colonial-like dependency (Trương 1985, 55).[14]

Foreign-led and funded modernization could thus be positioned as constitutive of, rather than antithetical to, decolonization and the party's espoused vision of "collective mastery" (*làm chủ tập thể*) over society (Lê Duẩn 1977a, 19–23). East German planners upheld this "enabling fiction" (Felski 1989, 168) by relocating agency. In the words of one visiting expert, "Urban planning was in the hands of the Vietnamese. They had the ultimate say. We were only

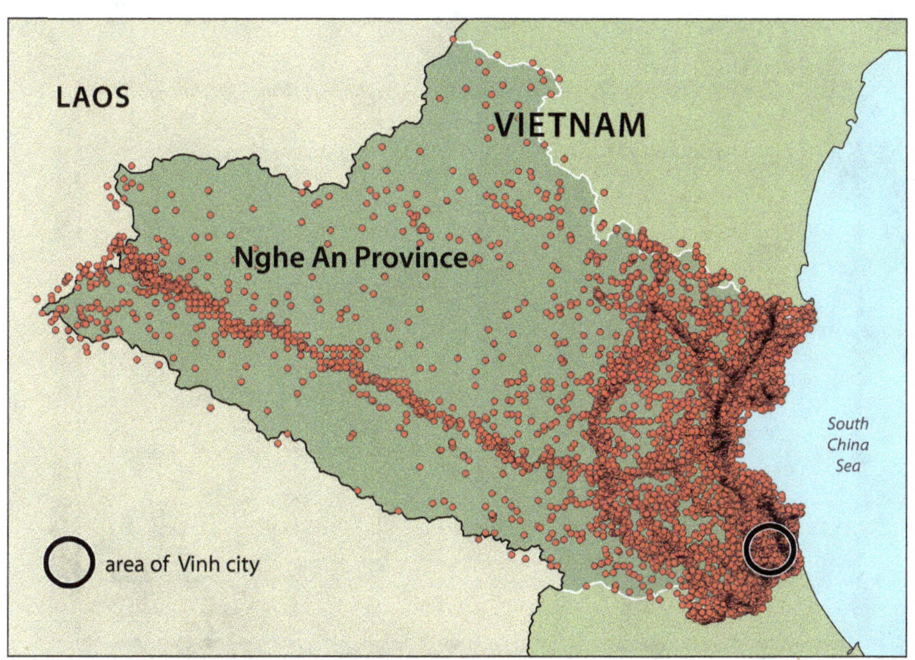

↑ Plate 1 Map of sorties carried out over Nghệ An province, October 1965–February 1973, using figures from CACTA/SEADAB database (NARA). Cartography by Jutta Turner. Base map: OpenStreetMap.

← Plate 2 "Nixon must pay the blood debt," 1972. Poster by Trường Sinh.

↑ Plate 3 GDR *Solimarken*, or solidarity stamps, from 1969 to show monthly donations to support the decolonizing world, including Vietnam.

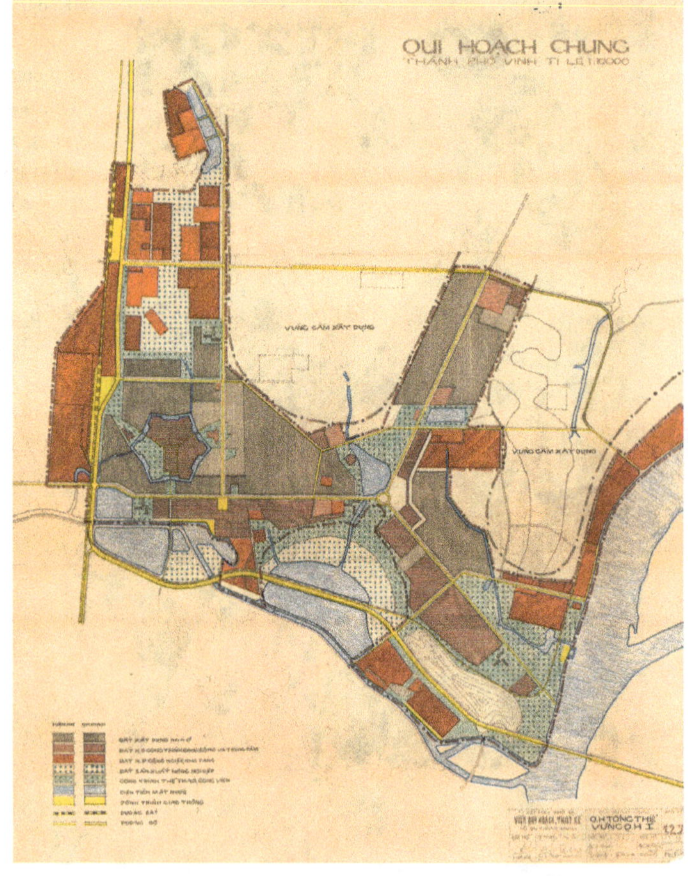

→ Plate 4 "Open hand" as master plan, 1975. BArch DH 1/28549.

↑ Plate 5 Horizontal design: residents access apartments through a shared, open-air corridor, 2011. Photo by the author.

↑ Plate 6 Altar to appease wandering ghosts in the corridor of block C6, 2011. Photo by the author.

↑ Plate 7 Not everyone complied with the directive to hang their flag for national holidays, 2010. Photo by the author.

→ Plate 8 Total makeover: collective corridor repair in A6, 2011. Photo by the author.

↓ Plate 9 Improvising safety in a C8 corridor, 2011. Photo by the author.

← Plate 10 Original kitchen with coal cooking (and water connection in washroom), 2011. Photo by the author.

↓ Plate 11 Renovated kitchen in the same housing block, 2011. Photo by the author.

↑ Plate 12 Larger and sturdier *cơi nới* in block C3 display stratification, 2011. Photo by the author.

↑ Plate 13 *Cơi nới* as an aspirational space of middle-class living, 2011. Photo by the author.

↑ Plate 14 Bird keeping in block B2: *gầm* as spaces for commercial and leisure activities, 2011. Photo by the author.

↑ Plate 15 Sprouting legs: new "toad" market in ward 9, 2011. Photo by the author.

↑ Plate 16 The New Modern as future utopia: proposed reconstruction of area C, 2010.

↑ Plate 17 On-site resettlement: the new Quang Trung, area A, 2019. Photo by the author.

there to support and advise them, to offer them solutions."[15] Another planner stressed, "We would never tell the Vietnamese what to do; we were there only to listen and to answer questions."[16] Vietnamese planners also contributed to this narrative; it was a source of pride that they facilitated the design of this high-profile project and ultimately controlled its outcome. "Look," one planner explained, "we worked together on the drafts and came to an agreement. These were not just ideas brought from Germany [*không phải từ bên Đức đưa sang đâu*]! We [at the Design Institute] were at the helm."[17] This image of the neutral, respectful foreign adviser helped to distance visiting GDR experts from the idea of *Hilfe* (aid) as paternalistic intervention and distinguished them ethically and politically from Western neocolonial development advisers—including those involved in administering West German aid to South Vietnam. As one GDR engineer wrote in an op-ed piece, "No paternalism in the form of colonial domination, just genuine assistance that guaranteed the autonomous development of their country."[18]

Sensitive to Vietnam's protracted struggle for autonomy, East German experts were keen to appease their hosts and accommodate their models of urban spatial planning. This stood in contrast to colonial knowledge formations that were less inclusive of local perspectives (Said 1993, xxi; Mitchell 2002), though of course colonized people reworked the transmitted ideas and merged them with other cosmopolitan borrowings (Kumar 2012, 58). Here, the exchange of Cold War socialist expertise was meant to augment the authority of the postcolonial state (Hecht and Edwards 2010, 285), rather than undermine or constrain it. In the complex planning encounters between Vietnamese nationals and well-intentioned but always suspect foreigners, blueprints and maps were not neutral objects for determining a rational course of action to achieve a collective goal, but moralizing technologies of mediation among different logics and arrangements of urban space (Verbeek 2005, 11). As such, they were far from equalizing.

Photographs of team-based planning-in-action offer insights into the power asymmetries of technology transfers and the masculine culture of design expertise that emerged. These images reveal the hierarchical relationships established within a coaching system that structured socialism's knowledge economy and its forms of international tutelage. A typical composition shows an exchange of expertise between men only, with East German planners at the center of the frame surrounded by eager Vietnamese cadres from the provincial Design Institute (see figure 5.2).[19] Blueprints and maps, as extensions of the power of the modern state (Mitchell 2002, 18), occupy everyone's attention. Trainers and trainees gather around these tutelary apparatuses in small

↑ Figure 5.2 Tutelage between East German and Vietnamese planners, circa 1974. BArch Bild Y12/152-22.

groups, the latter of whom are clearly learning new spatial "codes" for ordering the socialist city. Gesturing toward the maps in front of attentive audiences, foreign experts assumed the role of esteemed mentors, if not wise siblings, passing the charge of technical development on to their mentees.[20]

To be sure, the exchange of planning knowledge *was* multidirectional and also included South-South exchanges, such as the training of Vietnamese architects in China and Cuba. The success of rebuilding Vinh depended on sharing empirical data to manage resettlement and pace urban growth. As experts were careful to differentiate their altruistic assistance from that of the capitalist West—after all, East Germans were in Vietnam as guests, not invaders, I was reminded—they were fully cognizant of their more senior positions and their role to train future professionals. In interviews, they circumvented their uneasiness with social hierarchy by highlighting the authority of the Vietnamese state, which had deemed the pedagogical encounters to be benevolent and valuable to national building. This logic was evident in one architect's reference to "on-the-job training," in which nine Vietnamese interns shadowed six East German planners:

ARCHITECT: Each [GDR] expert had his double, the person who followed him around to learn our methods.
CS: But I thought that the Vietnamese were the head planners?
ARCHITECT: Well yes, it was a cooperation [*Zusammenarbeit*]. The Vietnamese side was in charge of planning and made the final decisions, but we still had a strong influence on them.[21]

From these words, we can infer that coproduction between donor (trainer) and recipient (trainee) did not mean equitable contributions to the final master plan, even as such fictions helped to legitimize foreign intervention in planning. Nor did cooperation amount to unity of vision and purpose among the multiple stakeholders, despite efforts to maintain the appearance of harmonious consensus. GDR planners shrugged ambivalently when I mentioned the multiple blueprint drafts I had examined in archives in Vinh and Berlin. Like their Vietnamese counterparts, they considered some of the designs incompatible with Vietnamese cultural values and material conditions at the time, a theme I develop in the next section. Certainly their paternalism was not as "heavy-handed," as Elke Beyer (2012, 311) describes Soviet planning in Kabul, Afghanistan, in her architectural history of socialist imperialism.[22] In Vinh, the "soft power" influence of foreign expertise on planning was subject to ongoing negotiation by differently situated actors. Some trainees ignored the suggestions of their trainers, while others expressed conflicting views about urban design and spatial organization.[23] This is most clear with debates over the city center, as rendered in a series of freehand sketches.

FREEHAND SKETCHES: DEFINING THE CITY CENTER

Despite attempts to accommodate both national and international visions of reconstruction, technical blueprints and freehand drawings revealed discordant approaches to socialist city making. This was not, however, a clear-cut instance of "competing local knowledges and world-views," such as Catherine Alexander (2007b, 175) observed in Kazakh ambivalence toward Soviet design in Almaty. In Vinh, differences did not map neatly onto a foreign-local binary but rather unfolded across a spectrum of hierarchical expertise within each work unit. For example, difference in opinion about spatial practices transpired at times between Vietnamese planners who had trained overseas and those who had been educated in country,[24] and among generations of East German architects, with junior experts questioning the universality of modernist planning and calling for "indigenous" (*einheimische*) solutions.

Modernization efforts often fractured around questions of scale and scope, as planners struggled to balance grand schemes with domestic needs, conditions, and possibilities. While there was general consensus on function (*chức năng*) and the type of city to build—that is, one organized around socialist relations of production to become a regional industrial powerhouse—there were discrepancies over the scale (*quy mô*) of projected future growth. For example, whereas Nghệ An officials projected a population increase to 120,000–150,000 residents over a five-year period, as evidenced in the provincial Report on the General Construction Plan from May 30, 1975,[25] some GDR planners had a larger scale of growth in mind, with 200,000–300,000 inhabitants (see also Purtak 1982, 90).[26] A more animated discussion centered on urban form and character (*tính chất*): what type of architectural façade should constitute the new public face of Vinh, and what sort of material base would best serve workers?

Iterations of the design for the city center and its environs showed competing ideas about transformative spatial design that would showcase Vinh's progress and new modern face. In contrast to blueprints that reduced the "complex sensory experience of space" to abstract lines and shapes (Buchli 2013, 54), freehand sketches rendered social life more visible and utopian futures more imaginable. They did so by shifting the perspective from flat horizontal planes to vertical dimensions, from a panoramic city seen from above to the everyday lived spaces below (de Certeau 1984). Drawings were replete with tangible shapes and identifiable spaces, including high-rise buildings, wide axial roads, automobiles, monuments, parks, and (faceless) people using public space in appropriate ways. Such street-view renderings were common in designs of GDR cities.[27] Other postcolonial cities seeking to modernize, such as Jakarta, also produced simulacra of orderly, idealized cityscapes (Kusno 2000). In Vinh, these drawings were entirely disconnected from the actual conditions of annihilation, even as they provided aspirational imagery. With its splendid monumentality, such utopian planning answered Hồ Chí Minh's call for a bigger and more beautiful city (indeed, one sketch featured a marble statue of the late president himself). In so doing, however, many of the plans more accurately reflected the living conditions and urban aspirations of contemporary socialist Europe than those of postwar Vietnam.

At the suggestion of the Vietnamese team, planners agreed to move the city center (*Stadtkern*; *trung tâm*) east from its traditional location during the colonial period along Quang Trung Road, the main north-south axis that ran into the central marketplace at "kilometer zero." However, they did not

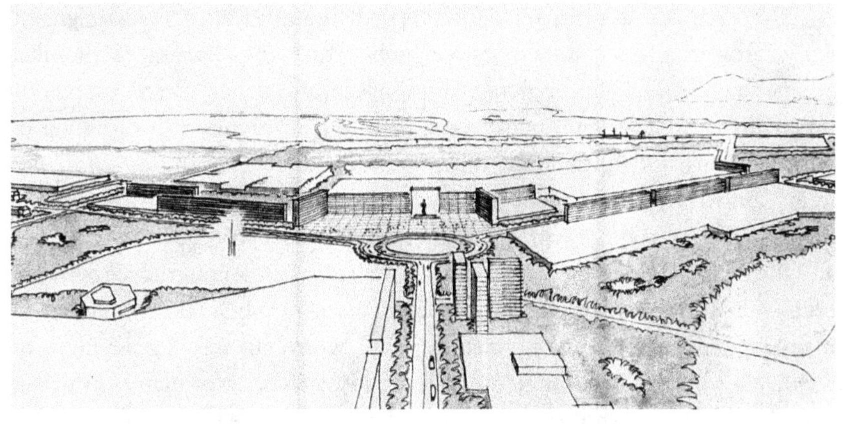

↑ Figure 5.3 Victory Square, proposed city center for Vinh, 1975. BArch DH 1/28550.

all agree on its purpose or appearance. Some of the East German architects were influenced by their country's Sixteen Principles of Urban Design from 1950, an ideological treatise that borrowed heavily from Soviet doctrine and emphasized the importance of the city center for socialist nation building.[28] In accordance with the sixth principle, the *Stadtkern* should be the iconic focal point of political power, prominently displayed through stately design and timeless architectural splendor. There should be large, open spaces for political and cultural activities, including jubilant parades and celebrations to reinforce the national fantasy of collective utopia. As Sonia Hirt has argued, this "big is beautiful" planning approach was applied to cities across the socialist world, producing a shared stock of built forms that included grand plazas, cultural palaces, mass housing, wide boulevards, people's parks, and national monuments (2013, S31–S32). Vietnamese authorities, especially in Hanoi, also took inspiration from these Soviet-based ideas of design (Logan 1995). But not all were convinced that monumental urbanism offered an appropriate scale of spatial development for Vinh.

In East Germany, grandiose urban designs were proposed for the model town of Stalinstadt, later Eisenhüttenstadt (May 2003), and for Berlin's center (Flierl 1998, 122–27).[29] GDR planners carried these ideas for radical reconstruction with them to Vinh, an equally symbolic city. Together with Vietnamese authorities (provincial and central government), they proposed a monumental city center to celebrate military victory and the power of state socialism, with a central east-west access leading to a majestic Platz des Sieges, or Victory Square (see figure 5.3).

The Vietnamese planners I interviewed disapproved of this design. In earlier research on commemorative architecture in Vietnam (Schwenkel 2009a, 102–26), I had encountered widespread ambivalence toward state monumentalism. So it was not unexpected when a local architect, his training in East Germany notwithstanding, drew on a discourse of "harmony" (*hài hòa*) to explain why he found such socialist realist schemes pretentious. They were, he explained, in conflict with Vietnamese "traditional" architectural practices and the logics of *phong thủy* (feng shui), which emphasize congruence between built and natural environments. He was not alone in this sentiment. East German respondents also gave a mixed response, which cut across generations of architects who had been influenced by the 1950s Stalinist principles of urban planning and those who revised those principles a decade later in an era of de-Stalinization. One cynical architect from the latter group saw the triumphal design as motivated by political ideology rather than the needs of the people that socialist planning aimed to serve. Planners like him preferred that the city center be a hub of social and economic life, not unlike Vietnamese market towns historically. These precolonial "cities" (*thành thị*) had formed more spontaneously around networks of trade or markets (*thị*) adjacent to fortified centers of feudal administration (*thành*) (Đàm 2005, 59). Another set of freehand drawings demonstrates shifts in the spatial logics of planning from the political to the social, from grand open spaces to more intimate urban spaces of daily life.

In their sketches of revitalized lived space (Lefebvre 1991), GDR planners depicted a dream world of socialist infrastructure, where a healthy and happy urban population maximized productivity. Drawing on "green city" (*die grüne Stadt*) conceptions circulating in East Germany at the time, combined with elements of tropical modernism, their designs foregrounded the lived experience of urban spatial planning with optimal distances between traffic, housing, and green zones (Schmidt, Linke, and Wessel 1969). One sketch of the north-south axis proposed remaking Quang Trung Road as "Palm Alley" (see figure 5.4). As in East Germany, separating spaces for motor vehicles and pedestrians would allow residents to move about safely and unhindered (Beyer 2011, 84). This people-centered iteration of the city remedied the cold emptiness of Victory Square, and yet cars appear as ghostly apparitions, specters of an unjust past and an equally uncertain future. Here, too, one finds the experimental prevailing over the practical, shaped by the Orientalist imaginaries of GDR planners. Palm Alley would offer residents standardized modern housing but also a broad, tree-lined street to stroll along, lit up at night with street lights. The diagram merged the technical—newly laid electrical lines and power stations—with the natural, a canopy of non-native trees that symbolized "the exotic" for

↑ Figure 5.4 Proposal for Palm Alley (Quang Trung Road), 1975. BArch DH 1/28550.

foreign experts, including for the green designer himself.[30] Depicting an illusory future, the sketch suggested a stable and prosperous postwar society, even though it would be years before power could be restored to the city (and even longer before there would be cars[31]). Like the proposal for Victory Square, my Vietnamese interlocutors considered the Palm Alley plan antithetical to their normative cultural practices. "Palm trees provide no shade!" exclaimed one planner who worked for the Design Institute during reconstruction.[32] As seen in figure 5.4, people are exposed to harsh sunlight as they walk and bike about the city without any protection from the elements.

Anticipation of a normative future on par with socialist development elsewhere was also evident in drawings for the shopping arcade or trade center. Here, the phantasmagoria of Vinh most resembled Benjamin's (1999) commodity culture as modernist fantasy. These sketches of the good life revealed an even stronger disconnect between idealized space and the reality of urban voids. In East German planning, leisure spaces served an important role in producing happy, healthful families. That these public spaces were associated with consumption provoked anxiety among some Vietnamese authorities about the bourgeois tendencies of East German socialism and their potential for moral contamination. Moreover, a "consumer town" mentality would create a desire for goods that the postwar state could not deliver (Dao 1980, 511). The sketches promised a lifestyle of socialist abundance centered on recreational consumption: in their free time, workers in Vinh could shop at kiosks,

↑ Figure 5.5 Visions of plenitude at the shopping arcade, 1975. BArch DH 1/28550.

get a haircut, buy a balloon, play table tennis, have a drink (beer or tea), grab a bite to eat, or enjoy an ice cream with loved ones, much as they might in Europe (see figure 5.5). In the future, they would park their cars in garages or take the bus to work (Nguyen et al. 1974, 14). Yet economic and material constraints made such outings unlikely for many years to come. For returnees struggling to secure their basic needs after years of evacuation, the "universalizing aspirations" of socialist modernization (Molnár 2005, 111) transmitted through architectural drawings were largely inconceivable. They spoke to the much higher standard of living in East Germany and that country's materialist fantasies more than to the pragmatic possibilities for Vinh's postwar recovery. Freehand sketches thus proved as detached from the lived experience of the ruined city as abstract blueprints and maps. After much disagreement, a generic trade center was eventually built, but without all the utopian frills.[33]

At the heart of debates over spatial design and planning of the socialist city—its form, function, character, and scale—was a larger concern with crafting a *Vietnamese* socialist modernity on the basis of universalist ambitions. These negotiations culminated in a surprising consensus: a rational master plan that Vietnamese architects came to identify, admiringly, as an organic, open hand.

THE FUNCTIONAL CITY

In May 1975, just a few weeks after the war's end on April 30, the Chairman of the People's Committee of Nghệ An province, Dương Văn Đạt, put forth the vision for the Master Plan for Vinh.[34] In the previous section, I showed how urban planning went through numerous iterations, as all sides discussed, revised, and rejected blueprints, maps, and sketches according to contrasting ideas about the design and use of urban space. The master plan that came out of this yearlong process of technological mediation established a multiscalar framework for a rationally ordered city that would position Vinh at the vanguard of socialist modernity. While the plan broke with the colonial grid system deployed by Ernest Hébrard and other French urbanists in Indochinese colonies as a technique of social control and colonial subjection (Wright 1991, 166), its aim was similar: bring spatial discipline to "unplanned," high-density settlements in order to govern more effectively. It did so by envisioning the city as a single interconnected organism.

East German spatial planning was shaped by discourses of scientific urbanism and technological modernism that were influential at the time. These modernist discourses were based on a totalizing notion of the city as an adaptive, socioecological system that could be anticipated, apprehended, and controlled through technical innovation and the application of universally measurable parameters (Gandy 2014, 11). In their distinctly materialist approach to the city, socialist planners embraced centralized planning and modern technology to achieve total social and economic transformation by reconfiguring the relations of production to eliminate class disparities and private property; in other words, by eliminating capitalism (Kotkin 1995, 35). This rationalist paradigm could be seen in the final blueprint of the Master Plan for Vinh. Notably, the proposal closely resembled the functional city of the Athens Charter, put forth by Le Corbusier at the fourth International Congress of Modern Architecture (Congrès Internationaux d'Architecture Moderne, or CIAM) in 1933. CIAM's rigid style—the zoned city—sought standardized solutions to the universal question of housing and land use. This idea appealed to architects in the Soviet Union (Mumford 2009) and influenced planners across socialist Europe, the capitalist West, and parts of the decolonizing South.[35] Vinh, however, offered a less industrial context, but it did offer a "blank canvas" on which to experiment with building a new way of life. To achieve maximum economic productivity, planners divided the city into functional, single-land-use zones with conjoining thoroughfares to optimize space, instill order, and increase efficiency. On the map, these demarcated zones were color coded to hierarchize space and distinguish between industrial areas, administrative districts, residential neighborhoods, agricultural land, traffic works, waterways, and green spaces—all of which formed a functional, integrated whole (see plate 4).

The application of scientific planning to urbanization, and the idea to use spatial organization as a method to transform society, enchanted architects and planners at the provincial Design Institute. For them, the abstract urban geometry of the master plan closely resembled the image of an open hand (*tay xòe*)—an organic metaphor of friendship and peace that complemented the fist of anti-imperialist solidarity (see chapter 3). Training and housing were concentrated in the palm—the city center—with each imagined finger serving as a connecting artery that led to a different sector of industry. Green belts, with recreational spaces for workers and plots of land for farming, bridged work and living areas, much as Le Corbusier envisioned. To woo local experts, the master plan represented Vinh as a stable circulatory system of heterogeneous parts that, working together organically, would ensure an expanding industrial economy and a higher standard of living. The rational organization of space would also order and manage everyday urban life. This view of Vinh restored and devoid of conflict presented society as a "set of conformable interests," where everyone stood to benefit from the healthful functioning and reproduction of an evolving social whole (Gibson-Graham 1996, 109).

It is important to note how this model of *planned* urban development broke with the *unchecked* growth and settlement that had characterized Vietnamese towns and cities historically (Dao 1980, 511), and why it so captivated Vietnamese planners. In postcolonial Vietnam, the government promoted centralized planning to develop heavy industry and eliminate rural-urban disparities in accordance with the party's first Five-Year Plan.[36] Like the Chinese "road to socialism," this approach prioritized smaller, provincial production units over larger industrial centers, as occurred in the Soviet Union (Bray 2005, 123; Lefebvre 1991, 421). Small cities were thus poised to become the regional motors of an expanding industrial economy. Regional development in towns with strong agricultural bases, like Vinh,[37] however, posed different challenges from industrial development in larger cities like Hanoi, where Soviet-guided modernization was proceeding (Logan 2000, 188–90). During the interwar years (1954–1964), rehabilitation (*khôi phục*) and growth in small towns was marked more by ad hoc infrastructure projects—a Chinese cement factory in one part of Vinh, a Soviet power plant in another—than by a comprehensive, future-oriented design for integrated urban development as proposed for the reconstruction (*xây dựng lại*) of provincial capitals in 1973 (Schwenkel 2015e). Local architects reminded me that before 1975 Vinh had yet to see such a detailed master plan for urban growth. Preliminary discussions for planning in 1961 and again in 1970 had been abandoned due to the air war. With a shortage of regional expertise, there was little experience in Vinh with multisector planning and none with scientific urbanism. One prominent architect in Hanoi shared his view that the disorderly character and spatial patterns of Vietnamese cities not only were a consequence of historical upheavals, like the U.S. war, but were also a product of culture.[38] His observations resonated with French colonial convictions about unruly spaces and subjects: a lack of planning strategy necessitated colonial government intervention to promote social order and the welfare of the urban population. Rational planning was thus appealing to this architect because of its capacity to mitigate urban unpredictability (explained by "culture") while applying Marxist-Leninist ideology to the synchronized development and management of cities (Tô 1985).

In depicting society as a functioning whole, the "open-hand" model fit neatly with the city-planning parameters and technical standards that socialist Europe was adhering to at the time. Configured as a set of entitlements, these parameters and standards were reflected in the call for balance among all facets of urban life in the GDR's Sixteen Principles of Urban Design: "The goal of urban design is the harmonious fulfillment of the basic human right to employment, housing, culture, and recreation."[39] Ample public green spaces (rather than elite gardens) were especially appealing to Vietnamese planners, who valued the emphasis on ecological harmony to ensure healthfulness.[40] But they also valued the scientific rigor of planning, which they saw as a radically different spatial approach to organizing society: "It was a science how they designed the city!" the architect who had been critical of urban disorder exclaimed. In contrast to dispersed settlements, he explained, the East German plan envisioned urban space as an orderly set of interconnected nodes and networked lines converging on a single, centralized place. "Everything was linked to the center," the vice director of the Design Institute said, using his hand to illustrate the system. "There were clear lines of traffic and a clear demarcation between housing and industry, with access through one of the main thoroughfares."[41]

In practice, rational planning was challenging to implement under postwar conditions, and residents were less convinced by its logic of spatial organization.[42] Suffering from food insecurity and acute shortages of goods, rural migrants flocked to Vinh to build provisional housing in green belts. Informal markets sprang up across the city, blurring the boundaries of single-use zoning (Lương n.d.). The master plan's goal was to banish such spontaneity and the porosity of space. But the Hanoi architect's words held some truth: culture *was* transformative of space (and not the other way around, as he had hoped), and it would come to play a strong role in the respatialization of the planned city over time (part 3).

BEYOND PLANNING: MATERIALIZING THE FUTURE CITY

There was more to the rational city than its plan. There was also its material realization in buildings and infrastructure that would redefine relations among labor, the state, and the family. In the previous sections, I showed how utopian planners with contrasting perspectives deliberated on the city of tomorrow through technical artifacts—maps, blueprints, and drawings of a rational world—and found consensus in the functionalist, open-hand design. As an exercise in virtual world building (Vidler 2000), planning was largely detached from the city's materiality and the lived experience of Vinh's obliterated spaces, however. In this section, I show how urban plans were put into purposeful action to create an orderly built environment that reflected the technological assurances of high modernism—an environment that was far from utopian for residents but still offered hope for a better future. The tasks of East German experts were planning *and* building, which introduced new forms of spatial control and strategies for the exercise of power (see chapter 4). For architects, this meant their experimental urbanism might take material form to remake Vinh into a model, people-centered city. For officials, grand modernist designs would generate new opportunities for urban governance and for the state to penetrate people's lives more deeply. Reconstruction would thus transform laboring subjects into consenting moral citizens who could be managed and molded into new socialist persons.

This was not tabula rasa urbanism, however, where architects imposed their modernist vision onto a blank-canvas landscape. Given the scope of the air war's destruction, it would be tempting to claim that an entirely new beginning was possible; certainly, the descriptions my respondents gave of the razed city would support such a claim. However, residues of the urban past formed a dense palimpsest of temporalities, not only in memories of loss and erasure (Huyssen 2003b, 7), but also in the traces of previous infrastructure projects, imperial and postcolonial. Past iterations of urban design, detectable in cratered roads, vacant lands, and crumbling architecture, would at times guide postwar planning and reconstruction of the "bigger, better and more beautiful" city. Upon their arrival in Vinh, East German experts found thirty-five kilometers of unpaved and badly damaged roads. Some of these, including Quang Trung Road, had been widened with Soviet assistance in the early

1960s to scale Vinh up from township to city. One critical task of modernization for civil engineers was to repair and expand the road network—or main "arteries" in the hand—to more than eighty kilometers (Purtak 1982, 94) in order to integrate Vinh's regional industry with the national economy. These roads would also guide workers along preferred pathways between zones of production ("fingertips") and social reproduction (in the "palm"). As aspirational infrastructure deemed vital to the city's development, roads materialized the banal presence of the state in everyday life (Harvey and Knox 2015, 286–87). This technique of social ordering was masked by the promise of mobility. Residents circumvented this spatial control, however, by carving out their own routes and shortcuts.

The construction of new public works—roads, electric lines, and sewage systems—was meant to undo colonial inequality, remedy the devastation of bombardment, and raise the living standards of the proletariat. At the same time, single-use zones of regulated activity would reform the population by taming urban unruliness. This politics of spatial containment to promote social and moral development can be seen in the building or renovation of social infrastructure that took place, including a sports stadium to improve fitness, a cinema to transmit ideology, and a marketplace to ensure proper practices of trade.

As a tool of disciplinary power intended to banish the specter of capitalism, the marketplace exemplified how modernist architecture could make citizens and their economic practices more legible to the state (Scott 1998). Like their counterparts in the South (Leshkowich 2011), petty traders in the DRV were commonly viewed with suspicion, if not as backward, especially in a small "red" town (*thành phố đỏ*) like Vinh. Newspapers commonly reported on *buôn bán trái phép* (illegal or black-market trading) in the years before the central market was renovated.[43] Built between 1977 and 1980 on the site of the colonial open-air marketplace and its postrevolution incarnation—bombed in 1968—the rebuilt market aimed to contain the spread of unruly commerce (see figures 5.6 and 5.7). Enclosing market spaces to produce a more orderly and hygienic city had also been a civilizing strategy of French colonialism in Saigon (Leshkowich 2014, 33–40). In Vinh, the new vertical market—two floors, each with a thousand square meters of covered space—was technologically modern, with electricity and a cooling system, and rationally organized to facilitate supervision and regulation of trade. It did not reflect how traders actually conducted their transactions, however, which were sometimes clandestine, including selling on the road to passing traffic. The rationalization of space and public infrastructure was meant to usher in a civilized urban life,

↑ Figure 5.6 Vinh's central market before rebuilding, 1974. Photo by Raimer Buntrock.

↑ Figure 5.7 Vinh's central market after rebuilding, 1980. Photo by Raimer Buntrock.

local in its practice and discipline and international in its design and technology. Ironically, reports of counterfeit and smuggled goods increased after inauguration of the new market.

To build this rational, future-oriented city, it was necessary to establish a building materials industry that could construct public works over the long term. This fit with the planning directives of the party, which saw national development of the construction industry as key to modernizing both Vietnam's rural and urban areas (Phạm Văn Đồng 1977, 45, 49). It was in the building materials industry that socialist progress—a trinity of modernization, rationalization, and mechanization—would materialize. Intrinsic to Cold War techno-politics (Hecht and Edwards 2010), socialist countries invested heavily in the research, development, and application of innovative building technologies, such as prefabrication, to mass-produce the built environment (Zarecor 2011, 225; Rubin 2016, 25). Financed by loans from East Germany, the rationalization (*Rationalisierung*; *hợp lý hóa*) of construction took priority in the postwar years in Vinh and across Vietnam (Cao 1978, 264), and was given precedence over the production of consumer goods (Norlund 1984). Apropos to the master plan, more than a dozen state enterprises in Vinh were slated for modernization to help build the material and technological foundations of socialism, including factories that produced cement, brick, pipe, lime, wood, concrete, sand, and gravel, as well as stone and marble quarries. This assemblage of modern construction technologies, intended to solve the problem of material underdevelopment, transformed the scale and scope of Vinh's industrial capacities but not without significant challenges and setbacks.

To maintain the targeted *Bautempo*, or pace of reconstruction, and promote technological enablement, the building materials industry underwent accelerated mechanization (*Mechanisierung*; *cơ giới hóa*). For Vietnamese officials, mechanization was key to rapid urban growth: it would increase productivity and enable self-sufficiency (Lê Duẩn 1977a, 81). For the East German technicians I interviewed, it was the lynchpin of progress that separated socialist Europe from Vietnam. Along with rationalization, mechanization defined the technological future according to new metrics of labor productivity. Machines would replace the drudgery of manual labor, with its lower efficiency—a change considered emancipating for women especially (see figure 5.8). Mechanization required a skilled and disciplined proletariat; to this end, in 1977 Vinh opened its first vocational school, modeled on an East German curriculum, which trained equal numbers of women and men.[44] Mechanization also required importing machinery and other equipment that Vietnam lacked. As Felix Guattari (1995) observes, there is more to the desired

↑ Figure 5.8 Brickwork as gendered, manual labor before mechanization, circa 1975. Photo by Raimer Buntrock.

technical object than its materiality alone. Imported technologies signified Vietnam's progress and recovery on the one hand and East Germany's prosperity and technological superiority on the other.

Imported machinery allowed for new infrastructural geographies to form, beyond the dominance of China and the Soviet Union. As Christian Joppke has argued, showcasing the GDR's technical prowess "suggest[ed] that the leadership role in the socialist camp was about to be passed on from the Soviet Union to East Germany" (1995, 45). In the years after the war, all vehicles, tools, equipment, and supplies for Vinh's reconstruction were transported by sea from East Germany. Only natural resources, like clay and sand, were sourced locally, but they allowed the city's character to be both technologically global and organically "Vietnamese." Such *Việt Đức* (Vietnamese-German) hybridity was important to maintaining a sense of horizontal collaboration, thus its use as a naming device in and beyond Vinh (a branding practice that continues through today). Arriving shipments were maritime spectacles that drew onlookers, marking the dawn of technological modernity. The first two cargos arrived in Vinh in April and May 1974, two months after the start of the project, with 1,227 tons of steel, 230 tons of fiber cement, 50 tons of glass panes, 50 tons of color pigment, 35.5 tons of water piping, 8.4 tons of repair tools, four excavators, a crane truck, and other vehicles and supplies, including food provisions for the technicians.[45] Between 1974 and 1980, over sixty cargo ships—on average, one every six weeks—embarked from the port of Rostock and delivered more than 5,000 tons of freight to Vinh.[46] Tensions surfaced, however, when the nautical performance of solidarity was disrupted and equipment arrived damaged, such as shattered glass, or was dropped into the sea accidentally.[47]

As emblems of an emergent modernity, imported technologies and new construction captivated the masses. They offered hope of emancipation from war, deprivation, disorder, and underdevelopment. One East German expert spoke of the air of excitement at the grand opening of the central market in 1980. Boasts that the market was one of the largest in Southeast Asia actually drew *too* many people to the inauguration, which ended in a stampede. Curious locals from far and wide pushed their way into the capacious structure to see the rows of dry and refrigerated goods displayed under electric lights—the good life had indeed arrived![48] This euphoria was short-lived. The new infrastructure broke down quickly; its premature obsolescence is a theme that I develop in part 3 of the book. The GDR technician responsible for machine repairs, who witnessed the stampede at the market, described the disenchanting effects of such disruptions. Not long after the market opened for business, the cooling system failed and the meat for sale spoiled. People refused to discard the rotten fare, he recalled, and instead boiled it—a reminder of the cruelty of optimistic attachments to utopian fantasies (Berlant 2011).

New infrastructure broke down because, in fact, it was often being *reused*. I discovered this while touring the Cầu Đước cement factory, which is still in operation. Cầu Đước was built in 1958 with Chinese assistance as part of earlier efforts to advance socialist urbanization. After the U.S. air war, the factory was in dire need of repair from bombardment, and its outdated technology needed modernizing.[49] The GDR donated machinery, which doubled the plant's prewar output. It did so despite frequent malfunction. "They were secondhand!" a retired architect explained when I expressed surprise. "They were in good enough condition but broke down at times."[50] Some criticized the GDR for sending "used" gifts to refurbish Vietnam's factories, which was mentioned casually in early negotiations with the DRV,[51] and later became a point of contention with counterparts in Hanoi, who chastised the delivery of "old" and "inoperable" machinery.[52] One Vietnamese engineer remarked that "the equipment was *lạc hậu rồi* [already obsolescent], stuff the GDR was discarding so they could modernize their industry," although he still pointed out its usefulness.[53] "It was a start," an East German specialist stated, describing how recycled technologies helped shift manual labor to mechanized production, one of the goals of GDR technical assistance. "Before those machines arrived, many things had to be done by hand."[54] In this teleology, "secondhand modernity" was a graduated advance toward socialist futurity, and while not ideal, it was still preferable to no step forward at all.

East German firms sent used equipment to Vietnam because it was in their best interest to do so. The system of material donations to the "Third World" worked as a socialist gift economy. In that system, the exchange of desirable goods as "favors" maintained valuable relationships and built political capital to be drawn on as needed in the future (Dunn 2004, 95). In Vinh, East German project leaders approached the directors of firms back home with annual "wish lists" (*Wunschlisten*) of items needed for reconstruction (which had been approved by the Ministry of Construction in Berlin) and asked for "solidarity donations" (*Solidaritätsspenden*). This involved much cajoling and bargaining, according to my interviewees, who explained how they navigated bureaucracy and a pervasive "economy of shortage" (Verdery 1996, 21–23) to convince directors to contribute coveted goods.[55] There were political and financial rewards for compliance. Directors received compensation for donations, based on the replacement, rather than the depreciated, value of their gifts—which allowed them to purchase new machinery and other material necessities for their firms.

This was one of the more fraught aspects of solidarity: GDR firms divested themselves of obsolete technology to help modernize their own country while publicly serving the cause of building socialism in Vietnam. That these donations were *schnell kaputt* (broken quickly)[56] reveals how East Germany's ascendance depended to some extent on keeping Vietnam from becoming *too* developed.

As the GDR's economy weakened (eventually to a crisis point), large donations from East German firms became harder to secure. Consequently, meeting the targeted *Bautempo* was in both countries' best interests. Rapid modernization of Vietnam's construction industry would reduce its dependence on costly imports—donations which were contributing to solidarity fatigue.[57] Moreover, a modernized construction sector would allow East Germany to move forward with its most ambitious project in Vinh, the subject of chapter 6: standardized mass housing as a critical node in the urban whole and an entirely new architecture of spatial control.

Urban Fragments 4

NHÀ TẦNG Ở VINH (HIGH-RISE IN VINH)

Những đồng chiêm đã nuôi ta lớn (Raised among rice seedlings)
Bằng mái nhà lợp toóc, lợp săng (In homes of myrtle and thatch)
Vẫn theo ta điều ăn nết ở (Still following our old ways of life)
Năm tầng cao chung một mái bằng . . . (Under the same roof of a five-story flat . . .)

Vẫn quen như đường làng ngõ xóm (Intimacy like in the village)
Lên cầu thang ai cũng hỏi chào (Greeting everyone on the stairs)

↑ Figure I.4.1 Building a new and civilized way of life, 1978. Photo by Raimer Buntrock.

Người tứ phương khác nhau nghề nghiệp (People from different places and occupations)
Mà biết nhau không sót gác nhau . . . (Know one another regardless of floor . . .)

Không cánh cửa khép buồn riêng được (Private units feel lonely so we don't close doors)
Có niềm vui năm gác chia ra (When we have something cheerful we share with all five floors)
Một gia đình con sắp vào bộ đội (One family's son will soon go to the army)
Tiễn đưa vui đủ mặt cả khu nhà. (The whole house gathers to see him off with joy.)

—XUÂN HOÀI, 1978[1]

6

UTOPIAN HOUSING

> Utopias share with the totality of culture the quality . . . of a knife with the edge pressed against the future. They constantly cause the reaction of the future with the present, and thereby produce the compound known as human history.
>
> —ZYGMUNT BAUMAN, *SOCIALISM: THE ACTIVE UTOPIA*, 1976

Under socialism, cities became malleable sites for full-scale makeovers of society (Pence and Betts 2008, 8). Vinh's devastated landscape, like that of cities in post-wwII Europe, provided fertile ground for architectural experimentation to create a modern industrial city inhabited by a trained, productive, and forward-looking proletariat. Building a new socialist city would entail a coordinated effort by thousands of laborers and technicians on multiple, interconnected fronts. By February 1974 alone, more than two thousand young, unskilled workers, a large percentage of whom were women, were mobilized to construct housing.[1] The vast majority were recruits from rural districts who received their formal training on the job: *vừa học vừa làm*.[2] Some recruits, such as high school pupils and pregnant women, violated labor policy, exposing how the road to socialist emancipation was plagued by exploitation early on.[3]

GDR experts sought empirical solutions to the infrastructural problems of urban devastation and underdevelopment. For visiting architects and planners, urban design was a project of social engineering that could increase labor productivity through the rational ordering of space. In their adherence to architectural determinism, they saw the built environment as an instrument that could inculcate the appropriate values, practices, tastes, and conduct of workers, while raising their quality of life. There is perhaps no better site to observe the relationship between technology, space, architecture, and governance than standardized mass housing, a quintessential institution of state socialism. In this chapter, I trace the creation of a radically new spatial, material, and sensory world out of the accretions of imperial warfare (Stoler 2016). And yet this utopian housing project introduced a logic of spatiality that was not entirely in sync with Vietnamese visions of urban futurity and socialist nation building.

RISING FROM RUIN: CEREMONIAL BEGINNINGS

> Stones can make people docile and knowable.
>
> —MICHEL FOUCAULT, *DISCIPLINE AND PUNISH*, 1977

On May 1, 1974, at the site of the most ambitious housing project in the country and before a crowd of government officials, planners, and workers from Vietnam and East Germany, the Minister of Construction, Đỗ Mười, laid the first bricks to rebuild Vinh (see figure 6.1).[4] The gesture symbolized an end to the city's dark era of suffering and a new socialist beginning that would radically transform both landscape and urban life. Otto Knauer, a Berlin architect and work unit leader, laid the second round of bricks to symbolize cooperation and included a small vessel with fragments from the wreckage of a downed U.S. bomber—literally, building imperial debris into the infrastructure of the future city (see figure 6.2). The ritual continued with Đinh Thị Bình, an aging heroic mother who used both hands to forcefully press the next set of bricks into place. These symbolic inaugural acts played out for the cameras, laying the foundation for what would become the most visible expression of horizontal solidarity and rational planning to "serve the people" of the city, like the heroic mother who would receive a "gratitude apartment." The resulting built forms showed visual continuity with the rest of the socialist world: high-rise, mass-produced buildings that in Vinh came to be known as Quang Trung housing estate (*khu tiểu*, later *khu chung cư* or *Wohngebiet Quang Trung*), after an eighteenth-century emperor and military general who founded the city (see introduction). And yet those first bricks also foreshadowed an *unfinished* utopia (Lebow 2013). Modern construction technologies would not replace conventional brick buildings to solve the urgent problem of postwar housing. Rather, poor material conditions and conflicting spatial practices inhibited the rapid construction of standardized mass housing, altering the plan and its intended social effects in significant and unpredictable ways.

↑ Figure 6.1 Laying the first brick at block A1, May 1, 1974. Photo by Hồ Xuân Thành.

↑ Figure 6.2 Laying the second brick at block A1, next to vessel with imperial wreckage, May 1, 1974. Vietnam News Agency.

The inaugural ceremony and performance of solidarity that launched the construction of block A1 on International Labor Day took place a year before the master plan for rebuilding Vinh was drafted, even before there was an approved design for the residential complex. Though the project was already beset by delays and obstacles (such as mobilizing labor), specialists also expressed their surprise at the speed with which the project was launched—a clear break from the sluggish bureaucratic rhythms of normative socialist time (McGovern 2017, 12). "It was remarkable to start so quickly—to receive all the necessary permissions, the materials imported, and a thousand workers on site and ready to go," a member of the first cohort of the GDR *Arbeitsgruppe* (work unit) commented. "It was an extraordinary feat!"[5] This language of accelerated time would underscore the urgency of the project of building a new socialist society from the ground up, by hand, brick by brick.

There was also an important performative dimension to the ritual. Bricks are a powerfully affective technology that convey cultural and ideological messages about cities and the people who build, manage, and live in them (Schwenkel 2013). In the groundbreaking ceremony to celebrate the first day of construction, bricks were aspirational objects that unleashed the imagination, inspiring hope for collectively building a better future—as swiftly as possible (and on the charred remains of imperial aggression). And yet, like the visionary planning that I discussed in chapter 5, utopian thinking about housing promised more than could be delivered. The bricks that indexed a definitive end to the *longue durée* of suffering would later signify a suspended modernity experienced as delay. This was because utopias tend to be "little concerned with pragmatically conceived realism" (Bauman 1976, 13), even as they aspire to the *possibly* possible. Building with bricks—the go-to manual technology that was used despite efforts to mechanize the building materials industry—revealed this condition and contradiction in Vinh.

In this chapter, I transition from the abstract technological artifacts of urban planning to the proximate and intimate spaces of mass housing by examining the construction of the Quang Trung housing estate (hereafter, Quang Trung). This planned living environment and architectural experiment, which was customized for local living conditions, embodied the functionalist ideals of the rational city and showcased East German technical ingenuity. The poem "High-Rise in Vinh," excerpted in interlude 4, captures the social and spatial world that broke with previous forms of dwelling and produced new sensory and material encounters with the rebuilt city. The design of the complex also enabled municipal authorities to institute new forms of social regulation and spatial control. Foucault (1977) observed how architecture had been deployed as a tool of governance to manage populations since the end of the eighteenth century. Like the school, hospital, prison, and factory, the housing estate in Vinh, with its similar panoptic spatiality, emerged as a key technology of state power and discipline.

As the first standardized housing blocks to be built in the region, Quang Trung complex became the prototype for modern (*hiện đại*) and civilized (*văn minh*) living quarters for workers and their families in Vinh, if not all Vietnam. Yet the apartments provoked ambivalence among residents, officials, and designers of different ranks. Efforts to foster equality and collective consciousness through standardization proved more difficult than anticipated. As ruined spaces were transformed into more comfortable and secure living environments, so too would people—especially rural migrants—be made into productive socialist persons. However, different approaches to socialism led to disagreements about the *type* of person and society that built forms should create.

For officials, the inaugural ceremony for Quang Trung signified the dawn of technological modernity and an age of deepening global integration, not isolation, as scholars are quick to claim about postwar Vietnam. Thereafter, solidarity could be seen, felt, and sensed in the urban fabric, from the buildings' materiality to the construction technologies distributed across the city. As the mayor of Vinh claimed, "Every stone, every house in the new Vinh represents our collaborative work and the deep friendship between our countries."[6] Contrary to Foucault's claim, these stones did not make Vietnamese officials docile and beholden to GDR support. As I show in this chapter, behind the drafted plan, conflicting spatial rationalities and ideologies of dwelling resulted in comprehensive changes to the design, construction, and allocation of modernist housing.

STANDARDIZATION: THE SOCIALIST HOUSING ESTATE

There are surprisingly few ethnographic studies of socialist housing estates, or microrayons as they are also called, despite their ubiquity across the former Soviet Union and Eastern Europe.[7] Microrayons were the building blocks for organizing and governing socialist society (D. Smith 1996, 74). They were prefabricated, state-managed settlements that housed large segments of urban populations and exemplified the imperative to standardize society.[8] Nestled between major streets, each large-scale, high-density complex was self-contained and grouped around basic amenities, including schools, markets, parks, and clinics—"everything right under your nose" (*Alles vor der Nase*), one man described of the GDR's showcase new town of Halle-Neustadt.[9] Because they could be built quickly and efficiently with costs kept low, socialist regimes prioritized their construction. Standardization was not only a practical solution to Europe's post-WWII housing crisis; it was also considered a moral responsibility (Lampland 2009). With housing framed as a universal right, uniformity presented the appearance of equality and the undoing of class distinctions (Fischer 1962). Industrial production of housing offered healthy, modern living environments for all, not only a select few (Molnár 2010, 62). Citizens of different social and occupational backgrounds would live side by side with equal access to infrastructure and the same functional floor plan. Though hierarchies and stratification persisted (Szelenyi 1983), to live in a modern microrayon at the time was a matter of pride and privilege. This contrasted with the stigma of living in public housing in the capitalist West, especially in the United States, where "towers in the park" quickly became racialized spaces of exclusion (Fennell 2015).

Historians have been more prolific than ethnographers in addressing socialist housing estates.[10] Despite the slogan "national in form, socialist in content," which captured the importance of local architectural expression to nation building, these histories point to commonalities in scale, form, and meaning across socialist urban spaces. Nevertheless, GDR experts promoted socialism's version of "glocalization" in Vinh by emphasizing the indigenization of development.[11] For example, the Construction Plan for Quang Trung aimed to strike a balance between modernity and tradition, suggesting internationalism tinged with a regional Vietnamese identity that was closely tied to nature: "All high-rises [in the residential area of Quang Trung] should combine modern socialist architecture with a national motif. They should have colorful accents . . . and the possibility to incorporate artistic works, flower gardens, and water fountains."[12] Today, one must look carefully to detect these "localized" details—such as a rice stalk that commemorates the first co-designed housing block, A5 (see figure 6.3), alongside the emblem "VĐ," which stood for Vietnamese-German (Việt Đức) solidarity (see figure 3.1). Such marks were intended to bring "local characteristics" to the unfamiliar vertical landscape emerging in the city center. Some residents were enchanted; others were perplexed.

One similarity in these historical accounts of socialist estates is the relationship between the provision of affordable, modern housing and the appearance of good governance. The speed and efficiency with which governments

↑ Figure 6.3 Vietnamese "accents" to block housing, 2011. Photo by the author.

addressed postwar housing crises were closely tied to their political legitimacy. Replacing rubble and voids with towering, modern buildings signaled a return to stability and normalcy in everyday life, and perhaps a dawning prosperity. As Paul Betts has argued of East Germany, the construction of mass housing not only augmented the state's credibility; it also conveyed the material benefits of a centrally planned economy (2008, 97–99). In the intimacy of their new urban dwellings, residents experienced—materially and sensorially—the utopian promises of socialist modernity.

Proactive government responses to housing shortages indicated concern for people's welfare, even in the face of bureaucratic indifference. As a tool of governance, state-sanctioned architecture was employed to improve health and living conditions while regulating conduct and productivity (Foucault 1980, 148). On the surface, people appeared to consent to the state's penetration into the intimate sphere of daily life: in the Soviet Union, as in Vietnam, families embraced the opportunity to move out of collective housing and into self-contained apartments (Attwood 2017, 246; Harris 2013), though in Vinh some found single-family housing lonely and alienating, as stated in the poem in interlude 4. Although there were large, open spaces for communal activities, the nuclear family was the basic unit of social organization in housing estates (May 2003, 65). In Vinh, the GDR's emphasis on single-family households a full decade before the shift in policy to a "family economy," or *kinh tế gia đình*, raised concerns among the Vietnamese officials who sought a balance between housing need and supply in an era of collectivization.

While providing assurance that the government was concerned with people's welfare, housing estates were also a spatial technology of control intended to create new socialist men and women (Crowley and Reid 2002). They did so by promoting a new way of life that affirmed the moral-political order of the socialist city. One GDR planner explained the larger task at hand: "We asked ourselves what kind of urban lifestyle did we want to develop [in Vinh]?"[13] In the Soviet Union, as in Vietnam, housing estates were explicitly civilizing projects to turn backward peasants into modern urban workers (Zavisca 2012, 28; Lebow 2013). These transformed men and women would be rational, forward looking, healthful, educated, productive, nonsuperstitious, and loyal to the regime. Trained in the arts of modern urban living, they would constitute "new cultured families" (*gia đình văn hóa mới*), whose happiness was secured through material comfort, social integration, and physical well-being in simple yet orderly households (see figure 6.4). As cultural histories of microrayons show, architectural façades and building interiors were equally important mechanisms of disciplinary power (Buchli 2013, 119). So, too, were discourses of the happy family, Sara Ahmed reminds us (2010, 45), which circulated through objects, such as photographs. Home furnishings became visual markers of both happy families and *fulfilled* material needs. Like standardized housing blocks, generic interiors reflected prescribed tastes (Bourdieu 1984), which indicated equality and abundance (Fehérváry 2012, 617). They also played a "decisive role in the larger Cold War struggle for ideological legitimacy" (Betts 2008, 98; see also Castillo 2010). Vietnamese officials, however, were uneasy about the growing consumer mentality in socialist Europe (see chapters 4 and 5). The emphasis on material accumulation to create a homey living environment suggested the spread of bourgeois domestic values that mimicked commodity fetishism in the West (Buchli 1999, 42).

Cultural histories of housing estates also emphasize a profoundly different experience of space that broke with previous modalities and sensibilities of dwelling. Residents were enthusiastic to leave behind the less favorable material and affective qualities of past dwellings for a brighter, more modern, and gratifying future.[14] There was a novelty to life in these high-density complexes, especially at first, when people were escaping miserable postwar living conditions. Aside from infrastructural improvements, large-scale architectural interventions dramatically altered sensorial encounters and

↑ Figure 6.4 Showcasing hominess and hygiene in new housing, 1978. BArch DH 1/ Bild-28568-10-06.

aesthetic sensibilities (Molnár 2010, 70), something that Foucault overlooks in his architectural analysis of space and power. As Eli Rubin observed of residents in the mass housing settlement of Marzahn in eastern Berlin, "Almost every aspect of their sensory worlds was new," including new sounds, smells, views, angles, sightlines, shadows, vegetation, and distances (2016, 77). Across Eastern Europe and the Soviet Union, these sensorial encounters were closely tied to relocation from inner cities (or rural areas) to unsettled urban edges, where microrayons tended to be built. This was not the case in Vinh, however. There, Quang Trung housing estate was located within the parameters of the city center, to separate the workplace from social reproduction.

EXPORTING TECHNOLOGIES: *PLATTE* IN VIETNAM

Another critical difference between the housing estates examined in the literature and the one in Vinh was prefabrication (*Vorfertigung*; *đúc sẵn*). This building technology came to define the socialist urban landscape as it was disseminated, adopted, modified, and applied across the Soviet Bloc. Often referred to as panel construction or *Plattenbau* (*Platte* for short; *pa nen* or *lắp ghép*), prefabrication was considered the most resourceful building strategy to deliver modern, mass-produced housing: concrete modular components—from large slabs to small decorative elements—were manufactured in factories then transported to construction sites for assembly into complete structures. Rows of prefabricated panel blocks came to signify the gray dreariness of socialism's concrete jungles (Fehérváry 2013). Yet as Kimberly Zarecor observes, the "most intensive research and experimentation" in socialist urban architecture occurred with precast building technologies (2011, 225). This experimentation unfolded amidst a Cold War techno-political rivalry, in which socialist infrastructure was built in competition with the capitalist West. Prefabricated construction also sparked rivalry between socialist countries and even resistance to Soviet models as planners developed their own prototypes (Molnár 2010, 68). A rapid and efficient architectural solution to Europe's own postwar housing crisis, the "prefab" model was exported to postcolonial countries—including Afghanistan (Beyer 2012)—where it standardized the construction industry and showcased socialism's technological ascendance.

East Germany promoted customized prefabrication in Vietnam as a viable building solution to place annihilation and to assert its technical dominance in the panel construction industry. Notably, it was the first to do so on a large scale, before even the Soviet Union.[15] Prefabrication was fairly new to Vietnam,[16] and its promise to quickly and cheaply produce standard mass housing appealed to government officials, given the urgent need (Phạm Văn Đồng 1977, 50). Architects were more skeptical. The first concrete panel factory initiative, launched in the early 1970s at Đạo Tú, held high political value for the GDR.[17] And yet panel construction in Vietnam was another poignant example of the disconnect between an imagined future and present reality. After its inauguration in 1977, the factory was projected to build one thousand apartments annually of fifty-eight square meters each. A retired architect from the Ministry of Construction who had studied in the Soviet Union maintained that these figures were far too ambitious. Because of aerial bombardment, little technical infrastructure remained; there were material shortages, few trained workers, and no passable roads linking the remote factory with the city. Moreover, cultural unfamiliarity among the population made prefabricated technologies challenging to transfer to Vietnam: "Panel housing was a foreign design that did not fit at all with Vietnamese ways of living."[18] Cultural and technological incompatibility meant that brick construction remained the standard, and the

← Figure 6.5 "Midday dreams of a lazy lad." *Lao Động News*, August 9, 1975.

imperative to modernize the building industry through *Plattenbau* was put on hold (see figure 6.5).

There were similar difficulties with the concrete factory built on the southern edge of Vinh in 1975, which was intended to produce prefabricated building parts for Quang Trung and surrounding industry. Given the constrained technological capacity at the time, this factory did not include large panel construction (as attempted at Đạo Tú), though authorities in Hanoi had proposed such a plant in early negotiations with East Germany.[19] Prefabrication was considered instrumental to maintaining *Bautempo*, or speed of construction, to sustain the pace of progress and recovery. And yet, as in Hanoi, the technology did not fit with the conditions of postwar Vinh, even for basic components of modular design. Transport was an issue, steel for molds was in short supply, machinery was lacking, and workers—70 percent of them women

(Nguyen et al. 1974, 4)—urgently needed training to shift from building by hand to machine-based manufacture.[20] In the end, infrastructural limitations meant that Platte in Vinh—despite their striking similarity to those in Eastern Europe—were not Platte at all but made of brick (see figure 6.6). Before the concrete factory became operational in 1976, precasting for concrete beams, plates, slabs, and other modular components was done onsite with wooden molds, and materials were carried by hand or bamboo yoke until heavy machinery and equipment became available (see figure 6.7). As one Vietnamese engineer joked with me of the project's early years, these were not efficient, high-tech, concrete panel buildings whatsoever, but labor-intensive, conventional structures assembled with manually prefabricated parts.

Despite being made of brick, the rows of multistory buildings across the city center symbolized Vinh's "rise from the ashes" (*tăng từ đống tro tàn*) of war. To understand how this architectural form and spatial organization impacted people's lives and provoked ambivalent reactions, I turn to Vietnamese housing policy and the dwellings that existed before.

ON THE HOUSING QUESTION IN VIETNAM

After World War II, housing emerged as a strategic Cold War policy instrument. Capitalist countries promoted private home ownership as the path to prosperity and self-fulfillment and even exported this model to promote democracy (Kwak 2015). Socialist countries, on the other hand, provided centralized, affordable housing to achieve stability and equality, and also promoted their model overseas. One East German architect who spent two years in Vietnam explained the *Wohnungspolitik* (housing politics) that the team brought to Vinh: "No privatization, everything should be state-given. Each person had the right to an apartment to help support production: *eine*, nicht *seine* [*one* (apartment) not *his*]. The goal was a better life for people."[21] Vietnamese leaders likewise proposed abolishing capitalism and redistributing land to solve their housing question, not unlike Engels's (1979) proposal a century earlier.

Although the right to housing is enshrined in the Vietnamese constitution, there was no centralized government response to the critical need for postwar housing, unlike the mass construction of *Khrushchyovka* (prefabricated panel or brick) flats in the Soviet Union in the 1960s or the *Wohnungsbauprogramm* (residential housing program) in East Germany in the 1970s. Leaders such as Phạm Văn Đồng did press for the rapid construction of permanent dwellings to enable people to resettle with their families and enjoy social stability (1977, 48). The second Five-Year Plan (1976–1980) called for fourteen million square

↑ Figure 6.6 Brickwork beneath a *Plattenbau* façade of block A5, circa 1975. BArch DH 1/Bild-28566-07B-01.

↑ Figure 6.7 Prefabrication of building components on site, 1974. Vietnam News Agency.

meters of residential housing to be built, of which six million were to be in cities and close to industry in provinces hit hard by U.S. air strikes. But it did not explain how this plan should be carried out. Rather, solving the housing crisis fell largely to local governments, which delegated responsibility to the workplace. Until this time, urban housing policy mirrored the Chinese collectivist model of the *danwei*, in which employers were responsible for fulfilling workers' basic needs, including accommodation. David Bray argues that the danwei in China offered members a sense of belonging and identity by providing a "complete social guarantee" of welfare services (2005, 4–5). Owing to wartime conditions, employers in Vietnam were unable to provide fully for their brigades (*đội*) and units (*tổ*), but they did offer simple provisions. This system of paternalism that was so integral to socialism, with its "quasi-familial dependency" between subject and state (Verdery 1996, 63; see also Siegelbaum 1998), had been in place in Vietnam since the end of French colonialism. This was a time when the drive for industrialization—and for achieving revolutionary social transformation—created jobs for migrant workers, who needed housing close to industry.

Like the danwei in China, the work unit in Vietnam was the center of cultural, material, and political life. Retired female workers who were my neighbors in Quang Trung—many of them had helped to build the blocks—explained that the workplace afforded an important sense of social cohesion, care, and belonging, especially in times of hardship. The emphasis on the communal—rather than the individual or the nuclear family—was instrumental to subject formation and to the operation of state power in the workplace. As Bray argues of the danwei, the work brigade was a "highly determined, regularized, and ordered spatial unit" that promoted the collectivization of daily life (2005, 9). In Vinh, it was also a space of spontaneity and blurred boundaries, contrary to functional urban planning introduced by GDR experts. For example, the state-run mechanics factory employed around three hundred workers from surrounding rural districts. The land allocated to this operation was used for industry, housing, sport, and agriculture. Workers were expected to become self-sufficient, particularly during the war and postwar subsidy years, when collective farming was necessary to supplement government rations. They also bore responsibility for housing construction.

For state agencies and enterprises, the solution to the housing crisis was collective housing (*nhà tập thể*). These were often rudimentary, single-story structures with shared facilities in the *nhà cấp IV* (housing level IV) style: the most basic shelter, according to state building standards ratified in 1969 known as TC-36–69. Occasionally they had two or three stories and were made of brick.[22] During and after the war, when construction materials were lacking, the structures were made of scavenged wood, thatch, and bamboo, and they had neither water nor electricity. In interviews, retired state employees—including former university faculty, civil servants at the Department of Culture, and workers at the confectionary factory—recollected how their brigades had worked collectively to build the makeshift nhà tập thể, before they were allocated modern apartments in the housing complex. They recalled the overcrowded living conditions without amenities during and after evacuation, when several people or families occupied single rooms. Winters were cold, and the winds and rains penetrated the porous walls, leaving them vulnerable to illness. These were unhygienic, noisy, and uncomfortable living conditions, but still legal, according to the building code.

For example, Ms. Lan, a bricklayer for Construction Company 1, returned from building roads on the Hồ Chí Minh Trail to work on the construction of Quang Trung. She shared a small room in the company's nhà tập thể with five to six other women. They took their meals communally at the workplace canteen, so there was no need for a kitchen. This cost her 21 VND per month, almost half her monthly income of 45 VND.[23] She married an older supervisor at Construction Company 2 (with earnings of 68 VND per month), who had been tortured at Côn Đảo prison for five years for his anticolonial activities.[24] He had also been a representative at the Quang Trung groundbreaking ceremony in 1974. After their marriage, the couple was allotted a collective family unit (*tập thể gia đình*) in block A3, where they continued to live through my fieldwork.[25]

Nhà tập thể were not the great equalizer, however, and not all state employees lived in them. Unmarried recruits, the vast majority of them low-skilled female workers from rural villages, as well as young families with absent husbands who had gone to war, typically lived in collective housing. Other families with access to land or with male heads of households—typically managers from the city—lived in provisional structures (*nhà tạm*) of wood and thatch. These tended to be randomly dispersed around the collective housing facilities but in close proximity to the workplace. According to a male supervisor for Nghệ An Pharmaceuticals, "At that time, people could lay claim to any piece of land, but only if they had the means to build their own shelter."[26] Male family members ventured into the forests to fell trees and gather bamboo for the rafters. "Women couldn't do this difficult labor alone," he claimed, though women then proceeded to help build the homes. This housing strategy reflected social divisions of labor in the workplace rooted in essentialist notions of gender and sexual difference, and in hierarchies between town and country:

many urban administrators had not been sent to war, unlike the husbands of low-skilled migrant workers. These divisions laid the foundation for gender disparities in housing access, as a claim to workplace land, in practice, required the presence of a male head of household.

Those with *nhà tạm* were fortunate in many ways, and that privilege accompanied evacuees when they returned to the city and were assigned a new domicile, as *nhà tạm* served as evidence of familial self-sufficiency. To illustrate the complex housing situation before Quang Trung was built, I offer the life history of a man who grew up on the outskirts of Vinh through a biography of his family house. I call him Bác, for "uncle," the term he used in our interview.[27] Bác was born in Vinh in 1950 and grew up in a fairly well-off family whose plot of land was large enough to require ten hired farmhands. He spent his early childhood in a spacious five-room thatch house (*nhà tranh*) with courtyard garden and orchard out back. During land reform, his family was categorized as a "medium landowner" (*chủ vừa*). Their land was seized, split up, and reallocated, reducing the holding from thirty-five hundred to five hundred acres. Because they were not considered wealthy (*giàu*), but only middle class (*khá*), no family member was tried in court. The house was burnt during the scorched-earth policy of the VIỆT MINH in the anticolonial war against the French. It was rebuilt after 1954 as a more modest, three-room shelter, also made of thatch.

Bác evacuated after the first bombs struck Vinh in August 1964. Throughout the air war, his mother worked alongside other women in an agricultural cooperative (*hợp tác xã*). Because his father, a civil servant, was required to stay in the city, the house was never abandoned, which saved it from squatters (chapter 5). Bác studied in his host village through the tenth grade before going to war. Though "no one wanted to go to the front," he was expected to do so as the eldest son. While the family's house was not bombed directly, it was damaged from attacks on neighboring factories and required rebuilding. In 1975, after the war, Bác studied chemistry in Hanoi at Bách Khoa University. Upon graduating, he accepted a job as a technician at the state chemical factory in Vinh. Because the plant was not far from his residence, he was given permission (as a bachelor) to live in the family's rebuilt nhà tranh, which over time they renovated to make larger and more durable (*kiên cố*). Bác explained that his situation was unique: the majority of factory workers, mostly women from the countryside, lived in the nhà tập thể. By his estimate, fewer than 10 percent of workers had the means to live independent of collective housing.

Workers typically aspired to having their own freestanding home. Despite having such a house, Bác envied the "elites" who were allocated an apartment in Quang Trung. "They were the tallest buildings we had seen in Vinh until then, and considered very modern," compared to his simple thatch house, he explained. To understand how a foreign-designed housing estate became the face of the city (*bộ mặt*), as Bác called it, and appeared, at least initially, to reverse workplace housing disparities, I turn to the negotiations that led to standardized mass housing organized around the nuclear family.

FROM THE COLLECTIVE TO THE INDIVIDUAL: COMPETING IDEAS OF MASS HOUSING

High-density housing had already been suggested as a solution to the postwar housing crisis even before GDR experts arrived, but on a much smaller scale. In November 1970, provincial architects proposed constructing a *khu tập kết*, or collective residential complex, in the city center, on the former site of the colonial railway station. The station was ruined during the French War and rebuilt on the edge of town in the early 1960s. This left twenty hectares of land largely vacant, save a few makeshift repair shops. Building a high-density settlement on this site meant that no compensation (*đền bù*) for homeowners would be necessary, although documents showed there were indeed families who had settled on this property.[28] Architects drafted a plan to build interim accommodation in low-rise, *nhà cấp IV* style for 3,410 cadres and state employees, while more stable workplace housing was constructed for returning evacuees, thus maintaining the danwei-like system.[29] The adoption of the term *khu tập kết* to describe the vision showed a different housing approach from that of Eastern Europe and the Soviet Union. It also differed from the model in Hanoi, of brick, multistory collective housing blocks in a single compound, or *khu tập thể* (classified as housing level III). Those in Hanoi typically had a shared kitchen, washroom, and latrine on each floor, more like the Soviet communal dwellings of the Stalin era (Trinh and Nguyen 2001, 53). By contrast, the proposed *khu tập kết* in Vinh would initially be transitory, single-story collectives (nhà tập thể) before more permanent housing could be built. The planned provision of space—twenty hectares of land for more than three thousand residents averaging sixty square meters per person—raised eyebrows among officials who rejected the plan.

Provincial planners introduced a modified proposal in the three-year plan (1973–1975) for rebuilding postwar Vinh. This roadmap for social and economic rehabilitation described the grave situation and need for immediate action: "The war of destruction carried out by American imperialists flattened

Vinh. All of our factories and enterprises have been annihilated. All public works, agencies, and facilities have been completely ruined. Our technical infrastructure has been heavily damaged, our transportation lines crushed. More than forty thousand square meters of permanent housing have been destroyed. Consequently, the work to recover and rebuild the city to meet the demand for production and the everyday needs of our workers is a matter of critical urgency [*vấn đề cấp thiết*]."[30]

With streams of evacuees returning to the city, housing construction took priority. The three-year plan proposed two options that showed changes from the 1970 proposal. One was temporary modular housing; another was permanent high-rises that would become the architectural façade of the city (*tạo bộ mặt kiến trúc thành phố*). Both remained collective in orientation, as in Hanoi.[31] Planners were advised to take families as well as unmarried workers into consideration—in other words, to think about variegated floor plans rather than spatial uniformity. In collaboration with the Ministry of Construction in Hanoi, planners designed the first set of housing blocks, A1–A4, on the southeastern edge of what would become the housing complex named after Quang Trung.

East German specialists brought an alternative vision. Ideologically, there was consensus between Vietnamese and East Germans: architecture (including housing) was key to governing and creating moral persons (Humphrey 2005). Deterministic thinking about the power of built space to shape socially desirable actions informed planning practice across socialist countries (Crowley and Reid 2002). There was less agreement, however, about the scale, form, and arrangement of space, or the spatial distribution of people.

When the first team of GDR experts arrived in Vinh, they were confronted with an informal and spontaneous built environment that they considered nonprogressive compared with the forward march of modernist architecture and functional planning. Respondents showed me photographs of scattered bamboo huts they first encountered—a cultural and temporal marker of primitivity (Brody 2010, 145). When they visited ruined factories, they saw the overcrowded, thatch nhà tập thể—another crude dwelling—and the integrated spatial unit of the workplace with mixed land use instead of single-function zoning. A review of planning documents also familiarized them with the proposal to create provisional collective housing on a mass scale in the city center. The idea of ephemeral architecture and multifamily dwellings concerned them; their vision of progress and urban futurity centered on permanent, stable buildings that encouraged individual rather than collective forms of living. One senior architect explained:

SA: We spent a lot of time thinking about what type of housing to build and how to create a new urban environment. It was a long discussion. We told the Vietnamese that we would not build anything temporary. . . . We wanted something that would last over the long term. So we proposed five-story, European-style apartment blocks.

CS: Were you concerned that residents might not be accustomed to this type of housing?

SA: Of course we were worried! We knew most people were from the countryside and wanted a freestanding home with a garden for their animals. But that was not practical. We wanted to create a new city, one that could provide a higher standard of living than life in the jungle. We were not there just to rebuild, you know, but to modernize and produce a new way of life.[32]

GDR experts thus dismissed provisional housing as a primitive relic from the past. In contrasting jungle life with their promise of modernity, they endeavored to not only improve living conditions but also to create an entirely new socialist civilization. This standpoint was also reflected in the photographs they showed me that positioned "the past" (thatch dwellings) alongside "the future" (modern housing blocks) within a single frame.[33]

These experts also expressed opposing ideas about spatial organization within the buildings. Their approach reflected a conception of the socialist subject that centered on *individual* cultivation and *self*-mastery to collectively transform society. They strongly advocated against communal dwellings, endorsing small, single-family apartments (*khép kín*) as the beacon of a prosperous society comprising self-realized, socialist persons (Reid 2009, 472). In contrast, the Vietnamese Communist Party emphasized *collective* mastery (*làm chủ tập thể*) as the basis for socialist transformation. As one Vietnamese architect explained, "When the East Germans came, they didn't want to invest in *tập thể* [collective] housing. It wasn't modern and didn't fit with their plan for urbanization."[34] Unlike the Soviet Union, the GDR did not have a history of building communal flats that decentered the nuclear family under the pretext of women's emancipation (Kaminsky 2011, 63). Its post-Stalin regime, however, did embrace a culture of domesticity centered around the nuclear family. Popular desires for the familial over the collective (and over the workplace) were also evident in everyday life; for example, in the aversion to taking communal meals at factory canteens (Weinreb 2017, 133). Shaped by these beliefs, the residential complex that GDR experts proposed would dramatically alter the material and social fabric of Vinh by moving workers and civil servants away from their workplaces and into high-density housing on a much larger scale than the Vietnamese state had envisioned. This was intentional. As I argued in chapter 5, rational planning prescribed the functional division of urban space to maintain social order, with clear lines between industry and housing. Modern urban workers would be more productive, and lead healthier lives, away from the pollution and stress of the workplace, one GDR architect explained. By advocating for a separate, occupationally mixed residential zone, East German planners broke with the spatial logics of the integrated, multifunctional work unit that suggested an incomplete urbanism. In separating work from social life, and the family from the collective, housing would no longer be communal but rather a mass individual experience (Reid 2009, 472).

EXTERIORS: VINH AS URBAN LAB

In *Spaces of Hope*, David Harvey identifies the visionary work of twentieth-century architects and planners, whose glimpses of utopian futurity merged an "intense imaginary of some alternative world" with a pragmatic concern for engineering urban space according to "radically new designs" (2000, 164). In Vinh, this utopian vision found material expression in Quang Trung. Achieving this required that planners turn the city into an urban laboratory, where behavior could be studied in a controlled setting. Much like their colonial predecessors, GDR planners conceived of Vinh as a source of empirical data acquired through observation and experimentation, and with a similar goal: to render the population more legible. In this case, however, experts appropriated colonial forms of knowledge-making to produce socialist epistemologies and predictive behavior-modeling to undo sociospatial inequality.

Turning Vinh into a creative laboratory for Western fantasies of modernity introduced a new scalar metric to the landscape. The *Wohngebiet* project dwarfed the housing proposal in the three-year plan, almost doubling the allotted land from twenty to thirty-four hectares. GDR planners helped design five separate areas of apartment blocks—A, B, C, D, E—spread over two microdistricts separated by Quang Trung Road, a main thoroughfare leading to Hanoi (see figure 6.8). The goal was to house more than fifteen thousand "priority" (*ưu tiên*) citizens, who had made notable contributions to nation building, a number that was almost five times that originally planned. The rapid construction of high-rises that followed would showcase East German scientific ingenuity. The sudden, almost magical appearance of imported technologies across the ruined city—bulldozers, cars, lorries, cranes, hoists, exca-

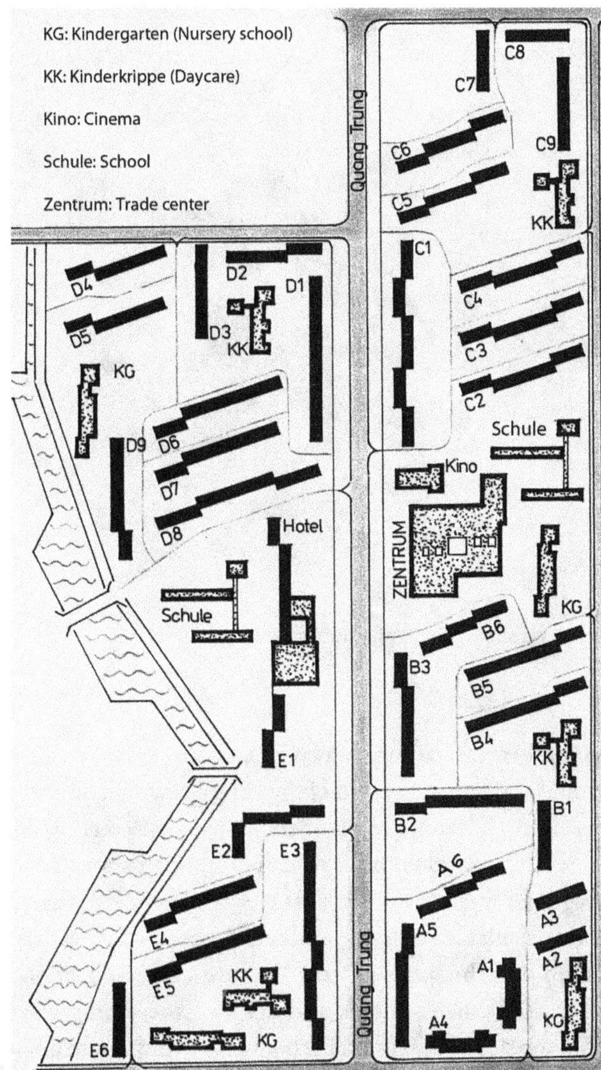

← Figure 6.8 Construction plan for Quang Trung residential complex, with housing blocks and public buildings. Only the east (right-hand) side would be built to completion. Source: Vietnam-Germany Friendship Association of Nghệ An.

vators, stone crushers, pumps, pipes, steel—was evidence of East Germany's technological power and prosperity. Such material abundance, along with knowledgeable experts, reinforced optimism that socialism was indeed the best path to modernization.

Like Le Corbusier's housing lab in Pessac (France), mass housing in Vinh represented a utopian social experiment (Boudon 1972, 2–3), which took the razed city as a site for amassing knowledge to create order out of chaos (Latour and Woolgar 1979, 33).[35] GDR ambitions to create a new society intersected with

↑ Figure 6.9 Quang Trung playground, circa 1978. Courtesy of Raimer Buntrock.

Vietnam's party goals to "build a new cultural way of life," or *xây dựng nếp sống văn hóa mới*. The horizontal and vertical design of the complex would be critical to this ideological project. Horizontally, planners focused on creating an extensive social infrastructure that would improve living standards for workers in the city. As in integrated microrayons in East Germany and elsewhere, public facilities were made available onsite or adjacent to housing to satisfy anticipated needs, including a shopping arcade, daycare centers, schools, youth clubhouse, a refurbished cinema, hotel, and library—everything residents would need to attain the good life. Vertically, high-rise living would offer more housing and more land for communal green spaces, as envisioned by Le Corbusier. Parks and playgrounds meant to uplift and restore the population averaged 1.5 square meters per person.[36] In this ecosocialist approach to urban planning, children, youth, and adults each had their designated commons to encourage sociality while promoting cultural and political activities for nation building (see figure 6.9).

Values of inclusion and egalitarianism were reinforced in designs for technical infrastructure that included new energy, water, and transportation systems. The provision of public utilities and services was to benefit all households equitably: electricity to illuminate homes and streetlights, fresh water and sanitation to enable indoor plumbing, sidewalks and internal access roads to facilitate mobility. This comprehensive approach to design differed from the focus in Hanoi, which prioritized housing construction over infrastructure expansion (Trinh and Nguyen 2001, 52).[37] In Vinh, social and technical infrastructure developed in tandem with housing to produce appropriate urban tastes, habits, and conduct. The shift away from collective dwellings would alter social and family responsibilities; single-family housing with modern amenities would—ostensibly—liberate women from domestic drudgery.

The GDR's "hyper-socialist" (Joppke 1995, 45) plan for Vinh proved too ambitious, however, even with a two-year project extension. The Quang Trung construction project came to an official close at the end of 1980, with twenty-two of the proposed thirty-six blocks completed in areas A, B, and C (and one in D), across twenty hectares, the size of the original 1970 plan. Over fifteen hundred units were allocated to approximately nine thousand tenants comprising the families of workers and civil servants from more than a dozen state factories and government agencies (see table 6.1). Only half the number of daycares and nurseries were built (two out of four in both cases), and half the number of primary and secondary schools, all on the eastern side of Quang Trung. A faltering GDR economy, recurring project delays, and mounting difficulties securing goods through patronage networks led to a decision not to further extend the agreement. This unfinished utopia, which risked East Germany's reputation as a technological leader, was not widely known: a senior architect who had been on-site from 1974 to 1975 continued to insist that the project had been completed, even after I told him otherwise.

Nonetheless, the housing estate brought Vinh national recognition. Its modernist design, rational planning, and ecological efficiency were on a scale that was unprecedented at the time. Curious spectators flocked to Vinh to witness the utopia-in-the-making, posing for photos against the backdrop of multistory buildings stretching into the distance. In 1978, the Ministry of Construction organized a conference in Vinh for a delegation of planning officials from northern provinces, who gazed upon the buildings like "palaces that had dropped from the moon" (*như từ trên cung trăng rơi xuống*), one attendee remembered.[38] With tremendously limited resources, GDR planners had, to all appearances, succeeded where others had failed. Much of the enchantment with the "palaces" could be attributed to what we today call green design, which I have described elsewhere as "eco-socialist planning" (Schwenkel 2017a). This approach adapted modernist styles and architecture originating in Europe to the social and ecological conditions of "the tropics" in Vietnam.

Table 6.1. Projected and realized housing.

Area	Blocks Proposed	Flats Proposed	Projected Tenants	Blocks Built
A	6	220*	2,180	6
B	6	420	2,310	6
C	9	880	3,870	9
D	9	920	4,140	1
E	6	500	2,535	0
Total	**36**	**2,940**	**15,035**	**22**

*Excludes blocks A1 and A4, used as office and hotel space.

ECOLOGICAL RATIONALISM

Blueprints from 1974 show how material reconstruction and environmental regeneration were inextricably linked. To accommodate Vinh's resource limitations, architects worked with landscape engineers to scrupulously design the Quang Trung grounds according to careful, systematic research they conducted on sustainable construction. Influenced by German public health discourses that emphasized ventilation as fundamental to "socialist hygienic modernity" (Hong 2015, 125), they amassed a vast store of scientific knowledge about Vinh, including meteorological data on its notoriously variable climate. With an eye to making the tropics familiar, they charted temperature patterns going back to 1907; wind frequency, strength, and direction; sun position, cloud cover, and shadow length; and correlations between human comfort and atmospheric pressure and humidity. They tracked, analyzed, correlated, and applied these findings to design climate-compatible (*klimagerecht*) housing.

These efforts to reconcile the built and natural environments made Quang Trung unique. In the resulting final plan, housing blocks were spaced at a calculated distance of one or more times the building height and arranged in a zigzag pattern at an angle of twenty-three degrees to facilitate air circulation (see figures 6.8 and 6.11). This differed from the rectilinear designs and sharp right angles of Hanoi's smaller and more compact housing complexes, which paid less attention to lighting and ventilation (Koh 2006, 210; see also conclusion). In Vinh, the nonlinear pattern along the east-west axis channeled the cooler northeast winds in summer, when the hot dry "Lao winds" were in full force, to act as a passive cooling system, or natural *Klimatisierung*. The blocks had a northwest orientation with a horizontal row design and shared external corridor (see plate 5), which protected units from the sun and encouraged *Querlüftung*, or cross ventilation. This orientation also provided natural lighting to lessen demand for already scarce electricity. Cultivation of native plants and trees around the housing blocks and complex perimeter, and along pathways, helped reduce solar heat gain in the apartments, while offering shade for assembly in the large open spaces between buildings. The use of sun and wind was considered healthful and hygienic: light and ventilation purified the air, reducing illness and exposure to smoke from wood-fire cooking, and helped control dampness and mold, especially in the cold, wet winters. From a legal point of view, the blocks complied with the standards of the housing code.

Local planners and architects praised the "science of wind" (*khoa học gió*) that informed the design and compared it with the Vietnamese practice of geomancy (*phong thủy*). Residents tended to agree. Some interpreted the staggered positioning of the housing blocks as an attempt by East German engineers to follow phong thủy principles. Others understood the spatial organization as a symbolic gesture of solidarity. When seen from above, several people told me, the shape of the buildings spelled out "Việt Đức" (Vietnam-Germany), inscribing the bonds of friendship onto the urban fabric.[39] East German experts chuckled when they heard these interpretations and denied any intention to act as geomancers, though they recognized that phong thủy shared similarities with their approach to *Energiesparen* (saving energy) and *Durchlüftung* (ventilation). And yet, green design could not be reduced to materialist or functionalist explanations of nonexistent infrastructure alone. Planners used urban ecology to improve welfare beyond the material and infrastructural constraints they faced, and to offer workers a reprieve. Parks, playgrounds, a central fountain, and a refurbished stadium helped create some sense of urban normalcy through leisure; this would ideally lead to increased labor productivity and urban sensibilities deemed desirable for urban proletarians.

The analysis of cultural habits and responses to climate conditions was an equally important component of eco-socialist design. This involved the application of ethnographic methods to observe daily practices, forms of sociality, and patterns of mobility to render the population knowable. GDR architects described to me their emic approach and efforts to "listen to what the Vietnamese wanted" or "see how workers lived," and to translate their needs into the built environment to "provide the best living situation possible." While they deployed scientific knowledge practices that were analogous to those used by colonial urbanists (Wright 1991, 6), if not contemporary sociologists, their objectives—emancipation not subjugation—clearly differed, even as postcolonial subjects became objects of knowledge for state-making projects in distinctly similar ways.

On the one hand, attention to local knowledge and dwelling practices distinguished embedded East German experts from other foreign planners, who exhibited strong paternalistic tendencies in their disregard of local epistemes.[40] On the other hand, their intimate knowledge produced Orientalist assessments of Vietnamese culture, such as claims that Vietnamese lived "closer to nature," a classic colonial trope of the native Other. Making the Vietnamese sociologically legible also rendered them abstract figures performing rote activity in flattened, two-dimensional space (Lefebvre 1991, 313). Planners undertook empirical studies that analyzed the ratio of time spent on work, recreation, and domestic responsibilities, with attention to kinship and gender relations. The diagrams, charts, and graphs that they then created as part of their repertoire of knowledge practices reduced housing design to a set of standardized calculations, formulas, and representations devoid of conflict and variation (see figure 6.10).[41] Susan Leigh Star and Martha Lampland point to the "enormous amount of work needed to stabilize knowledge, freeze action, [and] delete outliers" so that standards become common sense and an expression of authority (2009, 13–14). Similarly, sociological studies of Vietnamese lifestyles led to enhanced design, which in turn enabled new forms of state power. Air circulation, for example, enabled surveillance (Corbain 1986, 94): the row design with front corridor access created panoptic conditions for surveillants to peer into homes, I learned after moving into block C2 when the warden's assistant summoned me to a party meeting through my window (upon looking into my home, he reacted quickly: "Whoops—wrong person!").

Standardization was often based on idealized or projected indicators rather than objective or actual situations (Star and Lampland 2009, 24). Take, for example, the walk-out basement (*gầm*) that GDR architects designed. Vietnamese residences typically have a first floor that is level with the street, so people can sweep out their houses or convert them to storefronts. But based on their meteorological and cultural models that separated work from living (as per single-use zoning), GDR planners worried about typhoons, floods, and dirt; consequently, they put the first story on top of a 1.5-meter-high gầm to reduce the risk of flooding and to allow fresh air and light to enter the flats. "It was purely for climate-related purposes," one architect claimed. "Although it could also be used for storing bicycles," he added, referring to commuting methods observed in their study.[42] There were few bicycles at the time, however, and most people walked several miles to work because their housing

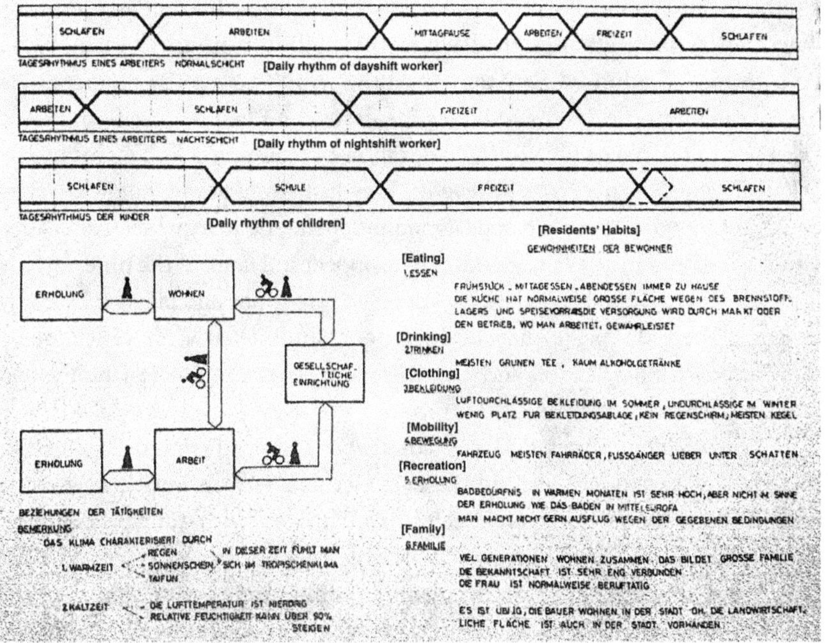

↑ Figure 6.10 Vinh as lab: Vietnamese daily habits and mobility tracked across time and space. Courtesy of Dr. Hans-Ulrich Mönnig.

had been moved away from the worksite to the city center between industrial areas. Despite the careful calculations of functional planning, this meant they had *less* time for recreation. Bikes were shared (or went to the experts), and no one would store them in the gầm anyway, since "locks were scarce and thieves a-plenty."[43] "I liked the idea of the gầm, but I didn't own anything to put in it. And I still don't!" the man who had been tortured at Côn Đảo prison told me.[44] Despite the efforts of GDR planners to incorporate Vietnamese knowledge and cultural practices into spatial planning, there remained conflicting ideas about how to design and make optimal use of space.

INTERIORS: DEBATING STANDARDIZATION

The presence of the Deputy Minister of Construction at the 1978 conference in Vinh concretized Quang Trung as a model of modern housing for the rest of the country, especially Hanoi. "At the time, it was the most ideal residential complex in Vietnam. It set new standards for the future," one Vietnamese architect remembered.[45] "It was meticulous planning [*quy hoạch tỉ mỉ*]," said another, who oversaw the plan's execution.[46] "It was just like in East Germany, where everything was designed with accessibility in mind to easily fulfill your needs." "I admired how they used the wind to keep the temperatures low," a planner reflected, "and it was the first time I had seen self-contained [*khép kín*] flats."[47] For the visiting delegation of planning officials, this utopia (*không tưởng*) was not to be believed: "They just gazed at the buildings. They could not imagine that we had designed independent apartments [*căn hộ độc lập*]!" Self-contained flats were starting to appear in Hanoi at the time, but the buildings there were seen as lacking adequate provisions and plagued by faulty design.[48] There was pride on both sides: poor, annihilated Vinh was suddenly more modern than Hanoi, and East Germany—not the Soviet Union—had helped to propel it there.

The enchanted professionals I quoted above knew this model well: all of them had seen and experienced the East German *Wohnkomplex* (residential complex) in situ as either architecture students or study-tour participants. Both groups had been impressed by the high living standards of East Germany: the spacious and orderly planned communities with shops, parks, schools, and trees, as well as modern housing with single-family dwellings. These specialists embraced the architectonics of the *Wohnkomplex* as an answer to Vietnam's housing crisis, though not without mediation. I asked one lead planner what had to change to make the design more appropriate for Vinh. He corrected me: "This was a cooperation; it was not the work of Germans. Their model needed to be adapted [*thích ứng*] to Vietnamese conditions and climate. It had to conform to Vietnamese standards."[49]

Conforming to Vietnamese standards often meant there were clashes between different conceptions of the urban and of relationships between people and inhabited space. Governance through design meant that banal matters, such as floor plans, had high political stakes. Like other forms of bureaucratic management, Vietnam's housing code provided detailed regulations for the planning, construction, and occupation of collective and single-family housing. These were devised to mitigate risk and promote optimal health and safety conditions across four housing categories (levels I–IV), each with its own criteria. GDR planners took these standards seriously in designing the housing blocks and individual units. And yet even with standardization, there remained considerable variation. As Lampland has argued, to standardize is not to homogenize: standardizing procedures always entail "complex techniques of differentiation" (2009, 124). This is an especially important observation to make for mass housing, which is routinely associated with drab uniformity and lack of innovation.

In fact, design variability (*Gestaltungsvariabilität*) was written into the Quang Trung construction plan, to create a "memorable urban ensemble" (*einprägsames städtisches Ensemble*).[50] Le Corbusier also used this tactic in planning at Pessac: "multiplicity in unity" was a way to reconcile desire for diversity with the need for serial production (Boudon 1972, 11). I noticed this multiplicity during my preliminary fieldwork visits to Quang Trung and observed them more closely when I lived in the housing blocks in 2010–2011. At a glance, they appear identical; foreigners who passed through Vinh often commented on this upon hearing where I conducted research. But in fact each building had some distinctive characteristic, such as a unique façade, design, or assembly method (see figure 6.11). There was a spatial pattern with some repetition to the small-group arrangement of housing blocks (such as B4–B5, C2–C4, and C5–C6). But the only consistent feature was height (five stories or twenty-five meters), and even that varied slightly between blocks with and without a gầm (A1–A4 in the latter case). The blocks *were* mass-produced: the basic building component was the *đơn nguyên* (*đơn* for short), or modular building unit. But eight typologies allowed for various configurations. Each đơn typically had twenty flats (four per floor), with some exceptions in area C. These freestanding units could be assembled, reversed, and conjoined to create nonlinear and nonaligned patterns that formed a distinct design (see C1 with its five alternating units). This architectural flexibility shows how Quang Trung emerged as a space of experimentation. Its design and assembly were marked by change and contingency—similar to contemporary notions of "urban labs" (Karvonen and Van Heur 2014), but not in the service of capital accumulation.

There was also spatial diversity inside the apartments, but this was only visible with more intimate knowledge of the housing blocks. Once I started surveys and interviews across areas A, B, and C with my team of student researchers, I observed a surprising number of floor plan variations. My informants identified two broad building typologies: *kiểu Đức* or "German style," and *kiểu Việt Nam* or "Vietnamese style." These styles mapped onto other distinctions that reproduced hierarchies between the GDR and the DRV, and also within Vietnamese society. Though Quang Trung emerged as a shining beacon of Vietnam's renewal and leap to socialist modernity, not all housing blocks in the complex were created equal. And while Vietnamese experts and provincial authorities gloated about the advanced ecological design of complex *exteriors*—interpreted as phong thủy by residents who added altars to the corridors to appease the wandering spirits (see plate 6)—there was less agreement about the *interiors* of the buildings.

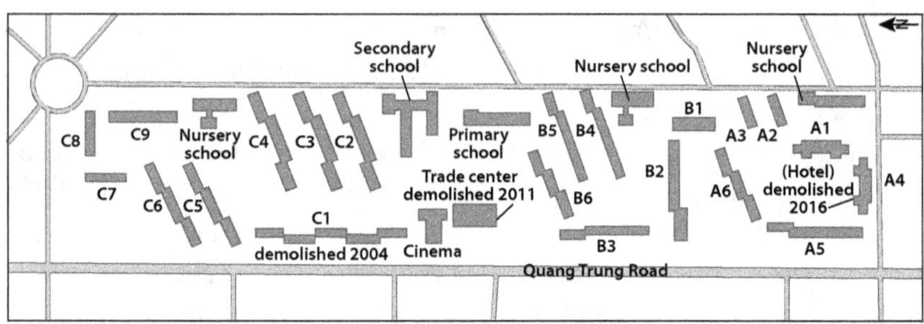

↑ Figure 6.11 Quang Trung's heterogeneous housing blocks. Situation as of 2017. Cartography by Jutta Turner. Source: Vinh City People's Committee.

"VIETNAMESE-STYLE" HOUSING: KIỂU VIỆT NAM

Plans for constructing blocks A1–A4, directed by the Ministry of Construction in Hanoi, were underway even before the first GDR specialists arrived in Vinh. Bureaucratically, these plans signaled a critical shift in control over housing from the workplace to the government. This gave more power to the municipal Housing Agency, under the provincial Department of Construction, which was responsible for administering and managing the apartments in coordination with state enterprises. The centralization of housing distribution moved workers and civil servants away from the worksite into high-density housing with people from other brigades and work units. This was more akin to the Soviet model than to the Chinese danwei (Morton 1980, 239), which became unpopular in Vinh with the new residential options. Vinh's postwar housing landscape thus reflected the waning power of China, with its Maoist spatial practices, and the growing influence of the Soviet Union, with its urban-centrism.

Blocks A1–A4 significantly improved living conditions for workers and civil servants who had spent most of their adult lives in workplace collective housing (nhà tập thể). They were the first five-story buildings ever to be built in Vinh, and as level II buildings they boasted higher construction standards than the rudimentary level IV workplace dwellings. Made of brick and reinforced concrete, they were structurally sounder than the makeshift dwellings. However, they remained basic, utilitarian, and collective. Such buildings have nostalgically been called "vertical villages," given the number of migrants who moved in and kept their "rural" habits (see chapter 7).[51] Because of the dire needs of returning evacuees, the ministry's goal was to provide stable accommodation to as many people as possible rather than promote a new

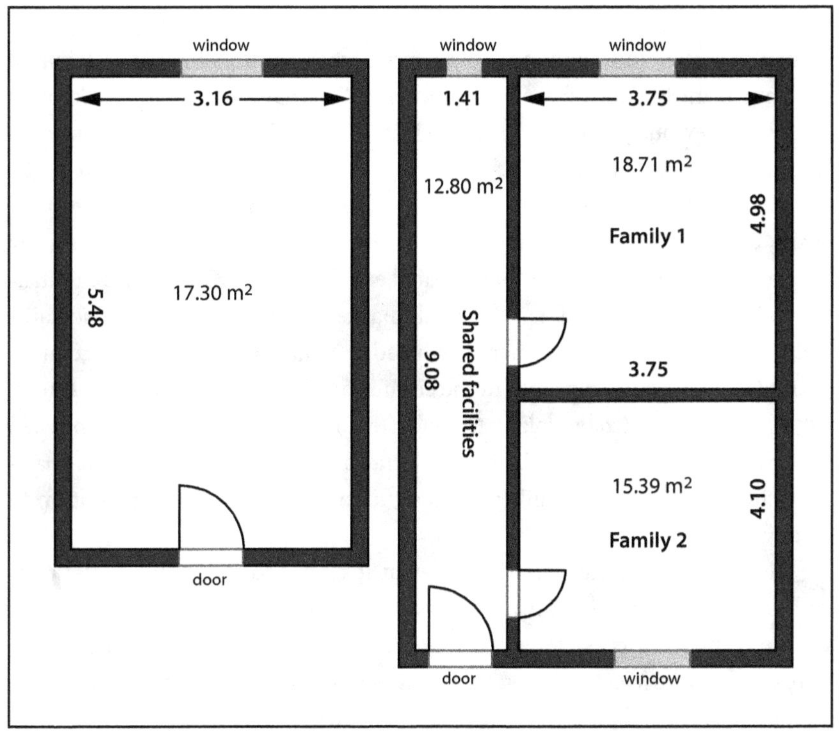

↑ Figure 6.12 Undifferentiated space: dormitory-style room in A1 (left) and two-family apartment in A2 and A3 with communal kitchen and bath (right). Drawing by Jutta Turner. Source: Vinh City People's Committee.

lifestyle. Accordingly, blocks A1 and A4, which were allocated to the Food and Beverage Company, were designed as offices and dormitories with shared facilities.[52] An average rectangular room in A1 measured seventeen square meters. At the standard allocation of four square meters of living space per worker (higher than in Hanoi), this was large enough to house four people in undifferentiated, multipurpose space for sleeping, socializing, or other activities (see figure 6.12).[53] Units had no kitchens or plumbing; gender-segregated toilets and washrooms were located on each floor at the back of the building close to the stairwell. With only a small window at the front and the entrance located at the rear, there was little air circulation, and rooms were dark and clammy.

In 1977, Construction Company 1 (*Công ty Xây dựng 1*) completed blocks A2 and A3. Though still considered Vietnamese style, these blocks marked an important design shift toward family housing. They remained collective—two families per flat (*tập thể gia đình*)—but were self-contained (*khép kín*). This was an infrastructural first: plumbing and kitchens in the unit. To understand what it meant to call these new apartments "Vietnamese style," I spoke with Mr. Huy, previously a planning supervisor with the Department of Construction. Huy still lived in block A3. As a young man he had participated in the scorched-earth resistance (*tiêu thổ kháng chiến*), joining the movement to destroy "every building, every column" to stop the French. Though he secretly longed to study medicine, he then studied engineering in Hanoi before returning to Vinh to help transform the small market town into a center of socialist industry. When the city was again reduced to ruins, he mobilized once more with his compatriots, swept up in the euphoria of building a new urban future. Like many of the (male) planners and (female) builders who had invested physically and emotionally in nation building, Huy was allocated an apartment in Quang Trung—a gift of infrastructure in return for contribution to its development.

Huy's answer to my question of what it meant to call a style "Vietnamese" was straightforward: "It means the blocks were designed by Vietnamese people at the Ministry's Design Institute, in accordance with Vietnamese standards."[54] "But how was the design *Vietnamese*?" I pushed, wanting to get at a deeper level of explanation. "The apartments were too large!" he said, changing the topic (the largest was seventy-four square meters). The spacious, multifunctional room was thus divided into two. There was a smaller, airy room at the front, overlooking a south-facing corridor with walkway access (a flip design of A1 with a rear walkway). At the back, there was a larger room that had less air circulation (see figure 6.12).

Another respondent, Mr. Chính, had worked at the Design Institute and had been allocated a larger back unit. For Chính, kiểu Việt Nam meant *tính chất tập thể*, or a collective character,[55] which GDR experts called "traditional" urban living. In A2 and A3, there were forty self-contained apartments for eighty families in each box-like building (no zigzag design here). A long and narrow *khu phụ* (kitchen and lavatory) ran the length of the two rooms, with the toilet at the back.[56] During my visits, I observed that the families who still lived collectively had set up small stoves next to one another in kitchen areas. They shared the space but not the cooking—their lives were separate but integrated and intimate. While a visual sign of progress toward a modernity that privileged high-rise buildings, straight lines, right angles, and concrete (Kusno 2000, 68), kiểu Việt Nam still fell short of the benchmark of socialist civilization and was quickly deemed obsolete. As Abidin Kusno observes, "No single meaning can be attributed [to the] most universal aesthetic of modernism" (2000, 67). A new model was thus necessary for the rest of the complex.

"GERMAN-STYLE" HOUSING: KIỂU ĐỨC

My Vietnamese respondents—planners, officials, builders, and tenants in Quang Trung—contrasted the *thiết kế cũ* (old design) of A1–A4 with the *thiết kế mới* (new design) that began with A5. Block A5 signified the commencement of the Việt-Đức *design* collaboration and a new architectural vision for Vinh. When I asked respondents to explain more concretely the differences between "Vietnamese" and "German" housing styles, they drew on value-laden binaries that exalted East German design as transformative and emancipatory, even as some remained critical of building choices (see table 6.2). Almost everything about the German blocks was considered more civilized (*văn minh hơn*): the front open-air corridors (rather than internal or rear hallways), back balconies, and walk-out basements (gầm), and the holistic planning that connected the buildings with walkways, parks, playgrounds, and gardens. Because few of these features could be found in Hanoi (Ngô 2016), they were identified as "modern" (*hiện đại*) and foreign or international (*quốc tế*) in style. Even the apartment-numbering system was considered more civilized, though my research team and I initially found it confusing.[57] A female accountant who had tallied Quang Trung project expenditures told me frankly, "The breezy and bright German-designed housing was superior [*ưu việt*] to that of Vietnam."[58] These architectural enchantments reproduced hierarchical difference as the natural order of things: East Germany could help save Vinh by offering a new way of organizing life in the city. GDR-style housing would not simply be utilitarian, but utopian.

East German planners did not use the same value-coded constructs. Instead, they drew on empirical data to discuss, in detached language, their observations about "traditional" Vietnamese building practices and cultural habits to craft a dynamic living environment that fit with their Western fantasy of urban modernity. Mass housing was to be enjoyable, not just inhabitable, to enable individuals to reach their fullest potential. Their accounts painted a culturally and historically sensitive portrait of Vietnamese people, albeit one that seemed essentialist and unchanging in its use of the ethnographic present: "In existing one–two story buildings, there are no kitchen-, wash-, or toilet- facilities. Like in rural areas, cooking takes place in outside annexes. The separate, dry latrine (at an appropriate distance from the building) is shared, as are washing facilities, located in the courtyard" (Purtak 1982, 119–20).

Table 6.2. Vietnamese vs. German styles (*kiểu*) of block housing based on descriptions by Vietnamese respondents.

Blocks A1–A4: Kiểu Việt Nam	**Blocks A5–A6: Kiểu Đức**
level II housing	level I housing
collective (*tập thể*)	self-contained (*độc lập, khép kín*)
old (*cũ*)	new (*mới*)
backward (*lạc hậu*)	modern (*hiện đại*); civilized (*văn minh*)
disorderly (*lung tung*)	orderly (*trật tự*)
low quality (*chất lượng thấp*)	high quality (*chất lượng cao*)
Vietnamese standards (*tiêu chuẩn Việt Nam*)	international standards (*tiêu chuẩn quốc tế*)
brick construction	panel construction
simple (*đơn giản*)	technical (*kỹ thuật*)
designed by Ministry of Construction	designed by Germany
supervised by Vietnamese engineers	supervised by German engineers
local materials	imported supplies
stuffy (*bí*)	airy (*thoáng*)

Enlightenment notions of self-actualization influenced the East German planners: the new socialist person would no longer live communally, and life would center on the nuclear family, not the work unit. Whereas danwei-like housing fostered dependency on the workplace (Bray 2005, 172), *independence* from the work unit was deemed essential to becoming modern.[59] These planning ideals reflected European values, including a "culture of privacy" that informed design practices in East Germany at the time (Betts 2008). The ideal family would be small with refined cultural practices that fit with urban life, even though the empirical studies conducted by GDR experts found multigenerational households to be the norm (see figure 6.10). Modern comforts in hygienic, self-contained units would hasten enlightenment, happiness, and material betterment. Private indoor amenities qualified the sturdier German-style buildings as level I housing according to Vietnam's building regulations, categorically placing them above the Vietnamese style of the ministry's design (level II).

In addition to civilizing amenities came efforts to civilize space. This was done by inserting walls into open, undifferentiated rooms. As a disciplinary device to shape conduct, walls introduced new arrangements, uses, and demarcations of space to redefine the family and divisions of household labor. Historically, the main living room (*phòng sinh hoạt chung*) in Vietnamese homes was multifunctional. As the largest and most important space at the center of the family, it was used for eating, socializing, sleeping, and ritual activities (Đặng T. H. 2009, 50). GDR planners noted this versatility (again, in the ethnographic present): "The living- and sleep-area is often furnished with French beds made with wood slat frames that are also used for sitting, eating and storage" (Purtak 1982, 122). As the disorderly city *outside* needed rational, single-use zoning, blurred spaces *inside* could be similarly resolved through functional spatial partitioning: "In the apartment, family sleeping rooms, living rooms, and guestrooms should be distinct from one another," and separated from the kitchen, toilet, and washroom. This would encourage new "living habits" and clearer boundaries between private and nonprivate spaces.[60] With the creation of separate rooms, gender stratification also became more spatialized (Massey 1994). It is perhaps not surprising that women came to spend time in kitchens cooking alone—not because this was a new division of labor but rather due to a new division of space that created an enclosed, designated "kitchen" (no longer an open area for cooking) and separated it more definitively from social activities in other rooms (see figure 6.13).

In his analysis of architecture as a technique of government, Foucault discusses the disciplinary power of walls, which introduced functional specification into undifferentiated space (1980, 148–49). Walls produce docile bodies, anchored in space to make them more governable. They also produce ethical subjectivities, especially among the laboring class: "The working-class family is to be fixed; by assigning it a living space with a room that serves as kitchen and dining-room, a room for the parents which is the place of procreation, and a room for the children, one prescribes a form of morality for the family" (1980, 149). Foucault's model took European spatiocultural practices as normative (for example, separating children from parents) and overlooked the role of walls in producing the middle class historically (see Löfgren 1984). Nonetheless, the fixing of people and practice in divided, utilitarian space was a similar design strategy used in Vinh to extend the reach of state power into the domestic sphere of the home, where it could shape conduct and transform residents into complicit socialist subjects (Foucault 1984, 190).

Walls were not a new phenomenon in Vietnam, of course. However, their function and effects were new in the German-style configuration of space—for example, in the creation of hallways in the flats. Walls had been used in buildings A2 and A3 to divide space *between* families. Partitioning space *within* single-family units created some ambivalence: people liked large rooms with open sight lines, and they preferred *rộng rãi* (capaciousness) to smaller, enclosed spaces, like the kitchen with only five square meters. To encourage air circulation and remedy the sense of containment created by walls, planners proposed higher ceilings, raising the Ministry's standard used in A1–A4 from 2.2 to 2.7 meters, but this did not open up space. I myself came to see walls in Quang Trung as unruly infrastructure. My apartment walls did not foster health, happiness, and hygiene but hazardous encounters with decay. Walls served as conduits for the spread of creeping, musty mold from the high humidity and broken pipes inside them and were a constant source of toxic dust from spores and chips of (what I feared to be lead) paint.

Residents were not ambivalent about the extra floor space they received in single flats. In the German design, floor plans varied to accommodate different-size families. While the new apartments were smaller on the whole—the largest in A5 was forty-nine square meters, as opposed to seventy-four in the *shared* units of A2 and A3—they significantly increased the amount of *individual* living space. In the Vietnamese-style buildings, families in tập thể gia đình enjoyed an average of twenty-five square meters (their private space plus half the shared facilities). The new design introduced the *buồng*, an extra room most often used as a sleeping area. Here, living space averaged forty square meters (areas 1, 2, 3 on the floor plan in figure 6.13), a fifteen-square-meter increase over shared units in A2 or A3. Even without the extra buồng (comprising a studio apartment; see areas 1 and 2 in figure 6.13), the single-family space still averaged thirty-one square meters, a 20 percent increase over A2 and A3. In the few apartments with two buồng, which were comparable in size to housing in East Germany,[61] living space was two times that of the shared units. These numbers revealed the "leaky borders" between standards (Star and Lampland 2009, 24). The German design more than doubled the Vietnamese allocation of urban living space of four square meters per person. This overprovisioning of space-per-person raised concerns among provincial authorities, who saw this allocation as excessive and wasteful for the circumstances.

Walls were also a spatial technology of population control. Studios and one-bedroom flats were the dominant designs for the standard *đơn*, or modular building unit. These floor plans encouraged small families by restricting available space. Typically, the middle of the đơn had a pair of one-bedroom units, with one room facing south and a slightly larger front room overlooking the corridor. These units were situated between two studios, one of which adjoined a stairway (see figure 6.14). Spatial allocation was tied to the nuclear family, even though Vietnamese households are typically patrilocal with three

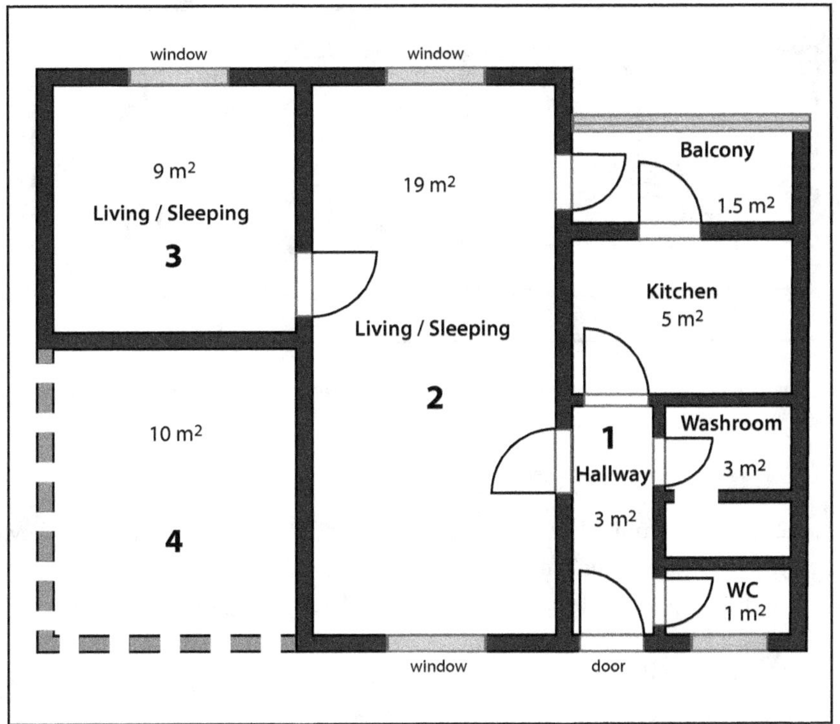

↑ Figure 6.13 Differentiated space: German-style single-family apartments. Drawing by Jutta Turner. Source: Vinh City People's Committee.

generations. Grandparents, whose affective labor plays a pivotal role in the household (allowing women to work, as Germans noted in their empirical study), were not expected to live in worker housing. Rather, the task of care-giving was to be taken over by daycares; readers will recall that the Quang Trung construction plan included one daycare facility per housing area (see figure 6.8).

Spatial allocation did not support family growth either. While small families were the desired norm, large families were common before the two-child policy of 1988 (Goodkind 1995). Families were anchored in their allotted space, however, no matter how many more children they had (or whether they assumed care of elderly parents). It was tedious to apply for a transfer to a new apartment (*xin chuyển*), and not guaranteed. Despite such spatial restrictions, over time families did grow in size, and three generations did come to live in the single-family units as original tenants became grandparents. During my research, one-third of families surveyed lived in three-generation households.

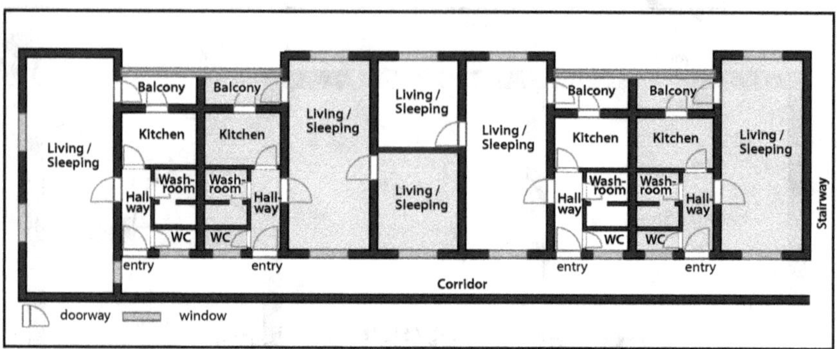

↑ Figure 6.14 Floor plan of a typical *đơn* with 1-2-2-1 room configuration. Drawing by Jutta Turner. Source: Vinh City People's Committee.

Notably, these families had less space than they did forty years ago when they first moved into Quang Trung.

As I got to know the blocks more intimately, I began to notice design variations: a few buildings had sliding doors and windows, some had kitchen ventilation (wood had been used as cooking fuel), end flats in staggered đơn often had an extra slat window, and so on. A surprise came in blocks C5 and C6, which housed civil servants. There, my research team and I discovered a new configuration: *three*-room apartments with 53.5 square meters, the largest of the German style in Quang Trung (see figure 6.13, areas 1, 2, 3 and 4).

When I interviewed key people involved in Quang Trung's construction, it was challenging to get beyond the story of a fruitful collaboration. Both sides were invested in this narrative, and certainly neither wanted to complain about the other (though one Vietnamese technician admitted that he found GDR attire on the construction site—shorts—inappropriate). I pressed with my questions, and the storyline began to crack as people became more reflective about disagreements and tensions in the project. These nearly always had to do with spatial politics of scale. East Germans attempted to constrain space, for example, by limiting building height. The Vietnamese team proposed six stories, but the German team insisted on five, citing technical limitations and practical considerations, such as the need for elevators at that height. Here, the Vietnamese side acquiesced. But GDR planners were also *too* generous with space; separate rooms were viewed as a "decadent luxury," similar to the perspective of early Soviet planners (Boym 1994, 123). Provincial authorities had conflicting ideas about the design, use, size, and purpose of living space. Should it produce a civilized life (*nếp sống văn minh*) for as many as possible, the Vietnamese rationale, or the good life for fewer, the German approach? As need remained high, especially for certain workplaces, and C5 and C6 grew into two-buồng apartments, authorities at the Department of Construction advocated for a return to the collective style or kiểu Việt Nam.

REFORMING THE GERMAN MODEL: RETURN TO KIỂU VIỆT NAM

The last blocks built—C7, C8, and C9—deviated from the ideal of one family per self-contained unit. In interviews, residents dismissed these three buildings as a disastrous modification of the standard *German* architectural form. Power struggles over spatial practices and the terms of urban planning played out most vividly as these blocks were modified. Vietnamese authorities had reservations about the socialist society that GDR experts aspired to build; it seemed at odds with the basic conditions in Vinh at the time and with the "spirit of collectivism" that mobilized support for the building of socialism (MacLean 2013, 84). While the spectacle of *joint* civil engineering bolstered a teleology of rational progress from imperial devastation to socialist liberation, the redesign of the last housing blocks revealed competing priorities to achieve social transformation. The vision of nuclear-family housing as the prototype for modern living conflicted with collectivist values and demands for housing that exceeded supply. Concerned more with quantity than quality, Vietnamese officials proposed the *cải tiến*, or reform of the housing plan, and a return to kiểu Việt Nam.

In the GDR plan, apartment layout was fairly standardized: units ranged between 30.3 and 53.5 square meters. They had a consistent, utilitarian division of space that fit the needs of individual families. Each had a *khu phụ* or latrine, washroom, and kitchen on one side, and living area and bedroom (contingent on family size) on the other (see figures 6.13 and 6.14). In C7–C9, provincial authorities pushed to reinstitute the tập thể gia đình model of A2 and A3 by allocating single-family apartments to multiple households. This required a redesign to distribute families across the space of the units more evenly.[62] The new design rotated the floor plan ninety degrees so that the *khu phụ* was at the front of the apartment—with the kitchen across from the toilet and washroom. The hallway separating food production from personal hygiene led to two rooms at the back (of eleven and fourteen square meters), each of which could accommodate a family with shared use of the facilities up front (see figure 6.15). This signified a 25 percent reduction in space for individual families compared with the tập thể gia đình design in A2 and A3 (and

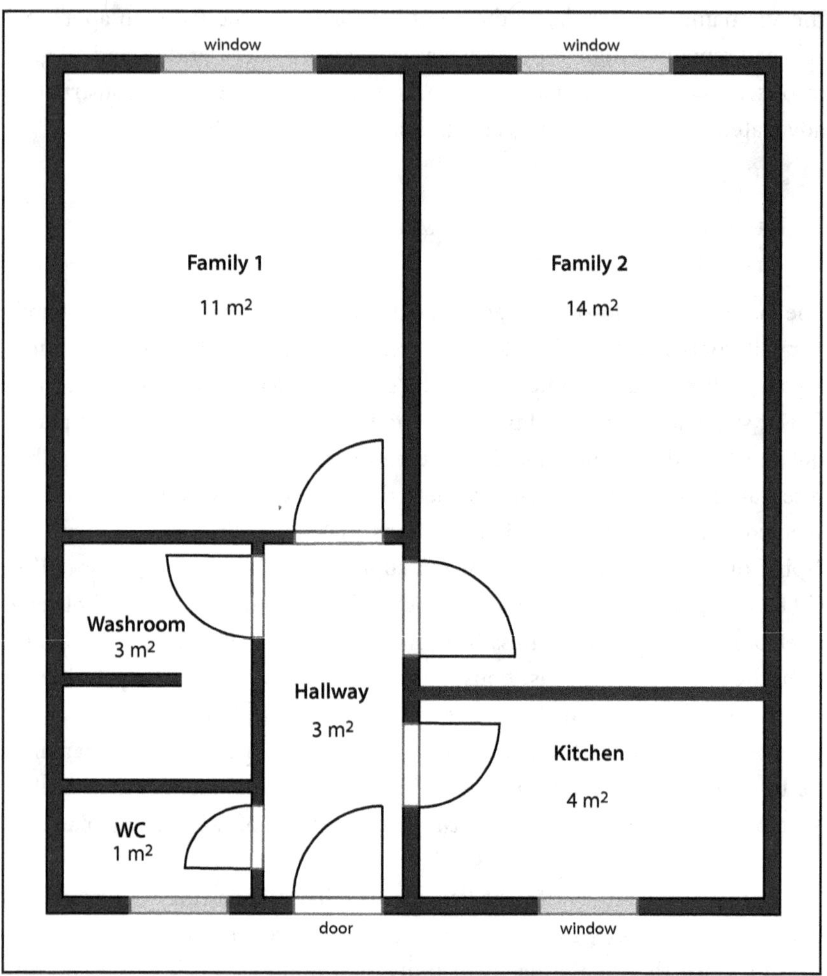

↑ Figure 6.15 Reforming the floor plan: *cải tiến* to accommodate two families per unit. Drawing by Jutta Turner. Source: Vinh City People's Committee.

over 50 percent less space than in single-family units). Changes not only cut costs by, for example, forgoing balconies, but they also enabled spatial control over an optimal number of bodies.

Vietnamese officials saw design "reform" as a practical, if not a moral, imperative to mitigate the acute need for worker housing and cut down on the wasteful use of space and construction materials. From the GDR perspective, "reform" undermined the science of rational planning. GDR architects had carefully calculated load capacity for the projected life span of the buildings, estimated at eighty years. They warned that the redesign would block airflow, creating stuffy, unhygienic, and overcrowded conditions, which would accelerate deterioration. Ideologically, the new design also undercut efforts to build a "new way of life" and negated a key value of European socialism: self-actualization of workers in service to society. GDR planners had no power over the final decision regarding housing scale and design. Despite their protests, Vietnamese authorities proceeded with the plan for cải tiến.

Upon their completion in 1979, the forty apartments in block C8 housed foreign (most Polish) experts temporarily until the units were allocated to eighty female workers and heads of household a year later. The flats of C7 and C9 were likewise allocated to twice the number of families. These blocks *would* decay more rapidly (see chapter 8). During my fieldwork, residents across Quang Trung disparaged these three blocks, but the tenants living in them made the harshest critiques. In interviews, they used binary terms to compare blocks A5–C6 with C7–C9: "Germans built those high-quality buildings. The grounds are orderly. Not like here; these were designed by the Vietnamese. That's why they have decayed [*xuống cấp*] so quickly."[63] From the outside, it is easy to spot the differences between "Vietnamese" and "German" design: the former favored no-frills, rectangular blocks set at ninety-degree angles, and the latter preferred long, zigzagged buildings of varied configurations (see figure 6.11). Visibly, kiểu Đức and kiểu Việt Nam had distinctive material and spatial properties. They also had different patterns of allocation.

ALLOCATION: WORKERS' PARADISE OR CELEBRITY TOWN?

> Quang Trung is predominantly a residential complex for the working class.
>
> —CONSTRUCTION AND DESIGN PLAN FOR QUANG TRUNG, 1974

> Originally the apartments were allocated to VIPS; now they house *người nghèo nhất* [the poorest people].
>
> —QUANG TRUNG TOUR GUIDE AND ARCHITECT, 2010

Quang Trung was a site of contradictions. As a spatial project, it embodied competing logics for how to organize society; as a social project, it represented different approaches to creating urban socialist men and women, who did not necessarily want to live in mass housing. At times, it was challenging to sift through the conflicting information I received, to get beyond appearances to the diversity of lived experiences. There was no tidy story to piece together, no triumphant narrative, or even consistent accounts. The housing blocks were ideal to some and flawed to others. The issue of allocation—the distribution of selected people across hierarchized space—was equally complicated, as the above quotations show.

To make sense of the confusion, I launched a survey to chart each block's history of design, allocation, and settlement, and to collect the stories of the families who lived in them.[64] To introduce my research team to the site, I asked a retired architect and former tenant to take us on a tour. As we wandered around the narrow lanes between the buildings, our guide peppered his history with amusing stories about the "celebrities" who lived in Quang Trung. The research team recognized many of them: the poet Minh Huệ in C4, the sculptor Đào Phương in C3, the writer Lê Thái Sơn in C2, and the folklorist Ninh Viết Giao in C3. These were the cultural workers (*văn công*) of Quang Trung, my neighbor, the former president of the Association of the Theatrical Arts, informed me. I had already learned that my building, C2, and C3 were considered the "intellectual" blocks, because elite cadres from the Department of Culture and retired professors from Vinh University (then: Vinh Pedagogical College) lived in them. There were also intellectuals in C4, C5, and C6, along with judges, doctors, and other professionals. I met these cultural elites during the survey; follow-up conversations took place in their homes, at the Film Café next to the restored cinema, and in the library in the former trade center. They were eager to share their histories and show me their works—poems, drawings, songs, books, and even plans for Quang Trung after its proposed demolition, such as turning it into a rubble memorial mountain. The musician Thanh Bảng, allocated a unit in 1981, even sang me an American protest song against the Vietnam War, translated into Vietnamese. I understood their enthusiasm as connected to their postreform decline in status as "socialist moderns" (Bayly 2008), which East German experts had also experienced (Schwenkel 2015b).

The guide's idea that Quang Trung was built for elites was not entirely true. The GDR vision was that the apartments would be allocated to *workers*. This was to be a proletarian utopia, and so it was in areas A and B (see table 6.3). I saw the eyes of my research team members light up when our guide told us that the Văn Sỹ soccer dynasty had working-class roots in block B5.[65] My neighbor in C2 was a worker: she had helped build Quang Trung. The idea that educated people had been given special consideration in housing allocation hurt her pride. She chuckled uncomfortably as she invited me into her studio on the fifth floor at the end of the đơn, where rain had leaked through the outside wall and ceiling, and asked me not to laugh at her poverty. "If those people of culture were so important, then why were they given housing last? They were less a priority than the workers," she remarked.[66]

She was right. Workers were allocated housing starting in 1977. In January 1978 the local press reported that three hundred worker families (*gia đình công nhân*) had moved into the high-rises and predicted that eighteen hundred more would receive housing later that year.[67] But there was still hierarchy: the Vietnamese housing code allotted more space to cultural elites in area C than to workers in areas A and B (and in C7–C9, with the redesign), as well as higher food rations.[68] The average spatial allocation per person was four square meters for workers, two for children, and six to twelve for civil servants, depending on rank. Even within worker housing, workers—mostly women—were given units on the less-desirable upper stories, while managers—mostly men—typically received the best apartments on the first and second floors, which had certain material advantages like pumped water and fewer stairs.[69]

Gender and occupational stratification happened both within buildings and across the complex. There were more female tenants in the worker-majority blocks of B1, B4, B5, and C8, for example, than in the cultural-majority blocks (see table 6.3). My neighbor's comments also suggested a persistent rural-urban divide in the complex, despite party efforts to eradicate disparities between countryside and city. This divide also mapped onto the worker–civil servant split of the housing blocks: areas A and B had a much higher number of rural migrants than area C (with the exception of the redesigned blocks in ward 9), which shaped people's aspirations, connections to the buildings, and sense of spatial *dis*/orientation. "We are not yet familiar with the names for the units [*đơn*], the buildings [*nhà*], or the streets [*phố*]," a couplet from the poem excerpted in interlude 4 read. "Out of habit we use the name of the village."[70] Rural workers remained leery of modernist mass housing and claimed they had been forced by their workplaces to move in ("bắt lên ở"). In contrast, cultural elites fashioned themselves as urban cosmopolitans who, like Europeans, desired high-rise living and felt privileged to be residents. "Remember, we were proud to live here at the time," our tour guide told us. His comment revealed a long-anticipated modernity whose break with the past was not just temporal but spatial and material. A sturdy, self-contained house was a world away from the ruined city and thatch communal dwelling where he had lived prior to his move to Quang Trung.

I learned about gender and occupational stratification quickly as I traversed the complex and spent time with my interviewees at their tea stalls, breakfast carts, vegetable stands, and grocery shops—in other words, at work.

Table 6.3. Distribution of state employees (workers and civil servants) in Quang Trung, based on 2010 survey conducted by the author.

Ward 1	# Households	Allocation	% Women
A2	41 (2 đơn)	Mechanical Engineering Co., Vietnam-German Machinery Co.	75.6
A3	43 (2 đơn)	Construction Co., Vinh Pedagogical College, People's Committee (PC)	77.4
Ward 2			
A5	80 (4 đơn)	Food and Beverage Co., PC	62.5
A6	60 (3 đơn)	Design Institute, Mechanical Engineering Co., PC	68.3
Ward 3			
B1	40 (2 đơn)	Printing Co., Food and Beverage Co., Department of Education	71.8
B2	80 (4 đơn)	Printing Co., Confectionary Co., Construction Co.	56.3
Ward 4			
B3	80 (4 đơn)	Woodworks Co., Vietnam-German Machinery Co.	64.6
B6	60 (3 đơn)	Confectionary Co., Woodworks Co., Construction Co., Food and Beverage Co.	53.3
Ward 5			
B4	80 (4 đơn)	Confectionary Co., Woodworks Co., Design Institute	72.7
B5	80 (4 đơn)	Food and Beverage Co., Woodworks Co., PC	72.5
Ward 6			
C2	80 (4 đơn)	Vinh Pedagogical College, Departments of Education and Culture	50
Ward 7			
C3	80 (4 đơn)	Vinh Pedagogical College, Departments of Education and Construction	62.5
C4	80 (4 đơn)	Electric Plant, PC, Vinh Pedagogical College, Post Office	58.8

(Continued)

Table 6.3 (Continued)

Ward 8

C5	70 (3 đơn)	PC, Department of Health, Post Office	58
C6	70 (3 đơn)	PC, Post Office, Confectionary Co.	58
Ward 9			
C7	40 (2 đơn)	Electric Plant, PC, Department of Education	72.5
C8	47 (2 đơn)	Pharmaceutical Co.	84
C9	60 (3 đơn)	Printing Co., Mechanical Engineering Co.	N/A

Note: I provide the number of households, which is higher than the number of units given shared residency in block C7 and collective family housing in blocks A2 and A3. The percentage of women is based on the registered names of people with user rights as of 2011; there may have been more women at the time of allocation. More than 60 percent of the original occupants still reside in the units. I do not include information for A1 in ward 1 given its status as an office and dormitory. Note that "departments" listed here refer to provincial-led government departments under the ministries in Hanoi and not departments at the pedagogical college.

The women I came to know in areas A and B ran small businesses to complement their monthly pensions that averaged 1.6 million VND (U.S. $80). Many of the women were widowed and received support from their children; their businesses brought them more social than economic sustenance. Like the cultural workers, they, too, supported my project but understood it, at first, more as policy work than as academic research.

Theoretically, the same allocation standards applied to workers and civil servants. In modern state bureaucracy, Weber (1978) argued, standardized procedures ideally govern conduct and prioritize reason over affect. Accordingly, housing allocation was based on an official formula that measured need and merit on a sliding scale. Workplaces assigned points to each employee according to standard criteria (*tiêu chuẩn*) that assessed, for example, activities during the revolution (*hoạt động cách mạng*), labor performance, family size, and housing need; more points led to preferential status. Despite the appearance of a rational bureaucracy, my respondents complained that these point allocations were arbitrary in the less objective categories, such as *thành tích xuất sắc*, or outstanding achievements. Typically, the point system determined who received one of three options: collective workplace housing (nhà tập thể), a plot of land, or an apartment in Quang Trung. These decisions were left to the workplace, not state officials. As bureaucrats at the Housing Agency explained, employers vetted workers and civil servants and decided who was assigned to live where.

People expressed cynicism about all these categories of housing. Life was miserable (*khổ*) in communal workplace housing, but rural migrants appreciated their access to land for gardens and livestock. Most workers I interviewed would have preferred a parcel of land to an apartment, which they considered unsuitable (*không hợp*) for a Vietnamese lifestyle: the blocks were too high (too many stairs to climb), too loud (despite noise regulations), and too crowded.[71] The vertical orientation detached them from the land and made daily chores like trash disposal cumbersome. Some preferred living at the workplace to the city center, which required long commutes on foot. Most despised was the institutionalization of a rent system in Quang Trung, which did not exist in workplace housing. Residents saw this illogical (*vô lý*) decision as a violation of the social contract: Germany had gifted (*tặng*) the blocks to the city to house workers—a sentiment that GDR engineers also expressed ("*ein Geschenk an die Leute*," a gift to the people)—and then the state began charging rent (and nominal fees for utilities). Rents were based on a standardized price table established in 1958, with fees increasing as building level descended: 0.12 VND per square meter on the fifth floor, 0.18 VND on the fourth, 0.22 VND on the third, and 0.25 VND on the first and second levels. I collected original rental agreements from the 1970s that showed monthly payments from 3.20 to 7.50 VND, with an average of 5.50 VND. This was close to 10 percent of monthly salaries, ranging from 40 to 75 VND, depending on skill level (*bậc*), which also determined food rations in addition to square-meter and floor allocation in Quang Trung.[72] This socialist rent system, which was not unique to Vinh, evokes Simmel's (2004) notion of value as an effect of desire: the less desirable, higher stories in the walkups housed lower social classes and commanded a cheaper fee for occupancy.

People were also ambivalent about land, which mostly went to those with higher *merit* (namely, men in management positions) rather than those with higher *needs*—namely, lower-skilled female workers with children. The state rationalized this as helping to stabilize households headed by women (Hoang 1999, 90). A retired civil servant explained, "Land had no value then, not like now. People had to pay a high fee of 200 VND for the transfer of user rights. And what could you do with land anyway? You couldn't build a house—there were no construction materials!"[73] A ready-made apartment was more convenient: "We were better off in the high-rises," one woman explained.[74] And indeed, some residents welcomed the life-changing experience of moving into Quang Trung, especially those who came later; it was the "pioneers" who most resisted this radical reorganization of their world. For example, Ms. Yến was the first in her family of rice farmers to leave agriculture to work in a state factory (in her case, at the pharmaceutical company). She settled in c8 in 1980. Yến explained the flat's meaning to her as a migrant to the city: "I was given a shared flat for me and my three children. My husband was away in the military so I didn't qualify for land. . . . But I liked the thought of moving into a modern apartment. It was a higher standard of living than in the nhà tập thể, more hygienic [*vệ sinh*] and civilized [*văn minh*]. It was the first time I lived in a brick building with a private lavatory!"[75]

Yến's nostalgic sentiments fit neatly with the state's teleological vision of progress. Officials encouraged such sentiments by praising the self-contained apartments as ideal for workers and their families, even if shared. Private facilities, like the indoor plumbing that excited Yến, were to replace the drudgery of collective living that led to fatigue and urban anarchy (Nguyen 1991, 57). Enchantment with modernity quickly dispelled, however; after tenants moved in, infrastructure broke down and the blocks decayed prematurely.

The final part of the book explores how this unplanned obsolescence played out in everyday life. The next chapters move from the planned city to the lived experience of modernist housing and its swift decline. While the master plans for Vinh and Quang Trung sought to help Vietnam "catch up" with the socialist world, residents had their own ideas about how to organize their living space. Against Foucault's prediction, stones and walls did not turn Vietnamese tenants into docile bodies that were "subjected, used, transformed and improved" (1977, 136). Despite attempts to create an "entirely new socialist person" (*xây dựng toàn diện con người mới xã hội chủ nghĩa*), architecture became a site of *in*discipline and subversion of the state's civilizing mission.

PART 3
Obsolescence

↑ Figure P.3.1 Quang Trung housing estate, 2011. Photo by the author.

7

INDISCIPLINE

It used to be that when people traveled through this area from north to south, and from south to north, they saw modernity. But today, they see only filth.

—INTERVIEW WITH VIETNAMESE PLANNER, 2010

We must, therefore, ask how dirt, which is normally destructive, sometimes becomes creative.

—MARY DOUGLAS, *PURITY AND DANGER*, 1966

We should not read the story of mass housing and visionary planning in part 2 of this book as a triumph of postcolonial progress and modernist experimentation in Vietnam. It was no spectacular re-creation of the built environment out of imperial ruins to liberate humanity—especially women. Like other utopian schemes to improve the human condition (see Scott 1998), Quang Trung housing blocks were plagued by the fragility of premature decay and dysfunction as infrastructure aged and broke down faster than experts anticipated, creating additional domestic burdens for female workers. Nor should we read the decay as pathological—as another predictable narrative of socialism's temporal disjuncture marked by ruin, crisis, and failure. In the following pages, I shift the analysis to the scale of social practice and to human-spatial interactions to argue for a more generative approach to filth and decay that draws attention to its anticipatory possibilities, rather than merely its destructive and precarious capacities, as Mary Douglas observed long ago. Just as ruins have productively contested state power and made new claims on the future (Edensor 2005; DeSilvey and Edensor 2012), decay emerged as a dynamic force in Vinh for mobilizing affect and action, creating new political subjectivities in the process. This argument makes an especially critical intervention in scholarship on Vietnam, some of which continues to cast people associated with the state as docile and without agency, power, or opportunities to transform their social worlds. Such a view overlooks the ways in which urban subjects, especially women, intervene in space to engage in urban provocations meant to alter or contest urban policy and daily forms of governance through infrastructure.

In its material and metaphorical registers as filth, decay produced new subjectivities, forms of sociality, and ways of making claims to urban space that undermined the rational master plan discussed in chapter 5 by inviting "disorder" and "crisis" back into daily life. It also produced civilizing discourses and scapegoat imaginaries, espoused by local experts, which were themselves highly gendered. The Vietnamese planner cited in the epigraph, who once lived in the housing blocks himself, showed his complicity with the pedagogical project of spatial ordering when he exclaimed, "We built this city, and then *they* undid it!"[1]—"they" meaning the gendered and classed perpetrators of filth and decay whose limited temporal horizons threatened to transform the model city of the future into a derelict place of the past. The reference to "them" likewise revealed stratification in the blocks along rural/urban, worker/cadre, and female/male divides, in addition to anxiety about failed efforts to modernize the population and produce "cultured" socialist persons. As this chapter shows, state interventions to improve the population would disproportionately target rural women and their conduct, which was considered disruptive and unbefitting of modern housing. In the end, the physical builders of socialism—rural migrant women who lacked a proper future orientation—were held responsible for the untimely decline of the city.

CREATING SOCIALIST PERSONS

> Muốn xây dựng chủ nghĩa xã hội, trước hết cần có những con người xã hội chủ nghĩa. (To build socialism, one must first have socialist persons.)
>
> —HỒ CHÍ MINH, 1961

Hồ Chí Minh's well-known dictum plays with the double meaning of a term commonly used to rally the masses around persuasive visions of possibility: *xây dựng*, or to build (*bauen*). As a verb, "xây dựng" is anticipatory and forward looking, and involves making with foresight to open a path to future emancipation (from predetermined form and practice) and inclusion through collective creation (Ingold 2013, 69). Hồ Chí Minh's use of the term reminds us that "xây dựng," which was peppered throughout Five-Year Plans for socialist development, sought radical material and ideological transformation of society—of base and superstructure, concurrently.[2] The term exemplified the Marxist belief that changes to the material conditions and productive forces of society were necessary to change social consciousness. The history of modernist mass housing in Vietnam is thus an account not only of its physical construction in urban space (in ways that deviated from visionary planning), but of the cultivation of certain kinds of persons, a fraught project that encountered significant disruption. As Heidegger argued, the verb *bauen* in German suggests dwelling as both (material) construction and (ontological) cultivation: "Building as dwelling unfolds into the building that cultivates growing things and the building that erects buildings" (1993, 350). Planners were aware that creating an entirely new living environment would require significant discipline and instruction to fashion urban sensibilities that were socially desirable and future focused. Peasants would need to learn how to live in modern apartments and use infrastructure to maintain social order and the structural integrity of buildings, as well as to raise "cultured families" (*gia đình văn hóa*) that exhibited positive traits in accordance with state directives (Kwiatkowski 2011, 26). More than shelter, the housing blocks became a site of intense socialization and moral development to establish a mass-housing habitus that would advance the country collectively toward socialism. Building, in other words, presupposed both making and awakening. If residents were skeptical of their high-rise living spaces—including those who had been seduced by images of modernity—they were even more so about the disciplinary technologies that the state deployed to enlighten them.

Mark Bradley traces twentieth-century discourses of civilization (*văn minh*) in Vietnam to the French colonial era, when Vietnamese anticolonial radicals identified the "emancipatory potentials" of civilizational thinking as "a space not only for the collective imagining of a future postcolonial state but also for working out new concepts of personhood" (2004, 67). Drawing from Western philosophical writings, these radicals appropriated and modified civilizational discourses to craft a vision of social order that broke with Confucian values to forge a more egalitarian relationship between self and society. Bradley claims that the turn to "collectivist paths" and political action (communism) rendered these aspirational discourses moot until recently, when (capitalist) globalization gave them new life. Indeed, Erik Harms's work on Ho Chi Minh City shows that postreform "ideas of civility, being civilized, and building a new kind of urban civilization" are still central to the project of twenty-first-century modernity (2016, 53).

And yet, civilizational discourse was not absent from what we might call the intermediate period of high socialism: other radical iterations of văn minh were tied to the joint projects of decolonization and *socialist* modernization (Schwenkel 2012). This should hardly come as a surprise. Socialist civilizational discourses originated from similar strands of enlightenment thought and utopian fantasies of modernity (Buck-Morss 2000). Moreover, scholars have traced ideas of Soviet civilization back to roughly the same era as when similar ideas were taking hold among the reform generation in colonial Vietnam (Kotkin 1995; Volkov 1990). Socialist discourses about *becoming* civilized were prescriptive; they sought to transform the tastes, manners, habits, and practices of the masses into those of the cultured elite (Volkov 1990, 214). In Vietnam, party campaigns launched after the U.S. war urged people to adopt a *nếp sống văn minh*, or "civilized way of life," including through the "new cultured family" campaign to produce moral socialist persons in the home. These were highly gendered projects directed at women especially, as Sara Friedman (2006) reminds us was also the case in China. Here, I examine "civilization" or văn minh as a similar set of gendered disciplinary practices deployed to stamp out cultural backwardness. In Quang Trung, municipal housing regulations aimed to reform conduct and create a forward-looking consciousness among rural migrants, particularly women, who were granted user rights to apartments in exchange for their labor. As I show, campaigns to civilize, discipline, and educate workers were often met with defiance as inhabitants sought to appropriate and "dealienate" urban space managed by the state, and to use it on their own terms (Purcell 2013, 149). Their tactics articulated a particular claim to the city that emerged spontaneously from domestic life.

Moving from conceptualization to realization of utopian planning raises questions about the transferability of design technologies that traveled from the socialist North to the postcolonial South and did not simply result in urban replication.[3] Rational planning, with its ordered lines, standardized forms, and functional segregation of space, was "translated" (Akcan 2012) and even undone by tenants in the housing blocks through a range of dwelling practices that I reveal over part 3 of the book. These acts of spatial-architectural-infrastructural intervention, some of which respondents commonly attributed to the sphere of domesticity, challenged top-down planning and, in so doing, raised moral anxieties about a failed urbanization and a "not-yet-modern" population. A dialectical relationship thus emerged between formalization and improvisation, and between civilization and backwardness, which threatened to slow the pace of socialist transformation. Rather than urbanizing the rural (*thành thị hóa nông thôn*), as Lê Duẩn and the party had advocated (1977b), the opposite seemed to occur: ruralization of the urban (*nông thôn hóa thành thị*). As the poem in interlude 4 suggests, migrant workers held on to their rural orientations and sensibilities as they struggled to adapt to an unfamiliar modality of dwelling in a new sensory-spatial environment intended to move them out of the past and into a more modern future.

Strategies of urban governance, Austin Zeiderman has argued, are anticipatory and motivated by projections of future risks and threats that may not come to pass (2016, 191). Similarly, housing officials—including Quang Trung wardens, who were also residents of the blocks[4]—governed domestic space and conduct in anticipation of disorder and crisis. As the household became a site for building and governing socialism (Friedman 2006), residents, especially women, responded with noncompliant acts that flouted regulations and challenged the larger state project of "urban civilization" (*văn minh đô thị*). Through these acts, we see that modernist housing and its infrastructure were anything but utopian or emancipatory. To develop this point, I focus on trash, which emerged at the crux of both the project to create an enlightened population and the crisis of looming dystopia.

Douglas's (1966) work on pollution and social order has, in recent years, inspired scholars to pay increasing attention to waste as symbolic matter that inscribes power and meaning. Anthropologists and geographers in particular have used waste as a heuristic to gain insight into rural-urban relations and class, ethnic, and gender hierarchies, including in Vietnam (Nguyen 2016). In addition to its social and economic significance, trash has important political valence (Fredericks 2014, 533). Douglas famously said that where there is dirt, there is system (1966, 35). And where there is dirt, there is also often political participation. Scholars have shown how, in an era of shrinking welfare provisions, waste manifests as vital materiality through which people mobilize around their rights and make claims to citizenship to effect social and political change. As an object of ethical intervention (Hawkins 2005), waste mediates the strained relationship between citizens and the state. In Quang Trung, waste exposed tensions between tenants and authorities, who held conflicting views about modernity.

Urban modernization has long deployed waste management and sanitation systems to create hygienic, orderly cities (Gandy 2006). And yet, public infrastructure in colonial cities involved racialized spatial practices that excluded many people from the benefits of modernity.[5] This means that today, rights claims in and through infrastructure, such as waste, are fundamentally claims to entitlements to the city (Chalfin 2014; Anand 2017). Similarly, migrant women in Quang Trung utilized waste to express their lack of confidence in the state and to generate particular social effects through noncompliance with modernization efforts. Their defiant acts of improper disposal of domestic trash transformed everyday filth into dangerous, unethical objects (Douglas 1966, 197) that threatened to destabilize the rational order of the socialist city by inviting in social and biological disease. For these women, filth was not a shameful or fearful substance, as it was for forward-looking city planners and party officials who associated cleanliness with the health of socialism (Buchli 1999, 52). Rather, it was a creative vehicle for contesting the spatial and infrastructural regime of housing by challenging its principles of order and hygiene (*trật tự, vệ sinh*). Through their defiance, women elicited anxiety among municipal authorities about the inability of socialist modernity to uplift the urban population and secure a future free from past "dirt" and division.[6] Indiscipline—coded as impending ruin, decay, disorder, and filth—thus coalesced in the figure of the female rural migrant, whose existence outside modern temporality risked turning back the clock on socialist development.

BECOMING URBAN

When I first met Professor Ninh Viết Giao, an expert on Nghệ An folk tales who passed away in 2014,[7] he told me, "If you want to understand the history of Quang Trung, you need to start with the countryside." In Vietnam, the countryside embodies a temporal contradiction as a site of imagined rural timelessness on the one hand, and the object of modernist collectivization plans on the other (MacLean 2013). I spent several mornings with Giao receiving lessons on what he called *nông dân thành thị dân*, or rural peasants *becoming* urban persons.[8] I understood his use of *thành*, or becoming, in a Deleuzian sense to signal an emergent, but ultimately elusive, subjectivity (Biehl and Locke 2010) that was socially desirable and state endorsed. "It never happened," he told me, but without the moralizing tone I detected in planners, who operated as experts of spatial ethics (Kusno 2011, 326). I was, however, uneasy with the suggestion that peasants occupied another temporality that prevented them from leaving behind their rural pasts. "Although they no longer farm, plow, irrigate, and transplant rice, their very essence, sensibility, and lifestyle are still those of a peasant," he said candidly, as the trope of the static Other, existing outside modern history, flashed through my mind (Fabian 1983). But Giao was not denying coevalness to rural migrants; he was arguing instead for dynamic resilience, if not urban resistance. "They may live in the city but they remain firstly rural people [*nông dân*]. They have not forgotten their habits," he added, evoking a line from the poem "High-Rise in Vinh" (see interlude 4): "Still following our old ways of life" (*Vẫn theo ta điều ăn nết ở*). Giao was hinting not at rural migrants' ignorance but at their tactical defiance of a new spatiotemporal regime that was at odds with their own subjectivities and ontologies of being in the world.

Giao's goal was to explain the ontological—and what I came to understand as political—reasons for the tenacity of a rural habitus, those dispositions that mark social difference and generate meaningful practice (Bourdieu 1984, 170). As a historian, he wanted me to understand peasants' sentimentalities as heterochronic (Foucault 1986, 26) or embracing both the past and the future: their historic ties to land, connections to ancestors, bonds with family and neighbors, and attachments to villages that structured their modern existence. This perspective allowed me to see both the poem's sentiments and migrants' practices as rejecting urban alienation as an inevitable condition of the modern metropolis, as Georg Simmel (1950) once predicted, while contesting new design technologies (high-rises) for administering the population through infrastructure. Giao also shared a secret: "We are all rural peasants!" Vinh, he reminded me, was a young city; nobody could truly say that they *gốc Vinh* (came from there). At best, people could claim a generation or two of residence; before that, the city had been a small market town interspersed with rice fields. Vinh never had clear town/country boundaries, as European cities might claim (see Williams 1975). In large metropolises in Vietnam, such as Saigon, only people living on the urban fringe are considered neither fully rural nor urban (Harms 2011). But in Vinh, town and countryside fused to coconstitute subjectivities for residents throughout the city, and they still do so for many. Even today, people I meet typically say they are from a provincial district, or the province of Nghệ An itself, not the city of Vinh (though this is changing with younger generations). So who, then, was the aspiring "urban person," and how might a rural migrant become one?[9] In Giao's view, people needed to synchronize their rural past with the urban present and change their thinking and conduct not to become civilized, per the state's goals of modernization (with which he fully agreed), but to become, simply put, good neighbors. Mirroring Lefebvre, Giao saw social cooperation and interconnectedness as critical to urban coexistence and human flourishing (Purcell 2013, 149). Mass housing with shared commons required everyone to adapt *collectively* to the rebuilt environment and its atypical dwelling practices, rather than act *individually*. Forging a new habitus was not something that could be done quickly, however, but was a product of developmental time: "I read books on France and know that this process of making rural people urban took place over the span of a hundred years," Giao explained, in teleological terms that saw "being rural" as a stage on the way to becoming "fully" modern.

Before I outline the habits considered outside modern time that were targeted for reform, let me take a step back to the early years of the blocks (1977–1978), when the housing of workers took precedence over offering units to cultural elites. Giao painted a picture of total confusion (*tất cả rối ren*) and urban turmoil, a view that other residents also expressed. The memories of one woman, who worked at the Department of Culture and moved to Quang Trung in late 1978, challenged the rationality of centralized planning: "At that time there was a lot of chaos. Things were not yet up and working; the rules weren't in place. So people randomly dumped water and waste. They did this all the time!" When I asked about current practices, she stressed synchrony with developmental time: "Now there is procedure and an orderly routine. That was a long time ago; more than thirty-five years have passed!" She then rethought her position: "Well, in truth, it's really still that way."[10] GDR experts, steeped in colonial imagery of tropicality, also noted the disorder and discontent among residents who felt spatially and temporally dislocated. "They were not satisfied with the apartments; they wanted to move out after a few days," one technician told me. I asked why. "They just weren't used to living in high-rise concrete blocks," he replied, affixing residents to a rural past outside modernity. "They were used to bamboo huts and didn't know how to live in constrained spaces," he continued, rendering tropical nature as timeless and fluid (Wilke 2015, 183). He explained how tenants expanded the possibilities for living in the city by making the complex more like their villages, and like the workplace *nhà tập thể* (collective housing) where they had previously lived (see chapter 6). "In A5, they closed off the balconies to create stalls for pigs and chickens," he said. "They used the green spaces for agriculture and turned the playgrounds into gardens. They just weren't happy with the buildings," he reflected with disappointment. The model of large-scale housing they exported to Vinh "didn't fit with their lifestyle," he voiced with regret.[11] Instead, tenants routinely snubbed the rules and regulations intended to maintain public order at Quang Trung, demonstrating their ambivalence about the elite tastes that had been pushed on them in a time of postwar instability.

GDR experts expressed their concerns about such conduct in material, rather than social, terms: they worried about structural integrity and building vulnerability (and the impact on resident safety), not how to make better urban persons. Vietnamese authorities, on the other hand, were more concerned with proper subject formation, as well as with Vinh's national reputation. After all, the housing blocks were solid, modern, high tech, and made by Germany. Their design had catapulted the annihilated city to the forefront of modernity, but tenants' conduct threatened to reduce its status to "filth," as the planner quoted in the epigraph forewarned. Officials worried that Nghệ An province, a frontier land of poor, backward peasants, would remain not-yet-modern in the national imaginary and be left behind by growth in Hanoi and Ho Chi Minh City. They responded swiftly with a series of civilizing tactics. The set of standardized regulations (*nội quy*) they issued in the late 1970s read like a page from Norbert Elias's (1994) *Civilizing Process*: "urinate only in designated areas," "cooking in the hallways is strictly forbidden," "use the housing space as intended, do not turn the kitchen into a bedroom," "maintain the water, drain, and septic systems; failure to do so will impact everyone's health and hygiene," and so on. Enforcement required a new regulatory regime, including unit inspections to monitor encounters with technical systems, and enforced collective cleaning of the commons. Media technologies, including signage (much of it torn or vandalized), public address systems, and community announcement boards, in each ward formed an arsenal of tutelary devices to discipline, train, and transform housing residents into civilized urban proletarians (see figure 7.1).

Giao described the behaviors and "ways of life" that authorities saw as uncivil, disruptive, and needing reform. These were all practices that in some form or manner affronted the senses. Take sound, for example: there was too much cacophonous noise, he said, laughing. People spoke and quarreled loudly. They yelled across floors and stomped up stairs.[12] They sang all night at weddings, which showed how "culture for fun" (*văn hóa cho vui*) in the anthropological sense exposed a "lack of culture" (*thiếu văn hóa*) in civilizational terms. This sonic experience was overwhelming, with "tenants shouting, cocks crowing, dogs barking, and cats meowing." Over time, residents learned to speak more quietly, he said, so neighbors could work or sleep. In my experience living in Quang Trung, the noise level did not seem to be strictly regulated, and I wondered how much more intense it had been in those early days, despite the rule in the nội quy. The 1970s version simply stated, "Do not make noise"; the iteration from 2006 was more specific: "Go lightly, speak quietly, and no noise during midday break."

Scholars have examined the relationship between modernity, the senses, and city life, from Simmel's (1997) urban overstimulation (like Quang Trung's sonic ruckus), to Seremetakis's (1996) sensory loss and displacement, to Bauman's "war" on senses like smell (1993, 24). With modern sensibilities came the spatial hierarchization of sensory experiences (Cowan and Steward 2007).

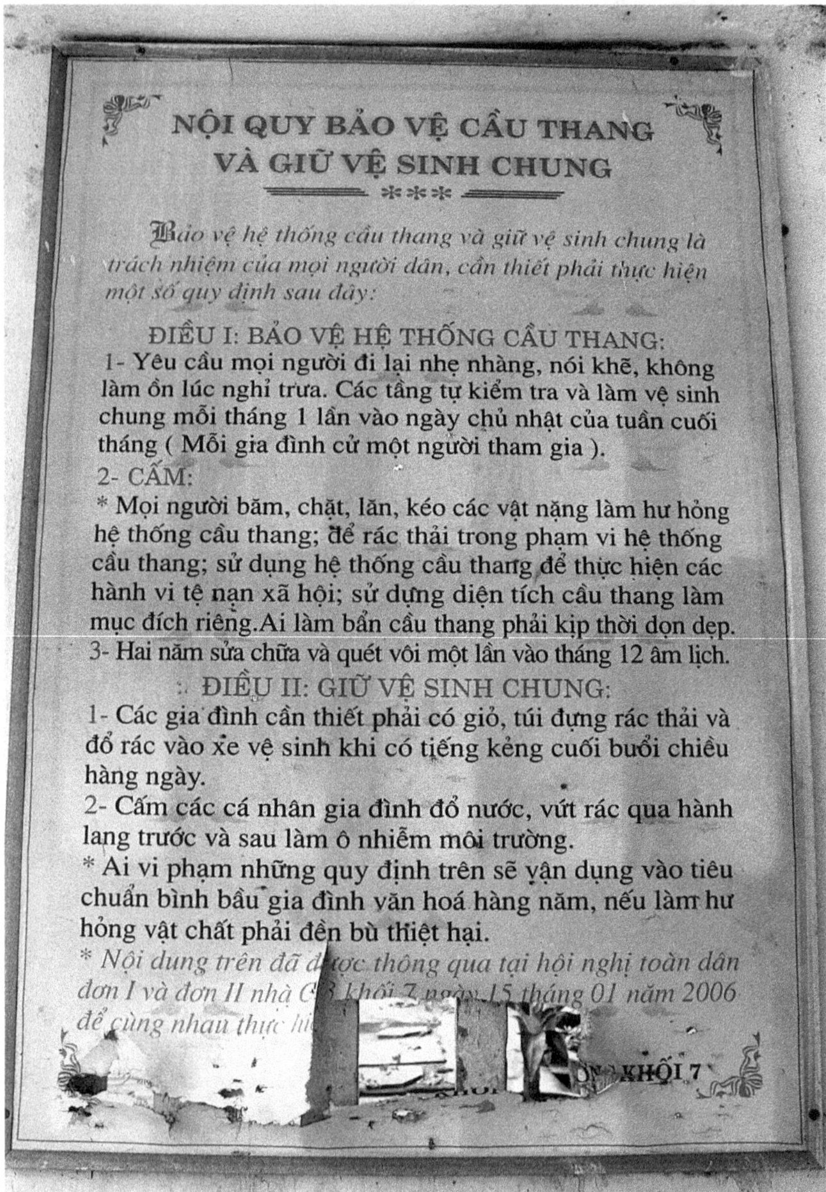

↑ Figure 7.1 Housing regulations for protecting the stairwells and maintaining communal hygiene, 2011. Photo by the author.

In Vinh, the regulation of dwelling practices was likewise an exercise in governing the urban sensorium to prevent crisis. Take the widespread claim I heard that residents disrupted the rational order of things by leading disorderly, untidy lives ("bừa bãi," "không trật tự," "lộn xộn"). When I asked people for an example, I often got the same response: pigs in the washroom, which produced dirty, malodorous homes (*bẩn thỉu hôi hám*). This postwar survival strategy was presented as a *multi*sensory violation of hygiene: of sight, since there was no place for a pig in a high-rise; sound, as the oinking added to the cacophony; and smell, not only from the daily waste, which backed up drains (leading to foul odors in the lower apartments), but also from the salty decay and lime peeling from the walls in the pigsty-washroom. Although cultural elites liked to point to the worker blocks as the sites where livestock were raised, I learned of this practice across the complex. Two married professors in my block, for instance, had kept seven chickens on their back balcony and a pig in the washroom. They had worried about being fined, but word spread before inspectors came around, so they could leave the house quickly to avoid them.[13] Moreover, though the nội quy forbade raising livestock in the housing blocks out of concern for order and hygiene, this rule was generally not enforced. In a gesture of proximate solidarity, officials looked the other way; they, too, came from the countryside, and some had kept pigs themselves to survive a desperate time. Nonenforcement based on expressions of *thông cảm*, or shared empathy, challenged the idea of a rational, technocratic state committed to discipline. Such empathy showed how affect became the "substance of governing projects" (Stoler 2004, 5) to maintain legitimacy while consolidating state and party power. Citizens were well versed in exploiting such sentiment to their advantage, I would learn (see also chapter 9).

No urban practice generated more civilizing rhetoric than the improper disposal of trash. This was also considered a threat to the hygienic order, and perhaps for good reason: rats. Along with pigs and loud talking, the random dumping of household waste was linked to gendered, rural bodies—the intended beneficiaries of civilization, reproached by those tenants who claimed more urban sensibilities. As one technician in C6 told me, using the third-person plural as a distancing technique, "They put garbage down the drains and hurled trash out their windows. They did not yet possess the right consciousness [*ý thức*]."[14] Professor Giao had a cultural explanation for this behavior too: "Yes, they dumped their trash wherever. But that's what people do in the countryside. They just toss it in their gardens." He was right to point out that impoverished rural areas did not have centralized waste management systems like towns and cities. What little disposable waste people generated, they recycled or burned, while organic materials were mulched for fertilizer or other agrarian use. But a new society, the technician implied, conjuring Hồ Chí Minh, required new people, cleansed of the "dirt" of their old ways (Buchli 1999, 53).

Giao then became more critical about the possibility of future crisis: "But that doesn't work here; we would be overrun with garbage—and vermin—in no time!" He concluded by warning me about the potential of filth to interrupt progress: "The matter of waste has been a big problem for the housing blocks, and it remains so." But there were also more pressing anxieties, such as drug use and other "social evils" that pointed to urban decline. As with the noise, I saw apprehension about waste grow across the posted rules over time. The 1970s nội quy mentioned trash only briefly, referencing its spatial distribution: "To maintain order and hygiene . . . do not throw garbage indiscriminately in the courtyards or the corridors." By 2006, however, proper forms of disposal were laid out with clearer material, spatial, and temporal parameters: "Waste dumping in the stairways is forbidden. . . . Families must have a basket or plastic bag for their waste and dispose of it in the trash cart at the sound of the bell every afternoon. It is forbidden to throw water or garbage from the front or rear balconies and pollute the environment." The threat of penalties—tenants who violated the nội quy would "receive a mark against their cultured family assessment," according to posted signage—did little to ensure compliance. Trash disposal remained a powerfully contested matter between housing authorities and residents, whose *anti*utopian practices became a distinctive form of agency that worked against the spatial and temporal imaginaries of the developmental state (Tonkiss 2013, 321).

WASTE AND DISORDER

As a technology to civilize both landscape and people, the East German–engineered waste and sanitation system offered the prospect of urban modernity for tenants in high-rise housing. Urban waste removal requires functional public infrastructure and trained sanitation workers, but also disciplined residents. The role that individuals play in trash management is often overlooked in anthropological literature, which tends to privilege waste collectors (formal and informal), the garbage itself (as nonhuman actant), or state infrastructure.[15] And yet, citizen-disposers are key actors: the urban social order itself is contingent on their disciplined participation in daily trash rituals. Urban governance in Vinh thus set out to produce trash-conscious citizens who would advance an orderly, hygienic city. The task—bringing garbage to the cart when the bell clanged—may seem intuitive, but it was a civic responsibility that had to be inculcated. Waste emerged as an ethical, if not pedagogical, tool of state intervention. Urban emulation campaigns, for example, often adopted litter, or waste out of place, as a rallying point for discipline and self-responsibility, especially during the monthly cleaning of communal spaces in Quang Trung. Such actions reinforced the divide between civilized (văn minh) and uncultured (*vô văn hóa*) engagements with trash that came to define—and distinguish—groups of people in the complex.

The "uncivilized" conduct of rural migrant workers thought to lack a modern waste sensibility was a constant source of frustration for municipal officials, as well as for other housing residents, such as the cultural elite who felt they handled waste properly. Misplaced trash wreaked havoc on the urban environment and prompted anxieties about the ruralization of urban space. In the disapproving words of one man, a retired teacher, "People used to toss their garbage out the window!"[16] It was a common lament that started soon after tenants moved in. Rather than walk down several flights of stairs, some people simply dropped their trash onto the ground below, in clear violation of the rules. An editorial in the local newspaper similarly chastised families for failing to "build a new and civilized life" in the apartment complex, even though they had received instruction on how to use infrastructure properly: "They indiscriminately throw garbage everywhere, also from the upper floors, and do not sweep the stairwells and other communal areas as required. They hang clothes out to dry and leave their children unsupervised to run wild outside."[17]

These complaints centered on domestic work typically associated with women, such as child care and laundry, which, the editorial suggested, should take place in the home to maintain a "civilized" environment. Without saying so directly, the editorial writer thus held women responsible for the lack of hygiene, aesthetics, and social order in the housing blocks. As Ann Marie Leshkowich has observed, disorder in Vietnam is often coded as feminine (2005, 188). Women's domestic labor in Quang Trung thus became a site of state discipline to modify dubious behavior and produce cultured families, an earned status that helped a neighborhood become recognized as a "cultural ward" (*khối văn hóa*). Actions deemed "backwards" and unbefitting of new socialist persons thus risked bringing shame on both individual families and the wider collectivity.

The author of the editorial pleaded with officials to increase education and mass mobilization (*phát động quần chúng*) of residents for whom high-rise living was a new way of life. While theoretically that could mean everyone in the complex, his words targeted rural migrants especially. Neighborhood leaders had a critical role to play in enforcement. Wardens, for example, monitored conduct and, at times, "outed" repeat offenders on announcement boards. There was palpable anxiety that Quang Trung would become the *antithesis* of a civilized city and undermine the entire project of socialist nation building, rather than lead that project as a model of urban futurity. Raising livestock in the complex also provoked such sentiments, and, like efforts at proper waste management, its ban was framed as a matter of public health. But while pigs and chickens were tolerated out of sympathy for tenants' poverty, misplaced trash was not.

Improperly disposed trash threatened to derail modernization. Public health and urban aesthetics aside, waste out of its proper place was thought to hasten the decay of infrastructure and the built environment. For example, some residents used the large, open sewers attached to squat toilets as trash receptacles. This clogged the pipes and created overflow in the lower apartment units, which were typically assigned to those of higher rank (all wardens I visited, for instance, lived on the first or second floors). As a retired architect and former resident complained, "People dumped their trash down the drain: paper, fabric, bamboo, and food. . . . They treated it as a disposal and obstructed the entire system."[18] Few acknowledged that these actions were often a response to infrastructure that was already broken, inoperative, or considered inconvenient, which the state failed to redress. Instead, rural migrants became a scapegoat for breakdown and their waste an unethical object that foretold of dystopian crisis.

Scholars have shown how people on the margins of society, like rural migrants, are often held responsible for housing disrepair rather than the "dirty materialism" that shapes their conduct, such as dry taps, broken pipes, or just plain bad design (Lea and Pholeros 2010, 205). Likewise in Vinh, few people pointed to the underlying structural issues in the housing complex that encouraged such practice: namely, the lack of a centrally organized waste management system. With Quang Trung's unique morphology of high-rise buildings, the routine of waste disposal that the nội quy prescribed was not sustainable. A retiree from the Department of Culture disparaged residents for throwing trash out the windows but also empathized with those who lived above him on the fourth and fifth floors: "The Germans did not design an efficient trash-removal system. When the bell rang, people were supposed to come out to toss their garbage. But there wasn't enough time to run downstairs! So people piled their waste elsewhere."[19] This observation undermines the common notion that rural migrants—especially women—were mystified by indoor plumbing and lacked basic knowledge of urban hygiene. Instead, there was need for a more efficient system for high-density living in multistory buildings. But rather than tackle inadequate design, city officials and tenants alike continued to cast rural migrants as ignorant and possessing the "wrong" urban habitus. Even two decades after residents first moved in, the Municipal People's Committee reported that despite persistent health campaigns and efforts to educate residents about civilized living (*cuộc sống văn minh*), most still did not comply with housing regulations or show awareness of proper waste management.[20] Rural migrants were more indifferent and defiant than they were unenlightened, however. If regulating waste disposal practices was a disciplinary technique to create modern urban subjects, as Foucault (1977) would have recognized, then denying waste its proper place was a refusal of this subjectivization.

NONCOMPLIANCE AS EVERYDAY GENDERED PRACTICE

These early incidents of waste incivility that tenants narrated to me showed how trash became a material expression of nonconformity in the housing blocks. More than any other practice, the refusal to submit to a new waste regime revealed a dissatisfaction with the state's vision of urban modernity as manifested in the high-density, high-rise housing where they lived. Efforts to civilize residents through proper trash disposal continued during my residence in Quang Trung, but with different methods to enforce compliance. While emulation campaigns to educate residents ended long ago, prescriptive efforts to train residents continue through signage. Among these, the community announcement boards (*bảng thông báo*), located at the bottom of stairways in each housing block, were most significant and provide a wealth of ethnographic information (see figure 7.2). These blackboards were a key technology of governance that residents encountered in their everyday lives—if they read them, that is. Wardens maintained the boards, which served several purposes. They offered practical information, such as when residents could pick up their pensions or pay their utility bills. They forged affective bonds in the community, as a space for death notices (*tin buồn*) and communications about social activities or health services for retirees. They also helped enforce good citizenship by encouraging attendance at party meetings and participation in community labor, such as cleaning the commons. In the spirit of transparency, all new government regulations were taped to the boards (a windfall for the ethnographer!), as were maintenance fees that households were

↑ Figure 7.2 Community blackboard calling on households to help clean the commons with "100% participation expected," 2010. Photo by the author.

required to pay. Wardens also used the boards to instill patriotism in the complex and to scold or publicly shame those who neglected their duties as loyal citizens. "One hundred percent of the households will hang the flag for Hùng Kings Day!" the chalk-written message on the board in my stairway instructed one day, though only 50 percent complied, the warden noted disapprovingly several days later (see plate 7). Unsurprisingly, then, the boards held warnings about misplaced trash.

Both time discipline and space discipline play important roles in the governance of urban waste disposal. In Vietnamese cities, household waste management is as much about accurate timing as proper placement: typically, women carry garbage outside to the cart in late afternoons when the bell sounds. Because the clang is loud and pulsing, and the female collectors who make the rounds do so unhurriedly, on foot, people know they have a few minutes to gather their rubbish. This had been my experience living in large and small cities, including Hanoi, Hải Phòng, and Cao Bằng. The housing blocks in Vinh had a slightly different system. After complaints by tenants on the upper floors that they did not have enough time to run downstairs with their trash, a collection spot was set up with a stationary cart, where resi-

↑ Figure 7.3 Garbage collection point with signage outside block c2, 2011. Photo by the author.

dents could discard household waste between four p.m. and seven p.m. (see figure 7.3). A female sanitation worker would come and haul away the trash in the evening. "No dumping outside these hours," the sign read. Waste disposal at other times of day and night often happened, however, and a reminder to follow the regulations would appear on the community board soon after. Such was the case at block c3 in December 2010, when the warden spotted an incident of after-hours dumping and wrote the next morning, "The duty to take out the garbage at the right time in compliance with housing regulations has been the subject of many public announcements. And yet, yesterday evening one household dumped a large bag of garbage (filled with baby diapers). Because communal hygiene is the responsibility of each person, please take note [of these rules]."

Though dumping after nightfall seems like surreptitious activity, this message revealed how waste disposal functioned as a tool of state discipline, not only through education and mass mobilization but also through public surveillance. For the system to work, however, the state had to perform its expected role in maintaining public infrastructure: a garbage cart needed to be at the collection site by four p.m. As I discovered early in my fieldwork, this was sometimes not the case, which meant that residents took the system far less seriously than I did.

In my case, the written reminder generated the intended effect: more self-discipline and anxiety about compliance, especially given my position as an American researcher and guest. I worried that I might violate a regulation unknowingly, come across as disrespectful, and find my name and apartment number written on the blackboard. The first time the cart did not appear as scheduled, I panicked. What to do with my small bag of garbage? There was already trash strewn haphazardly on the ground, but I hesitated to leave my own there, given the message of insubordination it might send. I turned to my neighbor who ran a small shop across the way; she waved her hand in dismissal and told me to toss my bag on the pile. I did, and quickly returned to my apartment on the fourth floor. After all, it was five p.m., and I was compliant with the time, just not the place (the cart). The next day, there was a message on the board from the warden informing residents that the cart would be back at four that afternoon—a message that was repeated over the public address system. "The new garbage dumping times are between four p.m. and six thirty p.m.," the loudspeaker announced, contradicting the posted sign and adding to the confusion. "At six forty-five p.m. the cart will be hauled away. Fellow neighbors are kindly requested to *not* discard their garbage at other times." To my great relief, no names or units were mentioned.

In addition to time discipline, the spatiality of trash—especially its disposal in *improper* places—remained an ongoing site of government intervention during my fieldwork. Though concerns about health, hygiene, and social order remained, an emphasis on waste as environmental and aesthetic pollution began to emerge. Despite the tireless efforts of wardens to enforce urban civilization, trash could be found all across the complex during my research, especially in communal areas between blocks that were intended as green spaces of leisure. Few places were left unsullied: even a community garden directly behind a collection point became a dumping site for household waste. In February 2011, the frustration of my block's warden intensified. One morning he wrote on the board, "It is senseless to throw piles of trash in the garden. . . . It pollutes [*gây ô nhiễm*] the area and makes it unattractive [*mất mỹ quan*]." Still, residents continued to ignore the exasperated, yet always polite, pleas to "kindly refrain from throwing waste" in undesignated locations.

Over time, I began to see these acts as taking an ethical stance of urban indifference that was as intentional as it was political (Tonkiss 2003). In some cases, residents made refuse—the very materiality of their modernist refusal—purposefully visible, as if to bring attention to the precarity wrought by disrepair (see chapter 8). For example, in blocks B3 and A5, which faced the main thoroughfare through town (Quang Trung Road) and served as the public face of the housing estate, residents dropped trash onto the corrugated rooftops of the makeshift shops below. This infuriated municipal authorities, as well as some tenants, as it reinforced an image of the housing blocks as poor and blighted—even a slum. "Uncivilized" trash in "civilized" spaces became even farcical at times. The retiree from the Department of Culture asked me, laughing, "Have you seen the piles of trash next to the 'Phố Văn minh' ['Civilized Street'] sign? Did you notice how the trash uses the signpost for support? Did you take a picture? I did!" This was hardly the orderly, utopian future that architects had envisioned. As the planner quoted at the start of this chapter observed, beset by filth, Vinh seemed set to become another example of the ruins left behind by socialism.

THE PROBLEM OF STAIRWAYS

Housing-block stairways were another embattled commons. As an ethnographer, I found stairwells (and their blackboards) exciting places to take the pulse of daily life, and I traversed them daily as part of my methods. In Vinh, stairwells were not just functional, enabling movement from one floor to the next, but heterotopias, or countersites that reconfigured state intentions (Foucault 1986, 24). In contrast to the dark spaces of alienation that Boym describes for Soviet stairways (1994, 140–41), in Vinh they were vibrant, gendered spaces for social activities. Recall the line from the poem "High-Rise in Vinh," excerpted in interlude 4: "Lên cầu thang ai cũng hỏi chào" (Greeting everyone on the stairs). Neighbors stopped on stairways to talk, especially near the announcement boards (which often prompted a cynical exchange); women cooked with coal, away from the apartments and in violation of posted regulations; men worked out with concrete weights; children played games, including drawing with chalk on the tiled floors; teenagers smoked and engaged in other "social evils"; and so on. East German architects had not intended such stairway sociability; like Soviet planners, they had envisioned clear boundaries between public and private spaces and activities. Disrepair, along with discarded rubbish, soon followed the socializing. Residents disregarded (or vandalized) posted regulations to "protect the stairwells and maintain communal hygiene." They remade the commons to be more responsive to their needs, and in doing so, subverted the state and the party's civilizing mission (see figure 7.1).

Stairways provoked widespread ambivalence, especially among female workers, who saw in them everything they disliked about living in an urban high-rise (including having to climb stairs). Given their "misuse," steps were often chipped and railings cracked; the whole apparatus was usually ridden with debris. Because they were public spaces for domestic practices, residents did not feel the same compulsion to keep these areas dirt-free, as they would their homes. And since there were no trash receptacles around the complex (only dumping grounds or collection sites at certain hours), residents often dropped food wrappers and other refuse in the stairways. Wardens devised various disciplinary actions to prevent littering and to institute a regular routine of cleaning. This cost residents time in community labor, and money to collectively fund repairs, which led to more indignation (and complaints on the stairs). Wardens threatened to give negative marks in their annual assessment of cultured families—which did not incentivize tenants to treat the stairways any differently. From their perspective, stairway disorder owed more to state neglect than to their individual conduct. Tense debates continued over who was accountable for the mismanagement of waste: negligent authorities or not-yet-enlightened residents.

Public filth, Susan S. Morrison has argued, not only "undermines the authority of public infrastructure"; it weakens state legitimacy (2015, 75). In Quang Trung, tensions about residents' indifference to trash came to a head during my fieldwork on December 31, 2010, when the municipal landfill closed before the new disposal site had opened. Over the next ten days, piles of rotting trash flooded streets across Vinh. While angry residents demanded a solution, they continued as usual to toss their garbage indifferently onto growing heaps. For them, the garbage crisis was just another disruption to urban infrastructure, one spawned through *state* disorder, not their defiant acts. An interim waste management system was hurriedly put into place, which required tenants to haul their trash *outside* the complex to adjacent main streets. And yet the trash piles in front of buildings *within* the complex continued to grow, prompting another intervention and disciplinary threat. The note left on the board by the block C6 warden created even more confusion: "For those who do not comply and continue to leave trash at the bottom of the stairs [i.e., at the collection point, per the usual rule of enforcement], we will bring it right back up to your apartment."

Conflicts between residents and municipal authorities around waste had been ongoing for more than three decades during my research. Authorities wielded domestic waste management as a tool of moral improvement to produce disciplined socialist citizens. Provided they did their part to keep mass housing free of filth, residents would enjoy a hygienic, utopian urbanism. But tenants, especially women, felt skeptical about the state's modernization agenda. For them, dumping waste where they saw fit was a way to express discontent with urban disorder, not to create it. A lengthy history of disrepair and decay had generated disenchantment with municipal governance and its goal of social betterment. Women's defiant acts of spreading filth rather than eliminating it (per gendered expectations) aroused anxieties about rural backwardness and the prospect of a belated urbanization. In this view, heaps of trash were a sign not of capitalist surplus and an excess of modernity, as in more prosperous cities (Gidwani and Reddy 2011), but of its absence. Because Vinh was a poor, provincial city struggling to rebuild its postwar economy, the accumulation of trash on its streets, gardens, stairways, and rooftops (and in its drains) challenged the teleology of socialist development by advancing decay of the complex.

8

DECAY

> Architecture . . . carries within itself the traces of its future destruction, the already past future, future perfect, of its ruin . . . [and] is haunted, indeed signed, by the spectral silhouette of this ruin.
>
> —JACQUES DERRIDA, "A LETTER TO PETER EISENMAN," 1990

By the time I moved into Quang Trung in September 2010, the buildings were in a severe state of decay and there was talk of their removal to avert looming crisis. The dominant temporal framing of Vinh's modernity had radically shifted: the city of tomorrow, as endangered present, was to become but a memory of the past's future. I encountered this temporal shift from anticipation to endangerment (Zeiderman 2016, 170), from hope to risk, in dystopian narratives of collapsing buildings. For instance, one day, while I was walking around to introduce myself, an elderly man in block C9 mistook me for an investor and asked, "Are you here to knock down my house and build a new one?" Sensing an ethnographic opportunity, I probed, "Do you want it demolished?" "Why, yes!" he exclaimed. "The quality has seriously deteriorated [*xuống cấp trầm trọng*], and we need new houses to move into." A neighbor, who held a conflicting view of the urban future—that of renovation rather than demolition—approached us and made an even stronger statement, telling me, "Go and see block C8; that's the worst one. People are going to die there."[1]

Within a short period of time, Vinh's status had fallen from model city to modernist "slum," so much so that even the U.S. press portrayed it as such.[2] While dystopian images of urban decline have long saturated the media (Prakash 2010), the use of the term "slum" rode a wave of capitalist triumphalism that was, at the time, reveling in the downfall of abject architecture as a symbol of socialism's collapse (van der Hoorn 2009). Once the prototype for the country—where viewers gazed at the spectacle of the unthinkable (*điều không tưởng*)—this wasteland turned utopia had abruptly earned itself the title of "least attractive city" in Vietnam, at least according to one American journalist and a host of Western travel guidebooks. As Vinh celebrated its 210th anniversary in 1998, mention of Quang Trung was all but absent from the press. Not a single image of the buildings was included in that year's September issue of the popular, Hanoi-based journal *Xây dựng* (Construction), which featured a glossy, two-page color insert labeled "High-quality buildings in Uncle [Hồ's] homeland." The new architectural face of Vinh was in urgent need of an overhaul, and undisciplined tenants, the rural female migrants especially, were to blame for its dramatic demise.

In this chapter, I outline Quang Trung's rapid change in temporality from future modern to outdated, blighted housing, and its residents from "preferential" (*ưu tiên*) to "poor" (*nghèo*) citizens, a morally tinged status reversal that cultural elites opposed (cf. Wing 2005). "Hey, big sister," said a friend of mine who grew up in Quang Trung and whose parents had worked at the Department of Culture, "did you hear that we are now the 'urban poor'?"[3] She laughed over our lunch, even though her young family was in fact struggling to make ends meet. It was difficult for people to accept the implosion of time and shift in image from being ahead of the curve to lagging behind, from being the celebrated proletariat to an "at-risk" precariat. Earlier projections of the future periodically resurfaced. "This housing was number 1—*Nummer eins*!" one planner reacted angrily to the clipping I showed him from the American journalist.[4] But the mad rush to achieve socialist timelessness had come to an equally swift halt (Ssorin-Chaikov 2006, 359): the ambitious *Bautempo*, or speed of construction, had been negated by the buildings' precipitous decline.

Derrida suggests in the epigraph that ruin was likely there in the very design, as the ghost of demolition lurks ominously in the shadows of modernist architecture (1990, 11). This notion of *planned* obsolescence, or creative destruction as the quintessential material condition of capitalism (Schumpeter 1942), draws on Benjamin's reflections on the distinctive temporality of urban modernity and its unraveling of history into ruins (Schönle 2006, 651). Vinh's architecture, however, did not quite conform to this analysis. Instead, it suggested that *unplanned*—indeed, unanticipated—obsolescence haunted the dream of utopia. Alexei Yurchak aptly captures this temporal paradox between socialism's appeal to eternity and its rather sudden fall in the title of his book *Everything Was Forever, until It Was No More* (2006). The grand architectural designs of socialism *were* built to last; in Vinh's case Quang Trung had a projected life span of eighty years, though deterioration set in almost immediately, reflecting an ironic "house of cards" quality to these "timeless" urban forms (Ssorin-Chaikov 2006, 359).

To be sure, the narrative of ideal-turned-undesirable architecture, upending the rush to the future, is far more complicated than an abrupt, straight decline into dystopia (Yurchak 2006, 4). That some residents felt forced (*bị bắt buộc*) to move into the high-rises had always complicated claims that the buildings *were* the desired future. Behind the modern concrete façade intended to convey a forward trajectory of uplift and recovery, accelerated decay and disrepair kept residents from enjoying the higher standards of living that modernity promised to bring them. As Patricia Morton observed, the afterlife of modern architecture "makes visible the transience of the 'new' and the lie of the promise of progress" (2006, 215).

In chapter 6, I argued that discussions of housing construction were future oriented. When residents talked about the buildings' deterioration, however, they shifted timescales to frame architectural achievement as triumph over an even more dystopian past. That is, the affective appeal of "the ideal" lay in memories of collectively building a better future, and of what the city had once suffered and lost. "At that time, the complex was outstanding, today it is inadequate," one male planner commented, while reminding me of what collaboration with GDR experts had accomplished after Vinh's destruction. "That history is close to my heart," he waxed nostalgically of solidarity.[5] As a narrative device, "the ideal" granted stigmatized buildings, and the people who built them, a place in history (van der Hoorn 2009, 8). Of course, the buildings still have a place in contemporary social life: the inhabited "ruins" of futures past remain first and foremost people's homes. In chapter 7, I showed how waste embodied the material, temporal, and moral ambiguities of modernization as "matter out of place." In this chapter, I show how decay concretized these ambiguities, signifying a changing relationship with municipal authorities and their management of infrastructure breakdown. As residents grew embittered by disrepair and more critical of state neglect, they deployed collective strategies to mitigate the risk of risky architecture.

In the following sections, I examine how Quang Trung residents lived with, responded to, sensed, and made sense of disrepair in their everyday lives. By using the term "disrepair," I point to the distinctive material and temporal experiences of *progressive* breakdown and decay of architecture that contributed to its ruin over the long term. This kind of ruination differed from the ruins of urban annihilation that I described in part 1, when buildings and their inhabitants met with sudden, violent death. A different scale, speed, and intensity of erosion clearly distinguishes deterioration from devastation (Gordillo

2014, 83), as well as from the unhurried decay of Simmel's (1965) aestheticized ruins. My use of "ruins" here is not intended to be romantic or, conversely, pejorative, but is meant to recognize the material "remainders and reminders" of a future that never came to pass (Boym 2008). And yet, all suffered a similar fate: "If architecture is invested with life, what [then] of its death?" (Cairns and Jacobs 2014, 13).

The severe decay of the housing blocks signified architecture's impermanence and its potential to disrupt future-oriented development. Indeed, construction presupposes destruction, Derrida reminds us. But abject "ruins" are also creative, inhabited sites where people strive to maintain their lives and livelihoods, and create new opportunities. As such, they embody "contested projections of meaning and memory" (Slessor 2017) that inspire a broad range of affects and practices while unsettling notions of progress. As with Douglas's dirt (see chapter 7), we can attend to the productive capacities of decay without denying its precarious qualities. Disrepair certainly put people, and especially women, at risk and added to their daily toil, as I show below. But it also generated transgressive possibilities to redefine their relationship to risk, as well as to one another, through risk management strategies in the absence of state protection. The lack of maintenance sparked outrage among Quang Trung residents, fomenting collective action in some cases and inaction in others. Breaches in the system generated an ethos of solidarity and "flexible, tactical collaborations" (Simone and Fauzan 2012, 130), as much as they exposed disparities and fragmentation. As I show below, tenants and municipal authorities debated the issue of responsibility for decay and its mitigation through the blurred metaphorical and infrastructural divide between *bên ngoài* (exteriors) and *bên trong* (interiors).

THE ROUTINE OF BREAKDOWN

Infrastructure breakdown is an intensely sensory experience. I learned this with the leak in my apartment, which had been ongoing for more than a week.[6] I heard the faint dripping, smelled the mustiness, and saw the puddles of water that felt cool on my toes, but I could not determine the source. I traced the leak to the bathroom ceiling, but on the advice of neighbors I decided to ignore it. Then, one winter morning, I woke to find the bathroom and hallway flooded with cold water. Leaks were one of the dystopian experiences in the decaying buildings that had once exemplified infrastructural modernity. Here, breakdown was not catastrophic but part of an everyday fractal, "always-almost-falling-apart" world (Jackson 2014, 222). Every household in

Quang Trung had water damage from leaks, though few people invested effort in tracing their origins. Such knowledge would have meant confronting the prickly issue of accountability and debating the ethics and economics of maintenance and repair. Most leaks eventually either stopped by themselves or were fixed with minor tweaks. Breakdown as routine meant a certain routine of breakdown that generated endless innovation and improvisation, as well as ambivalence—toward leaks, but also toward the state (*nhà nước*). Residents expressed their increasing disenchantment with municipal authorities, whose negligence made them vulnerable to precarious living conditions.

When I first mentioned the leak to my landlady, a divorced teacher who had grown up in Quang Trung, and my upstairs neighbors, who had moved in ten years ago, they shrugged.[7] Drips and trickles were not reason enough for repair work; besides, once fixed, they would inevitably continue elsewhere. But after the flooding incident, I decided to take action. I asked around for the telephone number of a plumber, assuming that a chronic state of disrepair meant there would be a bustling business in maintenance, but no one in my housing block used such services. Finally, a friend of a friend—a computer scientist with no plumbing experience and dressed in business attire—came and opened the ceiling. Water streamed out through an old plaster patch that could no longer hold back the tide. "Xuống cấp lắm" (bad deterioration), he said to my alarm. "Khó sửa" (difficult to repair).[8] He promised to find someone who knew about plumbing, and then left. My landlady started to show her irritation. "I take care of my house," she told me, revealing a moral stance beneath the façade that residents did not know who was responsible for upkeep. "Others don't take care of their flats, and now it's affecting me," she added, revealing cracks in the appearance of a united front. But when it came to repairs, she waved dismissively and told me I could worry about it if I pleased. She had no intention of investing her limited funds in fixing another glitch, when glitches were the normal routine.

A plumber eventually discovered that the leak was coming from the upstairs neighbors' toilet. But they also avoided responsibility, even though the cause was only an eroded steel nut. Had it been addressed earlier, it would have been a fairly simple fix. But now it had escalated to a structural problem, and given the building's advanced state of decay, the neighbors refused to assume liability. In a moral order where the state is expected to maintain infrastructure for the well-being of tenants, the source of the *interior* leak became secondary to its *exterior* damage: water seeping through already crumbling floors, ceilings, and walls. This launched a heated attempt at fault assessment, with responsibility passing among state and nonstate actors. Residents argued over the fuzzy boundaries between the building's exterior (*bên ngoài*), which they felt fell under the purview of the city's maintenance, and the home interior (*bên trong*), where tenant liability began. But even that distinction was difficult to make. In the end, my landlady and neighbors could not agree on a clear line of responsibility for the repair, nor on liability for damages—did it extend to her ceiling, for instance, which encompassed the liminal space between interior and exterior? Where did bên trong start and bên ngoài end?

My nonresident friend suggested that the municipal Housing Agency should be held accountable, and everyone laughed. The last major repair that residents remembered had happened in the late 1990s, when authorities had added iron braces to crumbling support beams along the corridor to avert their collapse. The lone on-site administrator at the Housing Agency (Công ty Nhà đất, formerly Housing Management Office)[9] confirmed this risk intervention. Mr. Nguyên oversaw daily operations in Quang Trung, including rent collection. He defended state inaction from his secluded office in the dangerously decrepit block A1 through claims to state fiscal insecurity. "Demands for repairs are high and funds are low," he told me defensively.[10] Because I had secured the necessary bureaucratic approvals from his higher-ups, affirmed on the paperwork I carried at all times, Nguyên was, to some extent, duty bound to talk with me. With its magic red stamp, my paperwork exemplified documents as nonhuman actants that "do things," like provoke a response and compel compliance (Cooren 2004, 378). This is frequently the case in hierarchical governance systems, as in Vietnam, where civil servants tend to adhere to rules and the chain of command (Le, Biesbroek, and Wals 2018, 2). Nguyên always made it clear, however, that I showed up at the wrong time and asked too many questions. Nevertheless, I think he actually enjoyed my visits—and my small tokens of appreciation. He seemed to take pleasure in calling me "em," or younger sister. He was the only bureaucrat to do so, and I saw this linguistic exercise of power as one of the ways he could exert authority in a lackluster government job with few resources to manage risk in the complex.

Nguyên liked to offer facts that were seemingly objective and thus safe to share with a foreigner. For example, Công ty Nhà đất received a budget of just 700 million VND (approximately U.S. $35,000) from the province every two years for maintenance and repair. I was surprised it was even that high, however, given the scale of disrepair in every housing block I had surveyed. Sixty-six percent of households reported needing repairs to the inside and outside of their homes, and 60 percent reported dangerous living conditions.[11] These numbers broke down differently across the complex: block C8 was in the lead, with a whopping 96 percent of households reporting hazardous decay, compared with 30 percent in my block (C2) and 35 percent in block A5, the first block built according to GDR design and known to be of the highest quality. When I pointed this out, Nguyên frowned. He was well aware of dystopian representations of the housing blocks, which the press regularly covered. Indeed, his office had produced the official evaluations of the buildings as dangerous, with estimates of remaining structural capacities ranging between 40 and 60 percent across the complex. But his hands were tied. To be fair, he was a disempowered, "street-level bureaucrat" at the frontline of municipal policy (Lipsky 1980)—and inefficiency. With a sigh, he told me, "With this money, we cannot carry out substantive repairs, only small jobs such as whitewashing the exterior [*quét vôi*, literally coating with lime]." When I mentioned this to a woman who lived in dilapidated housing in Hanoi, a city whose mass-housing stock suffered similar neglect (Koh 2004, 347), she responded cynically, "That's how they hide the decay!"[12] As a form of masking, whitewashing allowed officials to strategically maintain an outward appearance of upkeep, normalcy, and benevolent care, while neglecting critical structural deficiencies within. The woman in Hanoi seemed to suggest that quét vôi was an apt metaphor for the artifices of socialist governance and its façade of national development.

Who, then, was ultimately liable for unplanned obsolescence? Nguyên had a host of explanations for why the state could not fulfill its maintenance obligations as per the municipal housing regulations (*nội quy*). According to article 7 of those regulations, liability hinged on vague distinctions between temporality and intentionality, rather than spatiality, or between bên ngoài and bên trong. It states, "The Office of the Management of Housing bears the responsibility to repair damage to the buildings through natural causes that occur over time; damage that occurs as a result of a tenant's actions must be repaired by that tenant's household. If serious, the tenant can be prosecuted according to the law."[13] This directive left a lot of room for ambiguity. Simmel made a clear division between the natural, romantic ruin—a product of time—and the less spectacular, inhabited ruin, when "man makes himself the accomplice of nature" (1965, 261). In Vinh, progressive decay by "natural" forces and ruin by human intention were not so easy to distinguish. Simmel pointed to the role of indifference in the case of the inhabited ruin: "What strikes us is not, to be sure, that human beings destroy the work of man—this indeed is achieved by nature—but that men *let it decay*" (1965, 261, emphasis in original). In Simmel's view, counter to article 7, there are no "natural causes" for ruin when leaders passively allow a building to "die." Vulnerable tenants in Quang Trung would agree. Nguyên, however, saw things differently. After all, he was in charge of the numbers, and they did not add up. Besides, he confided, there would be no more repairs due to plans to rebuild the area "to đẹp hơn" (bigger and more beautiful). These words echoed Hồ Chí Minh's call for socialist reconstruction after the war (chapter 5), but now paradoxically applied to capitalist redevelopment after reforms (chapter 10). They suggested that keeping residents in a "state of protracted precarity" (Zeiderman 2016, 186) actually served the interests of the state, as decay would be a pretense for renewal and relocation.

CORRUPT ARCHITECTURES

Infrastructure neglect and the lack of state investment in building maintenance were topics of heated discussion in the housing complex during my research, and the substance of enduring criticism of housing officials. Some of the more vociferous critics accused the state of endemic corruption through the metaphor of *ăn tiền*, or "eating the money" that was supposed to go to housing upkeep. "Gifted" buildings that had once represented socialist benevolence, modernity, solidarity, and utopian futurity became the topic of rumors about "corrupt architecture" (van der Hoorn 2009, 2) that exposed a deep distrust of local government and a moral rift between tenants and higher authorities. Tenants generally saw the lower-placed ward- and district-level leaders and bureaucrats as their advocates. Indeed, several residents held those posts, blurring the line between state and nonstate actors in structures of urban governance. The most vocalized complaint involved rent, which remained heavily subsidized—averaging 30,000 VND monthly, or U.S. $1.50, during my fieldwork (less than 2 percent of monthly pensions)—and pointed to a breach of financial obligation. As one woman, a former bricklayer and builder of Quang Trung, calculated, "We moved here thirty years ago and have been paying rent to the state ever since. If you take all the households here and estimate length of time by amount paid monthly, then there should be more than enough to cover repairs."[14] A retired carpenter at Unification Woodworks who sold soft drinks outside block B4 agreed but pointed to a twofold betrayal of both the social *and* legal contract: "These apartments were a gift from Germany to the homeland of Uncle [Hồ] [*Đức tặng quê hương Bác*]. And then we had to pay rent! Where did that money go all these years? Not to maintenance! The state ate it!"[15] This woman's moral repugnance at having to pay for the bequest of material solidarity was bolstered by her anger at the unraveling of the social system that placed the interests of individual authorities ("the state") before the care of deserving tenants, a sentiment that scholars have also noted among populations in post-Soviet Central Asia (Alexander 2007a, 85).

Other rumors revived the socialist trope of German beneficence, magnifying the sense of municipal deceit and moral decrepitude. "[East] Germany provided aid to build these apartments, and now the government can't be bothered to even repair them!" one distraught veteran in block B3 declared.[16] Residents debated whether the GDR government had provided funds for building maintenance that had been subsequently "eaten," though Nguyên denied this. Another story circulated that the present-day German embassy had given the city money to refurbish the apartment blocks. After German reunification, officials in Bonn had maligned the buildings of the GDR's discredited socialist past, thus their eager demolition of the Palace of the Republic that had housed the East German parliament in Berlin (Bach 2017). Quang Trung was an equally symbolic site for the GDR's claims to political legitimacy. The story that the reunified government had revamped the façade of *đơn* (building unit) 3 in block B6 made sense against this background of architectural erasure and rehabilitation. The hasty replacement of the chipped, gray concrete front with sparkling white tile in 1998 seemed to announce, "Drab socialism be gone. There is a brighter future on the horizon!" (see figure 8.1). This facelift only served to mask the decrepit structure behind it, however; an apt symbol of the false promises of capitalist liberation. No one—not even Nguyên—understood, however, why the repairs had stopped at only one random đơn, which fueled further speculation: *ăn tiền*. "And where did that money from the German embassy go? The leaders ate it!" the soft-drink vendor alleged, her voice rising. These were just rumors, however. UN-Habitat, not Germany, had in fact supported the façade renovation (Shannon and Loeckx 2004). Nonetheless, the German government was involved in other refurbishment projects to "correct" the buildings' ailments, including upgrading the "faulty" wastewater system in collaboration with INFRAVI (see note 9). This happened as GDR loans (not gifts!) to Vietnam were converted into development aid that promoted structural adjustment programs. Rumors of corruption and indifference to decay on the one hand, and rescue tales of German (socialist and neoliberal) care and altruism on the other, showed how residents grappled with liability for breakdown and an acute sense of abandonment by the state.

COLLECTIVE MAINTENANCE

Scholars have argued that disputes over infrastructure generate possibilities for social and political collectivities to emerge around glitches, breakdown, and upkeep (for example, Chu 2014; Anand 2012; Graham and Thrift 2007). Through the encounter with the leak in my apartment, I was able to see how

↑ Figure 8.1 Facing a new future: updates to the façade of block B6, 2011. Photo by the author.

residents in Quang Trung responded collectively to problems with disrepair. Because the dampness from the seeping water had given my hallway a strong musty smell, and the walls and floor were starting to mold in the dank winter weather, I decided to ask the plumber to complete the job and offered to cover costs, despite my friend's protests that this was not my responsibility. Apart from bringing in an outside expert, the monetary intervention was, to me, the most expedient way to ensure a more healthful living environment. However, this decision violated the collective refusal to shift culpability from the state to the household. It also threatened to disrupt the established ethos of improvisation that hinged on collective, rather than individual, action. By "improvisation," I mean the social and moral practices of cocreation through which people make collective claims to rights and resources (Fischlin, Heble, and Lipsitz 2013, xi). These differ from the tactical, do-it-*yourself* (DIY) urbanism of megacities in the neoliberal North (Iveson 2013), which my response seemed to reflect. Rather, improvisation reflected a commoning strategy that coalesced around shared experiences of decay and difficulties with infrastructure. Since allocation of the housing blocks to tenants in the late 1970s, this ethos has generated important solidarities and informal mechanisms of maintenance as a nonstate response to chronic breakdown.

Even when reluctant to do so, residents typically funded, and at times carried out, repairs to *exterior* spaces collectively. Some of this collaborative maintenance was obligatory, though residents referred to it as "tự nguyện," or voluntary. The moral pressure that residents felt to contribute money and time kept most people compliant, not unlike the pressure surrounding GDR solidarity donations to Vietnam (chapter 3). For example, households in my block were asked on the community blackboard to contribute 100,000 VND (U.S. $5) toward patching up damaged stairs and handrails. A few households "forgot" to pay, which prompted a written reproach on the board soon after. When residents complained about lack of transparency, a detailed budget for upgrading the small meeting and parking house in my ward also went up on the board. Next to it appeared a list of those who had paid the "donation" of 120,000 VND (U.S. $6), which effectively outed households that had not contributed. We then received another request for 100,000 VND each to renovate street and stairway lights around the *entire* complex. If everyone complied, the total amount collected would be close to U.S. $6,500. This request pushed many people, like my neighbor Văn, a retired mechanic and war veteran who had studied his trade in East Germany, to the breaking point. It was not just the constant malfunctioning that irked him, but the state's deliberate *undoing* of modern infrastructure and with it, technological enlightenment that had once been in reach. On a frigid morning as we sat drinking warm tea, Văn shared his angry, and somewhat nostalgic, thoughts about the fated gift of urban luminosity:

> You know, when [East] Germany built these homes, we had electricity and lights on the buildings. The streets were lit up! We didn't have to pay anything.[17] And then the state came and cut it all. They turned off the lights and removed the bulbs to save money! . . . Today we have to contribute to everything: fixing the roads, funding repairs, support for flood victims. . . . And now we have to pay to reinstall the lights. It's ridiculous! My pension is 1.4 million VND [U.S. $70]. How should I pay for all of this?[18]

Văn's words captured the bitterness I observed among residents as the burden of infrastructural responsibility shifted from the state to citizens, depleting their limited resources. The *dis*assembly of new electrical infrastructure before the end of its "life" to cut state spending showed how quickly utopian dreams of brighter futures turned dystopic, plunging residents literally and metaphorically back into darkness.

Tenants also initiated repair projects themselves, as a citizen-led solution to state neglect and allegations of ăn tiền. That self-managed groups of networked neighbors took *collective* responsibility for maintenance shows that neoliberal governmentality is not by itself sufficient to explain "responsible subjects." Rather, as Susanna Trnka and Catherine Trundle have argued, multiple meanings and enactments of this concept call into question the tendency to "define and discuss responsibility in largely neoliberal terms" (2014, 136–37). As I argued in chapter 6, notions of self-actualization and self-sufficiency were central to ideologies of socialism, which were influenced by nineteenth-century liberalism and its colonial iterations of "responsibilization" (Rose 1999, 214). Discourses of responsibility in Vietnam have shifted with new modes of governance under market reforms (Schwenkel and Leshkowich 2012), even as tenants continued to look to the paternal state for their welfare and upkeep of apartments, bestowed for their role in nation building. In many ways, comaintenance was driven by a desire to uphold the social(ist) contract rather than engage in oppositional politics; this was not about protest but redress (Bayat 2013, 49). In avoiding the pitfalls of atomization (as in my self-concerned plumbing repairs), collective action affirmed the ethos of mutual care and interdependence that residents traced back to wartime suffering, and which motivated their practices of commoning and cooperation to protect their entitlement to safe housing.

Corridors were considered the most dangerous areas in the buildings, and thus were the best places to witness how collectivities formed around decay and disrepair. As shared spaces of mobility, corridors were a liminal zone of nebulous responsibility. Considered state property (*tài sản của nhà nước*) that was structurally exterior to homes, tenants assigned liability for crumbling beams, columns, panels, ceilings, and floors to the Housing Agency. Notably, these were all prefabricated components tied to imported technology. In their everyday use, corridors were porous spaces of improvisation between bên ngoài and bên trong. Benjamin described urban space in Naples in a similar way: "As porous as this stone is the architecture. Building and action interpenetrate" in shared spaces of habitation that "become a theater of new, unforeseen constellations" (1978, 165–66). GDR aspirations for family-centered, self-contained dwellings as the model for socialist living required new public-private divisions, created through spatial technologies such as doors and walls, which contained the domestic sphere (chapter 6). But much of life in mass housing unfolded in open heterotopic spaces like stairways, corridors, and courtyards, rather than behind shut doors, as I argued in chapter 7. Indeed, doors stayed open, resisting the divisions encouraged by these spatializing practices. The poem in interlude 4 captures this sense of cultural incongruence: "We don't close doors, private units feel lonely."

Urban porosity thus not only further blurred public/private, indoor/outdoor distinctions, historically ill defined in Vietnam (Drummond 2000); it also loosened the boundaries imposed to uphold a strict sociospatial order (Stavrides 2007, 175). Despite regulations to maintain safety, orderliness, and hygiene, corridors were convivial spaces brimming with altars (for wandering ghosts), flowers, herbs, cats, shoes, laundry, flags, and coal stoves with simmering pots of tea (see plates 6 and 8). Corridors connected up to four or five apartments and could be locked off and made inaccessible to nonresidents under certain circumstances. Their decay was therefore a matter of graver concern than that of other communal spaces, like stairwells. While everyone maintained that "nhà nước có trách nhiệm để sửa" (the state has the responsibility to repair) corridors, residents also saw the Housing Agency's attempt to stabilize crumbling columns with iron braces as ineffective (see figure 8.2). Individual actions, like the random patching of cracked ceilings, were deemed equally futile (see figure 8.3). Tenants in some buildings turned to a collaborative approach to repair as a solution to mounting architectural instability (see plate 8). An engineer in block C6 who had supervised construction of Quang Trung, and who organized his neighbors, explained, "We realized that if the state wouldn't fix the corridor, then we would have to ourselves."[19] But co-maintenance as a strategy to reclaim the commons from decay had its limits: on the engineer's floor, only three of the four households agreed to contribute 1 million VND (U.S. $50) to repair their shared space. In disrupting the routine of breakdown, collective action rendered the state unnecessary and in the process legitimized its neglectful, postreform policies that successfully shifted the locus of responsibility for upkeep to tenants (Roy 2005, 148).

Collective maintenance exposed where solidarity broke down among different groups of residents. One fault line fell along length of residence—for example, between original tenants with records of labor excellence who had been allocated apartments (*được phân*), including my landlady's family, and those who had bought into the complex (*mua lại*), mainly traders and small entrepreneurs who started arriving after the liberalization of housing in 1991, such as my upstairs neighbors. This moral-temporal distinction drew clear lines between belonging and nonbelonging through claims to a distinctive community of affect. The former group saw the latter, at times, as less cooperative; for example, the household that did not contribute 1 million VND to the corridor renovation was mua lại, while the three who did were original tenants. The được phân tenants also considered the mua lại tenants to be lacking in the *tình làng nghĩa xóm*, or "village neighborliness" (meaning, sense of close-knit community), that had bonded them in wartime and in the

← Figure 8.2
A state attempt at corridor repair in block C2, 2011. Photo by the author.

← Figure 8.3
A resident's attempt at corridor repair in block C5, 2011. Photo by the author.

early years in Quang Trung, creating emotional attachments to the complex. A chemistry professor in my block explained this demographic shift as the dispersal of consolidated affect, a common lament: "Things started to change after people began to mua lại [buy user rights] and move onto the premises. At first, we all knew one another and suffered hardships with each other. Afterwards, there were people we did not know, and sentiment started to decrease [*tình cảm đã giảm*]."[20] Unity did not break down only with "outsiders." As I argued in chapter 7, social distinctions endured between those with rural and those with urban subjectivities, which mapped onto gender, status, and occupation. To understand *đoàn kết* (solidarity) as a historically contingent social and moral practice that became a powerfully affective tool in disputes over decay, I turn now to tenants' early encounters with urban obsolescence through water infrastructure malfunction.

DRY TAPS

> You pump the water so carelessly
> It hasn't even ascended before it starts to go down!
> How miserable for the people who live on the upper floors
> They wait and wait at night until their eyes turn red with anxiety
> Their bodies dry and thirsty.
>
> —ANONYMOUS, VINH, 1986

The concentration of residents in high-rise housing required a hydraulic infrastructure at a scale unlike any in Vinh's history.[21] East German engineers were charged with designing a water and sanitation system that included treatment plants, storage facilities, pumping stations (so water could reach the fifth floor), and an extensive network of water and sewer mains. Teams of workers laid over fourteen kilometers of piping—7,884 meters to supply water and 6,608 meters for wastewater removal (Hội hữu nghị 2011, 54)—and built nine holding tanks across the complex with a total capacity of 520 cubic meters, enough for a projected average of sixty-five liters per resident daily. In area A, one cement tank had a capacity of 104 cubic meters, and areas B and C each had four tanks that held a total of 416 cubic meters. Every apartment was outfitted for private indoor plumbing—a first for tenants—with an imported, ceramic squat toilet in a water closet and an adjacent washroom with a water-supply line. Ideally, when the state turned on the pumps, tenants could fill a large concrete cistern with tap water for washing and cooking throughout the day in the confines of one's home, thereby reducing women's domestic labor. This system remains in place today, though plastic or metal tanks have replaced most of the concrete drums. Through the flow of water into, and wastewater out of, single-family flats, these modern facilities attempted to instill a "new moral geography of social behavior" that domesticated hygienic practices (Gandy 2004, 366–67), in contrast to previous forms of collective living. Like waste disposal in the last chapter, water distribution shows how disciplined urban citizens could be made and trained through the proper use of modern infrastructure.

Hope that the state would provide modern technology through dependable public services quickly evaporated, however, as residents moved in and taps in the upper apartments ran dry. The issue was not water scarcity but rather the technology of water flow: there was only enough pressure to move water up two stories. Nikhil Anand's (2011, 543) work on hydraulic pressure has shown how both material and social relations enable access to water. Likewise, in Vinh, inadequate pressure technologies, combined with a lack of electricity, meant that new solidarities and improvisational practices across the floors were necessary to facilitate water accessibility. It also revealed systemic rifts, as higher-ranking public servants typically were allocated units on the lower floors that had less water insecurity. Even so, that water was reportedly murky and "red as crab," as the anonymous poem addressed to the water company, excerpted in the epigraph, complained.[22] This imbalance undermined the ideal of egalitarian distribution of infrastructure and exposed stratification in the intimate spheres of daily life.

Water shortages on upper floors created immense difficulties for newly settled residents, especially women. Indoor plumbing was intended to free them from domestic work, but it paradoxically rendered many of their daily tasks even more cumbersome as residents struggled to gain access to water. Likewise, the attempt to domesticate hygiene—including bathing and laundering in the home—resulted in communal practices that planners sought to discourage. Men and children, for example, continued to bathe outdoors, as they had in shared housing without plumbing, and women continued to gather at wells to wash clothes together. Such acts undermined the values of self-mastery and the model of the nuclear family that GDR designs encouraged (chapter 6). Rural migrants had been skeptical of such spatial arrangements and values from the start, but even the cultural elites felt their initial excitement about self-contained apartments with modern amenities give way to a critical reassessment of the socialist project. "Ideal living, with no water or electricity? A symbol of socialism? Not one bit!" fumed a retired journalist in block C3.[23]

Feminist geographers have shown how water insecurity often exacerbates gender inequalities at the scale of households and communities (Truelove 2011, 145). I also found this to be the case in Quang Trung, with one important exception: during the early years, water scarcity necessitated the suspension of the gendered division of labor. Because families had to haul water (*gánh nước*) many times to fill the cistern in the washroom, residents abandoned the gendered labor practices that assigned women to water tasks. "It was so arduous!" recalled a retired female construction worker who had moved into the complex unwillingly. "Everyone in the family had to help."[24] Men and women remembered the exhausting nightly routine as a battle with time. Typically, the water would turn on at some point between eleven p.m. and two a.m., but the flow was not long or strong enough to reach the upper floors. Family members would descend quickly and race to the nearest public spout, sometimes blocks away, to stand in line to collect water. Each person could carry thirty liters: two buckets attached

↑ Figure 8.4 Communal washing and water collection outside the housing blocks, 1980. BArch DH 1/Bild-28565-06-02.

to the ends of a yoke. A man in block C3 who had worked at the Department of Commerce (and whose wife had been a war photographer) recalled his evening task: "It was burdensome! For years, we had to bring water upstairs in the middle of the night." But, he reasoned, the apartments were still more comfortable than the thatched collective housing where he had lived before. He waxed nostalgic about the sociality that formed around communal hardship among neighbors from different ranks and work units: "We were always on the stairs conversing with one another!"[25] This was in the early years, however, before UNICEF built wells on-site and the gender order was reinstated (see figure 8.4). Still, water would continue to remain a focal point of communal daily activity.

Residents' frustration intensified over time. This was the case not only for those without water on the upper floors, but also for those who lived on the lower floors, like my landlady's family, who recalled pitching in to help neighbors after filling their own cistern. "There was a lot of solidarity in Quang Trung then," my landlady recalled.[26] In 1986, economic reforms (*Đổi mới*) put an end to centralized distribution, including housing allocation and free health care and education. The same year, the local newspaper published the anonymous poem to the water company (see section epigraph). Applying political pressure through public chastisement, the poet berated authorities for their inaction, declaring that residents had waited long enough for a regular supply of clean water in their flats.

Although critics like the poet blamed indifferent authorities for the dry taps, housing officials and residents assessed accountability in more multifaceted ways. Their views revealed other measures of social distinction that structured daily life in the complex, including residents' *trình độ văn hóa*, or cultural capital and level of education. As argued in chapter 7, cultural elites who embraced the civilizing project of socialist modernity fashioned themselves as disciplined urban subjects who were more culturally refined than rural migrants. As with littering, migrant workers became the scapegoats for water-system dysfunction. In a moral order that identifies subalterns, or people of lower status, as incapable of living in modern housing, these female workers were held responsible for its breakdown. A year before the anonymous poem was published, an unsigned editorial appeared in the same newspaper that examined the causes and effects of water disruption. The writer asked readers to consider the impact of hauling water up several flights of stairs during the night on workers' health and productivity, and how it compromised nation building. While holding housing authorities responsible for technical issues with the new system, such as cracks in the pipes that contributed to pressure deficiencies, the author also faulted residents for their misuse of infrastructure, adopting language similar to that used to describe litterers: "Many people on the upper floors [that is, those of lower rank] have no sense [*không có ý thức*] how to use and care for the water-supply system"—for example, they left their tap open, which diverted pressure from others.[27] Such laments against the urban poor are not unique to Vietnam. "The unhygienic and undisciplined indigenous tenant who needs further tutelage in the arts of living in a house" is often the culprit of disrepair (Lea and Pholeros 2010, 197).

Ironically, the kilometers of pipes that symbolized a new democratic urban order (water for all!) came to undermine the project of technological modernity by exposing the aberrations and inequalities of infrastructure. Cultural elites also held female migrant workers responsible for disruptions in the wastewater system, even though modern conveniences like indoor plumbing were a novelty that everyone had to become familiar with. Susan Leigh Star has argued that infrastructures are learned arrangements that constitute membership in a "community of practice" (1999, 381). I, too, had to learn how to navigate the system. For one engineer who lived in block C5, however, migrants' persistent rural ways positioned them outside this community of practice and threatened to undo socialist development. His reasoning echoed Professor Giao's explanations: "There was a new wastewater system, but it was always backed up [*bị tắc liên tục*] because of misuse. The toilets were the most modern in Vinh at the time [*hiện đại nhất*]. But people didn't know how to use them and threw all sorts of things into the drains. These people were new to the city, and they continued to live like in the countryside [*sống như ở nông thôn*]."[28] Residents without water on the upper floors, mostly migrants who queued nightly at a public tap, thus failed to behave as modern socialist persons. Instead, they had their own ideas about the disposal of solid waste, which caused overflow on lower floors, where higher-ranked tenants lived. Such acts were not meant to protest stratification within the housing blocks, but they did suggest a refusal to comply with the use of modern infrastructural systems as instructed.

THINGS FALL APART

> In the process of decay, and in it alone, the events of history shrivel up and become absorbed in the setting.
>
> —WALTER BENJAMIN, *THE ORIGIN OF GERMAN TRAGIC DRAMA*, (1963) 2009

By the mid-1990s, almost twenty years after the first tenants moved in, most apartments had regular access to water. With water, however, came a condition that Cairns and Jacobs have called "obduracy-in-obsolescence": when a building falls out of time but remains in place and in use (2014, 111). When I started fieldwork in Quang Trung in 2010, new complications with the water system had emerged. Water did not just flow—it overflowed, as my ordinary story of the drip-to-leak-to-flood illustrated. Encounters with surplus water were part of everyday life in the complex and contributed, over the years, to the buildings' premature disintegration. They were a reminder that architecture is like any other material artifact that needs to be understood through processes of disarticulation, and not as a "stable entity with a durable physical form" (DeSilvey 2006, 324; see also Buchli 2013). This disarticulation was most evident in corridors: long-term water damage had eroded prefabricated components, exposing rusted steel rods and loosening pieces of plaster that fell from ceilings, subjecting residents to bodily harm (see figure 8.5).

← Figure 8.5
Eroded corridor ceilings as a safety risk in block B4. Photo by the author.

In contrast to the awe of attendees at the 1978 housing conference, who gasped at the sight of Vinh's surprising advance to modernity, visitors to Quang Trung today encounter rows of obsolescent housing blocks. Indisputably, block C8 has fallen into the worst disrepair and is at the center of narratives of risk in Quang Trung, shown in the conversation at the start of the chapter. Beset by overcrowded occupancy, it best exemplifies the precarity of "obduracy-in-obsolescence." The apartments in block C8 had been preferentially allocated in 1980 to female workers at Nghệ An Pharmaceuticals; it faced a busy street and an adjacent park with a water fountain built by the GDR as a departure gift (and reminder of the fruits of international socialism), and thus it once commanded one of the best views from Quang Trung (see figure 8.6).[29]

But by the time of my research, the building had emerged as a symbol of urban dystopia: compared with residents of other buildings, three times the number of surveyed households reported dangerous conditions either inside

↑ Figure 8.6 The city's central fountain in front of Quang Trung housing blocks c7 and c8, circa 1981. Photo by Hồ Xuân Thành.

or outside their units. This concurred with the official assessment of c8's precarity: according to the Housing Agency, in 2010 c8 had less than 40 percent of its original structural capacity, a number that is probably inflated, as anything lower would lawfully prevent its privatization and require demolition (chapter 10). Its notorious reputation earned it considerable attention in the local and national press, as shards of the building had fallen onto the heads of female tenants, injuring them.[30] There was no concerted state effort to manage such risk, however. Nguyên told me there were no funds to repair c8, nor were repairs necessary because the city had a plan for urban renewal. Because government officials did not take action—and in fact, rationalized inaction as good for the future—the block was emblematic of the inadequacies of urban governance and self-interested authorities. Housing policies in the postreform era of market socialism put the very female workers that the state had pledged to protect at great risk of bodily harm. Consequently, the women of c8, once the heroic subjects of history, became objects of public pity who needed protection. "Trước đây là ưu tiên, hôm nay là ưu phiền" (the priority of yesterday are the sorrowful today), one cultural elite explained, in a rhyming word play.[31]

The excessive decay of c8 is hardly surprising. Along with blocks c7 and c9, it had undergone a spatial redesign (*cải tiến*) to accommodate more residents (chapter 6). Despite objections from GDR planners, who held competing ideas about modern urban living, the Department of Construction allocated forty apartments in C8 to eighty female workers and their families. When I arrived in 2010, eight units remained occupied by paired families who had been sharing forty square meters of living space for thirty years. The decision to double the number of occupants in C8 continued to infuriate tenants, who saw the Vietnamese government's unilateral decision to increase occupancy, against the advice of foreign experts, as the cause of their unsafe living conditions. Yet residents still debated the scale and speed of the block's decay. I asked the elderly man in C9, quoted at the start of this chapter, why C8 had deteriorated so quickly compared with the other blocks. His answer revealed a distrust of the state: "Because it was the Vietnamese who supervised construction, not the Germans! And they changed the design!"[32]

Government officials were not the only people that residents distrusted, however. I asked a group of retired workers at a tea stand in area B, who claimed they lived in the best housing blocks, what had happened with ward 9 (C7, C8, and C9). "They stole [*ăn cướp*, literally, consumed] the cement," one woman exclaimed. I heard this charge often, even from construction workers involved in the heists. Armed with that knowledge, I probed gently, "Didn't they do that here?" The woman retorted, "How could they? The Germans were supervising! And they supervised closely!" Another chimed in, "They mixed in lime [in ward 9] to make up for the stolen cement so the construction is not as solid as here." A third woman interjected, "They also added sand!"[33] Such comments revealed an association of German technocracy with rational bureaucratic agency, much as Weber (1978) envisioned modern state organization: precision in regulation and procedural adherence, in this case, to assure the structural integrity of "high-quality" buildings. Residents did not hold German engineering accountable for the premature obsolescence, however, even as decay stemmed mostly from prefabricated parts. Instead, dangerous buildings signified the absurdity of the Vietnamese state for undoing sound planning and for the lack of oversight that encouraged the pilfering of materials, both of which led to structural deficiencies. Residents did not criticize the workers but rather the lack of competent management to prevent their misbehavior. One of the women explained with a proverb that rationalized petty theft as the redistribution of goods, "Đói ăn vụng, túng làm liều": One can eat on the sly without consequence when one is hungry and in need.[34]

Government officials and construction workers were not the only ones held liable for the rapid decline of the ward 9 blocks. Migrant women were also seen as agents of decay. Some tenants mentioned the lack of urban sensibility among households in C8, pointing again to the figure of the backward female migrant outside modernity. An architect involved in the construction of areas B and C told me, "Yes, there was theft of cement, but not enough to impact the buildings. *How* people used the buildings played a stronger role in decay." I asked him which people, and he replied, "People like the young women who left agriculture to go to war and then took factory jobs in the city."[35] Imaginaries of female rural timelessness bolstered distinctions between workers and civil servants, as well as divisions within the former category, as male cadres, often in management or technical positions, scorned their female subordinates. A neighbor in block C9, a wounded veteran who worked as a technician at the state printing press after the war, used the present tense to speak about the women, suggesting their refusal to adapt: "They don't know how to live in a high-rise! They only know life in a thatch hut!"[36] This ignored the fact that the women had resided for longer in the housing blocks than in villages, and also revealed anxiety about the feminine rural body in urban space that stands in the way of modernization, a common trope (Leshkowich 2014; Kim 2015). Regardless of the reasons for obsolescence, it was widely recognized that C8 tenants lived in the most precarious housing in the complex. Therein lay the potential value of ruins for the women who navigated the dangers of crumbling architecture that captured the attention of a sympathetic public (Fennell 2012), including property investors.

Across the housing blocks, tenants deployed the term "decay" (*xuống cấp*, literally: to decline in grade or status) not only as a moral judgment on the conduct of certain bodies but also to define a subjective experience to which they could relate. Each household, in some way, struggled with xuống cấp as an everyday, intimate sensorial encounter with the passage of time—Benjamin's decay of history mirrored in the slow violence of architectural demise (2009, 179). In C8, xuống cấp was both a metaphor for a decline in social status and a condition of material vulnerability that underpinned women's embodied experience of urban poverty. During my first visit to block C8 in November 2010, I received word that several residents were hoping to meet with me to discuss their living situation. As I climbed the dank, chipped stairway, a group of women gathered around me, pointing to the building's severe deterioration. A wooden rod held a concrete corridor slab in place, to keep it from tumbling four stories. The pillars had completely eroded, some held together by wire, and large pieces of the ceiling were missing. Residents had collectively built a makeshift awning out of recycled materials (see plate 9), including a propaganda poster on the two-child policy, to catch falling debris—an unintended statement on the moral decline of party ideology.

DeSilvey and Edensor have written about the potential of ruins to act as "political counter-sites" that mobilize collective anger and action against a shared sense of injustice (2012, 468–69). This was the case in block c8, but the alliances that coalesced around material decay shifted registers over time. These moved from an embodied display of vulnerability to protest the state's lack of public investments, to more direct organizing to impede market encroachments on the right to housing (chapter 10). I listened to numerous stories about chronic disrepair in c8 and read about it in the local press, even after I left the field. One account focused on a female labor hero who had been knocked unconscious by a large piece of falling plaster, forcing the women to wear conical hats in the apartments for protection, which I observed during my visits.[37] Because the palm-leaf hats really only shielded them from small, nonlethal debris, I understood this act as a performance of "maximized vulnerability" to expose the gendered violence of state neglect (Butler 2015, ii). They did so by appropriating their image as backward and needing state guidance to their advantage. This strategic essentialism afforded a symbolic advantage, much like the one enacted by the traders in Ho Chi Minh City discussed by Leshkowich (2014), by calling attention to their hardship as poor, rural women through an iconic symbol associated with the peasantry to elicit sympathy among the urban elite. Such an approach rendered the women as the victims of precarious decay rather than the perpetrators.

When I met with the women over the course of my fieldwork, they remained distraught that housing management refused to address the very risks of injury it had affirmed in its evaluation of structural uncertainty. From their perspective, this denied them their right to social protection in return for a lifetime of service. Many had served as volunteer youth militia (*thanh niên xung phong*) during the war and went on to work for Nghệ An Pharmaceuticals until retirement. At one point, an older woman pulled me aside and implored, in tears, "Can you help us? We have contacted authorities repeatedly, but they haven't responded to our appeals."[38] The women's desperation echoed across the hallways of block c8 during my visits. When I raised the matter with ward, district, and municipal officials, they all expressed genuine *thông cảm*, or empathy, reaffirming Danilyn Rutherford's observation that governance depends on the "sympathetic responses of variously located individuals, including public servants" to advance nation building (2009, 7)—but to what effect?, I wondered. Public servants like Nguyên quickly distanced themselves from such sentiments by claiming that their hands were tied, presumably by higher-ups in the bureaucratic chain. Moreover, the time was approaching when state ownership of the units would transfer to tenants, which made liability for disrepair even more inconsequential (chapter 10). Lack of response drove the women to use the traditional conical hat as a sign of their subaltern status to protest their abandonment, register trauma, and communicate everyday risk. During interviews, residents explained how hazardous conditions in their homes—from leaks to cracked walls and ceilings—adversely affected their health and encumbered mundane chores. They expressed palpable fear that the building would collapse (*sợ sẽ sập*). Indeed, soon after I began research, typhoon Megi prompted orders to evacuate C8 residents out of concern that the building would buckle under high winds, attesting to official recognition of the crisis conditions under which people lived.

This was not decay as patination, an aesthetic sensibility that values age and dirt, if not nostalgically then as political critique (Dawdy 2016). Here, the surface layer was dangerously alchemical and "hostile to the original architectural object" (Cairns and Jacobs 2014, 75). Block C8 was a ticking time bomb that created tremendous distress for residents. One day, I visited two women whose families had been sharing an apartment for over thirty years. From the corridor, the painted house number was the only evidence that the unit was divided into two: 131A/B. Walking in, I saw the washroom across from the kitchen, as per the Vietnamese reform of GDR design (see figure 6.15). The family in room A had claimed the kitchen, leaving the washroom to serve as the cooking space for the family in room B. They only shared the toilet. And yet the occupants moved fluidly across the space as if they were among kin. The women, who both had user rights in their names, invited me to sit down on a reed mat. This was the first time they had hosted a foreigner, and they were embarrassed at not having a table. In the room where we sat, the only pieces of furniture were a wooden chest and a bunk bed that accommodated three generations. I noticed dark patches on the ceiling, next to widening cracks, as if the tenants had tried, futilely, to stop the decay from spreading. I smelled the familiar odor of mildew. "The apartment is not safe," the woman from room B said, following my gaze. She, too, had been injured from loose plaster that broke off the ceiling. "How should we live with such danger?" she asked rhetorically. The press had covered the incident, making her critique of housing authorities intentionally public in a politically acceptable way: by stating residents' constitutional rights both to housing security (that is, no future demolition) and to a secure, no-risk home.

THE GENDERING OF RISK AND DISREPAIR

The above examples show that disrepair should not be viewed only as a negative and destructive force but can mobilize collectivities around decay and risk. The ethnographic examples I have presented here reveal claims to certain rights and protections that tenants, especially women, articulated in the aftermath of the ruin (and near collapse) of infrastructure. These rights, including the right to live free from bodily harm, involved the adequate provision, operation, supervision, and security of housing as entitlements of citizenship.

At the same time, unplanned obsolescence exposed the limits of GDR spatial logics of modernity, including the social and infrastructural organization that was intended to make Vinh the showpiece of Vietnamese modernization. Rather, exterior and interior breaks, fissures, and malfunctions precluded a higher standard of living. Ironically, tenants found themselves in conditions not unlike those of collective thatch housing. But now they endured increased risk and workloads: rain and water penetrated concrete living spaces, which quickly molded, while dry taps and clogged pipes forced residents outdoors to resume communal hygiene practices, which required hauling water, clothes, and household goods up and down flights of stairs. These risks and burdens were not shared equally. Infrastructure breakdown and decay disproportionately impacted women, even with the temporary suspension of the gendered division of labor. As I argued in chapter 6, the GDR design for mass housing redefined the family by privileging the intimate sphere of the household as a site for building socialism (see also Friedman 2006). This preceded the shift in Vietnamese Communist Party policy from that of collectivization to a family economy (*kinh tế gia đình*), which turned the household into a locus of national development (Werner 2009). Lisa Drummond has argued that this shift increased domestic labor, especially for female workers, who took over the role of caregiving from the state as the hearth resumed its social importance as a unit of productivity (2000, 2385). In mass housing, disrepair exacerbated this burden even further, instead of lightening it as planners had envisioned. Utopian, single-family housing, with the most modern infrastructure in Vinh, did not liberate women by any means; instead, discourses of self-sufficiency actually strengthened patriarchal institutions while allowing the state to retreat.

To be sure, not everyone aspired to decollectivize domestic work; planners, focused on the conveniences of modern technology, never questioned the assumption that it was desirable. But many women preferred the sociality of doing communal labor in outdoor spaces, which was culturally familiar, rather than working alone in their apartments, which was not. I regularly met older women cooking outside their units or washing clothes together at the well, despite having water and power connections in their flats (see figure 8.7). These activities were both gendered and generational, and were an

↑ Figure 8.7 Communal washing in the c6 courtyard, with the help of my research assistant, 2011. Photo by the author.

important part of sustaining cooperative relationships between neighbors. For the women in c8, intimate sociality was part of everyday life. The allocation of single units to two families in the block meant that there were even blurrier divisions between public and private. Moreover, I often observed women gathering water from the public wells around the complex to supplement household reserves and reduce utility costs that rose sharply after meters were installed in their homes.

With utility meters and fees for individual usage after Đổi mới came scrutiny of consumption. This included my own consumption practices. My monthly water use cost approximately 50,000 VND, or U.S. $2.50, for which the landlady—whose bill was 30,000 VND for her and her daughter—scolded me. Our incommensurable approaches to water consumption mapped onto differences in global North-South access to infrastructure. This was most apparent when I expressed concern that the water heater might be broken. The hot water in the shower ran out quickly—too soon for me to warm up on cold winter mornings. "It's fine," the landlady reassured me. She turned the shower on and counted to two, then switched it off. "Now you are wet and can soap up," she explained. Then she turned it back on, counted to five, and turned it off. "Now you are rinsed and there's still plenty of hot water," she declared. When it came to electricity, however, our usage was much more aligned—my electricity bill was usually under 100,000 VND, or U.S. $5, which earned me praise of *tiết kiệm*, or "thrifty with resources," from my neighbors. Tiết kiệm for my neighbors meant defying meters—a symbol of the loss of state care and subsidized infrastructure—by finding ways to circumvent fees, such as unplugging refrigerators (to use as storage) and maximizing public wells. Scholars have shown how metering devices have been at the center of postsocialist and post-apartheid conflicts as citizens resist the commodification of basic infrastructural services (von Schnitzler 2016; Alexander 2007a). Similarly, in Quang Trung I came to view communal tasks as small political acts that resisted increases in utility rates and the shift of infrastructural liability from local government to retired state employees. At the same time, some residents did *collectively* assume the burden of repair, and risk management, by improving building *exteriors*. In the next chapter I examine *individual* responses to decay believed to increase precarity: household upgrades to *interior* living spaces.

9

RENOVATION

> Outside things are broken and decayed, but the inside is still good.
>
> —INTERVIEW WITH QUANG TRUNG RESIDENT, 2011

In the opening vignette to his essay on the city as inhabited assemblage, the geographer Colin McFarlane described a unique house he visited in a favela in southern São Paulo. The owners built the structure incrementally over time by amalgamating "just about any object that came to hand," including waste and household objects that exemplified, for McFarlane, the city as processual dwelling and sociomaterial assembly (2011, 649). McFarlane was careful not to idealize the creative agency of the impoverished artist-cum-builder. As Ananya Roy, an urban theorist of the global South, has observed, the heroism of the poor is often the main plot in narratives of subaltern urbanisms (2011, 227). McFarlane's account of the remarkable house "in constant construction" does, however, accentuate another common theme in subaltern urbanisms: the "random" assortment and juxtaposition of gathered materials in informal urban spaces (2011, 651). In the interstices of the favela, the city as assemblage typified a hodgepodge urbanism of resourceful, ad hoc making.

McFarlane's processual framework of dwelling as assembly (and disassembly) is useful for thinking about living space in Quang Trung. Anthropologists have similarly argued that architecture does more than convey symbolic value or meaning but is itself a meaningful process extending beyond the finished product (Vellinga 2007, 760). This approach argues against a static and deterministic notion of the built form by showing how people and the material world coconstitute one another (Miller 2005; Daniels 2010; Buchli 2013). Housing in Quang Trung was also a generative process of doing and making that involved multiple state and nonstate actors negotiating the blurry divide between private and public life. Ontologically, it was a place of continuous becoming (Dovey 2010)—and undoing, rather than an already-formed, functional space, as the term "built environment" implies. This chapter argues that tenants' spatiomaterial interventions and transgressive acts of dwelling through interior renovations disrupted the temporality of ruins as a linear decline. Their physical and emotional labor, as well as their financial investments, countered the buildings' exterior decay, even as the press depicted such changes as accelerating ruin and turning back time. If ruins challenge the myth of progress (Edensor 2005)—and here suggest socialism's epic failure—then renovations to ruined modernist buildings problematize ruination as rupture by making new claims on the urban future (Dawdy 2010; Hoffman 2017). Affectively, renovation in response to *xuống cấp* (decay) defied the slow death of the housing blocks by recovering the ruin as home.

Such acts were not arbitrary. There is a tendency to assume that the urban poor merely "tinker" with their housing, perhaps impulsively as McFarlane's curious house seems to imply (2011, 659), while the wealthy, conversely, envision and plan. This reinforces an idea of urban informality as a vast dystopia of antiplanning (Roy 2005, 147). In this chapter, I argue against dwelling as ad hoc assemblage, symbolized by the bric-a-brac design of the favela house, and argue for tenants as designers rather than bricoleurs. People do, of course, improvise, and they make use of the resources they are able to claim while living in a state of precarity. In this sense, McFarlane is right to point to the enormous imbalances of power, resources, and knowledge that undergird the spatiotemporalities of urban assemblages (2011, 655). But poor people also plan. They, too, design cities, regardless of whether they live in shantytowns or socialist new towns like Vinh. To suggest otherwise affirms a false opposition between planned and unplanned urban spaces rather than viewing them as coarticulations, accretions, and fusions. As Michelle Provoost has argued, "The so-called 'unplanned' cities were also devised and built by the agency of people and are thus in a certain sense 'planned.' The difference lies in the identity of the planner" (2010, 11). In Vinh, many of these tenant-designers helped to build Quang Trung, and when conditions allowed—or indeed required it—they applied their expertise to remodeling their obsolescent flats. This demanded a high degree of organization and knowledge (both technical and consumer) from practitioners not formally trained in the craft. For local authorities, "unplanned" planning challenged the city's master plan, with its rigid regulations and functional zoning. As I show below, subversive planning practices to mitigate decay redefined tenants' relationships with the buildings and with the state by disrupting the normative spatial order of things

(Miraftab 2009). They produced aspirational dwelling spaces in response to diminishing social protections and a liberalizing housing regime that followed economic reforms. In so doing, they revealed the flexibility and adaptability of standardized mass housing that has been too easily misjudged as unimaginative and monolithic.

The previous chapter examined how a planned city aged; this chapter shows how an aged city was remade. In shifting from decayed exteriors to renovated interiors—from state neglect to the care that people lavished on their deteriorating homes—I trace the manifold ways that residents in Quang Trung brought the "dying" buildings back to life. These re-creations were a response to obsolescence and a new spatialization of inequality that made leaving Quang Trung cost prohibitive. To make the decaying complex more livable, and to fit with their changing needs and urban lifestyles, residents converted generic flats into vibrant spaces for homemaking, worship, socializing, and livelihood opportunities. As Krisztina Fehérváry observed of socialist housing in Hungary, "Families attempted to make apartment interiors into heterotopic spaces that transported their residents into worlds far removed from the walls of concrete in which they were situated" (2012, 626). Residents in Quang Trung accomplished this with decor and furnishings, but mostly through structural modifications, producing what I call, drawing on Svetlana Boym (2008), "off-modern housing" that challenged the modernist prototype. As a detour from the designed path to socialist progress, the off-modern emerged at the interface between scientific and symbolic practice; it did not so much reject the architectural remains of modernist planning as it appropriated and reclaimed them according to people's own cultural logics of spatial organization.

My use of "off-modern" differs from the urban spatial transformations that scholars have identified as "autoconstruction" among the urban poor in the global South. Both instances involve imagination and the self-managed production of urban space to achieve a better future in ways that actualize agency and political subjectivity, while butting up against formal planning (Holston 1991, 448–49). However, there are important spatial and temporal distinctions between them. Spatially, autoconstruction, as discussed in the literature, frequently unfolds at the margins of a city or in its vacant lots and derelict, even unfinished spaces, and for that reason it has been linked to a mode of urban expansion that scholars have called "peripheral urbanization."[1] The term also suggests a particular *social* location of marginalized persons whose spatial interventions form the basis of claims to citizenship (Caldeira 2017, 9). This was hardly the case with Quang Trung: as preferential, rights-bearing citizens, its residents were not spatially or socially peripheral. The temporality also differed: unlike autoconstruction, off-modern housing did not develop incrementally through "long term processes of incompletion" (Caldeira 2017, 5), as did McFarlane's house, nor was it makeshift or temporary (Tonkiss 2013).

Similar to autoconstruction, off-modern dwellings were remarkably diverse in the scale and scope of their designs. As instances of the "lateral potentialities of the project of critical modernity" (Boym 2008, 4), they expressed creativity and individuality in ways that standardized façades and floor plans did not. Boym dared her readers to look closely at the intimate spaces in socialist housing estates. I did so in Quang Trung and saw, like Boym, that they were not anonymous dwelling places marked by community disintegration—a common rendering of modernist planning that sees the "death of the street" and with it the disappearance of urban social life (Holston 1989, 104–5). Rather, they were dynamic social spaces of remarkable variability. While the topic of decay incited angry debate about futures that never came to pass (chapter 8), people were eager to discuss renovation (*cải tạo*) as the creation of place on their own terms. More than 90 percent of surveyed households had remodeled their apartments in accordance with their own ideas about a desirable "home." The majority of these households were in buildings considered most structurally sound, which tended to house cultural elites. Renovations thus not only inscribed rising economic inequality across the housing blocks; they also reflected enduring forms of stratification between factory workers and civil servants.[2] Variations in the scale of residents' spatial practices were material signs of disparities in social status and the horizons of urban possibility in Quang Trung.

The timescales of renovations also showed scalar shifts in how residents imagined the urban future to manage precarity in the present (see also Bunnell and Goh 2018). The first spate of relatively minor renovations that required fewer resources started after 1990 and spiked in 2000. A second, more comprehensive and costly round, carried out by one in four households, began in 2005 and plateaued in 2009, just before my residency in the complex. Renovations focused on modernizing the *khu phụ*, or auxiliary spaces of household infrastructure, such as bringing water lines, gas stoves,[3] and sinks to kitchens, changing "squat" to "sit" toilets, and adding bathroom showers and sinks, washing machines (one in two households), water heaters (two in three households), and air conditioning units (two in five households). Tenants remodeled just about everything according to their aesthetic tastes, spatial needs, and financial resources: walls, ceilings, doors, balconies, windows, and floors. They reconfigured and expanded space. Some renovations involved structural repairs, and others were cosmetic improvements, such as adorning square doorframes with decorative arcs. All required cash investments that exceeded average disposable income: households—with a median monthly inflow of 5 million VND (U.S. $250)—invested an average of 34 million VND (U.S. $1,700) into renovations, while 5 percent spent upward of 100 million VND (U.S. $5,000), a substantial amount for these low-income households, the majority of which comprised retirees. Such changes left few "original" (*nguyên bản*) apartments for comparison, but I did manage to find some, including one in my building. Only then did I grasp the extent to which residents had fashioned entirely new material worlds out of their austere, now obsolete flats, once branded "modern" apartments (see plates 10 and 11).

In this chapter, I examine three common apartment modifications to doorways, back balconies, and walk-out basements as transgressive spatial practices that respond to and mitigate uncertainty. In moving from the commons to the more intimate domain of the family, I show how interiors became sites where tenants solved problems of breakdown, decay, and stagnation by treating living space as malleable (Buchli 2013, 118). Efforts to harmonize, expand, and commercialize interiors gave rise to new material and social forms that deviated from planning policy and the spatial realization of socialism. Indeed, all of the residents' interventions I discuss below violated housing regulations, which prohibited changes to the form and structure of the buildings. Often depicted as the unlawfulness of the urban poor, these modifications were thought to contribute to disorder and insecurity. I argue, to the contrary, that these spatial arrangements and counterpractices became important markers of class distinction and upward mobility among enfranchised citizens. I thus take a stand with the literature that argues against the pathologization of informality and the people whose illicit architectural designs were largely tolerated by authorities to become a *durable* part of the urban fabric. The remaking of built space is a reminder that dwelling-as-process is itself tied to changes in both political economy and urban management policy, as people negotiated with state entities that were pulled between the rule of law and the right to survival in the city (Rao 2013, 772–73).

HARMONIZING SPACE: *PHONG THỦY*

Decay and obsolescence were not the only motivations behind renovation; "uncivil" design in "civilized" housing inspired action as well. While residents praised Quang Trung's ecological design, which kept the blocks cool, bright, and airy, they criticized apartment layouts. Exteriors demonstrated the principles of *phong thủy*, or feng shui, but interiors did not. "Không hợp [not appropriate]!" one resident after another informed me. Utopian planning had provided infrastructure to liberate women from domestic drudgery and serve the needs of workers and their families, but its proximity to spaces of ritual practices violated the cosmological order of the traditional "Vietnamese House."

To gain a deeper understanding of the Vietnamese House, and of residents' dissatisfaction with apartment design, I joined architecture classes at a local vocational school. I had studied architectural history and theory with Vietnam's distinguished architect Đặng Thái Hoàng (who was from Nghệ An) before commencing fieldwork. Now I was interested in architecture as practice and technique. I wanted to observe students-in-training to become familiar with the curriculum's intended goals and methods for transferring technical knowledge ("techne") while learning some of the tools and skills of the trade. The two-year program cost 270,000 VND, or U.S. $13.50, per month, at a time when the average monthly minimum wage for the area was less than U.S. $100. The classes I attended were composed only of young men, most of whom were from Vinh's urban margins or neighboring district towns. I observed classrooms with both female and male instructors. As a white American woman, and the first foreigner many of the students had met, my presence proved somewhat disruptive, and I stopped attending after two weeks.

While I did attend, I studied multiple iterations of the Vietnamese House across time and space in the Architecture Design (*Thiết kế Kiến trúc*) course. The textbook, *Thiết kế kiến trúc nhà dân dụng* (Civic architecture and design), published by the Ministry of Construction, focused on building typologies and the practical application of design principles to housing and public infrastructure. One lecture addressed the ordering of space in rural Kinh (Việt) households in Vietnam's northern regions.[4] Using examples from the book, the teacher explained the traditional spatial separation of the main house (*nhà chính*), which included sleeping and guest rooms, from the ancillary buildings (*nhà phụ*), or auxiliary areas for cooking and raising livestock, which should be located to the side or back for hygienic reasons (see also Đặng T. H. 2009, 49). In certain ways this spatial design was similar to the symbolic ordering of Bourdieu's (1970) Berber house, whose functional divisions inscribed a parallel set of gendered binaries: male/female, inside/outside, dry/wet, consumption/production, refinement/pollution, culture/nature.[5] In Kinh houses, however, such divisions are often transgressed, as gender relations tend to be more fluid and complementary than exclusive and oppositional (Errington 1990). Segregation of living and auxiliary areas had been possible in *nhà tập thể* (collective housing), where shared cooking and washing facilities had been located outside the main building (see chapter 6). This separation was more difficult to maintain in the city and impossible in blocks in Quang Trung that conjoined these areas within single-family units, to the dismay of some residents.

The ancestral altar (*bàn thờ tổ tiên*) plays a central role in this symbolic system, as its placement and care determine the well-being of the household. As well as for choosing a favorable move-in date, people often consult a *thầy bói*, or diviner, to find an auspicious, geomantically suitable location for the altar. Our course textbook made no mention of phong thủy, however, which evokes James Scott's (1998) notion of *metis*, or intuitive, place-based knowledge considered to be at odds with the codified logics of techne that the curriculum sought to impart. For example, recalling GDR experts' application of wind science to their designs, the text addressed the "physics" (*vật lý*) of architecture and the rational calculation of light, air, and sound exposure to produce suitable living environments. It provided students with key mathematical formulae needed to achieve good design, such as wind-flow modeling and lighting coefficients (K) calculated as a proportion of window area (Scs) and total room space (Ss), or K = Scs/Ss. Interestingly, the textbook did incorporate images of ancestral altars in its floor-plan diagrams for Kinh "folk housing" (*nhà ở dân gian*), including in Nghệ An, placing altars in the center of the all-purpose room across from the main entrance, but no explanation was offered. We discussed this spatial arrangement as one of the defining features of the Vietnamese House, but without any mention of phong thủy.

In the class time that followed this lecture, students worked in teams to create a viable housing plan drawn to scale. I joined a group that had designed a narrow, two-story villa of ninety square meters. On the second floor, they had added a room at the front of the house exclusively for the *bàn thờ tổ tiên*. One student criticized his teammate for positioning the altar room too close to the bathroom. "The altar should be here, on the other side of the house!" he argued. "No, it needs to have access to the balcony," another student responded, emphasizing flows of fresh air and light. "It has to stay in the nicest room, but not next to the toilet!" a third chimed in. I smiled: these were the same discussions I had begun to hear in Quang Trung. "Are you talking about phong thủy?" I asked, interjecting metis into the realm of techne, revealing their fuzzy boundaries. The students stopped quarrelling and looked at me before breaking into laughter.

TOILET TENSIONS

"If you could change one thing about the design of your house, what would it be?" I asked Quang Trung residents. Their responses were similar: expand space, and move the toilet to the back of the house. As I detailed in chapter 6, GDR-designed apartments had a consistent linear layout that fit with the East Germans' vision of modernity: a central hallway ran from the front entrance to the back balcony, directing traffic and separating the active "wet" spaces of infrastructure for sanitation and food preparation from the bright and airy "dry" spaces of living. Immediately beyond the entrance, there was a door to the toilet, then a door to the windowless washroom, which was directly across from the entrance to the living room, followed by the kitchen (see figure 6.13). In keeping with Vietnamese spatial and architectural distinctions, the Housing Agency referred to these areas as *khu phụ* (auxiliary area) and *khu chính* (main area). The areas held different economic, social, and symbolic values. For example, after liberalization of housing in 1991, rents were recalibrated according to the sizes of the main area (*diện tích chính* or DTC) and auxiliary area (*diện tích phụ* or DTP). The value of DTP was half that of DTC, so for a third-story unit, for instance, rental contracts stipulated DTC at 976 VND per square meter and DTP at 488 VND. In the Vietnamese House, women were associated more with the infrastructural labor of the outside nhà phụ—water transport, fuel collection, washing, cooking, and so forth—and men more with the social and cultural activities inside the nhà chính, though this was not absolute. As Bourdieu remarked of the Berber house, moist, dark areas of nature were coded female, in contrast with bright, dry areas of culture, which were coded male (1970, 153). For Quang Trung residents, the proximity of these areas rendered civilized modern space uncivilized (*không văn minh*) and posed problems with phong thủy that could be solved through renovation.

Residents especially disliked the placement of the toilet at the front of the house. In my interviews with Vietnamese and East German architects, both sides recalled this as a point of contention. As a retired civil servant explained, framing her sentiments with cultural generalizations, "The design is okay. The toilet should be in the back, however. You know, most Asians would prefer to have it outside the house."[6] To be sure, indoor plumbing *was* a novelty for most tenants at the time, but not everyone saw it as desirable or a sign of modernity, as East German experts did. "You have to understand, a small narrow bathroom in the house, and up front, was strange [*lạ*]," said a director at the Design Institute who had worked with the East German planners as a young intern.[7] Residents surmised that it was convenient (*tiện*) but also impolite (*bất lịch sự*): "It's the first thing a guest sees who walks in my home!" one woman bemoaned.[8] Where East German engineers saw indoor plumbing as central to a new hygienic order, Vietnamese tenants saw it as unsanitary (*không vệ sinh*) and dirty (*bẩn*). The north-south winds that blew fresh air through the flats carried odors from front to back. But the Germans had another rationale: if the toilet was placed at the back of the apartment, then the hot southwest summer winds would blow odors through the house. "There weren't many options," one Vietnamese architect conceded. Though it defied Vietnamese custom (*phong tục*), in this case German spatial imaginaries prevailed.[9]

Although residents were creative in renovating their flats, they came up against certain structural limitations. To deal with toilet tensions, people were forced to make use of the more malleable aspects of housing infrastructure. If they could not move the commodes—because of fixed pipes, drains, and sewer lines—they could redirect flows of traffic through the house by modifying doors and walls. One solution was to create a new apartment entrance, although this was cost prohibitive for many, and more strictly regulated. This redesign was most appropriate for corner units with extra space where the corridor ended. In these cases, builders sealed the original door to the hallway and created a new entry with direct access to the living room. Guests then bypassed the toilet, saving the host from shame. "It's a more practical design," a retired cook at Unification Machinery told me. Making this renovation, along with upgrades to the kitchen and bathroom, had cost her 40 million VND, or U.S. $2,000. It was a significant investment, but one she felt worthwhile.[10] Another solution was to remove the partition from between the latrine and the washroom. In this configuration, the door to the latrine was sealed, blocking the commode from sight (see figure 9.1). This transformed the washroom into an all-purpose bathroom.

DISHONORING ANCESTORS

Though it was intended to uplift them, tenants considered the spatial order of Quang Trung flats not just impolite and an affront to their spatial sensibilities but downright unlucky (*không may*). Worse than offending guests was the prospect of insulting the ancestors with bad phong thủy. As my neighbor, an avid geomancer and veteran of the war, explained to me, the position of walls, doors, and windows is critical to the flow of positive energy through the home. Openings that channel light, air, and sound help determine the placement of the ancestral altar, which protects the family and maintains harmony. A poorly

↑ Figure 9.1 Civilizing the hallway entrance in block C2, 2011 (dotted line outlines former toilet doorway). Photo by the author.

positioned altar is considered ominous and likely to incur the wrath of patrilineal forebears.

Good phong thủy prohibits certain doors from facing one another, particularly between living (khu chính) and auxiliary (khu phụ) areas. And yet, in the German design, the entrances to the main room and washroom were opposite one another. This alarmed residents, even more than the location of the toilet, for it positioned the sacred shrine directly across from spaces of sanitation. "That is taboo [*kiêng*]!" the geomancer decried.[11] "It is tactless and undignified [*không kín đáo*]," a retired electric worker affirmed.[12] Everyone I interviewed agreed: a bathroom across from the ancestors was completely unacceptable (*hoàn toàn không hợp*) and at odds with the core spatial principles of phong thủy.

The inauspicious design of the units risked disrupting the efficacy of ancestral rituals to bring health, wealth, and happiness into the home. But the narrow units presented few alternatives. An ideal altar would be placed high on a wall without openings, across from the main entrance to the nhà chính, as the textbook showed. In Quang Trung, the entrance to the khu chính was through the living room doorway, not the apartment entrance, which led to the hallway and khu phụ. Because altars should not be adjacent to sleeping

↑ Figure 9.2 An elaborate ancestral altar at the Lunar New Year, 2011. Photo by the author.

quarters, units with a bedroom had an additional door and wall to consider. A retired construction worker consulted a diviner about the altar for her husband, who had died after they moved to Quang Trung in 1977. Because they were the first high-rises in the city, the diviner was unsure where the altar should go. "He said that its location needed to comply with phong thủy, but the unit was cramped and presented too many difficulties," she told me.[13] Not everyone established an altar in their new apartments, as most rural migrants maintained a patrilineal shrine in the countryside. Food insecurity meant that people were less concerned about ritual practice as they struggled to meet their basic needs and stabilize their lives after the war.[14] Today almost all households have at least one altar.[15] The altars' arrangement has grown in scale and complexity (see figure 9.2), which has also been the case with ancestral veneration and funerary rites elsewhere in Vietnam (Shohet 2018). Recognizing the growing importance of family altars in Quang Trung does not negate their presence before reforms, which transformed socialist secular space (Schwenkel 2017b). But relocation of sometimes-grander altars from the countryside to the city does speak to residents' urgency to find a solution to bad phong thủy.

Rearranging doorways proved an affordable fix that could also be done clandestinely, beyond the peering eyes of housing authorities. The most common renovation I observed was relocation of the washroom door to the kitchen. "We redesigned our flat according to phong thủy," exclaimed a retired female postal worker, assuming the role of tenant-as-architect (Akcan 2018).[16] She had sealed the door to the washroom and opened the wall on the northern side of the kitchen. This preserved the dignity of the ancestral altar, her husband explained, since it no longer faced the dark, moist, polluting space of the bathroom. His wife saw another benefit: a reduction in household labor. Because there was no plumbing in the kitchens of units that had yet to modernize the water system, the redesign gave women direct access to the water spigot (and concrete drums) in the washroom. In this instance, apartment dis- and reassembly drew on inhabitants' cultural, moral, and ontological sensibilities, creating a flat that better aligned with their own expectations of modernity.

EXPANDING SPACE: *CƠI NỚI*

At the front of their homes, tenants altered walls and doors to harmonize living space according to their spiritual beliefs and sense of moral personhood. At the back, they renovated balconies to enlarge their units for both social and economic needs. Referred to as *cơi nới*, these lateral exterior extensions grew precariously wider and longer over the years. This planned spatial intervention reconciled socialist obsolescence with capitalist aspiration, as those who could not afford to move out of mass housing participated in modernity and consumer society by expanding their apartments. Technically unlawful, though tolerated by sympathetic authorities, cơi nới did not so much challenge the city's modernizing agenda as they realigned residents' relationship with the state.

Citizens who did not live in modernist housing projects criticized these illicit constructions and the tenants who built or commissioned them. From their outside perspective, assemblages of corrugated steel and metal sheets haphazardly attached to buildings signified social disorder, moral breakdown, and urban blight. The Vietnamese press has routinely published images of buildings "wearing backpacks" (*đeo ba lô*) to chastise residents for their dangerous constructions that further damaged public buildings.[17] These tales of unlawful modifications to state property have bolstered neoliberal arguments for privatization to transform negligent public tenants into responsible, middle-class homeowners (Tran and Dalholm 2005). By compromising structural integrity and hastening decay, cơi nới threatened not only housing safety and beauty but urban civilization itself (*văn minh đô thị*).[18] Residents, however, did not see cơi nới as contributing to a building's decline but rather to its upkeep and improvement. Outsiders often assumed that cơi nới signaled poverty. Within the Quang Trung housing complex, they were visual markers of social mobility. Like autoconstruction, cơi nới allowed residents to fashion positive images and identities to counter the denigrating information that circulated about them in society (Holston 1991, 462).

DEVELOPMENT OF CƠI NỚI

After I moved into the housing blocks in 2010, the buildings underwent dramatic morphological change as residents modernized their apartments by expanding floor space. The most pragmatic place to expand was via the small balcony behind the kitchen, which also connected with the main room. Competition among neighbors seemed to push everyone to extremes, and cơi nới became a topic of discussion, amusement, and envy across the complex.

This was not the first time tenants had modified their balconies without authorization. When Vietnamese tenants moved into block A5 in 1977 during the difficult years of the subsidy era, they raised livestock in the apartments, especially on balconies. Soon after, some families enclosed the open space with clay bricks, the only construction material available at the time, to create shelter for domestic fowl. As other materials became available following economic reforms, families enhanced their private balconies with wire-mesh fencing or an iron grill to create what they called "tiger cages" (*chuồng cọp*) for *external* domestic activities, such as washing and hanging clothes (see figure 9.3).[19] This was the case for my balcony in C2, which stored a washing machine and a water storage tank that also supplied the kitchen. By the late 1990s, the form, use, and durability of tiger cages had changed, shifting away from being open-air spaces for women's work. Cultural and political elites with the means to buy stronger construction materials built *enclosed* extensions onto their balconies to incorporate into the home. At first, these were modest in size and design and could hold the weight of a person. Over the next decade, increasing numbers of tenants experimented with ever more daring designs.

When I arrived in 2010, I saw simple but multifunctional cơi nới across the complex. They typically comprised a single room built of sheets of corrugated metal supported by a steel frame, with a wooden or cement floor and a small window for ventilation. The additional floor space was substantial for extended families living in the smaller studio units that averaged thirty-five square meters. Whereas the open tiger cage was a space for domestic chores as

↑ Figure 9.3 "Tiger cage" as space for women's domestic work in block c7, 2011. Photo by the author.

part of the khu phụ, new designs allowed for more versatile uses of the balcony as integrated living space of the khu chính.

From the outside, the backs of buildings were tapestries that told the history of spatial intervention and creative reinvention in Quang Trung through the changing materiality of cơi nới (see figure 9.4). Bricked-up balconies from an earlier era of scarcity nestled between mesh cages of various sizes, built after economic reforms. The different styles and configurations of cơi nới in recent years have signaled a burgeoning consumer market fueled by steady inflows of goods and capital to the city. Their variability likewise indexed growing inequalities within what had been a relatively economically unstratified population of "new socialist persons." They pointed to differentiation within the realm of informality (Roy 2005, 149), which allows aspiring middle-class populations to make claims on public property, especially when the "unplanned" structures looked planned and thus legitimate (Ghertner 2015).

Visual differences in cơi nới distinguished the better-off residents from the less fortunate. Within months of my arrival, the morphology of the housing blocks began to change quickly as a group of tenants in blocks c2, c3, and c4—which housed mostly cultural elites—began to build the largest cơi nới the complex had seen yet. Earlier generations of tiger cages and modest cơi nới had been built off the balconies only. The new cơi nới were

↑ Figure 9.4 Mosaic of tiger cages and early iterations of *cơi nới* in block B3, 2011. Photo by the author.

wider and longer, sometimes running along the entire side of an apartment (see plate 12).

I watched this process unfold in block C3 from the open corridor of my fourth-floor apartment across the way. Construction crews expanded the small, boxed cơi nới to the length of two rooms, approximately 5.5 meters long, which was double the span of earlier iterations. In larger units that had a back bedroom, cơi nới stretched across all three rooms, up to eight meters. They also became wider, at times surpassing two meters, extending far beyond the reach of the steel poles beneath (see figure 9.5). From below, cơi nới seemed precariously perched, although from the inside they felt sturdy to stand on—like a typical room. Their seamless integration into the household contributed to the illusion that they *were* stable and secure (see plate 13). Though cơi nới were a serious violation of housing policy, authorities were powerless to stop their construction and looked the other way as it increased.

THE LIMITS OF STATE POWER

Tenants did not try to dodge the authorities when committing these transgressive acts (as they had done with livestock in the apartments). Rather, they brought their cơi nới to the state's attention and feigned playing by the rules.

↑ Figure 9.5 Precariously perched: ever wider *cơi nới* in block c3, 2011. Photo by the author.

The script was already written for their encounters with urban bureaucracy, as both residents and city officials manipulated housing regulations to advance their own interests. Some tenants applied for a construction permit to build their cơi nới, thus demonstrating themselves to be law-abiding citizens. The permit was always denied (which they expected), but this did not dissuade them from undertaking the project, nor was it meant to. The inspector would show up at the site midproject and collect a fine of 500,000 VND (U.S. $25) for building-code violations, termed *phạt cho tồn tại*, or a fine for their existence (a twofold increase from 250,000 VND for first-generation cơi nới).[20] David Koh observed a similar practice in collective housing in Hanoi in the late 1990s: "In that way, the illegal builder will plead for compassion from officials because the construction work is almost done" (2004, 345). Assembly would resume after the inspector left, showing how informality was managed and, to some extent, even regularized by the state (Mains 2019, 88).

These bureaucratic enactments in Vinh demonstrated compliance with authorities, but they were notably devoid of any paperwork or documentation of such transactions. The transgression was officially acknowledged and penalized, without any record of it, enabling the possibility of petty corruption. Yet inspectors were not driven by greed alone; they framed these arrangements as ethical, if not compassionate (see also Endres 2014). One inspector told me that they did not ask tenants to remove the cơi nới, because they were poor, upstanding citizens in need of additional space. His statement illustrated that the Vietnamese state does not exclusively govern through the rational application of its laws and regulations but also manages populations through the "distribution of sentiment" (Stoler 2004, 5), especially at the lower levels of governance. As Shaun Malarney observed in a rural commune, effective political leaders in Vietnam are those considered "rich in sentiment" who express solidarity with the population through virtuous acts that may bend the rules to avoid inflicting hardship (1997, 912; see also Koh, 2006, 19–20). This instance of what we might call "empathetic bureaucracy" showed toleration of subversive spatial practices because they were viewed as an interim solution to outdated housing and thus allowed officials to rationalize their actions as moral, expedient, and contributing to public welfare.[21]

Koh (2004) interprets such "fence-breaking" (*phá rào*), or breach of regulations, as a sign of state weakness; my own findings confirm the challenges of negotiating the licit/illicit divide for urban governance (see also Rao 2013). At the same time, the boldness of the fence breaking suggests the conviction of residents as political actors who decided to take the matter of decay into their own hands and use it to justify their actions. To better understand the relationship between citizens and the state—between tenants' simultaneous commitment to and apparent defiance of state projects—I talked with Mr. Nguyên at the Housing Agency (Công ty Nhà đất), a key actor in the city's regulation of informality, or so I thought. When I knocked on his office door one afternoon to talk about the legal status of cơi nới, he seemed particularly cranky. I had interrupted his card game; moreover, he did not want to discuss the topic without prior notice of my questions so he could "properly prepare" (that is, call the central office to see if my inquiry fell within the scope of my research permissions). Without looking up from cards, he told me bluntly, "It is not allowed to build extensions onto the buildings."[22]

"But many people build them," I replied.

"We cannot stop them [*không cấm được*]!" he snapped.

"Are they fined?" I prodded gently.

"Yes, they are fined," he shouted, at last laying down his hand to look at me. "But they still build [*bị phạt mà vẫn xây*]." I asked if his office had to accept the cơi nới. "No," he continued, "we don't accept them, but we don't have the power [*không có quyền*] to ban them!"

"So who does?" I probed.

"I don't know," Nguyên retorted. "That's not my concern here! Maybe the District [Phường] or the Urban Management Office [Phòng Quản lý Đô thị]."

I posed a final question: "Can Công ty Nhà đất demolish illegal cơi nới?"

The reply was firm: "We don't have the right to do that!" Nguyên then returned to his card game, ending what had been a short but informative conversation. His admission that he was unable to enforce housing regulations and his lack of knowledge of (or refusal to tell me) where, administratively, regulatory authority lay to stop unlawful construction revealed the limits of state power to implement housing policy and to regulate urban space. Tenants took advantage of this legal ambiguity, and the agency's inability to intervene, to increase the number and size of cơi nới.

THE ARCHITECT

To contextualize this new phase of cơi nới construction and how it challenged many conventional ideas about "informal" building, I sought out another key player: Mr. Sơn, the local contractor responsible for most extensions in the area. I found his makeshift shop at the northern end of Quang Trung, behind block C9, which was one of the three buildings (along with blocks C7 and C8) that had been redesigned to reduce construction costs and economize space (chapter 6). This included doubling occupancy and removing balconies. As a result, there were virtually no cơi nới in blocks C7, C8, or C9, the most decayed blocks that housed some of the poorest families. As Sơn showed me around, he explained that residents in these buildings did not have the money or *dân trí* (intellectual sense) to expand their living spaces, unlike the people with culture (*có văn hóa*) in my area who were presumably more future focused. Although he avoided the controversial term "class" (see Bélanger, Drummond, and Nguyen-Marshall 2012, 6–9), he was in fact making observations about class disparities that were visible in the very architecture that had been intended to create an egalitarian society. These disparities had always been present in the complex, but given endemic postwar poverty they were more defined by cultural capital than economic. While decay, as a hindrance to progress, was linked to female, rural backwardness (see chapter 8), cơi nới as renewal revealed an aspiring middle class among cultural elites.

When I first met him, Sơn had been building cơi nới for more than a decade. During my fieldwork, he and his crew of five workers controlled the cơi nới construction market in Quang Trung. Sơn was a professional of the informal sector; although his work intersected with the formal economy, he had not received specialized training like other skilled professionals. Instead, his expertise lay beyond the accredited repository of "human capital" (Gidwani 2010, 49): he was self-taught, innovative, knowledgeable, methodical, and resourceful—traits often found with autoconstruction. Like certified architects, Sơn designed cơi nới in consultation with tenants. He described his work as *an toàn* (safe) and *chắc chắn* (secure), and indeed his reputation depended on producing sound structures. His off-modern cơi nới were a response to the obsolescence of the buildings, and they challenged the formal/informal binary by showing how grand modernist planning had produced a need for the unplanned and the unplannable (Roy 2005, 156).

It would be a mistake to see Sơn as an amateur builder and ad hoc producer of blight, as conventional accounts of urban informality might claim.[23] Rather, his efforts at place making opened up possibilities for residents to create a more inhabitable, beautiful home, or *nhà đẹp*, out of decay. Sơn's services were in high demand: between 2009 and 2012, he and his team built approximately sixty cơi nới across Quang Trung. These ever larger structures reflected changing consumer lifestyles: people needed more space for extended families but also extra room for more things. Cơi nới were no longer simply functional, Sơn explained, but aesthetic. They had to look good from both inside and out. To satisfy demands without sacrificing security, Sơn innovated and invested in high-quality construction materials. He regularly updated his skills and technique and his awareness of market trends. Building wider and longer cơi nới meant chiseling deep into the walls to fasten a sturdy steel frame. This required more planning and precision than attaching a thin metal rim onto the balcony, as he had done previously with the much smaller and less ambitious tiger-cage cơi nới.

Such modifications were costly and indicated an increase in disposable income among certain families. On average, expenditures climbed from 15 million VND (U.S. $750) for a basic cơi nới—already a sizable amount for households whose median monthly income was 5 million VND (U.S. $250)—to more than 30 million VND (U.S. $1,500) for a more impressive addition. The most expensive cơi nới that Sơn built was for Bà *thầy bói*, the female clairvoyant, whose popular trade made her comparatively well-off. Bà was a *người mua lại*—she had not been allocated a flat as an original tenant but purchased user rights in 1995 for a few hundred dollars. Bà's three-room-long cơi nới of roughly fifteen square meters increased her living space by 30 percent and cost 70 million VND (U.S. $3,500) to build. Knowing it would be rejected, she had not applied for a building permit and subsequently paid the fine of 500,000 VND. The lengthy room was divided into two functional spaces: one for taking meals and receiving guests (for her trade), the other for sleeping (for her son and his wife). "It's totally secure!" Bà reassured me.[24] Sơn confirmed that the bulky assembly had been fortified with eleven steel beams supporting a concrete

↑ Figure 9.6 Setting new trends: engineer inspects the frame for an eight-meter-long *cơi nới*, 2011. Photo by the author.

↑ Figure 9.7 Completed project two weeks later (note original balcony on lower left), 2011. Photo by the author.

foundation (see figure 9.6). Formica laminate walls enclosed the structure, which had three acrylic louvre windows. I had witnessed the construction from my front window; my neighbors also watched, chuckling with envy at its size and opulence. Topped with a corrugated metal roof in matching green, the custom renovation achieved a clean, modern look on the otherwise obsolescent building (see figure 9.7), far from a bricolage assembly.

There was an irony to these material displays of wealth among the urban poor. During my fieldwork, the municipal government was transferring ownership of the flats from the state to tenants who had legal user rights, as per Decree 61/CP. This was a fraught process (see chapter 10). Residents supported Decree 61/CP in theory, but they were dismayed that it involved an exchange of capital since, in their view, the property had been gifted from the GDR and they were the rightful inheritors, also through their long-term occupancy. Far worse than requiring that tenants purchase their apartments was the fact that the buildings were slated for demolition after the handover was complete, and investors had proposed compensating residents at a below-market rate that *excluded* nonpermitted structures. This was significant for two reasons: First, it meant residents might be subjected to a classic capitalist condition of accumulation by dispossession (Harvey 2003), which was radically at odds with the more familiar notion at the time of collective ownership. Second, from a rational-economic perspective, investment in cơi nới would not maximize future returns since they did not add value to the homes. For example, in 2011 Bà, the fortune-teller, paid U.S. $1,450 to purchase her flat from the state and invested U.S. $3,500 in the construction of a cơi nới, as mentioned above. Such investments were perceived by outsiders as foolish and prompted critique: "Those impoverished families are wasting their money!" one cultural elite who had the financial means to leave Quang Trung exclaimed.[25] What he failed to see was that for people like Bà, cơi nới challenged the "poverty" label and its associations with the social and moral failure of residents who remained in Quang Trung.[26]

Tenants did not subscribe to the same cost-benefit analysis as the man who had moved out of Quang Trung, but there was a sound logic to their investments. Their vulnerable position between a state-controlled housing regime and a speculative property market influenced decisions around renovations. Sơn, for example, began cơi nới projects even as notices of town hall meetings to discuss resettlement circulated among the blocks. Tenants who built elaborate attachments—often using pooled family resources—might appear affluent compared with neighbors, but they still were unable to buy themselves out of Quang Trung, Sơn reminded me. The U.S. $3,500 that Bà spent on her cơi nới would buy her just one square meter of prime land within the city, or four square meters of living space in a new condominium. Residents weighed their options carefully and concluded that it was better to remodel. More critically, their willingness to channel scarce funds into decayed housing, even under the threat of its demolition, signaled popular discontent and a lack of confidence in the state's plans for urban redevelopment. With the widespread belief that such a project would face interminable delays—suspending them in an endless meantime (Jansen 2015)—residents proceeded to spend more disposable income on upgrading their units than at any other time in the history of Quang Trung. This included beautifying the interiors of cơi nới.

INSIDE CƠI NỚI: AESTHETIC ASPIRATIONS

As symbols of distinction in otherwise neglected buildings, cơi nới were a twist on the "problem" of urban informality. Building cơi nới allowed cultural elites and others to display their upward mobility, much as owning a motorbike had done in the 1990s (Truitt 2008) and buying automobiles more recently (Hansen 2016). They were signs not of encroaching urban poverty and blight, but of what Alison J. Clarke (2001) has aptly called the "aesthetics of social aspiration." Cơi nới not only expanded living space; they enabled new urban lifestyles and modern subjectivities based on the accumulation of things. Scholars of Vietnam have drawn on Bourdieu to show how consumption practices, as a performance of status, defined an emerging middle class that enacted new forms of personhood after market reforms in 1986 (Vann 2012). In this case, residents explicitly "classed up" cơi nới interiors to show their middle-class aspirations as discerning and tasteful consumers—rather than "classing down" to conceal them (Leshkowich 2014, 185).

More than any other renovation, cơi nới reconfigured social relations within the family. As Victor Buchli has observed, the "productive work of kinship" is at the center of architectural malleability (2013, 75). Spatial arrangements that emplace people according to gender and seniority convey important cultural messages about kinship systems. Cơi nới reshaped daily household practices and the use of space by creating firmer divisions between public and private life at the front and back of the apartment, respectively. This is not to suggest that Vietnamese homes are rigidly "organized according to a set of homologous oppositions," as in Bourdieu's Berber house (1970, 157). Indeed, Waterson's study of Southeast Asian houses showed that "ideas of gender hierarchy do not provide the dominant mode of [spatial] organization" (1990, 170). Space is gendered, but not immutably so. In certain cases, cơi nới reinforced hierarchical and patriarchal relations, and in other instances they undermined them. In all cases, cơi nới created more personal spaces that accommodated rising demands for privacy that accompanied apartment remodeling. For example, in the quest for more marital independence, some newly wedded couples used cơi nới as a private sleeping area in extended, patrilocal households (like the example of the clairvoyant's son).

In other instances, cơi nới expressed shifting notions of personhood and self-fashioning under market socialism (Leshkowich 2014; Tran 2015), especially among a younger generation of consumers who placed a higher value on originality. Interiors embodied a modern urban aesthetic and included imported furnishings made popular by slick magazines like *Nhà Đẹp* (Beautiful house). The relationship between the desire for global commodities and articulations of middle-class identity has been noted across Southeast Asia and has prompted moral anxieties about consumerism (Jones 2010), not unlike the apprehensions that GDR designs triggered in the 1970s (see chapter 5). After economic reforms in Vinh, the household's emergence as a site of material investment and expressive individuality (see Clarke 2001, 24)—fashioning "class" out of a "classless" society—was an aesthetic counterpoint to the buildings' exterior decay and state disinvestment.

Cơi nới were aspirational spaces of beautification that showcased taste and a chic hominess, with wooden walls, tiled floors, and modern furnishings. They proudly displayed possessions that would have been unthinkable a generation before: wall hangings, curtains, fish tanks, houseplants, wardrobes, televisions, shelves, books, clothing, clutter—material articulations of social capital (Clarke 2001, 25). In contrast to communal, multipurpose space at the front of the house, cơi nới privileged individual, productive activities at the back, beyond the peering eyes of passersby in the corridor, creating a more rigid spatial divide between public and private. Such individuated spaces of self-regulated practices have become emblematic of neoliberal regimes (Rose 1999). In Quang Trung, computers turned cơi nới into personal offices and studies, treadmills into exercise rooms, and drafting tables into art studios (see plate 13). These desirable lifestyles did not so much undermine socialist political visions as they evinced the success of modernization and of state efforts to produce a civilized population that now shows loyalty through consumption (Schwenkel and Leshkowich 2012, 383). At the same time, in creating a sense of interiority, such spaces "reduced the accessibility of the family to the public," making it more difficult for government officials to exercise their power (Yan 2003, 124–25), for example, in their attempts to seize time and summon residents to meetings.

There were important gender dimensions to the new spatiality of cơi nới that turned the utilitarian flat into a place of affective homemaking. One is reminded here of the geographer Doreen Massey's astute observation that the spatial is always gender relations writ large (1994, 2). Many cơi nới were male spaces of consumption that reflected larger spatial and temporal transformations in everyday life: first was the growth of privatized leisure and hobbies as signs of middle-class subjectivity displayed through notions of "free" time, especially among male retirees. And second was a generational shift of recreational activities from outdoor communal areas to the interiors of flats. They also reflected a gendered redistribution of space. Apartment interiors were ordered around the kitchen in the back, where I usually found women busy at work, and the living room in the front, where men spent more time, often with guests. During my visits, men tended to remain seated, conversing, as women bustled about, chiming into the discussion from another room. Only a few times did couples sit together during interviews. These were not spatial absolutes: women used living rooms for their own purposes, to eat with family and perform ancestral rituals. However, I rarely saw men in the kitchens. Proportionately, women accessed more household space than did men; there was no exclusive male space in the socialist-designed home.

With cơi nới, a stronger division between male and female spatialities emerged. While small tiger cages had expanded women's space for domestic work, larger cơi nới were often private male spaces. Male teenagers studied and played computer games in them, a sign of parents' growing investment in their children's education, especially for boys (Bélanger and Liu 2004). For older men, cơi nới were not unlike the "man caves" found in American basements and garages—"vernacular museums" of memory, where masculine identity is reproduced through nostalgic objects and personalized space (Browitt 2017, 207). They were also socially intimate places where male friends could gather informally—and only by invitation—leaving the front room for receiving more formal and unannounced guests. One cơi nới I frequented was a site for poetry readings. Built with a cement floor and supporting steel beams, it housed the poet's archive and served as his workroom. It was unique in its inclusion of a less secure tiger cage attached to a wooden plank for hanging laundry—a precarious extension of an extension (imagine a knapsack attached to a backpack) that reflected, in Massey's term, the gendered spatial division of labor in the household.

Shelves lined one side of the poet's room, holding his books and documents. Nearby hung his stylish collection of caps and ties, next to the black beret he wore to meetings. There was also a yellow hard hat from his time working at the electric plant, which he donned in the afternoons to park motorbikes for housing management to earn some cash.[27] These nostalgic accessories sustained a meaningful shift in his postretirement identity, as the poet moved from being an intellectual by day to an enterprising state subject in the evenings. A photograph of General Võ Nguyên Giáp, whom he had met during the war, and the national poet, Tố Hữu, hung next to a drawing of Hồ Chí Minh, around which he had arranged his poems. Indeed, I saw several portraits of Hồ Chí Minh in cơi nới. Private male spaces for leisure, consumption, sociality, and self-expression were affectively and semiotically rich places of patriotism that upheld the values of the nation (Browitt 2017, 207).

Cơi nới were also entrepreneurial spaces, especially for upwardly mobile women with limited resources. Female, middle-class entrepreneurs were typically involved in affective service industries (Freeman 2014), including child care and tutoring (*dạy thêm*). As in other urban socialist societies (e.g., Humphrey 1999), relocating enviable or suspicious businesses, such as divination, from Vinh's public sphere to the home kept them under the radar, and their proceeds off the books. For some, auxiliary businesses run from cơi nới supplemented meager state salaries. This was the case with my neighbor, Phượng, who was an English teacher at a local primary school. Like the fortune-teller's, Phượng's cơi nới was three rooms long, and a source of envy because of its income-generating capabilities. Her mother-in-law, a retiree from the Department of Construction who had worked on the master plan for Quang Trung, had designed the space, and Sơn had built it for 26 million VND (U.S. $1,300). Phượng's husband was the head of household (his father had passed), so the couple slept in the bedroom, and his mother slept in a section of the cơi nới. The rest was open space that Phượng transformed into a lucrative English-language classroom for children several nights a week, an example of cơi nới as aspirational spaces of academic achievement (see figure 9.8). Female entrepreneurialism showed the heterogeneous ways that women combined homemaking, child rearing, and commerce to create wealth for their families while exhibiting status and mobility through the scale and materiality of their cơi nới.

COMMERCIALIZING SPACE: *GẦM*

Instead of bringing commerce into the home, renovations to *gầm*, or walk-out basements, extended the home to commerce. More than any other modifications, gầm renovations signaled a radical shift in the city from large-scale, industry-led modernization to small-scale, "entrepreneurial urbanization"

↑ Figure 9.8 Preparing the next generation for the future in a *cơi nới* classroom, 2011. Photo by the author.

(Datta 2015). Vinh's attempts to achieve emancipation through industrialization had been largely unsuccessful. The city's residents endured crushing poverty and hunger in the postwar subsidy years, or *thời bao cấp*. Owing to state inefficiencies, devastating floods, and a border war with China in 1979, industry in and around Vinh slowed and in some cases came to a halt. People described their lives at the time as *cực kỳ khổ*, or insufferable hardship. *Đổi mới* reforms may have liberalized the economy and ended state subsidies in 1986, but people's lives in Vinh did not improve, at least initially. "Slowly, life started to change in the 1990s," one retired designer recalled.[28]

Indeed, for many, Đổi mới made life more difficult. With economic restructuring, thousands of workers were laid off in 1989, as per Decision 176.[29] Across Quang Trung, the proletariat encountered what was once unthinkable: unemployment. Many took lump-sum compensation—one month of salary for each year they had worked, with no retirement benefits—and invested it in new businesses. "I was rich!" laughed a female worker from the Food and Beverage Company, who opened a grocery kiosk after losing her job. "My salary, fifty-seven *đồng*, for eighteen years of work all in one payment—that was a lot of money then!"[30] By disconnecting people from the workplace—their lifelong source of material support and social identity—Decision 176 drastically altered their lives and sense of self. It also transformed Quang Trung's built environment, as laid-off workers—mostly women—were forced out of the state sector and into the informal economy.[31] Unplanned economic activities across the complex began to encroach on communal spaces of "ongoing politics" and state-making projects, like courtyards (Laszczkowski 2015b, 137). Renovated walk-out basements were at the center of this transformation and became opportune sites for livelihood creation that diversified building façades and created a flourishing gầm economy.

As a distinctly GDR design concept, gầm made Quang Trung—and Vinh—unique. No other housing complex in Vietnam had them; all were built at ground level in a style called *nhà trệt*. This was also the style of blocks A1–A4 that the Ministry of Construction had designed before East German experts arrived. Despite the extra cost, provincial authorities recognized the benefits of an elevated first story that the ground-level gầm made possible, so they kept them in the redesign of blocks C7–C9. Residents appreciated the extra space and the additional height they afforded, though they did not always use the gầm as intended. In many cases, disuse led to their deterioration. The nhà trệt style, however, had an important advantage: after Đổi mới, ground-floor apartments were turned into private businesses across Vietnam. Because liberalization made the Quang Trung trade center obsolete, there was a need for shops and services in the complex, but no ground floors existed.[32] The gầm offered the most practical solution: tenants could use their cellar storage spaces for small-scale business opportunities or rent them for additional income. A few families even opened the floor to access the gầm directly from their first-story flat (see figure 9.9). In the gầm, we see the most extensive appropriation of state infrastructure for private commercial activity, and the biggest challenge to the GDR's spatial ordering, where concerns about ecology (how to avoid flooding) took precedence over culture and livelihood strategies. Rather than marking clearer divisions between public and private spaces in the home, as I argued occurred with cơi nới, gầm made those divisions even blurrier.

Housing administrators had allotted each household a gầm, which was not calculated as living space for rent purposes. This meant that, like the cơi nới, a remodeled gầm did not add property value and, later, would not be calculated for compensation. A typical *đơn*, or modular unit with twenty flats, had a minimum of twenty gầm, half of which opened toward the front courtyard and half toward the back garden. Gầm were fairly standard in size, averaging 3 meters long, 1 meter wide, and 1.5 meters high (see figure 9.10). In recent years, these narrow, dark spaces have been repurposed in diverse and creative ways, which sometimes involved removing weight-bearing walls.

↑ Figure 9.9 *Gầm* store, with access from first-floor apartment in block C7, 2011. Photo by the author.

An important class distinction here once again shows the limits of egalitarian politics. Unlike with cơi nới, most of these renovations occurred in blocks allocated to (predominantly female) workers. To increase the size of their businesses, tenants widened and lengthened their gầm by incorporating adjoining lots, at times attaching metal shacks, or kiosks (*kiốt*), onto the front. Because such structures encroached on public space, users were required to pay a land-use fee to the Housing Agency of 1,000 VND (U.S. $.05) per square meter, another example of state efforts to formalize informality. Like the fine paid for cơi nới, this quarterly payment showed authorities that residents were upstanding citizens, despite their damage to state property. In a few cases, people moved into the renovated gầm. One homeless family lived discreetly in a dank gầm in block C9; an elderly nurse, who could no longer climb the stairs to her fifth-floor flat, lived in a widened gầm in block A6 that was outfitted with electricity and a lavatory with running water. Whereas cơi nới were places of middle-class aspiration and affective home making, renovated gầm were spaces of precarity and economic possibility for a more vulnerable urban population.

Mainly women used renovated gầm to run small businesses, including workers laid off by Decision 176. This confirms Massey's observation that gender

↑ Figure 9.10 Original *gầm* in block B3, used for storage, 2010. Photo by the author.

also plays a vital role in the organization of economic space (1994, 180). One exception was a senior in block B2, a bird keeper who turned his hobby into a lucrative business. "Bird keeping is a man's activity," he explained, showing me his collection of colorful, feathered pets in bamboo cages, which were for sale (see plate 14).[33] This was not a pastime for men of small means: prices for each bird and cage ranged from 200,000 VND to a few million VND (U.S. $10 to U.S. $100). The bird business was unique in its focus on a leisure activity. A comparative study of gầm across blocks A5–C9 showed that the majority of businesses involved food (cafés, soup stalls, noodle shops, tea stands), wellness (beauty salons, barbers, dentists, pharmacies), groceries (packaged foods, dry goods, nonfood items), textiles (tailors, clothing), repair (appliances, motorbikes), and commercial storage (for rice, flowers, incense, and fowl). In block B3, close to the main street of Quang Trung, I found a bustling gầm restaurant, established in 1991. Nearby was a pillow production enterprise (see figure 9.11) that the son of a *liệt sĩ*, or war martyr, had founded with his wife in 2001. This man's mother had received a rent-free apartment in 1978 as a *nhà tình nghĩa*, or charity house gifted to "heroic families." His wife ran the operation, and with another female worker they sewed polyester pillows to sell to vendors in Vinh's central market down the street, which provided the main source of income for their family.

↑ Figure 9.11 Pillow factory in block B3: *gẩm* as spaces for manufacturing, 2011. Photo by the author.

Gẩm generated profits not only through private business ventures like the pillow operation, but also through a system of rents. In ways that socialist planners had never imagined, former proletariats made "modest forays . . . into petty rentiership" (Levien 2011, 476) by converting utilitarian gẩm into property assets. The value of gẩm was based on location: those closer to schools, day care centers, markets, and main roads commanded higher rents. For example, the total monthly overhead for a woman in block C7 who sold rice porridge in the morning at the local *chợ cóc*, or "toad market" (where traders "hopped" around to avoid the police), was 600,000 VND (U.S. $30): 500,000 to the landlord (the tenant with user rights to the gẩm), 60,000 to the Housing Agency for use of the land on which the attached kiosk stood, and 40,000 for electricity. One of the most valuable strips of gẩm ran across the front of block C5, adjacent to an informal market. There, a tailor paid 1 million VND (U.S. $50) to the legal tenant of the gẩm that she rented for her shop. Her business was one among many in Quang Trung that demonstrated a new precariat-in-the-making in Vinh: five young female workers, without any labor protection, hunched over sewing machines in the airless, dimly lit gẩm.

As refurbished gẩm expanded commerce across the complex, they reintroduced the specter of urban disorder by appropriating the commons. Generous open spaces, a hallmark of socialist planning—in Quang Trung comprising 60 percent of the complex—filled with activities associated with microenterprises, such as a makeshift barber shop between B4 and B5 (see figure 9.12), goats grazing behind B3 (see figure 9.4), and a spontaneous chợ cóc between C4 and C5 that grew to fill the internal roads and shared spaces of wards 8 and 9 (see figure 9.13). In a similar display of empathetic bureaucracy that I witnessed with cơi nới, authorities tolerated these spatial transgressions, though the press criticized them for *lấn chiếm sân chung*, or occupying the commons, and for violating the order of urban civilization (*trật tự văn minh đô thị*). Within Quang Trung there was no stigma attached to these informal economic activities, as observed elsewhere in the global South (e.g., Gidwani 2010, 48). Itinerant traders and market vendors used communal resources daily, washing their produce at wells and taking naps under Quang Trung's many trees. They were not, however, allowed to hawk their wares within the blocks.[34] These migrant women also reconfigured planned space and challenged its prescribed functions in Quang Trung. Unlike in Hanoi (Turner and Schoenberger 2012) and Ho Chi Minh City (Kim 2015; Leshkowich 2005), their presence did not incite moral panic and a new ban on street vending meant to "civilize the city." In fact, the toad market eventually was formalized as Quang Trung Marketplace, demonstrating the women's influence on municipal planning and policy. In this instance, the "unplanned" became coopted by authorities and integrated into top-down, formal planning with its own set of rules and regulations that traders continued to flout. Quang Trung Market swelled and grew new legs in the courtyards between blocks C7, C8, and C9, where some of my neighbors also sold goods (see plate 15). This flexible use of public space for small-scale economic activities was reminiscent of the spontaneous trade in the 1970s that Vietnamese authorities and GDR experts had attempted to contain through similar municipal strategies of formalization (see figure 5.6).

Repurposed gầm helped to enable this spontaneity, which zoned urban planning had sought to eliminate (chapter 5). This was clearest when I visited gầm at dawn and dusk—when markets opened and shut down—and saw how they were used as storage and even as parking for vendors with larger operations. Their cool, dark atmosphere was ideal for preserving produce, flowers, dry goods, and other wares that outside vendors stored overnight for a fee. As they expanded, the gầm and the market integrated and served one another through the collective occupation of public space, offering tenants both vending and rental opportunities as well as convenient shopping. Unlike cơi nới, gầm and adjacent spaces constituted a vibrant "infrastructure of common life"

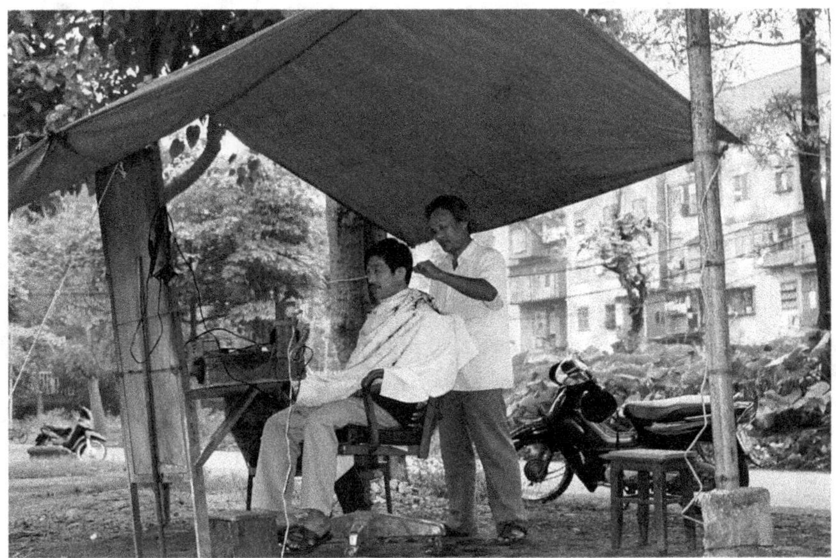

↑ Figure 9.12 Appropriating green space: barber shop in area B, 2011. Photo by the author.

↑ Figure 9.13 Appropriating the commons between blocks C4 and C5: Quang Trung market, 2011. Photo by the author.

for distributing urban resources, from material goods to care and social support (Tonkiss 2013, 322). Many of my elderly neighbors bought groceries at Quang Trung market every day, and still others worked there. Some, like the hot-tea vendors, made little money but enjoyed the company of regular customers, who preferred the small stalls to new cafés across the street. Shoppers at the market considered the goods to be cheaper, fresher, and more local than those available in supermarkets, where they almost never shopped, even after a Big C Supercenter opened a block away. My neighbors felt more at home in the commons of Quang Trung than in the (for them) awkward spaces of consumer capitalism. There were also practical reasons for this: the ability to buy fresh food daily meant there was no need for a refrigerator, which reduced utility bills. These repurposed spaces of routine exchange and sociality were essential to people's livelihood and to fulfilling the social and economic needs of an aging population with restricted mobility.

In doing away with the "organized outdoors" of socialist utopias (Boym 1994, 127), off-modern housing began to resemble the chaos of unplanned "capitalist cities" that had once vexed GDR architects. It also bore a resemblance to the sprawling Vietnamese market towns that socialist planners had tried to abolish because of their "profiteering." The proposed solution to socialism's crumbling utopia was to revitalize Quang Trung through urban restructuring to keep pace with rapid economic growth and development in other cities in Vietnam. While residents used deteriorating conditions to justify their spatial transgressions, the state, too, appropriated the logic of obsolescence to advocate demolition, sparking revaluation of the ruined buildings by residents who rejected the vision of a new future city.

10

REVALUATION

> Houses are like people: they do not live forever; they have a life cycle. One day they will also become old and need to be rejuvenated or replaced.
>
> —INTERVIEW WITH EAST GERMAN ARCHITECT OF VINH, 2012

On March 24, 2011, a magnitude 6.9 earthquake struck eastern Shan State in Myanmar, sending tremors all the way to Vietnam. In my fourth-floor apartment in block C2, I felt nothing. A friend on the fourteenth floor of a nearby condominium—in fact, Vinh's first skyscraper, built on the former site of block C1—called me in a state of panic after experiencing forceful swaying. Our different experiences of the earthquake affirmed what my neighbors had known all along: that the most durable and disaster-resistant housing in Vinh was East German–made. The irony was not lost on me: wealthier owners of spacious apartments in the new condominium tower appeared to be at higher risk of catastrophe than poorer people in cracked and crumbling modernist mass housing.

This understanding intensified the lack of trust in renewal projects—what I call the "New Modern"—executed by Vietnamese public-private partnerships and the revaluation of socialist architecture as a durable housing model for the city's future, despite needing urgent improvement. The foreign-designed structures were seen by many of my respondents as high quality and stable, even in their advanced state of decay, and were preferred to locally engineered buildings, considered even less safe. How this logic unfolded, as a refusal of spatial rupture, is the focus of this chapter and goes something like this: Unlike Quang Trung's housing blocks—made to be sustainable, but neglected and misused—faulty design marred new Vietnamese construction, which was built from a desire to accumulate wealth rather than to improve people's well-being. For older generations in Quang Trung, it was the shoddy constructions of "wild capitalism" (Harper 2005)—rather than those of socialism (Fehérváry 2012, 634)—that foretold of social and ecological ruin.

Recent scholarship has emphasized the extraordinary scale and speed of urban development in Vietnam since economic reforms (*Đổi mới*). Its authors commonly argue that housing liberalization in 1991, and the real estate booms and busts that followed, respatialized inequality. Urban development has also wrought new forms of social upheaval and spatial segregation, connected to land grabs and gentrification (Harms 2016; Labbé 2014; Gough and Tran 2009).[1] With these changes has come a new "affective atmosphere" (Anderson 2009) around the built environment. Sentiments such as exasperation mobilized social and political subjectivities as well as feelings of indifference and apathy, particularly among women. In Quang Trung, the transition from a policy of universal, state-managed housing to one of private ownership generated considerable anger and despair among residents, who enjoyed the benefits of the former and stood to lose the most from the latter. As Simone (2010, 62) observes, the extension of market forces over urban institutions is "never a smooth accomplishment," especially in centrally planned cities like Vinh that were organized around the *collective* ownership of the means of production.

Privatization of the socialist commons radically altered the relationship between tenants and the state (Alexander 2007a), as well as between tenants and architecture, inspiring both reverence for socialist aesthetics and disidentification with spectacular postmodern structures (Laszczkowski 2015a). As in larger Vietnamese cities, new forms of stratification, some with their roots in socialism, contributed to rising inequality and social fragmentation across Vinh. Driving these uneven geographies of redevelopment were aspirations to a free-market economy, especially among the younger generations enchanted with the New Modern, and an enduring commitment to socialist utopian imaginaries among others—two different paths to the same goal of progress. Among the latter, tenants who were most skeptical of liberal housing regimes rejected the aesthetic sensibility and vision of futurity that came to prevail in Vinh during my fieldwork. In response, they valorized East German design and technology over the aesthetics of global capitalism and recast ruined buildings as the most desirable housing in the city.

Scholars have noted how discourses that pathologize socialist architecture as "poor quality" have been used to justify its removal from the built environment. Microrayons, in particular, have been maligned as drab, hulking monstrosities that prevent communities from flourishing (Fehérváry 2013; van der Hoorn 2009). It is not without irony that the material legacies of modern history's perhaps most humane housing policies, where architects applied their skills to improving society rather than achieving fame, are now discredited as inhumane abominations (Hatherley 2015, 92). And yet, older residents in Quang Trung inverted this aesthetic order, and along with it, conventional East/West, socialist/capitalist binaries. In so doing, they undermined the rationale of "creative destruction" to maintain profitability through constant innovation (Harvey 2003) and the planned obsolescence of buildings (Cairns and Jacobs 2014; Derrida 1990). Retirees defended the social and ecological achievements of Quang Trung, a place rich in memory and meaning for them, and linked dystopia instead with the New Modern, even as they struggled themselves with the dangers of decay in their living environments. In arguing for the renovation and preservation of their buildings, they consciously resisted the erasure of place thick with affect (Casey 2001) and their history of struggle along with it. They sustained the notion of modern architecture as a public good to fulfill social needs rather than a tool of capital to serve private interests (de Graaf 2015).

During my fieldwork in Vinh, privatization and redevelopment were at the center of anxieties about urban change and uncertainties about the future of housing. This final chapter outlines the affinities that formed among a generation of Quang Trung residents and their coordinated responses to the greatest disruption in their lives since the end of the war. For state officials and developers, the unplanned obsolescence of Quang Trung had sealed its fate: the buildings held little value and needed to be removed. Residents thought otherwise and contested this devaluation. In the previous chapter, I showed how decay allowed tenants to imagine alternative *material* possibilities through renovation. Here, I show how decay inspired new *political* opportunities to challenge the logics of value that underlay spatial and architectural transformation, and to push for other ways to qualify "worth" (*giá trị*). Two case studies illustrate the revaluation of the ruined buildings as they moved between registers of economic, aesthetic, and historical value, and other measures of meaning. In the first, residents refused to move out of Quang Trung and into new housing; in the second, they refused to accept developers' offers of compensation. In both, residents' deep historical and affective ties to one another and to the built environment generated novel forms of valuation and political participation that were communal and consensual but not indissoluble. Residents filed grievances with the city, attended public meetings, told their stories to the press, submitted petitions to authorities, voted as a block against redevelopment, and called attention to their lifelong service to the state. Through these civic acts, they claimed rights to material security and the possibility of human flourishing threatened by the retreat of the state (Friedmann 2000, 466). Consequently, they contested the market logics that encroached on socialist planning and threatened to undo the "people-oriented" (*định hướng con người*) design of their city. In their attempts to exert some control over the future, residents questioned the processes of valuation they encountered in redevelopment and the assessment of their homes as expendable.

THE PRIVATIZING CITY

> We built tunnels and fought under the rain of bombs for this?
>
> —INTERVIEW WITH FEMALE YOUTH VOLUNTEER AND QUANG TRUNG CONSTRUCTION WORKER, 2011

No topic infuriated residents more than the privatization of Quang Trung, as per Decree 61 of the Central Government (61/CP) from 1994. In witnessing this highly contested process, I came to grasp how the imaginary of a benevolent state masked and reproduced systemic inequality. I also came to view residents, including the wardens who represented both state and nonstate interests, as housing activists who were passionate about asserting their rights to the city. Privatization provided residents with a platform for political participation that fit with the state's rhetoric of democratic socialism. It also enabled citizens to proactively shape redevelopment through narratives of belonging and reciprocal entitlements. While residents could not stop the forces of privatization, they did have the power to collectively disrupt them.

Decree 61/CP followed on the heels of the Housing Ordinance of 1991, which allowed the purchase and sale of residential property, and the Land Law of 1993, which permitted the transfer of user rights while maintaining land as a public asset (Nguyen 2010). Decree 61/CP transferred ownership rights to residents in mass housing through the sale (*bán*) of state property at a rate that corresponded to its "remaining value" (*giá trị còn lại*). But Quang Trung residents considered their apartments social goods, not commodities. In their view, the decree's use of the term "purchase" (*mua*) signaled a betrayal by the state. Tenants considered themselves the rightful owners of their apartments, which they had received for their "outstanding achievements" (*thành tích xuất sắc*) and commendable "service to the revolution" (*công với cách mạng*). Their moral economy was driven by a logic of reciprocity that affirmed the basic tenets of their social contract with the state: rights and protections for duty and loyalty.

Residents also expressed a clear economic rationale for this claim: having been liable for rent and upkeep for more than thirty years, they had long paid for their "gifted" housing. Across the complex, I heard the sentiment "Đức cho, người phải mua. Vô lý!" (Germans bequeathed, people have to buy. How ridiculous!). Neighborhood leaders were equally vocal about the state's extraction of money from the city's poorest residents. A female construction worker who had served on the Hồ Chí Minh Trail complained, "It's outrageous that we have to pay for our apartments! They were given to us. We built, maintained, and paid for them each month."[2] Labor, habitation, and remittance made Quang Trung flats an inalienable possession for retired workers and civil servants, who refused a property-rights conception of ownership initially. Despite decay, their homes were prestige symbols of their status and role in nation building that the state's commodification threatened to annul.

The state, in contrast, framed privatization as benevolent. One intellectual in C4 was particularly troubled by the timescale of 61/CP—which had taken fifteen years to implement in Vinh—just another sign of how the city always lagged behind, in his view. He said, "61/CP was designed to secure housing rights for the poor. It should have taken place years ago. The government has no intention to take care of the people."[3] Whereas this man interpreted *stalled* socialist time as a lack of concern for poorer residents, the state framed it as favorable and in line with party policy. Municipal officials described the delay as a protective measure: Quang Trung tenants did not have the capital to purchase apartments in the 1990s—unlike in Hanoi, where people had become legal property owners in 1995. Officials were correct that growth and stability took longer to establish in the much poorer Vinh. And yet their paternalistic rationale worked against tenants' long-term economic interests and created regional inequities. As per 61/CP, the square-meter price for units would be assessed at *current* market rates (in this case, 2010), while mandated deductions for state service remained at 1994 rates (the year 61/CP was ratified). This was a critical point of contention between housing authorities and residents. Delay-as-protection meant that residents would pay more for their apartments than their better-off compatriots in Hanoi—in some cases, up to ten times more, enraging tenants who cried foul.[4]

The first step in the shift from user rights (*quyền sử dụng*) to legal ownership (*quyền sở hữu*) was the calculation of gross living area (*diện tích*) per household, which happened in early fall 2010, around the time I moved into Quang Trung. This offered another opportunity for authorities to claim benevolence, though it did not maximize residents' welfare as claimed. Carefully written calculations were posted on community boards around the complex at

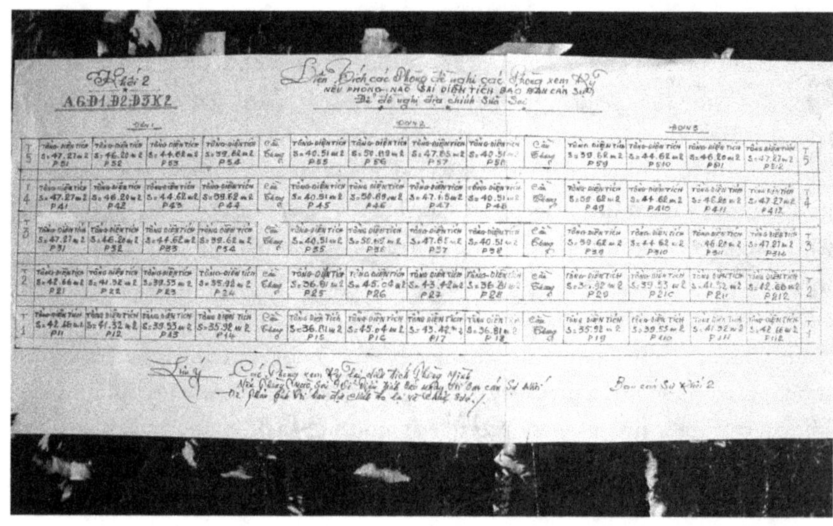

↑ Figure 10.1 Calculations of gross living area per unit, posted in stairways, 2010. Photo by the author.

the start of November, along with a request that residents either sign in agreement or report errors to management (see figure 10.1). Whereas wary residents anticipated that housing authorities would *over*estimate their living space, in fact they tended to *under*estimate it to save residents money; for example, they did not include balconies or *gầm* in their measurements. The secretary of ward 9 explained this practice as the outcome of benevolent care: "The state is not insensitive to the people! Residents complained about the high costs per square meter, so the state decided to exclude those [exterior] areas. That saved people a lot of money!"[5] This proved beneficial for the poorest residents—retired female workers—because it lowered the purchase price for their units. Perhaps the state was indeed looking out for its most vulnerable citizens. But later, during compensation negotiations with developers, a lower diện tích proved disadvantageous, especially for cultural elites who had expanded their living space through balcony renovations (chapter 9).

Residents spent months contesting the appraisals. I viewed their insistence on precision as a tactic to assert control over a process they considered unjust and demoralizing. One frustrated warden, however, saw it differently: as stemming from the low education (*trình độ văn hóa thấp*) and lack of economic rationality that he attributed to the poorest residents, the migrant women. "They don't understand and argue over a few square meters!" he told me. "They only think about the amount paid now and not future returns."[6] Later I would encounter, in another circumstance, the opposite complaint that was equally disparaging: that these women were actually too calculating and possessed too much market logic for their own good and that of Vinh's development (see under "The Offer" below).

Privatization was fast-tracked, reflecting the attempt to shift to an "acceleration society" under capitalism (Wajcman 2014, 17), contrary to the deceleration of socialist time experienced by Quang Trung residents after Vinh's fast rebuilding. By December 30, 2010, a reported 99.84 percent of Quang Trung households had settled on the calculated living space and "voluntarily" (*tự nguyện*) registered to purchase their apartments. A government memo taped to blackboards announced that only two households had failed to register. Many of those who did register felt coerced (*bị bắt buộc*) and without options. They anxiously awaited the next step: the posting of final amounts to be paid in March 2011. After wardens released those numbers, residents approached the boards with trepidation, paper and pencil in hand to record the figures. Many walked away in silence; others grumbled about errors. To get the pulse on my neighbors' thoughts, I went to my favorite early-morning haunt: Ms. Xuân's popular tea stall in B5.[7]

Long, heated conversations were common at Xuân's gầm-kiosk. I spent many mornings there talking with residents and listening to their concerns about 61/CP over cups of hot green tea. One spring morning, as Xuân lit the charcoal stove, I visited with Ms. Mai, head of the local Women's Union, and Ms. Mỹ, who was known to complain about government corruption. The women were comparing how much they owed the state to transfer ownership and concluded that their apartments were appraised at too high a value: Xuân, who lived on the fourth floor, owed 30 million VND (U.S. $1,500); Mai, who lived on the fifth floor, owed 29 million VND (U.S. $1,450); and Mỹ, whose apartment on the first floor was the most expensive among the three, owed 61 million VND (U.S. $3,050).[8] Xuân and Mai were extremely distressed: "Bị bức xúc nhiều!"[9] Both lived on retirement salaries of less than U.S. $100 per month and had no way to pay what was, for them, an exorbitant amount. Mỹ announced that her son in Germany had promised to send her the money. Mr. Thành from the neighboring block stopped by and reported that his apartment would cost 58 million VND (U.S. $2,900). He was also unsure how he would obtain that kind of money and believed that his apartment, too, had been overvalued.

Having been persuaded that privatization was in their best interest, upon seeing the numbers my neighbors felt duped by the state's assessment of value. How could their run-down flats cost so much? And how could retirees be expected to pay for the space they had lived in for decades, especially when those apartments had been granted for their hard work to defend and rebuild the country? One warden had served in the army's special command forces for forty-five years. Xuân had spent twenty years varnishing furniture at a woodworking factory. Both suggested that the apartments should be gifted (*tặng*) in recognition of their allegiance to the party and for the losses their families had suffered in wartime. After all, Quang Trung had been a solidarity gift from East Germany, and the state had no right to profit from its sale as a commodity, they explained, insisting on a clear separation of gift and transactional market economies (Mauss 2000).

Residents spent the following months appealing to authorities. The circulation of bureaucratic artifacts—government decrees and the petitions that followed—facilitated a cycle of "affective interaction" between citizens and the state (Navaro-Yashin 2007). Collective forms of civic engagement generated new political subjectivities, especially among elderly male residents, who embraced every opportunity available as citizens to *phàn nàn* (complain) and *đóng góp ý kiến* (express their opinions) at town halls and other public forums. Their methods of claiming rights—negotiation rather than confrontation—did not challenge municipal authority so much as reaffirm its sovereign power and legitimacy, and that of the Communist Party. For these men, the state was not imagined as distant and indifferent (Gupta 2012). Rather, their tactics revealed both familiarity with centralized authority and belief in its commitment to social betterment as the basis of good governance, a perspective that was lacking in other, more cynical residents.

One morning in May 2011, discussion at Xuân's tea stall turned to *chế độ miễn giảm*, or state-mandated deductions to apartment prices. As per Decision 64 by the prime minister in 1998, these deductions were based on number of years of state employment and military service: 100,000 VND (U.S. $5) per year for the former and 180,000 VND (U.S. $9) per year for the latter.[10] Mai criticized these amounts as ridiculously low and out of sync with inflation over the past ten years. She said, "100,000 VND does not buy much these days. In 1998, you could buy several kilos of rice for that amount. Not today. The rate should be increased to 300,000 VND to reflect current prices." Her declaration echoed the demands in her ward's petition to the state that she and others had signed. Like Mai, women across Quang Trung tended to use the price of goods as their basis of comparison, while men used the value of gold (see Truitt 2013). But all came to a similar conclusion: if deductions and credits were adjusted for inflation, then ownership would not cost them a đồng.

Thành left our group suddenly, returning moments later with a set of documents that roused emotions among the group: two petitions, dated October 2010 and April 2011, that all nine wardens had jointly sent to the district, municipal, and provincial People's Committees. These petitions had appropriated state discourse to generate sympathy (Schwenkel 2015c) by reminding officials that the people most impacted by privatization were those who had helped to "liberate the country, build socialism, and defend the Party and democratic rule of law." The signatories pleaded with officials to reduce the hardships wrought by 61/CP (*giảm bớt khó khăn*). Authorities answered the second appeal, but only to inform residents that their demands would not be met. By claiming that "everything has been done in accordance with the law," the state revealed its less benevolent face to embittered Quang Trung tenants. "Lừa đảo! [such deception!]," Mỹ declared as the documents passed around the table. Although they did not achieve the desired results, the petitions were successful in organizing residents to demand more transparency and to make their voices heard in discussions of redevelopment.

After months of opposing the terms, tenants slowly began to pay for their apartments using pooled family resources. Some continued to hold out, citing inaccuracies (*sai*) and uncertainties (*chưa rõ*)—for example, a receipt that said "tax payment" (*nộp tiền thuế*) and not "home purchase" (*nộp tiền mua nhà*). "We will not pay until this error is corrected!" the daughter of cultural elites in C3 declared.[11] "This is not a tax; we are purchasing property." "Which should be free!" her father chimed in from the next room. Tenants' defiance revealed an underlying distrust of state power that conflicted with their deep sense of patriotism, even as they remained committed to nation building (MacLean 2013). In all, the state earned more than U.S. $2 million from the sale of the nineteen buildings that comprised Quang Trung, with each block selling for between U.S. $60,000 and $170,000, based on posted apartment figures.

Urban redevelopment catapulted people into a different temporality of compulsory waiting, Erik Harms (2013) observed of Ho Chi Minh City. Likewise, in Vinh, paying the fees (for both apartment ownership and land use) did not end residents' distress, but subjected them to another spell of stalled socialist time as they waited in legal limbo for property titles, or *bìa đỏ* (red certificates), to arrive. In blocks C8 and C9, tenants had been told that processing would take up to two weeks, but one month passed, and then another. Rumors began to circulate that provincial authorities had decided to withhold distribution of the bìa đỏ "in the interest of the people." My neighbor in C9, a war invalid, was outraged. One summer day I found him in the courtyard tending to his chickens. "They won't give us our bìa đỏ!" he told me angrily.

"They said I could have a photocopy, but I refused. We all refused. We paid our money, and those titles belong to us."[12] I went upstairs to visit a retired print operator and his wife, who sold rice cakes in the market. The husband had already filed a complaint with the Housing Agency. "They think we might lose the bìa đỏ, so they are holding on to them for safekeeping," he said, shaking his head. Controlling title distribution meant controlling the bundle of rights that titles conferred. "The state fears we will give the titles to the bank [as collateral] and they won't be able to proceed with land clearance. But this has nothing to do with the state anymore," the print operator exclaimed indignantly. "We paid for these apartments. It's now between us and the investors."[13] For tenants, payment and its bureaucratic artifact—the title—involved more than the legal transfer of property: it signified their definitive estrangement from the paternalist state.

RENOVATE OR REBUILD

Competing visions of urban futurity were most evident in the proposal to rebuild Quang Trung. Decision 553/QĐ-UBND of November 2010 was another highly contested urban matter that inscribed new forms of political agency: the ability of people, as sociopolitical actors, to "make choices that further their own goals" (Leheny 2018, 22). In the city's action plan for sustainable growth, Quang Trung's obsolescent blocks had been slated for demolition. Here was clear indication how decay had served state interests: Three joint stock corporations, in which the government held controlling stakes, proposed razing areas A, B, and C. In their stead would be spacious condominiums, sold as a modern paradise. But few original Quang Trung residents were convinced by the glossy renderings of the New Modern posted around the complex (see plate 16). Nor did they agree to the proposed compensation laid out in Decision 553. Demolition meant that residents would have to pay for their housing *twice*—first in Quang Trung (privatization) and then in the rebuilt complex (redevelopment). This added insult to injury and took a toll on personal health. The doctor who had spent the air war struggling to save lives in evacuated zones (see chapter 2) explained the impact of 61/CP and Decision 553: "I am so exhausted from the stress of the situation that it has made me ill. I can barely talk about it anymore. It has given me high blood pressure. After all I have done for the state. *Mệt thôi* [I am so tired]."[14]

Others were skeptical that reconstruction would ever take place—especially women, whose experience with socialist time was punctuated by delays and anticipation. When I asked Ms. Hương, a neighbor in C9, if she was worried about relocation, she waved her hand dismissively: "They have been talking about this for five years now. That's Vietnam. All talk and no action. I'll worry when it happens."[15] This timescale was different from compulsory waiting in the case of bìa đỏ. Hương was not suspended in urban developmental time; rather, she practiced a politics of refusal to even subject herself to the temporal regime of endless waiting and to suffer its emotional toll. Her husband, Minh, however, *was* distraught—not with time, but with the devaluation of his service to the military. Pulling a gently folded copy of the decree from the plastic bag where he kept important government documents, including his disabled-veteran certificate, Minh explained that Decision 553 was an affront to his time on the battlefield. It proposed an in-kind compensation rate of 1.3 square meters in a new apartment for every current square meter of living space. "That is not enough!" he declared. "We demand a rate of at least 1.5 square meters. What they are doing is illegal! They should deliberate with the people, and the people need to agree." To negotiate with investors, however, tenants needed to be the official apartment owners, and for that, they needed to possess a bìa đỏ.

Quang Trung's reconstruction (*xây dựng lại*) began in 2004 with land clearance of C1, which made way for Vinh's new modern face: the "luxurious" (*sang trọng*) twin TECCO towers.[16] These were Vinh's first skyscrapers, which reestablished Quang Trung as the most desirable location in the city.[17] Reconstruction propelled the government to push through 61/CP by the end of 2010. Authorities alleged that the transfer of apartment ownership would protect tenants from insecurity and increase their bargaining power with investors, but that power resided in the bìa đỏ. The coveted red certificate assumed a sacred, talismanic quality: tenants perceived bìa đỏ as powerful and empowering, as having agency to effect change, inspire hope, and control outcomes (Gell 1998). The veteran in C9 who waited months to receive his bìa đỏ placed it gently on the table when I visited him. Proudly he told me, "This certificate gives me certain rights, fundamental rights [*quyền cơ sở*] that I did not have before. They cannot deceive me anymore."[18] Like an amulet (see Tambiah 1984), bìa đỏ conferred protection from the malevolent forces of capitalist restructuring and helped to manage its uncertainty. As per Decision 553, demolition could only begin with a two-thirds vote of approval among new apartment owners. The efficacy of the bìa đỏ helped tenants reach a consensus: they would not agree to the terms of compensation and resettlement. There was less agreement, however, on the future of Quang Trung, whether it should be renovated or rebuilt.

Liberalization of housing policy in 1991 had brought major demographic changes to the complex as more "outside" people purchased flats. The shift had begun in the late 1980s, when a few tenants swapped (*đổi*) or passed on (*để lại*) their units or illicitly sold their user rights (*mua lại*), mostly to other workers and civil servants. By the mid-1990s, 15 percent of tenants were *người mua lại*, or people who had purchased user rights. This increased to 20 percent after the economic growth of the early 2000s. Ten years later, when I started fieldwork, 30 percent of surveyed households had purchased user rights to their flats from other tenants. Original tenants still comprised 60 percent of Quang Trung's population, mostly in the worker blocks (cultural elites tended to have better relocation opportunities).[19] Two important distinctions shaped residents' attachments to and revaluation of Quang Trung: length of residency and mode of unit acquisition. Unlike the original "ưu tiên" (preferential) tenants who had been allocated Quang Trung housing, most mua lại tenants did not qualify for housing price deductions; they had no recognized service to the state. These distinctions also shaped opinions about what to do with the deteriorating buildings.

Residents had conflicting ideas about the urban future. In surveys and interviews, newcomers were more likely to support demolition and reconstruction than original residents, who preferred renovation. This is in contrast to the revaluation of GDR architecture in Germany, where newcomers have been *less* likely to reject prefab panel housing and consider "Platte" desirable and trendy (van der Hoorn 2009, 101). In Vinh, a surprising two-thirds of respondents overall wanted Quang Trung to be refurbished, not razed, almost all of whom were original tenants. Some even advocated valuation of the blocks as a heritage site, similar to Hanoi's Old Quarter, to commemorate East German solidarity and the built environment that emerged from that period. "The issue is not use value [*giá trị sử dụng*], but its value to humanity [*giá trị nhân văn*]," one man wrote in an emotional plea for preservation of Quang Trung despite its loss of habitability (Ngô 2016, 11).

There was also a generational divide. Many newcomers were younger—single mothers or new families for whom a crumbling apartment was the only affordable housing option in the city. With no attachments to the place or its community, they saw the buildings as old (*cũ*), degraded (*xuống cấp*), dangerous (*nguy hiểm*), and low quality (*chất lượng kém*), and thus proved more likely to favor reconstruction. New apartments in high-rise developments were more modern (*hiện đại hơn*), spacious (*rộng rãi hơn*), convenient (*tiện hơn*), and beautiful (*đẹp hơn*)—all the qualities that Quang Trung's obsolescence lacked for them. The vision of urban modernity among young mua lại tenants fit with ideologies of free-market capitalism and upward mobility in line with national development policy. Like low-income urban residents elsewhere

↑ Figure 10.2 Nghệ An PetroVietnam towers looming over block A5, 2011. Photo by the author.

in the global South (see Ghertner 2015), they championed the built forms of redevelopment, even when it undermined their interests or fostered their exclusion. Many praised, for example, the spectacular twin towers across from Quang Trung, though none could purchase a unit in them (see figure 10.2). This gleaming vertical modernity was not a viable way out of Quang Trung; rather, praise for the New Modern towers embodied the yearning for escape from the social immobility of life seemingly caught in an endless meantime (Jansen 2015).

While original tenants also dreamt of urban betterment, they had a different vision of the future. What younger generations found alluring—commanding, vertical steel structures—was disenchanting to the elderly. Despite its decay, older tenants expressed a deep attachment to Quang Trung, ascribing social, historical, and affective value to the aging buildings. Its demolition would mean a loss of home, identity, and sociability, as well as abandonment by government authorities. In the words of a retired female accountant from the Design Institute, "I've lived here for most of my life by now and am fond of the neighborhood. This is all I know. There is a strong sense of village community [*tình làng nghĩa xóm*], and the blocks hold many memories [*kỷ niệm*] for me."[20] For these tenants, demolition threatened the city's unique social and material history, which was closely tied to its status as "German-made." A retired journalist attempted to halt redevelopment by sending his own protest letters to local government, demanding recognition of the value of the collectively built forms, which were still adorned with the symbol "VĐ" (for Việt Đức, or Vietnam-Germany), showing that Vinh had once been modern—and international, too. "Quang Trung needs to be preserved [*bảo tồn*], not rebuilt!" he insisted, while reflecting nostalgically on a time he considered more cosmopolitan than the present. "Reconstruction will destroy the character [*bản sắc*] of our city!" he warned, and by that he meant its *global* identity.[21] As the city struggled to attract foreign investment, removal of the most visible signs of its transnational connectivities could potentially downgrade Vinh to a mere *local* metropolis.[22]

From the perspective of older residents, spectacular new constructions were culturally and environmentally incompatible with their ideas of Vietnamese modernity. They were also potentially unsafe, as the earthquake revealed. These residents saw the Vietnamese-designed private condominiums as inferior built forms. Because local government had political and financial stakes in these ventures, residents' idealization of East German architecture can be understood as a veiled reproach of redevelopment and its new path to progress. Local authorities made concerted efforts to persuade people otherwise.

THE TOUR

The Nghệ An PetroVietnam buildings towered over the city during my fieldwork (see figure 10.2). Standing eighty-five meters tall, the twenty-five-story twin towers surpassed the celebrated eighteen-story TECCO condominiums, just down the road, as the tallest structures in Vinh. Soon, they too were surpassed by even taller structures in the competitive rush toward a vertical city.[23] At the time, the towers' foreboding presence owed as much to their clean, modernist, steel-and-glass façades as to their uncanny emptiness—an ominous sign in Vietnam, as vacant lots can invite wandering spirits. One January morning in 2011, officials cut the red ribbon on this newest iteration of urban modernity. Months later, as summer approached, the still-empty towers remained dark against the night sky, though real estate agents claimed that the majority of the units had already been sold. They were quick to drop their price, however, when attempting to convince me to buy into the new Vinh.

The towers had a ghostly aura. That they remained devoid of the vibrant activities that unfolded every day in the courtyards and hallways of Quang Trung was one reason that residents rejected their design and the lifestyle they promoted. Another was the terms of compensation offered by PetroVietnam, whose next project was to redevelop area A of Quang Trung. Residents were haunted by the specter of C1 tenants, who had been relocated to the margins of Vinh after demolition of their block, as has also happened with the dispossessed in other global cities. In-kind compensation of apartment space in rebuilt area A, however, would avoid a similar disintegration of community through "on-site resettlement" (*tái định cư tại chỗ*), which meant that these "urban poor" would remain in the city center—if they could afford to do so. The rate of resettlement—1:1.3 square meters—meant that residents would receive only a share of a new unit and would need to pay for additional space. As argued above, the state had underestimated gross living area in Quang Trung, purportedly as a protective measure. But to maximize their share in the new development, residents would need to take on even more debt to pay up to twenty times the price per square meter they had paid to the state for their apartments in Quang Trung. For example, residents in an average forty-square-meter apartment would receive fifty-two square meters in a new unit. Additional space would come at a reduced market rate of 13.5 million VND (U.S. $675) per square meter (down from 18 million). Given that the smallest units started at sixty square meters, residents would still need to pay for at least eight square meters, at a cost of about $5,400. Those living in studios and shared apartments with less space fared even worse. "They should have included my renovated gầm!" one man exclaimed. "That would have been an extra ten square meters in a new apartment!"[24] Original tenants—low-income pensioners who opposed paying for the right to state-guaranteed housing—considered such resettlement terms absurd.

To allay anxieties about the New Modern, municipal authorities and PetroVietnam organized tours of the towers for residents of ward 2. A typical tour moved from offices and shopping areas on the lower levels through the higher stories with their upscale (*cao cấp*) apartments and ended in a penthouse with a panoramic view of the city. Participants were unconvinced by this splashy show, commenting that there were a lot of stairs to climb if the electricity went out. While intrigued by the spacious layouts and modern facilities, they remained skeptical of the culturally alienating buildings and the lifestyle offered (not unlike rural migrants' suspicion of socialist housing, as argued in chapter 6). The warden, a former colonel who had fought at Điện Biên Phủ and in Saigon, was unimpressed with this new dreamworld that transcended existing built forms that were more familiar to him. "Không phù hợp [not suitable]!" he declared along with many others, reminding me of early critiques of Quang Trung.[25]

Residents did not reject redevelopment; rather, they had their own ideas about Vinh's future that differed from the vision promoted by the state. Contrasting the crumbling façade of his building against the sleek towers in the background, the colonel said, "Most of us want better housing and a more beautiful city, but we do not want to live in a high-rise [*cao tầng*]. It's just not harmonious with its surroundings." Five stories—the old iteration of cao tầng—were more aesthetically pleasing and practical in his view, especially given random power outages. Others maintained that the quality of all new high-rises was poor, in contrast to the old. This was because "the old" (Quang Trung) functioned like a branded object of value creation (Foster 2008). A retired planner who projected a short life span for the New Modern buildings demonstrated this branding when she ascribed more value to the crumbling blocks because of their association with *German* engineering: "Germans built Quang Trung with German equipment and German technology. After thirty years our homes are still structurally sound [*kết cấu vẫn chắc*]. Vietnamese companies are building these new high-rises. In a few years, they will be in worse condition than Quang Trung."[26] By refusing to see size, newness, and speed as a desirable modernity (Osborne 2011), the residents recast market development as inferior in quality (*chất lượng thấp hơn*) to the familiar scale of socialist reconstruction that was cracked but resilient and still standing solidly (*vẫn chắc*). In so doing, they resisted rupture with their socialist past, which has defined the social and material conditions of global capitalism in other late- and postsocialist cities.[27] At the same time, their claims about socialist quality drew on longstanding cultural perceptions about the superiority of German craftsmanship, which elicited a strong "brand" trust and conferred symbolic status and meaning on the city.

The lack of quality and workmanship in the tower design was of particular concern. Residents contrasted its hostile architecture with the people-friendly approach in Quang Trung. While Quang Trung's horizontal rows and *external* corridors enabled air and light to flow through adjoining units (see chapter 6), the towers had a vertical layout with *interior* hallways and doorways that faced one another around a central elevator. Consequently, the tower apartments seemed dark and stuffy to the visitors, who considered them unhealthful. To maintain comfort, summers would require air-conditioning that no one could afford. There were no balconies on which to dry clothes or conduct morning exercises. Spatially, the New Modern encouraged an internalization of social relations (Harms 2009; Yan 2003), not unlike the intention behind East Germany's design that residents subverted. The visiting warden surmised that to have privacy, the door would need to stay closed—an uncommon and unnecessary practice in Quang Trung owing to its design.

Residents were also concerned about the lack of commons. Generous open spaces have been an emblem of socialist cities (Hirt 2013). Likewise, Quang Trung's abundant parks, courtyards, and walkways were essential to quality of life and social well-being. This was especially the case for retirees. Seniors spent much of their time outdoors, gossiping and drinking tea, playing board games, tending gardens, visiting markets, or playing badminton. For many, Quang Trung comprised their entire social world, and they seldom left the complex. "I love meeting people on the stairways," effused one elderly man, who exercised every morning with a group of neighbors he signaled at six a.m. sharp by clapping his hands.[28] This thriving sociality meant there were always "eyes on the streets," which helped maintain a sense of security through informal surveillance (Jacobs 1961). "People are always watching," the elderly man said, aligning everyday, informal policing with urban safety. In contrast, the New Modern appeared socially and ecologically unsustainable. There were few places of assembly and no greenery of any kind, despite glossy ads that promised otherwise. Social infrastructure was also lacking. "I don't want to move there," a retired postal worker acknowledged. "There is no space, no air, no trees! Those new buildings are not like here."[29]

Redevelopment also threatened to eliminate green space, one of the most praised qualities of Quang Trung. Like elsewhere, urban renewal meant the death of urban nature in Vinh (Schwenkel 2017a). Investors viewed the GDR's open landscape design as unproductive, "wasted land" (*lãng phí đất*) that could be turned into lucrative developments. "Their goal is profit maximization, not space for people," a senior architect warned of conflicting forms of land valuation (Ngô 2016, 11). Where residents saw vital public parks, developers saw untapped commercial potential. As one designer explained, "Back then there were a lot of open spaces in Quang Trung. Through our eyes, we saw that as normal. Then came marketization, and people began to see the land differently; through their eyes it was a place of golden opportunity."[30] My neighbors had a reason to be leery. They watched as bulldozers demolished C1 and replaced it with twin condominiums and a concrete parking lot. The only landscaping comprised bonsai trees in cement pots. "This is what the future of development will look like," cautioned Mr. Văn, an avid gardener.[31] Construction of the Handico tower between C6 and C7 in 2011 affirmed that this vision would come to pass. Residents complained about loss of a sports field and obstructions that left their overshadowed blocks without air and sun. "It's just chaos [*lung tung*]," Văn complained, echoing socialist critiques of disorderly capitalist cities. For senior residents, capitalism—not socialism—produced a drab, inhospitable living environment. In the end, the condo tour failed to persuade residents of the merits of the New Modern, and instead heightened their angst about relocation and Quang Trung's impending demolition.

THE OFFER

While residents in area A expressed reservations about resettlement, those in area C, especially the retired female workers in block c8, disputed the terms of compensation. Their opposition also generated novel forms of agency and collective organizing that made me attentive to the possibilities for political life in the complex among women. But rather than assessing the ruined buildings of Quang Trung as high *design* quality, the women called attention to their high *market* value.

At the time of my research, 142 *khu tập thể* (collective living quarters) continued to house workers across Vinh, all of which were in serious disrepair.[32] While liberalization had led to innovative solutions, such as community planning at former workplace dormitories (Kaiser 2016), in most cases the problem of obsolescent housing was left to market forces to resolve. This reliance on the private sector deepened the social and gender hierarchies that socialism had failed to abolish. My findings among the women of block c8 confirmed what scholars of gender have long observed: that northern Vietnamese women have generally fared worse under market reforms, even losing some of the revolution's important gains in redistributing domestic responsibilities to the state, like daycare (Werner 2009).

The strategic essentialism that I detailed in chapter 8—retired workers calling attention to their hardship as poor rural women—elicited sympathy because of Quang Trung's dangerous state of decay. Empathy gave way to admonishment, however, in negotiations with developers. Like other Quang Trung residents, the women in c8 were anxious about the privatization of their units. They faced particular difficulties raising funds for the legal transfer of state property. "We paid rent for thirty years, and now we are forced to buy these crumbling apartments!" one woman in a shared unit complained.[33] Each household in her apartment had paid 15,000 VND (U.S. $.75) every month. Privatization would cost an additional 10 million VND (U.S. $500) per family—more than five times her average monthly pension.

Women like Ms. Hiền, who lived in a shared unit, weighed their financial options carefully. A widow, Hiền spent her days selling tea and cigarettes in front of C8. She had left the countryside at seventeen to take a job with the pharmaceutical company after her brothers had been sent to the front (both returned). In 1980, Hiền moved to Quang Trung with her husband, a veteran, who died soon after, leaving her with two small children to raise on an income of thirty VND per month. In 1990, Hiền took early retirement following Decision 176 (see chapter 9), and at the time of my research, she received a monthly pension of 1.6 million VND (U.S. $80). Because Hiền's family could not help her financially, she applied for a commercial bank loan to finance her apartment, with an interest rate of 13.3 percent.[34] She was one of a handful of people in Quang Trung to do so, and the only woman in C8, to my knowledge. Many elderly residents did not use banks—they collected their monthly pension from the District People's Committee—and were suspicious of new forms of finance emerging in Vinh at the time. These "under-banked poor" (Storm 2018, 303) preferred to remain debt free, but Hiền saw no alternative. Her share of the first-floor apartment cost 25 million VND (U.S. $1,250), and her deductions (including those of her husband) totaled 8 million VND (U.S. $400). Paying in a lump sum would save her an additional 10 percent—a benevolent "gift" from the province to show sympathy for residents' hardship. Hiền's loan of 15 million VND (U.S. $750) was approved shortly after we met. Her monthly mortgage of 800,000 VND (U.S. $40) over two years would cost her an extra 4 million VND (U.S. $200) in interest, for a total payment of 19 million VND (U.S. $950) for her half apartment. Like financial inclusion schemes elsewhere, Hiền's example is a reminder that economically vulnerable households disproportionately carry more debt relative to income than households that are less vulnerable. The same is true of households in the global South, which carry more proportional debt compared with those in the global North (Storm 2018, 309).

There was also palpable anxiety in C8 around redevelopment. The women were distressed by the news that the developer had proposed their temporary relocation to the adjacent Handico tower until a new condominium with low-income housing could be built—with *two* families per apartment. That the state allegedly agreed to this proposal without consulting with the residents further undermined its credibility as a benevolent actor serving their interests.

This rumor infuriated Hiền's neighbor Ngọc.[35] A Vinh native, Ngọc had received her degree from the Pharmaceutical University in Hanoi in 1974 and returned to work in management at Nghệ An Pharmaceuticals. Unlike the rest of the women in C8, she came from a prominent family—her father had been a high-ranking official at the Provincial People's Committee. Ngọc and her husband had subscribed enthusiastically to the ideals of socialist modernity and its notions of urban personhood. They had been eager to move out of collective workplace housing and into a modern family apartment in the city center. For Ngọc, Quang Trung promised inconceivable conveniences for the time, even though her building was crowded and afflicted with unstable infrastructure. When she moved in, eleven people shared the split unit: a mother (and wife of a martyr, or *vợ liệt sĩ*) and her five children, along with Ngọc, her husband, and their three children. In 1992, the other family moved out, and Ngọc's family, now extended to three generations, was permitted to keep the flat for themselves. Ngọc was unsure how they would come up with 17 million VND (U.S. $850) to assume legal ownership of the apartment. Like most tenants, she appealed to her kinship networks. Ngọc was more worried about relocation and its impact on their tight-knit community, which extended back to the war and evacuation: "It would be nice if we could stay together—that's how we have lived for much of our lives." To add insult to injury, it was rumored that C8 families would be relocated to the highest floors of the Handico tower, which had the lowest value. "Two families in one new apartment on the upper stories after thirty years of sharing? What deceit [*bị lừa*]!" a neighbor proclaimed angrily from the doorway. That a similar promise of "interim" sharing had been made in 1980 only magnified the women's distrust of the state.

This condition of uncertainty, risk, and precarity strengthened affinities across ward 9 and emboldened the women to contest the inequities of capitalist restructuring by giving new value and meaning to the crumbling ruins of C8. Whereas previously tenants had called attention to the threat of bodily harm from decaying buildings (see chapter 8), now they emphasized dispossession as a threat of social alienation and community disintegration, appropriating market logics to secure what they felt was a just resettlement package. A housing activist—the son of a fellow coworker—supported the women, earning their trust with his "high education" (*trình độ văn hóa cao*) and experience with state bureaucracy, which most female migrants did not possess, I was told. An administrator and resident of C8, the activist became the women's representative in spaces of government they felt to be inaccessible. At a town hall meeting with the People's Committee at the start of 2011, for example, he spoke to provincial authorities on behalf of the women. Appealing to their sentiment (*tình cảm*), the activist highlighted the affective dimensions of the social contract as mutual protection (Shanks 2015). He described the bare living conditions the women endured as labor heroes and as citizens who had suffered war casualties and yet dedicated their lives to socialist nation building. Who was protecting their rights and interests, he asked insistently.[36]

The activist's advocacy and the women's own participation in negotiations with developers showed the public that they were not vulnerable victims but people with intention and agency—and a tinge of market rationality. Herein lay a quandary for those public observers and for the other residents of Quang Trung. One month after the town hall, C8 tenants negotiated a higher rate of compensation. A new decree ratified an in-kind exchange of 1:1.5 square meters, while the original 1:1.3 rate remained for the other blocks. This seemed to be a victory. However, after rumors circulated that resettlement would entail *co*habitation, the women retaliated by voting unanimously to reject the new offer. The retirees recognized the commercial value of their building, marking a critical moment in their "reckoning with ruins" (DeSilvey and Edensor 2012) as owners of now private property. The crumbling blocks were no longer abject architecture in need of clearance; instead, the women recast C8 as desirable and profitable real estate. In a petition filed with provincial authorities in August 2011, *after* they had received their bìa đỏ, residents called attention to the auspicious location (*vị trí đắc địa*) of their building. Block C8 faced a major intersection on *đất vàng*—golden land for speculative investment that promised a high return. The view of the park with fountain—the GDR's departure gift—added further to its worth. As legal owners and rational economic actors, they demanded a share of future profits through a reciprocal swap—one property for another (*đổi nhà*)—that would ensure their inclusion in the New Modern with no additional payment for a modest, individual apartment.

The press followed these developments carefully. Its coverage essentialized the women as the heroic female face of the urban poor and the future dispossessed. In response, developers crafted a counterdiscourse of working "collectively and humanely" with distraught pensioners. In pledging to resolve the situation in the "best interests" of tenants, they presented Quang Trung's redevelopment as benevolent and embedded in moral practices of compassionate capitalism. At the same time, they fretted about the women as obstacles to wealth and value creation. Public opinion moved between pity for the elderly women and derision. Some of the people I spoke with saw their actions as irrational, calculating, greedy, and naïve. "They are asking for too much," reasoned one man. "This is not Ho Chi Minh City!" said another, as if rural female workers deserved less than their cosmopolitan contemporaries. Others framed their recalcitrance in temporal and aesthetic terms by accusing the women of holding up Vinh's beautification and standing in the way of its progress. Like the gendered and classed discourses about indiscipline and the causes of decay (chapters 7 and 8), these sentiments shifted accountability for

Vinh's stagnation from the state to migrant women who continued to be held morally responsible for obstructing the path to modernity.

At the time of my last visit, in early 2019, the apartment owners were still living in C8 and in the rest of Quang Trung, except for A1 and A6. The toad market (see chapter 9) bustled as usual in the courtyard. The renewal of area C had stalled due to the rippling effects of the global financial crisis, though Vietnam had fared better than other countries in the region. Still, many blamed the deceleration of capitalism on the elderly women. New investors remained leery of their refusal to adjust their demands for redistribution of speculative wealth. Emboldened, the women and their allies continued to hold a two-thirds voting majority against redevelopment, even as other, especially younger, residents grew impatient. For these retirees—the builders of socialism—the constitutional right to housing in return for their *công* (meritorious work) was non-negotiable. With their bìa đỏ secure, the fate of the housing block lay largely in their hands.

The aspirational politics on the other side of the complex had a different outcome. After a three-year delay, developers proceeded with *cải tạo*, or "renovation," of area A. The use of "renovation" rather than "reconstruction" (*xây dựng lại*) marked a small victory for residents; recall that in surveys, two-thirds had advocated for the former. Cải tạo offered an alternative model of urban renewal that did not displace poor households to urban peripheries. Rather, a distinct project temporality—build, resettle, and then demolish—meant residents remained in the city center, transferring to adjacent, low-income housing only *after* its construction was complete. In 2015, the sports field between blocks was transformed into a construction site. Developers then erected two modest towers alongside A5, so close that some walls nearly touched the *cơi nới* (see plate 17). To all appearances, developers had incorporated residents' ecological ideas of "good design" influenced by the GDR: the condominiums were simple, bright, and airy, with balconies and windows for light and ventilation. At fifteen stories, they were not excessively high, nor were they intended to rival the spectacular New Modern structures elsewhere in Vinh. Apartments were spacious at sixty square meters, with two bedrooms and two small bathrooms, but not ostentatious. In fall 2017, residents in block A6—the tour participants—resettled in the buildings, just a few meters away. The sight of the eerie, lifeless shell of A6 rekindled calls to establish Quang Trung—or at least one block—as a heritage site, a kind of melancholic monument to urban futures past (Bunnell and Goh 2018).

When I saw the new towers inhabited later that year, I was hopeful that authorities had listened to the angry, desperate voices and would treat the residents of areas B and C, who continued to linger in a long drawn-out meantime (Jansen 2015), with similar compassion. At the time of writing, the new Quang Trung seemed to be something more than another story of gentrification, wealth concentration, and accumulation by dispossession. Instead, it seemed to offer a more humane and inclusive model of redevelopment that put people back at the center of design and kept them in the center of the city.

CONCLUSION

ON THE FUTURE OF UTOPIAS PAST

How are we to make sense of the passing of utopian dreamworlds while aspirations to realize those dreamworlds persist and continue to inform a sense of place, self, history, and social imagination of the future? I asked myself this question as I watched the people at the heart of this book—the German and Vietnamese designers, builders, and residents of Quang Trung—grapple with the dissipation of their modernist fantasies while fragments of their dreams retained an affective charge and inspired imagined possibilities anew. The unmooring of utopian fantasies from grand narratives of historical development, Susan Buck-Morss reminds us, has enabled these spirited fragments to travel and enter new constellations of meaning (2000, 68).[1] I was reminded of this during a dinner in 2012 with two younger friends in Hanoi, Lan and Hàng. Intrigued by my research, Hàng, who was from Vinh, asked about my experience living in Quang Trung. "What's Quang Trung?" Lan interjected. Hàng vividly recounted how Germany had built a modern-day paradise with bright, spacious apartments surrounded by lush trees and vegetation in the city center. She described Quang Trung's vibrant sociality and the moral codes that structured interactions within the complex: "People look out for one another. There are parks, markets, daycares, and schools *on-site*—you don't even have to drive anywhere!" "I would love to live in a place like that!" Lan exclaimed, moved by the picture of an ideal living environment that was free of the problems that accelerated growth had brought to Hanoi. But the utopian imagery was of Quang Trung when it had been hailed as the cutting edge of modernity, unveiled to awestruck crowds in the 1970s. Today, Quang Trung signifies the very urban crisis from which Lan longed to escape. One person's lived dystopia was another person's fantasy of urban possibility.

Hàng's yearning for utopia revealed the gap between image and reality and called to mind Baudrillard's simulacrum. As I have shown throughout these pages, life in Quang Trung bore little resemblance to its plan. The affective atmosphere turned quickly from one of hope in a grand rebound to despair and disappointment: infrastructure intended to liberate women workers from domestic labor failed or broke down, prompting residents to appropriate public goods to meet their basic needs. For example, both German experts and Quang Trung residents recalled the park fountain—a simulated spectacle of socialism's bounties (see figure 8.6)—as a place to wash clothes and bathe children, until shortages forced the state to turn off the water. Hàng's description was not a false representation, Baudrillard would argue, but it did "rejuvenate the fiction of the real" by substituting signs of the real for reality itself (Baudrillard 1994, 12–13). In many ways, this book is about the seduction of East German fantasies of progress and its marvel of engineering—Quang Trung—as appearance, aspiration, and ambiguous modernity.[2] Like in colonial settings, socialist subjects consumed seductive images and information about modernity in fragments with delay and uncertainty, and thus could not escape feelings of inadequacy since "what they had access to was not the sound whole" (Yoo 2001, 435). Even so, my ethnography shows that the dream of good design was neither distorted illusion nor delusion, as critics might claim, but was productive of lived social and material experiences of the city. Quang Trung *was* built through a tremendous amount of coordinated labor—physical, logistical, and affective—that hierarchized the socialist world as much as it opened spaces for solidarities to form across cultural divides. Despite its insufficiencies, the housing stabilized people's lives and provided a material basis for their social and spatial sensibilities for decades after the war. Indeed, the complex continues to be an important repository of affect, memory, and identity, even as it falls further into disrepair and disassembly.

Hàng's favorable portrayal of Quang Trung was not entirely inaccurate. Like many of my interlocutors, she had good reason for refusing to dismiss it as a "failure," a common trope for the unrealized visions of socialist construction (Alexander 2007a, 86). As I have argued, Quang Trung represented an experimental rush to the future to help Vietnam modernize on par with the socialist North. Its architecture would facilitate urban governance and the management of everyday life through modern "things" like infrastructure (Foucault 2007, 96–98). While some residents contested their subjectivation, others took pride in the new world they had helped to build. Hàng was right to point out that Quang Trung was an intensely social environment in which historical affinities created a moral imperative of mutual support. It was also surprisingly green: Quang Trung had more urban nature and open spaces than collective housing in Hanoi, and the apartments *were* larger. By chance, we were eating at a soup stall attached to one of Hanoi's largest and most dilapidated housing estates, which I had recently visited. Spatially, its units were considerably smaller, with no room divisions and lower ceilings than those in Quang Trung; moreover, the facilities were shared. The sensory experience also differed: there was no breeze or sunlight, few windows, and no *gầm* (walk-out basements). Without open corridors, the interior halls and stairways were dank and dark. There were fewer public spaces to gather and fewer trees. Like many of my colleagues in Hanoi, my dinner companions lived in such flats and had only a few square meters of space. By comparison, Quang Trung seemed to offer better material and spatial conditions, even though its residents also had to deal with the "attritional violence" of accumulative decay (Nixon 2011). At one time, such differences had allowed Vinh to claim that it was "more progressive than Hanoi" and, indeed, the rest of war-torn Vietnam (Ngô 2016, 9).

Hàng's description also revealed her enchantment with German technology, which for both women signified a superior global brand and commodity. Pictorial and textual narratives of Quang Trung had once showcased East German rational planning and methods of standardized construction (*xây dựng đồng bộ*) as liberation from the cycles of imperial violence that had prevented Vinh from modernizing previously. Party discourse deployed spatial and temporal metaphors such as "catching up" and "rising from the ashes" to frame this narrative of rescue through architecture as conversion from imperialist wasteland (*đất hoang*) to the fantastical and unimaginable—*không tưởng*, or the utopian. The ambition of GDR and Vietnamese planners was such that modernist mass housing and its infrastructure would bring Vinh out of the darkness of "prehistory"—what U.S. military technocrats called the Stone Age, the temporal object of their obsessive bombing—and into the contemporary socialist world, propelling the rebuilt city and its enlightened population into a brighter future of progress and prosperity.

That anticipated future was tenuous and ephemeral. The Marxist narrative of linear historical development, from decolonization to socialist transformation, proved less plausible in material practice. The rapid industrialization and urbanization that followed aerial warfare came to an abrupt halt after foreign advisers and experts returned home. The socialist city had indeed been built, but low production capacities combined with inefficiencies in urban governance amounted to an absence of the material conditions necessary to sustain the pace of change. These challenges registered quickly and materially through the buildings' decay, which became a pretense for their removal but also for residents' spatial and architectural interventions as risk mitigation and livelihood creation. Vinh's postwar ascendance and precipitous decline demonstrates what James Ferguson has called the "mythology of modernization," where "optimistic teleologies" are replaced by fears of "slipping backward" to a less civilized time (1999, 13). Dread of backwardness shaped residents' attempts to understand—and cast off—unplanned obsolescence. A Vietnamese architect and former Quang Trung resident captured this anxiety when he led a tour of the complex for my research assistants. "You might not know this, young people," he began, "but in the past, Germany brought the first tower cranes to Vinh." Turning to me, he explained, "When the Phương Đông Hotel was built in 2000"—it was the tallest building in Vinh at the time, constructed on the site of the proposed Victory Monument—"a young journalist claimed they had used the first ever tower crane in Vinh. I called to set him straight! I told him, 'You were born after reconstruction and have no idea.'" A student giggled. Looking at her, he said with melancholy in his voice, "We were modern before."[3] In this man's view, Vinh was no "city yet to come," as AbdouMaliq Simone (2004) has described the misunderstood metropolises of Africa, but a city that had come and gone all too quickly, not unlike other planned socialist cities (Ringel 2018).

The oft-heard refrain "không hiện đại nữa"—not modern *anymore*—signaled that residents were recalibrating their temporal relationships to past and future modernities. Apartments that had once been spacious were now cramped with too many people. "They served their purpose at the time," the Vietnamese engineer in block C6 suggested, "but they no longer fit with modern life today."[4] Residents had also undergone a status reversal: those who had once been considered privileged socialist workers were now seen as old-fashioned, poor, and vulnerable. The scales of urbanization, too, had drastically changed. From the viewpoint of capitalist redevelopment, Quang Trung's abject materiality, its decay and obsolescence, suggested that socialist modernization was *not yet* modern. East German experts had once used the "massive" (*đồ sộ*) tower crane—the largest machine shipped from East Germany to Vinh—as a powerful symbol to show that Vinh was indeed advancing toward modernity (see figure 6.6). The architect's cries—"We had cranes! We were modern!"—evoked the emotions that had coalesced around iconic construction technologies. But the now pitifully small crane had devolved into an emblem of Quang Trung's decline. Our guide narrated this downfall by describing how it stood neglected and unused for a decade after the experts left, during the state subsidy period, or "time of hunger and crisis," until it was dismantled by recyclers for scrap metal. Both the crane and its product—Quang

Trung—symbolized future aspirations that, like other socialist utopias, ended in detritus and ruin.

Vinh's annihilation, reconstruction, and obsolescence is a tale of an aspirational city, always on the brink of modernity, always trying to catch up, but somehow lagging behind—a city of simultaneous forward, sideways, and backward movement. Women who had built and defended socialism were often held responsible for this undoing, I have argued. Decline and backwardness were attached to unruly female migrant bodies and their conduct (Leshkowich 2014, 182), which hastened the demise of the model city and threatened to turn it into yet another "modernist wasteland" (Brown 2015). Gendered anxieties about the ruralization of the city deflected attention from state neglect that contributed to urban decay and underdevelopment. It also obscured the "secondhand modernity" that East Germany had gifted Vinh through its politically expedient export of used machinery and aging technology to aid reconstruction efforts. As a space for industrial throwaways, Vinh had been destined for obsolescence even before it was rebuilt.

In this book, I have shown the limits of visionary socialist planning and its elusive modernity that seemed, in the most optimistic moments, almost in reach. At the same time, I have documented the heterogeneous ways that people imagined to resourcefully build that better future and the enormous collective effort undertaken to achieve it. Imagination as collective fantasy manifested not as "opium for the masses" (Appadurai 1996, 31) but as action, agency, and affect that bound citizens to one another and to the state. For Vietnamese and East German visionaries alike, traumatic histories of war profoundly shaped their sense of collective mission and their hopeful imaginaries of an egalitarian futurity, even as those visions diverged. Imaginaries of past and future "feed off one another," Liisa Malkki (2001, 328) has argued, and may indeed be "different chapters of the same narrative story"—in this case, a shared national story of ruin, rebirth, and growth (see also Leheny 2018, 19).

Dominant discourse has typically associated socialism with a lack of imagination and limited sensations or dullness: people were considered plain (Berdahl 1999), their lives generic (Fehérváry 2012), and the housing unimaginative (Ghodsee 2005). When imagination was allowed to exist, the presumption was that cultural constructs of a desirable, more vibrant West had inspired it (Yurchak 2006). In contrast, my account provincializes the capitalist West and reveals imagination as central to the historical experience of socialist decolonization. Utopian traditions from the socialist North—Vietnam's "West"—traveled to Vietnam as world- and future-making strategies: the building of socialism. But people in Vietnam did not unconditionally accept modernist utopian design; they reworked and translated it, ideologically and architecturally (Akcan 2012). Competing spatial logics and ideas about how to organize and build a better society reflected different cultural practices and theories of socialism circulating in the world at the time, undermining claims to universality.

It is therefore impossible to speak of a uniform "socialist city," if such an urban construct even existed (Hirt 2013), or to see modernist forms as devoid of any cultural specificity. People did share ambitions and ideals of a more just future, free from the violent dislocations of imperialism, but the meanings attached to functional forms and spaces differed considerably. Vinh still bears the imprint of this global aspiration, which may soon disappear. In a time of capitalist restructuring, when international experts are training a new generation of Vietnamese architects to see public space as ripe opportunity for urban speculation, where land's value now comes before people's needs, it may be worth preserving the traces of this past dreamworld of future possibility.

NOTES

INTRODUCTION

1 The names of all research respondents in this book have been changed to maintain anonymity.
2 For recent compelling urban and village ethnographies, see especially Harms (2016) on Ho Chi Minh City and Meeker (2013) on *quan họ* folk singing in Bắc Ninh province.
3 David Lamb, "Country's Least Attractive City Trying to Put on a New Face," *Los Angeles Times*, July 9, 1999.
4 See, especially, contributors to the edited volume *Comrades of Color* (Slobodian 2015b), as well as book-length studies by Hosek (2011) and Hong (2015).
5 I recognize that this is changing among a new generation of scholars, for example, in research on the "Black East" (Schenck 2018).
6 Though the context differs, here I draw on Neil Smith's notion of the "urban frontier," where both environment and people, imagined at the intersection of wilderness and civilization, are progressively "tamed" (1996, xv).
7 Throughout history, Nghệ An and its southern neighbor, Hà Tĩnh, have been at times merged into the region of Nghệ Tĩnh, most recently between 1976 and 1991, the period between Vietnam's reunification and the Soviet Union's dissolution.
8 In October 2018, Vinh celebrated its 230th anniversary since the founding and its tenth anniversary as a "Grade 1" city.
9 A common observation about Nghệ An is that people *học giỏi vì nghèo*, or study hard to escape poverty. Because a number of preeminent national scholars come from the region, and its students place at top universities, Nghệ An is also referred to as *đất học*, or land of the studious (Chu 1998, 62).
10 A string of schoolgirl attacks and lynch mobs occurred during my fieldwork.
11 Gia Long later built citadels in Quảng Bình (1812), Nam Định (1814), and Quảng Trị (1824).
12 Even before France annexed Nghệ An in 1885, urban stratification "reflected the dominance of the alien [Chinese] merchant class" (Woodside 1971, 32), who lined Vinh's main street with their two-story brick-and-tile houses (Chu 1998, 40–41).
13 While there is no consensus on who exactly coined this term, historians generally agree that it came out of the "Soviet Nghệ-Tĩnh movement," as the uprisings were called.
14 Figures show that the anticolonial VIỆT MINH destroyed more than thirteen hundred structures (including bridges, buildings, and factories), dug up access roads and

turned them into trenches, and pushed more than three hundred railcars and locomotives into the river to thwart the advance of enemy warships (Phạm 2008, 111).

15 *Nghệ An News*, May 20, 1964.

16 The use of the term *Liên Xô* to identify foreigners was so common after the war that Swedes working on aid projects in the 1980s playfully wore T-shirts that read, "Không phải Liên Xô" (Not Soviet).

17 Because of the violence suffered, Vinh is known for "hating Americans," and this was most likely the case for many years after the war, but I found that this sentiment had decreased significantly since I first began visiting Vinh in 2000. Individual hostility toward the United States remains, understandably so, but people tended to direct their anger toward the U.S. government rather than its population (a common expression in Vietnam). Over the course of my research, three people declined to talk with me based on my nationality.

18 Such costly possessions were rare. Only three households in Quang Trung owned cars at the time of my research. As of publication (2020), cars are a common means of transportation.

19 For an overview of the material changes to the city at this time, including the demolition of Quang Trung building C1, see Schwenkel (2012).

20 I continued my research in Vinh, and in archives in Hanoi, through summer 2011 and have made annual visits since.

21 While framed as voluntary, all donations were recorded on the community boards to ensure compliance. Making these contributions raised a host of questions about my moral obligations in relation to war reparations for U.S. atrocities in Vietnam: What was an appropriate amount to give to the various causes posted on the blackboard—floods in central Vietnam, Agent Orange victims, earthquake in Japan—without calling attention to my economic status, which could be seen as pompous? Would I be considered stingy if I paid a similar amount as my neighbors? Would people think I was denying the violent history of U.S. empire that made funds for Agent Orange victims necessary? I decided in the end to make public donations equal to those of my neighbors, and to give extra money privately to the wardens. My neighbors laughed and thanked me when they saw my name on the board, but I felt ashamed that my contributions could never compensate for the tremendous damage and losses they had endured.

22 Respondents gave a number of reasons why they refused to participate, including concerns about time and reluctance to share information about private finances. One man—irate at the government—wanted to talk to me and not to a student, and one household refused because I was American. Not being chosen for the survey created tension as well. In one area, people that I did survey used my foreign status to make neighbors who had not been surveyed envious. In another area, false information circulated that I paid respondents for their participation.

23 The president of the Association of Agent Orange Victims of Quang Trung, whose daughter was born with severe disabilities due to his exposure to toxins in wartime, shared these numbers with me.

24 One of the last major ruins—the student dormitory—was demolished in fall 2010. On the ruins of war as haunted landscape, see Schwenkel (2017b).

25 Personal interview, Germany, August 21, 2012. Note that throughout this book, I do not specify location for interviews that took place in Germany. Many of my German respondents live in cities and towns small enough that naming those places would reveal the respondent's identity.

26 For example, in 2011, German television executives declined to support a film project on Vinh that I was involved with. Since 2015, however, there have been two programs on the afterlives of GDR projects in Vietnam: on coffee plantations in Đắk Lắk and Vietnamese students in the GDR.

CHAPTER 1. ANNIHILATION

1 Bernard Weinraub, "Leader of the First Raid on North Returning to U.S.," *New York Times*, January 20, 1968.

2 Though Urban claimed that indiscriminate bombing was not condoned, strong evidence exists that it nonetheless took place. See Schwenkel (2009a, 200) for an account of the dumping of excess bombs over a residential area of Hải Phòng by a young girl fleeing the city with her father.

3 For example, Thrift and Forbes (1986). For an exception, see Logan (2000) on Hanoi.

4 Huntington estimates that the RVN's rural population decreased by 20 to 25 percent during the 1960s, making it the most urban state in Southeast Asia after Singapore (1968, 648).

5 In addition to the bombing of Hanoi and Hải Phòng, 28 of 30 provincial capitals were bombed (twelve of which were demolished), and 96 of 116 district capitals were bombed. More than half of the DRV's four thousand villages were also targeted by air raids (Thrift and Forbes 1986, 96).

6 By contrast, maps produced in Hanoi at the time show the country as united. As political projects, maps were an especially important tool of socialist world making, used to prove that there was only one legitimate Vietnam under communist rule. Militarily, this meant there could be no North "invasion" of the South, which was the rationale for aerial bombing.

7 Officially, according to the U.S. military, this operation lasted from March 2, 1965, to November 1, 1968 (U.S. time; Vietnam was one day ahead). Bombs fell on Vinh, however, outside this time frame. According to the DRV, the War of Destruction started on August 5, 1964, and continued through the end of January 1973.

8 "171 U.S. Missions over North Vietnam Set Record for War," *New York Times*, September 13, 1966. At the time, it was U.S. military policy to reveal the number of attack missions carried out but not the number of jets involved.

9 Again, bombs fell on Vinh outside the official U.S. military time frame for this operation, which lasted from May 9 to October 23, 1972.

10 White House memorandum for Henry A. Kissinger, September 5, 1972, 1. National Archives and Records Administration (NARA), Nixon Presidential Library (NPL), Vietnam Subject File, Box 97, Folder 4.

11 For example, on April 21, 1966, the *New York Times* reported that, over the previous week, antiaircraft fire had brought down two planes in the vicinity of Vinh, with only one pilot rescued. "U.S. Planes Bomb outside Haiphong for a Third Day."

12 This phrase is from the Operation Priming Charge quoted in the epigraph, presented to Nixon by the Secretary of Defense on December 7, 1972. NARA, NPL, Vietnam Subject File, Box 97, Folder 4.

13 See, for example, Yoshikuni Igarashi's argument that "through the bomb, the United States, gendered as male, rescued and converted Japan, figured as a desperate woman" (2000, 20).

14 Department of the Army, *Aerial Observer Techniques and Procedures, Field Manual* FM 1–80, December 1968, 4.

15 On state infrastructural warfare as geopolitical strategy, see Graham (2005). In this historical examination of U.S. airpower, Graham does not reference Vietnam (or Laos and Cambodia), demonstrating how one of the largest bombing campaigns in U.S. history remains neglected in academic scholarship.

16 For example, attacks on LOC sites (targets associated with lines of communication) in the panhandle in the month leading up to Operation Linebacker averaged 34 per day, compared with none over Hanoi and Hải Phòng, in the northwest LOC area. During Operation Linebacker, attacks increased to an average of 233 per day in the panhandle LOC versus 29 per day in the northwest LOC. Assessment of the Air and Naval Campaign against North Vietnam, November 28, 1972. NARA, NPL, Vietnam Subject File, Box 97, Folder 5.

17 Rules that constituted "limited" warfare prohibited air assaults on water-management infrastructure, such as dams, dikes, and locks (thus preventing Commander Urban from striking the busy docks at Hải Phòng). Despite the November 1, 1968, bombing halt, the authority to fire at DRV targets was granted on November 27 under the pretense of self-defense. Originally, permission was given to attack below the nineteenth parallel only (which included Vinh); this was extended to the twentieth parallel in 1970 per a request to Nixon from the Secretary of Defense on March 2. NARA, NPL, Vietnam Subject File, Box 99, Folder 5. Note that the U.S. government claimed that reconnaissance air missions did not violate the November 1, 1968, agreement since such missions were not an "act of force."

18 For example, an intelligence memorandum on foreign shipping to North Vietnam during December 1968 reported that four "free world" ships transported cargoes from Hải Phòng to Vinh, including a delivery of rice from Cyprus. In March 1969, an East German freighter, *Naumberg*, the first GDR ship to arrive since 1964, docked in Hải Phòng. NARA, NPL, Vietnam Subject File, Box 69, Folder 3.

19 Historical accounts of the air war offer tallies of damaged material things, like transport vehicles, based on government data. For example, in *Vietnam in Military Statistics*, Micheal Clodfelter reports that, by the end of the first year of Operation Rolling Thunder, "about 1,500 waterborne logistic craft, 800 trucks, and 650 pieces of railroad rolling stock had been destroyed" (1995, 218). The year 1966 saw the destruction or damage of "4,084 vehicles, 2,314 railroad cars and locomotives, and 9,500 vessels" (1995, 219).

20 "U.S. Bombers Pound 50-Truck Convoy in North," *New York Times*, March 23, 1966.

21 The abstraction of Vietnamese deaths through linguistic subterfuge so deeply structured military thought that truck kills were converted into *saved* American lives. In the words of General Westmoreland, "For every bomb we drop on a truck, we destroy five hundred bombs and rockets that won't fire shrapnel and steel into the hips and bodies of American boys" (quoted in Van Dyke 1970, 209).

22 White House memorandum for Henry A. Kissinger, September 5, 1972, 14. NARA, NPL, Vietnam Subject File, Box 97, Folder 4.

23 "Bomb Damage Assessment of Bridges in North Vietnam through 1966," May 1, 1967. General CIA Records, Document number CIA-RDP78S02149R0001000 70004-9.

24 For example, a March 2, 1970, Memorandum to the President advocated a shift in command authority to Washington, given the "high" uncertainties and risks involved in air operations: "It is frequently not clear what base an aircraft is operating from, i.e., it may take off from one base and land, if only for refueling, at another. It is likewise not clear, at times, precisely which GCI [ground control interception] site is controlling." NARA, NPL, Vietnam Subject File, Box 99, Folder 5.

25 Due to, for example, unfavorable weather that hindered strikes and damage assessment.

26 The Joint Chiefs of Staff memorandum for the Secretary of Defense, November 3, 1969, 4. NARA, NPL, Vietnam Subject File, Box 99, Folder 7. Another unintended consequence of the air campaigns was, of course, that U.S. pilots were taken as prisoners of war.

27 As the author, Major Alexander P. de Seversky, wrote: "Total war from the air against an undeveloped country or region is well-nigh futile" (1942, 102).

28 CIA intelligence memorandum, August 22, 1972, 4–5. NARA, NPL, Vietnam Subject File, Box 97, Folder 4.

29 United States Senate, Committee on Foreign Relations, *Bombing as a Policy Tool in Vietnam: Effectiveness, A Staff Study Based on the Pentagon Papers*, 92nd Congress, 2nd Session, Study No. 5, October 12, 1972. U.S. Government Printing Office, 1972.

30 White House memorandum for Henry A. Kissinger, September 5, 1972, 10. NARA, NPL, Vietnam Subject File, Box 97, Folder 4.

31 Vietnamese figures report that the plant was subjected to three hundred air strikes that released an estimated 2,319 bombs and 149 missiles, and was repaired twenty-six times (Bùi 1984, 158).

32 According to Micheal Clodfelter, between 1965 and 1968 seven hundred sorties released more than 12,500 tons of explosives on the bridge. Twenty-nine American aircraft, or 4 percent of fighters, were lost in the effort (1995, 223).

33 CIA intelligence memorandum, August 22, 1972, 4. NARA, NPL, Vietnam Subject File, Box 97, Folder 4.

34 Moscow: Pravda Publishing House, 2320201003, Douglas Pike Collection: Unit 06—DRV, The Vietnam Center and Archive, Texas Tech University.

35 Personal interview, Vinh, May 25, 2011.

36 Personal interview, Vinh, November 2, 2010.

37 Records from CACTA files, compiled between October 1965 and December 1970, and the Records about Air Sorties Flown in Southeast Asia from SEADAB, amassed between January 1970 and June 1975, contain aggregated data on the sorties flown over the entire region of Southeast Asia. They are accessible through NARA. Thank you to Phan Văn Hùng at Project RENEW for sharing the extracted data on Nghệ An with me, which was used by the Technology Centre for Bomb and Mine Disposal to produce an extensive report on unexploded ordnance across Vietnam's most heavily bombed and mined provinces.

38 The Vietnamese government claims that 7.85 million tons of bombs and shells were released over the country, a number that is significantly higher than the 5 million tons typically reported in Western scholarship—1 million over the DRV and 4 million over the RVN (High, Curran, and Robinson 2014, 90).

39 As mentioned, CACTA records are incomplete: several months are excluded from the database (though other sources confirm that raids took place at this time, including the *New York Times* article and the attack map cited above), including December 1965, April 1966, June–July 1967, October–November 1967, and September 1968. I have taken the monthly average of sorties during Rolling Thunder and multiplied it by fourteen months (March 1–October 1, 1965, before CACTA records began, and including the omitted months) to get a more representative figure, though it does not account for air strikes before the start of the campaign (for example, on August 5, 1964). CACTA and SEADAB data also overlap one year (1970), though mission redundancy seems to have been corrected.

40 An estimated 6.7 million tons of ordnance were dropped over Laos, Cambodia, and Vietnam (McCoy 2012, xv), or more than double the tonnage released on Europe during World War II. Other scholars cite figures upward of 8 million tons (see Harrison 1993). This does not include the 400 million tons of napalm and 19 million gallons of herbicide, including Agent Orange, that were sprayed across the southern part of Vietnam, with devastating ecological consequences that continue to severely impact the population (Fox 2007).

URBAN FRAGMENTS 1

1 Trong trận oanh tạc ngày 5–8, địch bị bắn rơi 8 máy bay và bị thương 3 chiếc khác. (In the August 5 bombardment, eight enemy aircraft were shot down and three were damaged.)

2 Published in *Nghệ An News* on August 15, 1964, ten days after the first air strikes.

CHAPTER 2. EVACUATION

1 Some of this subterranean architecture remains and is now utilized for tourist and pedagogical purposes, including the Củ Chi tunnels (Schwenkel 2006) and the Metropole Hotel bomb shelter, where Jane Fonda and Joan Baez sat out strikes on Hanoi (Schwenkel 2017c).

2 Personal interview, Vinh, May 28, 2011.

3 Scholars rarely access provincial collections. The Director of the Nghệ An Provincial Archives, housed on the grounds of the Provincial People's Committee, told me in October 2010 that I was the second foreigner to work with the archival materials. (I could not find a record of who the previous person was or the purpose of their visit.) My access was first approved by the Chairman of the Provincial People's Committee. Because I had his signature in hand, the director generously allowed me to read and photograph all the files I requested.

4 The term "urbicide" is also used to describe the destructive capacities of capitalism and urban renewal and to bring attention to the variegated forms of racial violence done to landscapes and communities. One of the more famous examples is Benjamin's (1969a) critical account of Baron Haussmann's nineteenth-century reconstruction of Paris.

5 This was not entirely true. Only two *salvageable* buildings remained, one of which became a guesthouse for foreign experts. Other standing structures were mere skeletal frames and wreckage.

6 On the history of the prison, or *nhà lao* Vinh, see Phan (2005). On the rethinking of historiography of the Nghệ Tĩnh Soviets, see Del Testa (2011).

7 This is not to claim that the Vietnamese state has not exploited war photographs for propaganda purposes, but that this image collection serves a different documentary purpose in the contemporary era, by offering an alternative iconography to dominant historical memory in the United States. On "exhibitions houses" (*nhà trưng bày*) as sites of public documentation for the display of "war crimes" in Hanoi, Đà Nẵng, and Ho Chi Minh City, see Schwenkel (2009a, 163–64). In Vinh, city officials organized a photo exhibition on what came to be known as the "August 5 [1964] Victory" (Chiến thắng ngày 5 tháng 8); fifteen years later, in 1979, a photography exhibit titled *Victory over the Chinese Military Invasion* (Chiến thắng quân Trung Quốc xâm lược) opened on the occasion of Hồ Chí Minh's eighty-ninth birthday.

8 Such images draw on the cultural construction of Vietnamese women as inherently nonmodern and backward (Leshkowich 2005; see also chapter 7).

9 Schwartz goes as far as to argue that "the battle in the Tonkin Gulf was fabricated out of thick air, not thin, and was less the spawn of militarism or imperialism than, at first, of noise" (2011, 26). I would argue that these cannot be disentangled: militaristic and imperialist proclivities led, in the first place, to the fateful misinterpretation of radar "spooks."

10 Personal interview, Vinh, May 28, 2011.

11 Personal interview, Vinh, April 17, 2011.

12 Personal interview, Vinh, April 9, 2011.

13 Personal interview, Vinh, July 21, 2011.

14 Personal interview, Vinh, April 9, 2011.

15 For example, during the difficult subsidy years of the 1980s, noodle soup without meat, a basic fare, was called "soup without the pilot" (*phở không người lái*) in jesting reference to unmanned reconnaissance craft.

16 Bảo Ninh, "The First Time I Met Americans," *New York Times*, September 5, 2017, www.nytimes.com/2017/09/05/opinion/vietnam-war-writers.html?mcubz=1. Bảo Ninh's famous work, *The Sorrow of War* (1993, published in Vietnam ten years later as *Nỗi buồn chiến tranh*), was one of the first published accounts of the horrors, rather than the glories, of battle.

17 Personal interview, Vinh, May 24, 2011.

18 Personal interview, Vinh, May 31, 2011.

19 In German the term is *Blindgänger*, or "blind" devices, implying a loss of sight rather than the inability to make sound and be heard like *bom điếc*. Nonetheless, both terms, *Blindgänger* and *bom điếc*, suggest links between weaponization, errant technologies, corporeal debilitation, and imperialist desires to maim (Puar 2017).

20 Đồng Lộc junction, at the start of the Hồ Chí Minh Trail, was one of the hardest-hit areas in the region. The site is famous for the ten female youth volunteers killed there on July 24, 1968. A memorial marks the spot today.

21 Personal interview, Vinh, January 19, 2011.

22 Personal interview, Vinh, April 9, 2011.

23 Nghệ An Administrative Committee, Report on the request to expand Vinh City, October 13, 1966, Nghệ An Provincial Archives (NAPA), File 51.

24 This is in contrast to East German films, many of which were shot in Vinh and surrounding rural districts (see chapter 3).

25 Nghệ An Administrative Committee, Statistical reports on the living situation of civil servants and workers in Nghệ An province 1968–1970, NAPA, File 1056.

26 Nghệ An Administrative Committee, Statistical reports on the living situation of civil servants and workers in Nghệ An province 1968–1970, NAPA, File 1056.

27 Personal interview, Vinh, April 26, 2011.

28 Personal interview, Vinh, April 17, 2011.

29 Nghệ An Administrative Committee, Statistical reports on the living situation of civil servants and workers in Nghệ An Province 1968–1970, NAPA, File 1056.

30 Personal interview, Vinh, July 19, 2011.

31 Personal interview, Vinh, April 21, 2011.

32 Personal interview, Vinh, May 28, 2011.

33 This idiom is difficult to translate into English but conveys an affective commitment to the collective care of fellow compatriots. "Xã luận: Phòng không Sơ tán" (Editorial: Air Defense Evacuation), *Nghệ An News*, May 11, 1972.

34 Personal interview, Vinh, April 11, 2011.

35 Personal interview, Vinh, December 18, 2010.

36 According to CACTA and SEADAB data, between November 1, 1968, when a total halt was instituted, and the start of April 1972, when air attacks resumed, the city was hit by twenty-three sorties involving fifty-eight aircraft. Most of the bombing of Nghệ An during that time (522 missions) took place close to the Lao border in an effort to stop the movement of people and goods along the Hồ Chí Minh trail.

37 Report on the current situation in Vinh City, September 1970, NAPA, File 50.

38 Personal interview, Vinh, May 28, 2011.

URBAN FRAGMENTS 2

1 Hoover Institution Archives, Stanford University, Vietnam Subject Collection, 1950–1990.

2 Excerpt. This song was first played on the radio on May 31, 1973. It was written on the occasion of the proposal at the 9th Party Congress to support, at Hanoi's request, the reconstruction of Vinh. *Neues Deutschland*, June 1, 1973. The song confuses the city of Vinh in the DRV with the district of Vĩnh Linh, another hard-hit area called the "steel rampart" (*lũy thép*), which lay close to the border with the RVN. Today it is known for the Vịnh Mốc tunnels in Quảng Trị province.

CHAPTER 3. SOLIDARITY

1 As Hồ Chí Minh stated at a reception in his honor, "Like you, the Vietnamese people endure deep pain and suffering over the temporary division of the Fatherland. Like you, they have the same enemy, the imperialist aggressors" (Foreign Languages Publishing House 1958, 8).

2 Tuong Vu argues that the term *đoàn kết* emerged in the 1950s as part of nationalist rhetoric to reduce conflict between workers and state enterprises (2005, 339).

3 Report by the prime minister on economic, technical, and scientific relations with the GDR, 1955–1973. Vietnam National Archives (VNA) III, Văn phòng Phủ Thủ tướng (PTT) 1954–1985, Vol. 3, File 9132. Wernicke claims that total aid to Vietnam by 1975, including donations omitted by the Vietnamese government, amounted to 1.5 billion marks (2003, 317).

4 "Vietnams Kampf ist unser Kampf" [Vietnam's struggle is our struggle], *Junge Welt*, February 17–18, 1968.

5 Dieter Stöhr, "Solidarität in Aktion" [Solidarity in action], *Die Brücke*, no. 8, 1981.

6 Repeated Chinese warnings to Hanoi also likely influenced this ambivalence; the Chinese leadership cautioned that Soviet aid was insincere and intended to gain control over Vietnam (Khoo 2011, 33–36).

7 Ambivalence toward Moscow went beyond party leadership. While people with fond memories of studying and living with host families in the Soviet Union often claimed Russia as their second homeland, others had a less positive view. In jest, Russians in Hanoi were referred to as "Americans without dollars" at the time, suggesting imperialist intent behind their assistance with little financial benefit. For a contrasting view, see Vu (2008).

8 VNA III, PTT 1954–1985, Vol. 2, File 5590. An earlier version of this report, submitted to the Ministry of Construction on July 18, 1973, can be found in NAPA, File 51. The trip lasted from June 21 to July 21, 1973. I provide a context for this visit below.

9 While *cảm*, as a cognate, is linked to affect or sense (as in *bị cảm*, or to catch cold), *thông* implies transmission, as in *thông tin* (news).

10 Personal interview, Germany, September 7, 2011.

11 Such contributions are documented in reports on "solidarity among the GDR population with a fighting Vietnam (*kämpfenden Vietnam*)." Bundesarchiv (BArch), SAPMO, DY 24/117905.

12 *Die Zehn Grundsätze der sozialistischen Moral*. Commandment 10 in German reads, "Du sollst Solidarität mit den um ihre nationale Befreiung kämpfenden und den ihre nationale Unabhängigkeit verteidigenden Völkern üben."

13 See, for example, Kunze and Vogel (2010), Hosek (2011), Weis (2011), Hong (2015), Kroiber (2017), and the edited volume by Slobodian (2015b).

14 Surprisingly, there has been little research on this support. For a notable exception, see Mark et al. (2015) on antiwar demonstrations in Hungary, Poland, and Yugoslavia. Mark et al. argue that the Warsaw Pact countries of Hungary and Poland used solidarity with Vietnam as an opportunity to also criticize Soviet imperialism (458–59).

15 Personal interview, Germany, August 17, 2012.

16 This exhibition can be found at the War Remnants Museum in Ho Chi Minh City and was previously displayed at the Army and Air Defense museums in Hanoi.

17 I take this phrase from a female worker in Suhl, who had donated fifty marks to the solidarity fund to support "das kleine tapfere Volk" (the small and proud folk); presumably, she made the donation out of *Herzensbedürfnis* (heartfelt need) to support the heroic struggle against an imperial power. "Überall in der Republik Solidarität mit Vietnam" [Solidarity with Vietnam everywhere in the republic], *Neues Deutschland*, February 4, 1973. Her maternalism is an example of the intrinsic sense of racialized difference that informed encounters with the subjugated Other.

18 Li (2010, 218) argues that between 1965 and 1970, more than 320,000 Chinese forces served clandestinely in Vietnam. Though no official records in Russia have been released to date, Li estimates that more than 4,000 Soviet military personnel served during the war (66). These men are not officially recognized or given veteran benefits in the Russian Federation today.

19 Personal interview, Germany, August 18, 2008.

20 Personal interview, Germany, December 17, 2015.

21 This is not to be confused with the "Soli" tax, or solidarity surcharge (*Solidaritätszuschlag*) to help develop the "new" federal states in eastern Germany after reunification.

22 Email communication, July 25, 2017.

23 Weis makes a similar claim for African solidarity: "Donations were not obligatory, but the moral pressure to donate could be quite strong" (2011, 360).

24 Slobodian (2015a, 32), for example, cites Andrew Port as describing the "disgruntlement of ordinary workers at making contributions to Solidarity Funds for Vietnam in the 1960s, believing that the funds would only prolong the war and detracted from more pressing domestic concerns." My own findings do not support this generalization about workers as a whole, though it is important to pay attention to distinctions across social lines as well as across rural-urban divides and even gender.

25 "Geschenke für Vietnam" [Gifts for Vietnam], *Neues Deutschland*, April 4, 1956.

26 Following renovation, the name changed to Bệnh viện Hữu nghị Việt Nam–CHDC Đức (Vietnam–Democratic Republic of Germany Friendship Hospital). Public works projects with GDR assistance, 1955–1972, VNA III, PTT 1954–1985, Vol. 3, File 8892.

27 See also Hong (2015). In 1991, the name changed once more to the Vietnam-Germany Friendship Hospital (Bệnh viện Hữu nghị Việt Đức), erasing the history of East German humanitarian support.
28 I read these types of reports, for instance, in the archives of the Martin Luther University Halle-Wittenberg and the Burg Giebichenstein University of Art and Design Halle.
29 Personal interview, Germany, August 17, 2012.
30 This generic Orientalness was evident in the interchangeability of Asian people: photographs of men and women from other Asian countries, like North Korea, sometimes stood in for images of "Vietnamese" at war in factories or on the battlefield.
31 "2,500 Bonner Söldner in Südvietnam" [2,500 Bonn mercenaries in South Vietnam], *Junge Welt*, February 9, 1966.
32 Terms that conflated imperialism with fascism and national socialism were taken from the *Berliner Zeitung* in 1972.
33 Personal interview, Germany, November 4, 2017. The journalist wept while telling me this still-painful story about the grieving mother and the translator's callous response.
34 *Neues Deutschland*, December 29, 1972. See also the subheading on the front page of the *Berliner Zeitung*, December 31: "In two weeks 22 B-52s annihilated."
35 "USA betreiben Massenmord am vietnamesischen Volk" [USA carries out genocide against the Vietnamese people], *Berliner Zeitung*, December 29, 1972. On the figure of the POW-perpetrator in the four-part television series *Pilots in Pajamas* (*Piloten im Pyjama*), produced by Walter Heynowski and Gerhard Scheumann in 1968, see Schwenkel (2014a); for an alternative reading, see Alter (1997).
36 The GDR produced more films about Vietnam than any other socialist country in the 1960s and 1970s; to give an idea of the scope, Vietnam was the subject of fourteen of the approximately seventy documentaries produced by the renowned directors Walter Heynowski and Gerhard Scheumann.
37 Anna Mudry, "Für Vinh gab es keine Stunde Null" [For Vinh there was no zero hour], *Berliner Zeitung*, August 12, 1973. For an account of her experiences as a female journalist in the war, see Mudry (2017).
38 *Junge Welt*, February 17–18, 1968. The subheadings announced that GDR youth had donated more than six million marks to Vietnam by 1968 to purchase electrical equipment and medical supplies.
39 Detailed plan for the Vietnam bazaar "Solidarity Supports Victory," October 18–20, 1968. BArch, SAPMO, DY 25/2199.
40 Over time, and especially after the fall of the Berlin Wall, the Vietnamese students and trainees who once embodied the beneficence of solidarity would trigger xenophobic anxieties about the presence of Others in East German society (Schwenkel 2015d, 20–21).
41 Crew (2017, 147) observes that *Inferno Dresden*, written by the mayor of Dresden, became the basis of GDR popular memory and government propaganda.

42 Huyssen notes this in a cursory way. In his article, "Germany" stands in for the FRG, erasing the East and relegating it to a mere footnote in history. Respondents in my study reversed this construct: their use of "Germany" and "Germans" referred to the GDR, a practice that I continue in this book to provincialize the West.

43 In this historical narrative, World War II was depicted as a "forerunner to the Cold War, and both were reduced to a communist struggle" against fascist imperialism (Kelly 2010, 138). This perspective differed from the moral equivalences drawn between Allied bombing and the crimes of Nazi Germany by Holocaust deniers and revisionists, such as David Irving in his discredited book on the destruction of Dresden (Shermer and Grobman 2009, 260–61).

44 As Roy Scranton notes in his review of Verso's 2017 edition of *War Primer* in the *Los Angeles Review of Books*, GDR censors originally rejected Brecht's manuscript for being too pacifist and not critical enough of the Allied "imperialist warmongers." https://lareviewofbooks.org/article/the-shipwreck-of-history-bertolt-brechts-war-primer/.

45 This is not to suggest that East Germans denied the Holocaust; as Heins and Langenohl (2013) and Vees-Gulani (2008) argue, it was simply not as dominant in East German memory as it was in the FRG.

46 "Wie der kalte Krieg begann" [How the Cold War began], *Neues Deutschland*, March 15, 1967.

47 See, for example, "Luftpiraten griffen Umgebung der Stadt Vinh an" [Air pirates attack area of Vinh City], *Neues Deutschland*, January 11, 1967.

48 GDR Solidarity Committee, Vietnam Commission, 1974. "Vinh: Bericht über eine vietnamesische Heldenstadt" [Vinh: Report on a Vietnamese heroic city], Berlin, 3.

49 Hellmut Kapfenberger, "Neues Kapital in der Chronik der Stadt Vinh" [New chapter in the chronicle of Vinh City], *Neues Deutschland*, August 12, 1973. This article was published the day before Mudry's article in the *Berliner Zeitung* that I discussed above, suggesting media coordination to familiarize readers with the name of Vinh.

50 Personal interview, Germany, August 18, 2008, also quoted in Schwenkel (2012, 446).

51 The text reads, "Dresden was like the moon now, nothing but minerals. The stones were hot. Everybody else in the neighborhood was dead. So it goes" (Vonnegut 1969, 178). *Slaughterhouse-Five* was published in 1972 by the East German press Volk und Welt, another example of the role Dresden played in national memory.

52 Personal interview, Vinh, September 28, 2010.

53 See chapter 2 in Hong (2015) for an account of the GDR project in North Korea.

54 My respondents cited the date of March 16, 1973, as the start of negotiations for the reconstruction of Vinh. For details of this meeting in Hanoi between GDR and Vietnamese officials, see Kaiser (2016, 70).

55 This letter is part of a dossier on GDR assistance to Vietnam with the design and construction of Vinh City, Nghệ An from 1973–1979, VNA III, PTT 1954–1985, Vol. 3, File 11167.

56 See Decision 02-61/II.3/73 of the Office of the Council of Ministers, BArch, SAPMO, DC 20 I/4 2875.

57 As reported on the front page of Vinh's local newspaper on June 14, 1973: "Cộng hòa dân chủ Đức giúp ta xây dựng lại thành phố Vinh" [The Democratic Republic of Germany to help us rebuild Vinh City], *Nghệ An News*. Honecker's speech to the Central Committee was quoted in the article at length. Two weeks earlier, on May 31, this timeline was also reported in the People's Army newspaper, *Quân đội Nhân dân*.

58 See, for example, "Solidaritätsspenden zum Aufbau der Stadt Vinh" [Solidarity donations to build Vinh City], June 5, 1973, and "Schüler wollen der Stadt Vinh helfen" [Pupils want to help Vinh City], June 17, 1973.

59 On June 20, 1973, the Chairman of the Central Committee, Willi Stoph, confirmed in a two-page letter to Phạm Văn Đồng that the party and government had tentatively agreed, as an expression of the fraternal bonds between the countries, to Hanoi's request, pending the findings of the five-person delegation. VNA III, PTT 1954–1985, Vol. 2, File 5590. As mentioned above, the tour took place from June 21 to July 21, 1973.

60 Personal interview, Germany, August 21, 2012.

61 The tour lasted from September 25 to the end of October, 1973. Ministry of Construction, Agenda for the Vietnam delegation to the GDR to study construction problems in connection with the rebuilding of Vinh City, September 18, 1973, BArch, SAPMO, DH 1/28526. A Vietnamese report of this visit can be found in VNA III, PTT 1954–1985, Vol. 2, File 11167, dated November 13, 1973. A likely reason for the change of location from Dresden was the roster of experts chosen to redesign Vinh. By no coincidence, a chief architect of Dessau and Halle-Neustadt went on to lead the project in Vinh. His expertise in rebuilding destroyed cities made him an attractive candidate, he told me.

62 "Eure Solidarität ist wahrer Internationalismus" [Your solidarity is true internationalism], *Neues Deutschland*, October 21, 1973.

CHAPTER 4. SPIRITED INTERNATIONALISM

1 Personal interview, Germany, August 17, 2012.

2 A list of these treaties can be found in VNA III, Văn phòng Chính phủ (CP) 1957–1995, File 7409. Most important for the discussion here is the Agreement on Technical and Scientific Cooperation, ratified on March 14, 1956, and extended on February 9, 1966, the details of which can be found in BArch, SAPMO, DC 20/9189.

3 For example, Hungarian support established an electrical plant at Thanh Hóa; Czechoslovakian support built a shoe factory in Hải Phòng; Romanian support refurbished the cement plant outside Hải Phòng; and Mongolian support developed cattle breeding, to name but a few of the projects from the post–French war era of rehabilitation (*khôi phục*), before the first American bomb strikes in 1964. "RGW Länder helfen Vietnam" [CMEA Countries Help Vietnam], *Neues Deutschland*, September 2, 1963. For an explanation of CMEA, see note 14. A more comprehensive

list, and detailed project files (including moneys spent) broken down by country, can be found in VNA III, PTT 1954–1985, Vol. 2.

4 On military aid and the printing of Vietnamese currency in East Germany, see Schaefer (2015); on the training of Vietnamese intelligence officers and police by the Ministry of State Security (Stasi), see Grossheim (2014).

5 The glassworks factory went into operation in 1962, and the cannery in 1963. The latter could produce 3,000 tons of canned fruit per year with machinery imported from the GDR. "Vietnam würdigt DDR Hilfe" [Vietnam highly values GDR assistance], *Neues Deutschland*, May 20, 1963.

6 Joachim Krüger (1991, 823) puts the first cohort of Vietnamese students in the GDR as early as 1953. Following ratification of the 1956 scientific cooperation agreement, thousands more went to study in East Germany to acquire technical skills to rebuild their homeland.

7 "Enge Zusammenarbeit mit Vietnam" [Close cooperation with Vietnam], *Neues Deutschland*, March 16, 1956. Note that the terms "solidarity," "mutual aid," "co-operation," "friendship," and "equality" were similarly used to flatten hierarchies between Han rulers and ethnic minority groups in Maoist China (Litzinger 2000, 163–64).

8 This letter was included with a collection of official dispatches from the Administrative Committee, Fourth Military Zone, from July to September 1957. VNA III, PTT 1954–1985, Vol. 1, File 07.

9 Bernhard Harrass, "Glaswerk Haiphong" [Haiphong glass factory], *Neues Deutschland*, October 6, 1962, Beilage No. 40.

10 One famous example was the "kitchen debate" between the United States and the Soviet Union, in which home appliances and other consumer goods became arenas of conflict between capitalism and socialism (Baldwin 2015, Castillo 2010). See also Day and Liem (2010) on the cultural Cold War in Southeast Asia.

11 See also Kotkin (1995, 150–51) for a discussion of historical debates over the nature of the Soviet socialist city.

12 The first Five-Year Plan was disrupted by the onset of the air war; the second Five-Year Plan (1975–1980) was then delayed for ten years.

13 According to the Five-Year Plan, heavy industry (*công nghiệp nặng*) would be given priority (*ưu tiên*), but the country would simultaneously "strive for the comprehensive development of agriculture and the development of light industries," including the food and beverage sector.

14 Council for Mutual Economic Assistance, which, at that time, consisted of the Soviet Union and Eastern Europe (Poland, Bulgaria, Romania, Hungary, East Germany, and Czechoslovakia), as well as Mongolia, which did not contribute aid, and, after 1972, Cuba, which had eleven projects in the DRV between 1967 and 1974 and was not included in above number.

15 Office of the Prime Minister, Report on the status of public works projects signed with the Soviet Union and Eastern Europe, 1974, VNA III, CP 1957–1995, Vol. 2, File 5578. The Soviet contribution for these early projects amounted to 344 million rubles, followed by the GDR with 54 million rubles, and then Poland and Hungary,

each with 35 million rubles. Note that these figures do not include humanitarian projects, like hospitals, or reconstruction of cities that I discuss below.

16 Situation on the public works projects signed with Soviet Union and Eastern Europe (as of June 15, 1974), VNA III, CP 1957–1995, Vol. 2, File 5578.

17 Review of plans to invite foreign experts to Vietnam in 1978–1979, VNA III, CP 1957–1995, Vol. 2, File 1922. Among socialist countries, the Soviet Union had the most in-country technicians (1,661), followed by the GDR (357) and Cuba (185). Among nonsocialist countries, Sweden had the highest number (334), followed, surprisingly, by France (160) and Japan (69). There were no American experts, according to the report, and no experts from nonaligned countries. On the Swedish-funded construction of Vietnam's largest paper mill at Bãi Bằng in the 1970s, see Jerve (1999).

18 The legacies of both socialist and nonsocialist projects still have a presence in Vietnam and continue to contribute to national development. Beyond Vinh, my research took me to the former Đạo Tú concrete panel factory (GDR), now Xuân Mai Construction, to the expanded Bãi Bằng factory and "Swedish village" that once housed experts in the 1970s, and to the "Finnish village" for experts on the Phà Rừng shipyard project in the early 1980s in Hải Phòng.

19 BArch, SAPMO, DC 20 I/4/2875.

20 For details on the Soviet plan for Hanoi, see chapter 6 in Logan (2000).

21 Planning and design of cities and townships, February 1974, VNA III, CP 1957–1995, Vol. 2, File 5578. There are some discrepancies between the German telegram and map and the Vietnamese records, which I take as the authority source. In Vietnamese documents, Cuba would concentrate on technical and agricultural projects in Quảng Bình, south of Nghệ An and close to the Demilitarized Zone, but no mention was made of Vĩnh Linh, as marked on the map.

22 Planning and design of cities and townships, February 1974. VNA III, CP 1957–1995, Vol. 2, File 5578.

23 Personal interview, Germany, September 9, 2011. During the war, experts flew with Interflug, East Germany's national airline, from East Berlin's Schönefeld Airport to Hanoi via Moscow and Karachi (Pakistan), where the plane would refuel (also at times in Tashkent). Experts received a U.S. $10 bill for the layover, which another specialist recalled saving as a souvenir.

24 East Germany made this suggestion in October 1973, on the occasion of the signing of the bilateral agreement to rebuild Vinh. In a memo dated January 19, 1974, Phan Mỹ, Head of the Office of the Government, confirmed the prime minister's endorsement of the proposal. VNA III, PTT 1954–1985, Vol. 3, File 9428.

25 "Những người con xứ sở Các-Mác trên quê hương Bác Hồ" [The children of Karl Marx's country in the homeland of Uncle Hồ], *Nghệ An News*, October 7, 1974. This issue was devoted to the twenty-fifth anniversary of the founding of the GDR in 1949.

26 Personal interview, Vinh, December 7, 2010.

27 This letter, along with the original request and the final agreement, is part of a dossier on GDR assistance to Vietnam with the design and construction of Vinh City,

Nghệ An from 1973 to 1979. VNA III, PTT 1954–1985, Vol. 2, File 11167. The final agreement can also be found in File 5590, in addition to NAPA, File 51.

28 Internal reports in Hanoi also show that design and construction were part of the negotiations during the first fact-finding mission, with the aim to transform Vinh into a major economic center. Ministry of Construction, Report on the results of the GDR delegation visit to assist with planning and construction of Vinh City, July 18, 1973, NAPA, File 51.

29 Reflecting the ideas of Lê Duẩn, Võ Nguyên Giáp (1975, 59) described the New Socialist Man as a "patriot with revolutionary consciousness" oriented toward proletarian internationalism, who demonstrates a "spirit of collective mastery" (*tinh thần làm chủ tập thể*), possesses good health and a high level of cultural proficiency (that is, has overcome backwardness), and is loyal to the party and government—values assessed as positive and necessary for modern urban life.

30 For example, Romania worked on the design of Nam Định City and North Korea on Bắc Giang town from 1973 to 1974. VNA III, PTT 1954–1985, Vol. 3, Files 9528 and 9336, respectively.

31 The extension was ratified on July 4, 1978. VNA III, PTT 1954–1985, Vol. 3, File 10648. (For the same documents in the German language, see: BArch, SAPMO, DF 4/23679.)

32 Personal interview, Germany, August 21, 2012.

33 Personal interview, Germany, September 7, 2011. Having a family also influenced the decision not to accept an assignment in war-torn Vietnam. One respondent who was recruited for the panel factory project in Đạo Tú turned down the offer for this reason.

34 According to their labor contract with the Vietnam Task Force (*Arbeitsstab Vietnam*) under the Ministry of Construction, experts were entitled to twenty-four working days of annual vacation leave, in addition to one day for every calendar month worked, for a total of thirty-six days of paid leave per year, or six weeks based on a six-day work week. Per the field doctor's recommendation from July 18, 1974, experts were advised to use their vacation time in East Germany to reunite with families who were not allowed to accompany them, and as respite from the climate and adverse living conditions. BArch, SAPMO, DH 1/28526. Destinations within Vietnam varied, as did freedom of movement: later cohorts had more flexibility after the end of the war, but they were far from free-touring vacationers. Earlier cohorts, for whom travel was still difficult and dangerous, were restricted to group outings arranged by their Vietnamese counterparts. Those in higher positions had fewer restrictions on their movements, as their job often depended on frequent travel between Vinh and Hanoi.

35 These numbers are based on a list provided to me by the provincial government in Vinh, which I cross-referenced with names given to me by experts, including those who attended reunions, and which I found in documents in Germany.

36 Personal interview, Germany, August 26, 2018.

37 The procedure for employing wives (*Ehefrauen*) in the field was drafted on July 16, 1974, as part of the "Ground protocol for management of the Vinh Work Unit,"

and endorsed two days later by the field doctor, who confirmed that improved living conditions would make their deployment possible. The assumption was clearly that women—who were thought to be more susceptible to tropical illnesses—would only serve the mission as wives and not as recruited technicians. BArch, SAPMO, DH 1/28526.

38 Planning and design of cities and townships, February 1974, VNA III, CP 1957–1995, Vol. 2, File 5578. The report also noted the different project temporalities: Romanian and Polish planners had already collected data on their first trip and would return to present preliminary plans in March and June 1974 respectively, while Czechoslovakian planners had yet to travel to Vietnam. Soviet planners were at that time in Vietnam gathering necessary documents. On the short trips to Hanoi made by Russian architects and planners, see Logan (2000, 193–94).

39 Illness and injury led some experts to break their contracts and return home, despite having an East German doctor on site, as documented in medical reports from the field. Several interviewees commented that such afflictions led to the early deaths of their colleagues. My Vietnamese respondents knew well the circumstances surrounding the death of the electrician and recounted it to me in tragic detail—how he climbed a utility pole (to which they would point) after hours to fix a power line on his last night before he was scheduled to return to East Germany for good—illustrating his ethical commitment to solidarity to the bitter end.

40 Author's personal collection.

41 Trần Doãn Qưới and Nguyễn Hường, "Cảm nghĩ chân thành" [Sincere feelings], *Nghệ An News*, October 7, 1974. This was published on the twenty-fifth anniversary of the founding of the GDR.

42 Group interview, Germany, September 9, 2011. This group later erupted into conflict, divided along the lines of planners and tradespersons—in other words, elite apparatchiks and laypeople.

43 A Polish team, for example, was periodically in Vinh to work on a friendship hospital (see Schwenkel 2015e), as were Soviet teams for other regional projects, including a radar installation close to the Lao border.

44 Personal interview, Germany, August 20, 2017.

45 Personal interview, Germany, September 6, 2011.

46 Personal interview, Vinh, February 26, 2011.

47 Personal interview, Germany, August 21, 2012. Even among the pioneers, there were tensions between the elite planners on shorter-term assignments and skilled professionals who stayed much longer and developed closer relationships with the local population.

48 For example, single rooms with en suite bathrooms, air conditioning, and refrigerators. Office of the Prime Minister, Report on the status of public works projects signed with the Soviet Union and Eastern Europe, 1974, VNA III, CP 1957–1995, Vol. 2, File 5578.

49 Personal interview, Germany, August 17, 2015.

50 Examples of labor contracts can be found in BArch, SAPMO, DH 1/28526. On average, specialists earned from 1,000 East German marks to upward of 1,500,

showing significant income inequality between lay and professional experts. As a point of comparison, the median income of women I interviewed was 650 marks.

51 The per diem for those with income over 1,500 marks was 11 VND. The original amount of 30 VND was reduced because of the free lodging and meals. Vietnam Task Force, Sample contract for overseas deployment to Vietnam, October 25, 1973. BArch, SAPMO, DH 1/28526. There was no currency conversion at this time.

52 GENEX (Geschenkdienst und Kleinexport GmbH) began as a hard-currency, mail-order retailer for West Germans to purchase gifts for their relatives and friends in the East. For its history, see Zatlin (2007, 270–77).

53 Personal interview, Germany, August 17, 2015.

54 The creator of the postcard attached the caption to a photograph from a nursing home. It represented the ability to buy "something extraordinary" (*irgendwas Außergewöhnliches*), one female respondent, the wife of an expert, explained. Email communication, June 10, 2019.

55 VNA III, PTT 1957–1995, Vol. 2, File 5590. An earlier version of this report, submitted to the Ministry of Construction on July 18, 1973, can be found in NAPA, File 51.

56 Thus, as Michael Barnett argues, humanitarian agencies emphasize the technical aspects of their work to appear apolitical, which "facilitates their ability to work without triggering the suspicion of the state or the local elites" (2011, 40).

57 Personal interview, Germany, September 8, 2015.

58 Personal interview, Vinh, May 27, 2011; also cited in Schwenkel (2017b, 425).

59 Personal interview, Germany, August 18, 2008.

60 Attitudes and work habits deemed harmful to the project or to relations with Vietnamese counterparts were included in "Situation Reports" from work unit leaders in Vinh under a section on "political and ideological assessment." BArch, SAPMO, DH 1/28668.

61 See also Hong (2015, 62–63) for similar concerns about racial arrogance and misconduct among East German specialists in Hamhung, North Korea, in the 1950s, when leaders were anxious to disassociate their country from National Socialism.

62 Personal interview, Germany August 17, 2015.

63 Most statistics were outdated regardless, since mass data collection halted when U.S. bombing began. Planning documents in the 1970s tended to use statistics from 1966 or earlier. On December 15, 1973, Nghệ An officials submitted an urgent request to Hanoi for permission to provide visiting experts with maps of the city center and diagrams of infrastructure systems. Planning and construction of Vinh City, 1973–1974, VNA III, CP 1957–1995, Vol. 2, File 5590.

64 Planning and construction of Vinh City, 1973–1974, VNA III, CP 1957–1995, Vol. 2, File 5590.

URBAN FRAGMENTS 3

1 Excerpt. Published in *Nghệ An News*, April 30, 1974, in the same issue as figure I.3.1, the day before the first brick was laid to build Quang Trung.

CHAPTER 5. RATIONAL PLANNING

1 This statement was made during a speech at the Sixth Session of the Second National Congress of the Communist Party in 1963, as printed in the newspaper *Nhân Dân* on May 3 and 4, 1963.

2 The International Congresses of Modern Architecture (CIAM) and Le Corbusier's vision of the Radiant City inspired socialist modernism, as I discuss below. On the intersections between CIAM and Marxist-Leninist ideology in communist urban planning, see Mumford (2009). On Le Corbusier in Moscow and the reception of his ideas among Soviet planners, see Cohen (1992).

3 Thạch Quỳ, "The Rubble of Vinh," *Nghệ An News*, February 18, 1966.
(Is there any other city like this one
Where you cannot find a radiant red building
But find only traces of red in the crushed brick?)

4 Personal interview, Vinh, April 9, 2011.

5 Report on the planning of a residential complex for state employees returning to Vinh City, November 5, 1970, NAPA, File 51.

6 Draft of three-year plan to build Vinh City, 1973, NAPA, File 51.

7 Though the suggestion that this model *was* transferable and that East Germany's approach to recovery should provide the template was evident in the Vietnamese delegation's visit to rebuilt cities in the fall of 1973 (see chapter 3).

8 Personal interview, Germany, August 21, 2012.

9 By the end of 1973, more than seven thousand hectares of craters had been filled, with the assistance of a few bulldozers and tractors, according to the Provincial Planning Committee's report to Hanoi. VNA III, Văn phòng Ủy ban Kế hoạch nhà nước, File 975.

10 Deutsche Bauakademie, "Thesen zur 1. Theoretischen Konferenz der Deutschen Bauakademie" [Theses of the first theoretical conference of the German Building Academy], *Deutsche Architektur*, 1960:9(10), supplement.

11 Some of these plans can be found in NAPA, File 1087, Documents on the evacuation of state enterprises to the countryside, 1972–1975.

12 In German documents, this was sometimes abbreviated as WTZ for *wissenschaftlich-technische Zusammenarbeit*, or scientific-technical cooperation.

13 For scholars of Vietnam, this metaphor will bring to mind the famous 1960 photograph by Lâm Hồng Long of Hồ Chí Minh conducting the national orchestra, titled "Chủ tịch Hồ Chí Minh bắt nhịp bài 'Đoàn kết'" [President Hồ Chí Minh keeps pace with the song "Unity"].

14 Tuong Vu made a similar argument for Vietnamese-Soviet relations: "Despite the asymmetry of the relationship, they refused to think of it [aid] as another form of colonial dependency in which the USSR supplanted France as Vietnam's patron" (2008, 258).

15 Personal interview, Germany, August 29, 2012.

16 Personal interview, Germany, August 18, 2008.

17 Personal interview, Vinh, November 1, 2010.

18 Dieter Stöhr, "Solidarität in Aktion" [Solidarity in action], *Die Brücke*, 1981, no. 8.

19 The work of the Nghệ An Institute of Planning and Design (Viện Quy hoạch Thiết kế Nghệ An), or the Design Institute hereafter, fell under the auspices of the Ministry of Construction (Bộ Xây dựng); it served a similar function to the state-run Design Institute in China, which centralized architectural production with the assistance of the Soviet Union (Roskam 2015).

20 This role made some uncomfortable. Certain GDR experts made the conscientious decision not to play the part of socialist big brother: "If the Vietnamese took the lead and attempted to solve a technical problem, we held our mouths and didn't say a word, even if we knew the solution." Personal interview, Germany, September 7, 2011. The desire to empower Vietnamese planners to realize their intellectual capacity was arguably a tactic to make training appear more egalitarian and less threatening (see also Babül 2017, 122).

21 Personal interview, Germany, August 29, 2012.

22 On other North-South transfers of design expertise among socialist countries, see Stanek (2012). On the training of East German planners in the Soviet Union that resulted in the Sixteen Principles of Urban Design in 1950, see Flierl (1998).

23 For example, one team leader's report to Berlin from August 28, 1979, mentions that recommendations were either "sluggishly" (*schleppend*) implemented or disregarded. BArch, SAPMO, DH 1/28668.

24 On the overseas trained expert as carrier of suspect knowledge, see Schwenkel (2015d).

25 Nghệ An Administrative Committee, Report on the general construction plan for Vinh and preparation for selected projects, May 30, 1975, BArch, SAPMO, DH 1/28549.

26 The East Germans predicted more accurately: by 1978, municipal officials recorded Vinh's population at 125,000, a number that surpassed Vietnamese expectations for that year (Nguyễn 2005, 229).

27 See, for example, the sketches in Flierl (1998), where ghostlike figures move serenely through space and use objects, such as park benches, in orderly fashion.

28 The GDR Council of Ministers approved *Die sechzehn Grundsätze des Städtebaus* on July 27, 1950, following a study tour to the Soviet Union, referred to in the literature as the "Reise nach Moskau" (Trip to Moscow). The Khrushchev-led push toward standardization and industrialization in the following decade prompted a reformulation of these principles, which had introduced more socialist classicist forms—for example, the monumental Stalinallee in Berlin (now Karl-Marx-Allee). The subsequent revised General Principles of Planning and Design of Socialist City Centers (*Grundsätze der Planung und Gestaltung sozialistischer Stadtzentren*) was published in 1960 by the Deutsche Bauakademie in *Deutsche Architektur*, vol. 8.

29 As May observes, such extravagant monumentalism in East Germany bore uncanny similarity to Nazi town planning (2003, 57).

30 Personal interview, Germany, November 10, 2017.

31 Dalakoglou (2012, 572) has also argued that highway construction in Albania was more about spectacle and allusion to a particular futurity than it was about instrumentality, given the lack of automobility at the time.

32 Personal interview, Vinh, June 1, 2011.

33 A 1978 report by the Nghệ Tĩnh People's Committee noted that the trade center was a site of divergent visions, which slowed down its construction: "There have been delays with the trade center owing to a difference of opinions between the experts and Vietnamese cadres. Many issues are not yet agreed upon." VNA III, PTT 1954–1985, File 11167.

34 Nghệ An Administrative Committee, Report on the general construction plan for Vinh and preparation for selected projects, May 30, 1975, BArch, SAPMO, DH 1/28549.

35 Boyer (1983, 153), for instance, traces functional planning in American cities and strict, single-land-use zoning policies to protect private property back to 1914. See also Holston (1989) on Brasilia, which he considers the quintessential "CIAM city."

36 Woodside (1970, 716) claims that decolonization policies of "coordinated development" to close the urban-rural gap have their roots in early VIỆT MINH doctrine, which was influenced by Maoist spatial models of "simultaneous advancement."

37 In Vinh in 1974, for example, 38.5 percent of the urban working population was employed in agriculture and only 20.8 percent in industry, according to the provincial report on the general construction plan for Vinh from May 30, 1975. BArch, SAPMO, DH 1/28549.

38 Personal interview, Hanoi, August 15, 2010.

39 Second principle from *Die sechzehn Grundsätze des Städtebaus*, 1950.

40 Early Soviet planning also recognized that urban nature was critical to the health and restoration of the labor force (Bittner 1998).

41 Personal interview, Vinh, May 23, 2011.

42 Ironically, the master plan was never approved by Hanoi. Kaiser (2016, 94–95) offers explanations based on GDR archival materials. My Vietnamese interlocutors chalked up this lack of approval to government inefficiency, showing their disenchantment with bureaucracy.

43 "Buôn bán trái phép ở chợ Vinh" [Illegal trading at Vinh market], *Nghệ An News*, December 27, 1974.

44 The Việt Đức Vocational School had two-year, coed programs in mechanics, bricklaying, concrete work, carpentry, welding, and electrical engineering. Its graduates encountered a similar temporal regime that structured industrial socialism as E. P. Thompson observed of industrial capitalism (1967). The problem of labor rhythm, time discipline, and training was an ongoing concern: "[There existed] limited work discipline on account of the unfamiliarity of the majority of the workforce with regular, fixed work times in set work places with the same work tasks to perform" (Purtak 1982, 19).

45 Planning and construction of Vinh City, 1973–1974, VNA III, PTT 1954–1985, Vol. 2, File 5590.

46 BArch, SAPMO, DH 1/28526.

47 Tensions frequently erupted over damaged, missing, and delayed freight. In interviews, German respondents described the difficult work of unloading freight at Cửa Lò, where, due to shallow waters, goods were moved via crane to local

vessels two kilometers offshore—a technical feat in itself. Owing to rough seas, loads sometimes dropped into the water during transfer. After roads improved, ships docked in Hải Phòng, and freight was delivered via lorries, which posed additional challenges. Problems with freight (and complaints by Vietnamese counterparts) were commonly mentioned in reports from group leaders in Vinh. BArch, SAPMO, DH 1/28668.

48 The GDR expert had been onstage during the ceremony and watched his colleagues hide behind columns to escape the tide of people. As he described it, "There was a mass of people as far as I could see, who were edging their way excitedly into the market to view all the goods on display." Personal interview, Germany, September 6, 2011.

49 Before Cầu Đước factory opened in 1959, the region relied on the main cement factory in Hải Phòng, built in 1899. That factory, which had supplied much of French Indochina with cement during the colonial era, was a target during the French and American wars due to its importance to the construction industry. It was rebuilt after both wars with Romanian aid.

50 Personal interview, Vinh, June 4, 2011.

51 There is bracketed mention of the proposed delivery of "some specialty used or refurbished machines and equipment" in an early draft of the agreement between the GDR and DRV, dated September 28, 1973. BArch, SAPMO, DH 1/28526.

52 These concerns were expressed at a working session on the problems of cooperation that took place in Vinh on January 21, 1977, as captured in the minutes. BArch, SAPMO, DH 1/28668.

53 Personal interview, Vinh, February 26, 2011.

54 Personal interview, Germany, September 12, 2011.

55 According to one team leader, "It was not easy for me to get the supplies I needed. How could I persuade directors when they also had shortages? How could they reach their productivity goals if they gave me one of their trucks? I had to convince them it was the right thing to do to support the solidarity fund." Personal interview, Germany, August 18, 2008.

56 Personal interview, Germany, September 12, 2011.

57 This meant withholding certain information from the East German public, such as the resale of donated trucks.

URBAN FRAGMENTS 4

1 Excerpts. Published in *Nghệ An News*, November 14, 1978.

CHAPTER 6. UTOPIAN HOUSING

1 Nghệ An Administrative Committee, Report on the provision of labor to build Vinh City, February 20, 1974, NAPA, File 330. This represented under half the targeted number of five thousand recruits, however, showing how labor mobilization was a challenge for district governments.

2 Planning and construction of Vinh City, 1973–1974, VNA III, PTT 1954–1985, Vol. 2, File 5590. A GDR work unit leader expressed concern about these untrained workers in an inception report to Berlin on March 25, 1974. Information about the activities and results of the work unit in Vinh from February 15 to March 31, 1974, BArch, SAPMO, DH 1/28668.
3 Nghệ An Administrative Committee, Report on the provision of labor to build Vinh City, February 20, 1974, NAPA, File 330.
4 In press releases, "Đặt viên gạch đầu tiên xây dựng lại thành phố Vinh."
5 Personal interview, Germany, August 21, 2012.
6 "Jedes Haus des neuen Vinh ein Stück Zusammenarbeit" [Every house in the new Vinh a part of cooperation], *Neues Deutschland*, September 6–7, 1975.
7 See Jansen (2015) on a housing complex in Sarajevo, and Laszczkowski (2015a) on Soviet-era housing blocks in Astana, Kazakhstan. On the privatization of socialist housing and the making of a postsocialist middle class, see Fehérváry (2013) on Hungary, Zavisca (2012) on Russia, and Zhang (2010) on China.
8 While utilitarianism took precedence, aesthetics were not abandoned; GDR architects debated the *künstlerischer Charakter*, or artistic character, of socialist architecture in housing estates (Author collective 1972, 7).
9 Personal interview, Germany, June 28, 2018.
10 See Zarecor (2011) on Czechoslovakia, Rubin (2016) on East Germany, Lebow (2013) on Poland, and Harris (2013) on the Soviet Union.
11 Similarly, see Hirsch (2005) on Soviet nationality policy, and Litzinger (2000, 163–69) on China's ethnic policies in minority regions.
12 "Konzeption für die Bebauung und Projektierung des Wohngebietes Vinh—Quang Trung" [Construction and design plan for Quang Trung residential complex in Vinh] from May 15, 1974, BArch, SAPMO, DH 1/28549.
13 Group interview, Germany, September 9, 2011.
14 This was also the case with 1950s housing estates in the United States. See J. S. Fuerst's (2003) book of oral histories, *When Public Housing Was Paradise*.
15 Two concrete panel factories (*Plattenwerk*) were built to serve Hanoi after the war: one by the GDR in the 1970s at Đạo Tú, north of the city, and another by the Soviet Union in the early 1980s, south of Hanoi at Xuân Mai. After economic reforms, Xuân Mai took over the Đạo Tú factory and merged into the Xuân Mai Investment and Construction Company to become a major player in the upscale condominium industry. As of my visit to Đạo Tú in 2017, the factory remains in full operation.
16 Prior to the air war, North Korean engineers had used more rudimentary and smaller-scale prefabricated technology to build the Kim Liên housing complex in Hanoi for political elites, well before Đạo Tú. While the use of precast *bloc bê-tông* (concrete blocks) at Kim Liên broke with the conventional use of bricks and cement, it was not large panel technology as developed by East German engineers at Đạo Tú, an architect in Hanoi familiar with both projects explained. Personal interview, Hanoi, June 21, 2011.
17 The East German newspaper *Neues Deutschland* recorded the handover of the plant at the start of October 1977. "Erstes Plattenwerk Vietnams mit DDR Hilfe

fertiggestellt" [Vietnam's first prefabricated factory with GDR assistance completed], October 3, 1977. The date was originally set for the end of 1974 as per the July 26, 1972, agreement, but was delayed on account of the air war. A copy of the original agreement between the GDR and DRV Ministries of Construction can be found in BArch, SAPMO, DH 1/28526.

18 Personal interview, Hanoi, July 31, 2017.

19 Ministry of Construction, Report on the results of the GDR delegation visit to assist with planning and construction of Vinh City, July 18, 1973, NAPA, File 51. The GDR rejected this request as unsuitable for conditions (Kaiser 2016, 81).

20 A high percentage of workers in the building materials industry were women: in stone quarries, women made up 51.7 percent of the workforce, in limestone 63 percent, and in brickwork 77 percent (Purtak 1982, 24). A majority of Quang Trung construction workers were also women. One supervisor who oversaw 129 workers estimated that 70 percent were women; most had served as youth volunteers during the war and trained at the Việt Đức Vocational School afterward. Personal interview, Vinh, January 17, 2011.

21 Personal interview, Germany, August 29, 2012.

22 See, for example, figure 2.4, of the bombed two-story house for workers at the electric plant.

23 Costs were also prohibitive in the Soviet Union and affected men and women differently. According to Victor Buchli, "Economies of scale kept the prices of the few functioning communal dining rooms high and out of reach of the single female worker" (1999, 31).

24 Built by the French, Côn Đảo prison was notorious for its "tiger cages." Born in 1923 in southern Vietnam, this man went north to Nghệ An in 1949 to fight the French. After the division of Vietnam in 1954, he stayed in the North to participate in national reconstruction. Personal interview, Vinh, December 15, 2010.

25 The age gap of approximately twenty-five years between the couple speaks to the difficulty that female youth volunteers had marrying within their age cohort upon their return from the war. These women were considered by society to be "polluted" and *ế rồi*, or beyond marriageability. See Phinney (2006) on state reproductive policies that allowed for these single women to "ask for a child" out of wedlock.

26 Personal interview, Vinh, April 27, 2011.

27 Personal interview, Vinh, July 19, 2011.

28 Report on the current situation in Vinh City, September 1970, NAPA, File 50.

29 Report on the planning of a residential complex for state employees returning to Vinh City, November 5, 1970, NAPA, File 51.

30 Draft of three-year plan to build Vinh City, 1973, NAPA, File 51.

31 Though in the case of Hanoi, workers remained close to industry outside the city center (Đặng 1985, 100–7; Logan 1995, 453–55).

32 Personal interview, Germany, August 21, 2012.

33 I also saw this photographic practice in the Bundesarchiv; see, for example, Bild 183-N1105-424, called, "DRV: Past and future next to one another."

34 Personal interview, Vinh, July 20, 2011.

35 Le Corbusier designed the housing complex, Cité Frugès de Pessac, in the early 1920s. H. Frugès, the investor-industrialist behind the project, was reportedly excited by the prospect of standardization and serial production (Boudon 1972, 11).

36 Construction and design plan for Quang Trung, BArch, SAPMO, DH 1/28549.

37 The Soviet-inspired housing projects in Hanoi tended to be built on a smaller scale than the GDR project in Vinh and were not typically integrated with public facilities.

38 Personal interview, Vinh, September 28, 2010.

39 This was explained to me as follows: "If you view from above, you will see that Quang Trung spells out the letters 'Việt Đức,' with block D2 as the rising tone." My neighbor told me how this rumor had circulated among the female bricklayers: "Sometimes I would go *đi chơi* [hang out] with friends at the vocational school and heard this story! I don't know if it's true. Why don't you go in an airplane and have a look?" Personal interview, Vinh, March 22, 2011.

40 Douglas Pike reported that the Soviets made simplistic assumptions about Vietnam in the 1980s, revealing a "lack of serious sociopolitical analysis (and no perceived need for any)" (1987, 171). Catherine Alexander identified a similar imperial arrogance in Soviet postwar planning in Kazakhstan, noting that it "paid little heed to local environmental factors" (2007b, 167).

41 Interestingly, these same indicators were proposed as tools for a planning team in Zanzibar working on a mass housing project there (Nguyen et al. 1974, 3), showing belief in the transferability of standardized design. See Wimmelbücker (2012) on the outcome of this project.

42 Personal interview, Germany, August 29, 2012.

43 Personal interview, Vinh, June 1, 2011.

44 Personal interview, Vinh, December 15, 2010.

45 Personal interview, Vinh, September 28, 2010.

46 Personal interview, Vinh, June 2, 2011.

47 Personal interview, Vinh, May 23, 2011.

48 "Vietnam Advances: Housing, a Real Problem," *Vietnam Courier* 18, no. 4 (1982).

49 Personal interview, Vinh, October 29, 2010. An accountant on the project disagreed: "This was a German design; the Vietnamese side only participated!" Personal interview, May 22, 2011.

50 Construction and design plan for Quang Trung, BArch, SAPMO, DH 1/28549.

51 See, for example, the artist Nguyễn Mạnh Hùng's 2011 diorama, "Living in Paradise," which captures, and in some way idealizes, the rural characteristic of housing blocks in Hanoi.

52 In 1975, the provincial government approved a request by the Food and Beverage Company to use both blocks as hotels. Because there were so few visitors, municipal authorities eventually reclaimed A1 as office space and housing. Bulletin no. 84 on the allocation of housing in Quang Trung, October 24, 1975, NAPA, File 37. A4 remained a guesthouse until its demolition in 2017, and is not included in figures I cite below.

53 There were eighty-eight rooms in block A1, ranging from 14.3 to 26.4 square meters. Because A1 housed offices and single workers, no original residents remained when I conducted research. Living space in Hanoi averaged 2.5 square meters per person at the time, though this number fluctuated across workplaces. Report on the construction and distribution of housing in Hanoi, 1973–1974, VNA III, PTT 1954–1985, Vol. 2, File 5660.

54 Personal interview, Vinh, June 2, 2011.

55 Personal interview, Vinh, November 2, 2010.

56 A2 still had one shared unit during my fieldwork, while A3 had three. Typically, when one family moved out, the remaining family took control of the entire flat, unless another family was assigned to the unit. On the spatial and ontological division of Vietnamese housing into *khu phụ* (auxiliary areas) and *khu chính* (main areas), see chapter 9.

57 Each block (*nhà*) was assigned a letter (according to area) and a number; for example my block was C2. Because apartment numbering was inconsistent across area A, my survey team dubbed it the confusing (*lung tung*) "Vietnam" system. From B1, a standardized system was in place that assigned each flat a number according to unit (*đơn*), floor (*gác*), and flat (*căn hộ*) in relation to the stairway. My flat, 143, was in *đơn* 1 (numbered from house left to right), on the fourth floor, in the third apartment counting from the stairway out. While confusing for visitors, my research team called this "German" system orderly (*trật tự*) and civilized (*văn minh*).

58 Personal interview, Vinh, May 22, 2011.

59 One engineer noted, after the end of cooperation, that this process was ongoing: "The separation of living from the work place is still in development" (Purtak 1982, 38).

60 Construction and design plan for Quang Trung, BArch, SAPMO, DH 1/28549.

61 By comparison, the average one-bedroom apartment in the new town of Halle-Neustadt was fifty-five square meters, with a target of sixteen square meters of space per person.

62 A similar spatial reallocation took place in Kim Liên housing in Hanoi, built with the support of North Korea more than a decade earlier. Large, self-contained apartments intended for party cadres were allocated to two families, as I learned from visits and interviews with residents and architects in 2012.

63 Personal interview, Vinh, March 2, 2011.

64 As explained in the introduction, the survey targeted 50 percent of households in each of the nineteen buildings (n = 647). My team and I divided households equally across đơn and stories. For example, because each standard đơn had twenty households, or four per floor, we surveyed two per story (selected randomly), or ten per đơn.

65 The Văn Sỹ soccer dynasty consists of the brothers Hùng, Sơn, Linh, Ngọc, and Thủy, along with their father. The family grew up in B5.

66 Personal interview, Vinh, March 22, 2011.

67 "Thêm 300 gia đình công nhân đến ở nhà cao tầng" [300 employees and their families move into the high-rises], *Nghệ An News*, January 20, 1978.

68 See Building Standards and Norms for Housing, TC-36-69, by the Ministry of Architecture, 1969. Workers discussed receiving four hundred grams of meat per month or more, depending on their position; low-level civil servants received four hundred grams, and midlevel ones received six hundred grams.

69 Despite their higher status, cultural elites also endured hunger in the postwar years. A young woman recalled peeling peanuts with other university families as a child and selling them collectively at the market to earn money to purchase food. Personal interview, Vinh, May 31, 2011.

70 Xuân Hoài, "Nhà tầng ở Vinh" [High-Rise in Vinh], *Nghệ An News*, November 14, 1978.

71 Hong (2015, 71) reports similar ambivalence toward multistory apartment buildings in Hamhung, North Korea, that were designed by the GDR.

72 After the 1991 Housing Ordinance liberalized housing and ended workplace allocations, rents increased to an average of 1,000 VND per square meter, where they remained until 2011, when the units were privatized. Vernacularly, this change in housing regimes marked a bureaucratic shift from *phân* (allocate) to *thuê* (rent) state housing—that is from the state as provider to lessor—even though the contractual language of *thuê nhà* (house rental) had been adopted from the start. Median monthly rents were 30,000 VND (U.S. $1.50) at the time of my study.

73 Personal interview, Vinh, March 22, 2011. This man explained that it took time to accumulate enough points through union activities and participation in emulation campaigns.

74 Personal interview, Vinh, November 5, 2010.

75 Personal interview, Vinh, April 23, 2011.

CHAPTER 7. INDISCIPLINE

1 Personal interview, Vinh, September 28, 2010, emphasis added.

2 "Two essential and pressing goals are to build the material-technical infrastructure of socialism and to reform the material and cultural life of the people" (Lê T.N. 1977, 18).

3 I emphasize this point after being struck by the number of colleagues from former socialist countries who recognized their own childhood homes in the images I showed them from Vinh. It is too easy to see Quang Trung as mimicry, which itself has the potential to be subversive, as Bhabha (1994) observed.

4 At the level of local urban governance, the warden, or *khối trưởng*, is a two-year elected position, nominated and voted for by residents. During my time living in Quang Trung, the majority of the nine khối trưởng were former commanders of the French and American wars. The khối trưởng reported directly to the Chairman of the District People's Committee and earned a monthly salary of 548,000 VND (U.S. $27). Under the khối trưởng are the vice warden (*phó khối trưởng*), secretary (*bí thư*), and residential leader (*tổ trưởng dân cư*), who was responsible for an average of forty households.

5 On the racialization of infrastructure in Hanoi, see Vann, who examines French sewer systems as a form of urban apartheid, which "dictated that whites and nonwhites would not share modernization equally" (2003, 193).
6 Here I speak of "dirt" metaphorically to refer to customs and practices that were considered antithetical to socialism (see also Buchli 1999); by division, I mean socioeconomic or class distinctions, particularly under colonialism, as well as division of the country until 1976.
7 For significant works, see Ninh Viết Giao (2003, 2006, and 2008).
8 These conversations took place in March and April 2011.
9 For a contemporary analysis of rural-urban migration and the process of becoming urban in Hanoi, see Nguyen et al. (2012).
10 Personal interview, Vinh, May 22, 2011.
11 Personal interview, Germany, August 17, 2015.
12 The poem excerpted in interlude 4, "High-Rise in Vinh," also had a line about urban sound: "Hurriedly and noisily we stomp up the stairs" (Đi vội vàng dẫm mạnh cầu thang).
13 Personal interview, Vinh, March 9, 2011.
14 Personal interview, Vinh, January 17, 2011.
15 See, for example, notable recent works by Nguyen (2016), Chalfin (2014), and Fredericks (2014).
16 Personal interview, Vinh, March 23, 2011.
17 Tủ An, "Xây dựng nếp sống mới ở tiểu khu Quang Trung" [Building a new way of life in Quang Trung], *Nghệ Tĩnh News*, May 26, 1981.
18 Personal interview, Vinh, February 26, 2011.
19 Personal interview, Vinh, April 23, 2011.
20 Municipal People's Committee, *Báo cáo hiện trạng thu gom—vận chuyển và xử lý chất thải rắn ở thành phố Vinh, Nghệ An* [Report on the current status of collection, transportation, and disposal of solid waste in Vinh City], 1997.

CHAPTER 8. DECAY

1 Based on field notes from September 2010.
2 David Lamb, "Country's Least Attractive City Trying to Put on a New Face," *Los Angeles Times*, July 9, 1999. I brought this article with me to the field. People who had shared information with Lamb were deeply offended by the portrayal.
3 Personal interview, Vinh, January 2, 2015.
4 Personal interview, Vinh, November 5, 2010.
5 Personal interview, Vinh, August 16, 2011.
6 A revised version of this ethnographic account can be found in Schwenkel (2015f).
7 My landlady had spent her early years in a thatched *nhà tập thể* until 1983, when her family of high-ranked educators was allocated a first-floor apartment in C2. A child of six at the time, she understood the move as a transition from vulnerability to security. In 2000, she obtained her own fourth-floor unit, where I lived during my fieldwork, while her parents remained on the first floor. Such expansion of kin networks across the complex was not uncommon: 32 percent of

surveyed households reported having family members in other apartments. As with my landlady's family, these were most often second-generation residents—the children of civil servants and workers—who had purchased user rights from departing tenants. Though these extended families might live in discontinuous space—on different floors, and often in different blocks—their lives were integrated and not unlike multigenerational households within a single spatial unit. For example, I observed that extended families continued to eat together, and grandparents minded grandchildren while parents were at work. The transfer of units among "insiders" meant that original residents and their kin remained a significant majority across the complex, close to 80 percent.

8 Quotes from field notes, December 20, 2010.

9 Công ty Nhà đất is the colloquial term that tenants used to refer to Công ty Cổ phần Quản lý và Phát triển Hạ tầng Đô thị Vinh, or Urban Infrastructure Development and Management Joint Stock Company (INFRAVI). Formed in 2005, INFRAVI is an example of an entrepreneurial bureaucracy: a quasi-private, government-controlled enterprise that facilitates urban development (McGee 2009, 239). State and private actors share 51 and 49 percent stakes in INFRAVI, respectively. Personal interview, INFRAVI Director, February 24, 2011.

10 Personal interview, Vinh, March 8, 2011.

11 Of the 60 percent that reported dangerous living conditions, 28 percent reported unsafe conditions within the home; 23 percent identified dangerous conditions outside (in corridors and stairways especially); and 9 percent reported both interior and exterior dangers.

12 Personal interview, Hanoi, August 5, 2011.

13 *Nội quy sử dụng nhà ở do nhà nước quản lý* [Regulations on the use of state managed housing], Vinh City, January 10, 1977.

14 Personal interview, Vinh, November 8, 2010. Planners contested this. Based on 2010 rates, rents brought the Housing Agency U.S. $2,000 per year, hardly enough for regular maintenance and repair. As early as 1991 (and before a new price table was instituted), stipulated rents were recognized as "irrational" and grossly insufficient for budgeted administration and maintenance costs (Nguyen 1991, 69).

15 Personal interview, Vinh, May 26, 2011.

16 Personal interview, Vinh, November 12, 2010.

17 This was not entirely true. As Alexander (2007a, 83–84) similarly noted of Almaty residents (Kazakhstan), in Quang Trung there was a common perception that utilities had been free during the subsidy years, though tenants had paid a nominal fee based on communal usage since individual meters did not exist at the time.

18 Personal interview, Vinh, December 2, 2010 (also quoted in Schwenkel 2018).

19 Personal interview, Vinh, January 17, 2011.

20 Personal interview, Vinh, March 9, 2011.

21 This section is adapted from Schwenkel (2015f).

22 "Gửi nhà máy nước Vinh" [To the water company of Vinh], *Nghệ An News*, July 1, 1986. The poem even claimed that the water sometimes had tadpoles swimming in it.

23 Personal interview, Vinh, April 9, 2011.
24 Personal interview, Vinh, December 18, 2010.
25 Personal interview, Vinh, March 22, 2011.
26 Personal interview, Vinh, March 20, 2011.
27 "Thấy gì trong việc cấp nước cho các khu nhà cao tầng ở thành phố Vinh" [Findings on the provisioning of water in high-rises in Vinh City], *Nghệ An News*, October 11, 1985.
28 Personal interview, Vinh, February 26, 2011.
29 For an analysis of the water fountain as spectacular infrastructure, see Schwenkel (2015f).
30 For example, Hồ Hà, "Chính sách chưa thông, dân không di dời" [Policy not yet given the clear; residents not to relocate], *Gia đình và Xã hội*, December 1, 2008, http://giadinh.net.vn/xa-hoi/chinh-sach-chua-thong-dan-khong-di-doi-20081201080236418.htm.
31 Personal interview, Vinh, June 1, 2011.
32 Personal interview, Vinh, November 8, 2010.
33 Field notes, May 25, 2011.
34 Personal interview, Vinh, February 24, 2011.
35 Personal interview, Vinh, September 29, 2010.
36 Personal interview, Vinh, January 18, 2011.
37 Mỹ Hà, "Di dời nhà C8 Quang Trung (TP Vinh): Cần hài hòa 3 lợi ích" [Relocation of block C8 in Quang Trung, Vinh: The need to balance three benefits], *Nghệ An News*, November 2, 2011.
38 Quote from field notes, November 3, 2010.

CHAPTER 9. RENOVATION

1 Though Teresa Caldeira recently challenged the term's spatial connotations: "What makes this process peripheral is not its physical location but rather the crucial role of residents in the production of space" (2017, 4).
2 Three-quarters of the 10 percent of households that reported no substantial renovations were in the worker blocks of area B and blocks C7, C8, and C9 (ward 9); the latter were the most dilapidated in the complex.
3 A total of 88 percent of surveyed households used propane gas stoves, and 32 percent used coal as a cheaper, supplementary cooking fuel. One in ten households used coal exclusively, and two households continued to cook with wood in the original *bếp củi*, or woodstove with ventilation duct designed by GDR engineers.
4 Vietnam has fifty-four officially recognized ethnic groups. The Kinh are the dominant group and represent approximately 86 percent of the population.
5 Note that the outward orientation of female areas and inward orientation of male spaces in Kinh architecture invert the cosmological duality of the Berber house, where women were "protected" from outside intrusions (Bourdieu 1970, 155).
6 Personal interview, Vinh, January 24, 2011.
7 Personal interview, Vinh, May 23, 2011.

8 Personal interview, Vinh, April 20, 2011.

9 Personal interview, Vinh, January 14, 2011. East German experts had been more concerned about pollution from kitchen smoke than contaminating bathroom odors since people cooked with woodstoves at the time. A kitchen in the back was thought to reduce health risks in the flat.

10 Personal interview, Vinh, March 4, 2011.

11 Personal interview, Vinh, April 25, 2011.

12 Personal interview, Vinh, March 5, 2011.

13 Personal interview, Vinh, May 22, 2011.

14 Karen Fjelstad (2006, 105–6) makes a similar observation about precarity and religious practice among Vietnamese refugees after their arrival in the United States.

15 Several people had individual shrines for deceased children, which were positioned below the ancestral altar. Some retired male cadres and cultural elites had simple shrines placed even lower to commemorate (*tưởng niệm*)—not worship (*thờ cúng*)—Hồ Chí Minh. Several families also maintained protective shrines in the corridor to prevent hungry, wandering souls from venturing inside. "No need to worry about ghosts from the war," the geomancer—who had fought on the battlefield in the South—reassured me, pointing to an altar he had constructed in the corridor (see plate 6). "They are well fed and at peace now."

16 Personal interview, Vinh, November 15, 2010.

17 Minh Cường, "Sẽ cưỡng chế các chung cư cũ không chịu di dời" [Forced relocation for residents in old housing who refuse to leave], *Vietnam Net*, December 16, 2015, http://vietnamnet.vn/vn/bat-dong-san/se-cuong-che-cac-chung-cu-cu-khong-chiu-di-doi-279205.html. According to this article, 100 percent of the fifteen hundred housing blocks in Hanoi have cơi nới attachments. This was far from the case for Vinh.

18 Nguyễn Tú, "Bó tay với nạn chung cư xây 'chuồng cọp'" [Apartment buildings and "tiger cages" go hand in hand], *Tiền phong*, November 26, 2012; "Lại tái phát cơi nới 'chuồng cọp'" [Back to the "tiger cage"], *Tin tức*, November 25, 2015.

19 Not to be confused with the notorious prison "tiger cages," referenced in chapter 6. None of my interlocutors made this connection.

20 Sanctions are increasing in cities with lucrative real estate markets. Most recently, Decree 139/2017/NĐ/CP has aimed to stop the practice of *phạt cho tồn tại* by requiring more remedial measures, especially for large investment projects that ignore regulations.

21 The toleration of small-scale illegal construction has been proposed as one explanation for why Hanoi does not have the "slums" of other industrializing countries with large informal settlements. See, for example, Lauren Quinn, "Hanoi: Is It Possible to Grow a City without Slums?," *The Guardian*, August 11, 2014.

22 Personal interview, Vinh, April 27, 2011.

23 Notable recent works that challenge these narratives include Caldeira (2017), Ghertner (2015), and Lombard (2014).

24 Personal interview, Vinh, April 20, 2011.

25 Personal interview, Vinh, May 24, 2011.

26 Poverty assessment is a relatively new and contested process in Vietnam (Nguyen and Tran 2014). In Quang Trung, different uses and meanings attach to the term "the poor," or *người nghèo*. Economically, the official designation *hộ nghèo*, or poor household, applied to urban families earning less than 500,000 VND (U.S. $25) monthly per person. Only four households in Quang Trung qualified as *hộ nghèo*, though many were *gia đình chính sách*, or policy families who received some state support for their personal losses in war. In the words of one housing activist in block C8, "No one is poor here! Everyone has a pension! There are people facing hardship, however." Personal interview, Vinh, January 20, 2011. People resisted being called poor for social reasons as well: in classic neoliberal form, poverty is increasingly cast as individual failure (Wacquant 2012) rather than tied to Buddhist notions of karma as previously understood. During the war, everyone was "equally poor," or *nghèo bằng nhau*, which lessened the stigma of poverty. Today, the inability of some cultural elites to improve their material conditions and move out of Quang Trung signals personal inadequacy to turn their social capital into economic gain. To some extent, this was a source of shame for those who stayed and a matter of speculation for those who left (who were also suspect for their wealth, I should add).

27 For more on this poet, including an analysis of his poems as expressions of his affective ties to energy infrastructure, see Schwenkel (2018).

28 Personal interview, Vinh, November 10, 2010.

29 The Central Committee's Decision 176/HĐBT, on the reorganization of labor in state-owned enterprises (*Quyết định về việc sắp xếp lại lao động trong các đơn vị kinh tế quốc doanh*), was ratified on October 9, 1989.

30 Personal interview, Vinh, April 9, 2011.

31 Informal or "second-economy" activities, which operated in the interstices of state-controlled planning and production (Verderey 1996, 211), were common under socialism. In Vietnam, factory workers and civil servants engaged in multiple family-based initiatives to survive the *thời bao cấp* years—for example, selling pigs raised in the apartments (see also Đặng P. 2009), which residents also did in Quang Trung. These survival strategies were largely tolerated by sympathetic authorities also struggling to survive. Respondents who engaged in such practices contrasted their actions with the stigmatized work of *con phe*, or market profiteers, keeping their moral worlds intact. This ethical distinction continued after reforms: "original" tenants (state employees) distinguished their livelihood activities from those of *mua lại* residents, whose work during the *bao cấp* years, often as traders, was beyond the purview of the state-run economy and therefore suspect. The Nghệ An press heightened such distrust with its postwar coverage of smuggling and sales of counterfeit goods in Vinh's marketplace by "*bọn*" vendors—a prefix indicating activities that undermined the revolution.

32 The trade center was eventually turned into a municipal library. In the fall of 2010, the library relocated to the outskirts of Vinh on Lenin Avenue, near the airport, and the trade center was demolished, along with a movie house from the 1950s that had been restored by the GDR after the war. A cinema multiplex, built in French colonial style, replaced it.

33 Personal interview, Vinh, December 14, 2011.

34 Signs posted around the complex read, "Nghiêm cấm mọi hình thức mua bán hàng rong trên khu vực nhà tầng" (All forms of vending within the buildings are prohibited).

CHAPTER 10. REVALUATION

1 For similar observations on China, see Ho (2015) and Zhang (2010).

2 Personal interview, Vinh, May 22, 2011.

3 Personal interview, Vinh, July 20, 2011.

4 I made this calculation using payment data collected from Quang Trung wardens and from interviews with residents and wardens in collective housing in Hanoi, some of whom received their flats at no cost because of the low market rate at the time combined with deductions for state service.

5 Personal interview, Vinh, June 3, 2011.

6 Personal interview, Vinh, May 27, 2011.

7 This account at the tea stall appeared in altered form in Schwenkel (2015c).

8 Price per square meter was calculated according to floor level and building condition. The first floor average was 1.5 million VND (U.S. $75); the second, 1.14 million VND (U.S. $57); the third, 960,000 VND (U.S. $48); the fourth, 800,000 VND (U.S. $40); and 600,000 VND (U.S. $30) on the fifth floor, which was usually the most dilapidated.

9 On *bức xúc* as exasperated response to perceived bureaucratic injustice, see Harms (2012).

10 These deductions, which applied to 80 percent of households in Quang Trung, impacted women disproportionately, since "military service" did not include the youth volunteer forces (*thanh niên xung phong*), which had comprised mostly women working on the Hồ Chí Minh Trail and those who had built Quang Trung. Credit was also granted to people with *công với cách mạng*, who had contributed to the revolution, as per Decision 118-TTg of 1996. This included families of fallen soldiers, heroic mothers, war invalids, and former prisoners of war. From half to two-thirds of the households in each building received this adjustment to their apartment price.

11 Personal interview, Vinh, July 10, 2011.

12 Personal interview, Vinh, July 21, 2011.

13 Personal interview, Vinh, July 21, 2011.

14 Personal interview, Vinh, April 26, 2011.

15 Personal interview, Vinh, April 11, 2011.

16 TECCO is a joint-stock technology and construction company based in Ho Chi Minh City.

17 "Nhà ở C1 Quang Trung thành phố Vinh: Lý tưởng cho cuộc sống gia đình" [Quang Trung C1 housing block in Vinh City: Ideal family living], *Lao động Nghệ An*, February 7, 2007.

18 Personal interview, Vinh, December 21, 2011.

19 The other 10 percent had either traded or inherited their flats. Note that *mua lại* tenants included family of original tenants, who also worked for the state (approximately

5 percent of the total number of *mua lại*). Survey statistics showed that original residents stayed longer in Quang Trung when they lived in predominantly worker wards, compared with wards housing more upwardly mobile cultural elites.

20 Personal interview, Vinh, May 22, 2011.

21 Personal interview, Vinh, April 19, 2011.

22 During my research in 2010–2011, the city was struggling to develop its international portfolio, and municipal officials frequently asked me how Vinh could attract foreign investment, or ODA (Official Development Assistance), funds to help grow the city. There was virtually no international tourism to Vinh, and few foreigners resided in the city. The transformation of the city over the past two decades that I have witnessed (2000–2019) has been propelled by domestic ventures mostly.

23 The neighboring Mường Thanh Luxury Sông Lam hotel extends to thirty-three stories; its modern rooftop bar commands the best view of the city, making the no-frills TECCO café on the eighteenth story, which had been a center of nightlife during my research, now obsolete.

24 Personal interview, Vinh, July 20, 2011.

25 Personal interview, Vinh, May 27, 2011.

26 Personal interview, Vinh, November 12, 2011.

27 For ethnographic accounts, see, for example, Pozniak (2014), Fehérváry (2013), and Zhang (2010).

28 Personal interview, Vinh, April 24, 2011.

29 Personal interview, Vinh, January 8, 2011.

30 Personal interview, Vinh, December 19, 2017.

31 Personal interview, Vinh, January 11, 2015.

32 Hoàng Vĩnh, "Nhiều vướng mắc trong giải phóng mặt bằng" [Problems with land clearance], *Nghệ An News*, September 4, 2011.

33 Personal interview, Vinh, November 3, 2010.

34 Because her pension placed her above the poverty line, Hiền did not qualify for lower-interest loans from a state bank.

35 The accounts of Hiền's and Ngọc's lives are based on a series of conversations from November 2010 through May 2011.

36 Personal interview, Vinh, January 20, 2011.

CONCLUSION

1 Though Buck-Morss writes of intangible memories and images, these fragments are also material. See Schwenkel (2014b) on the use and circulation of GDR material culture in Vinh and Vietnam more widely, where it continues to hold value.

2 Starostina (2009) makes a similar argument about French colonial engineering in Vietnam.

3 Personal interview, Vinh, September 28, 2010.

4 Personal interview, Vinh, January 17, 2011.

REFERENCES

Agamben, Giorgio. 1998. *Homo Sacer: Sovereign Power and Bare Life*. Translated by Daniel Heller-Roazen. Stanford, CA: Stanford University Press.

———. 2005. *State of Exception*. Translated by Kevin Attell. Chicago: University of Chicago Press.

Ahmed, Sara. 2010. *The Promise of Happiness*. Durham, NC: Duke University Press.

Akcan, Esra. 2012. *Architecture in Translation: Germany, Turkey, and the Modern House*. Durham, NC: Duke University Press.

———. 2018. *Open Architecture: Migration, Citizenship, and the Urban Renewal of Berlin-Kreuzberg by* IBA*-1984/87*. Basel: Birkhäuser.

Alexander, Catherine. 2007a. "Almaty: Rethinking the Public Sector." In *Urban Life in Post-Soviet Asia*, edited by Catherine Alexander, Victor Buchli, and Caroline Humphrey, 70–101. London: UCL Press.

———. 2007b. "Soviet and Post-Soviet Planning in Almaty, Kazakhstan." *Critique of Anthropology* 27(2):165–81.

Alter, Nora M. 1997. "Excessive Pre/Requisites: Vietnam through the East German Lens." *Cultural Critique* 35(1):39–79.

Amin, Ash. 2006. "The Good City." *Urban Studies* 43(5/6):1009–23.

Anand, Nikhil. 2011. "Pressure: The Politechnics of Water Supply in Mumbai." *Cultural Anthropology* 26(4):542–64.

———. 2012. "Municipal Disconnect: On Abject Water and Its Urban Infrastructures." *Ethnography* 13(4):487–509.

———. 2017. *Hydraulic City: Water and the Infrastructures of Citizenship in Mumbai*. Durham, NC: Duke University Press.

Anderson, Ben. 2006. "'Transcending without Transcendence': Utopianism and an Ethos of Hope." *Antipode* 38(4):691–710.

———. 2009. "Affective Atmospheres." *Emotion, Space and Society* 2(2):77–81.

Appadurai, Arjun. 1996. *Modernity at Large: Cultural Dimensions of Globalization*. Minneapolis: University of Minnesota Press.

———. 2004. "The Capacity to Aspire: Culture and the Terms of Recognition." In *Culture and Public Action*, edited by Vijayendra Rao and Michael Walton, 59–84. Stanford, CA: Stanford University Press.

Appy, Christian G. 1993. *Working-Class War: American Combat Soldiers and Vietnam*. Chapel Hill, NC: University of North Carolina Press.

Arendt, Hannah. (1963) 2006. *On Revolution*. New York: Penguin Books.

Armstrong, Charles K. 2005. "'Fraternal Socialism': The International Reconstruction of North Korea, 1953–62." *Cold War History* 5(2):161–87.

Atanasovski, Srđan. 2016. "'The Song Has Kept Us': Soundscape of Belgrade during the NATO Bombing." *Südosteuropa* 64(4):482–99.

Attwood, Lynne. 2017. *Gender and Housing in Soviet Russia: Private Life in a Public Space*. Manchester, UK: Manchester University Press.

Author collective. 1972. *Wohngebiete: Grundsätze und Kennziffern zur Erarbeitung von Bebauungskonzeptionen* [Residential areas: Principles and indicators for the development of housing design]. Berlin: Institute for Urban Planning and Architecture, Bk. 42.

Azoulay, Ariella. 2012. *Civil Imagination: A Political Ontology of Photography*. Translated by Louise Bethlehem. New York: Verso.

Babül, Elif M. 2017. *Bureaucratic Intimacies: Translating Human Rights in Turkey*. Stanford, CA: Stanford University Press.

Bach, Jonathan. 2017. *What Remains. Everyday Encounters with the Socialist Past in Germany*. New York: Columbia University Press.

Baldwin, Kate A. 2015. *The Racial Imaginary of the Cold War Kitchen: From Sokol'niki Park to Chicago's South Side*. Hanover, NH: Dartmouth College Press.

Bảo Ninh. 1993. *The Sorrow of War*. Translated by Phan Thanh Hao. New York: Riverhead Books.

Barnett, Michael. 2011. *Empire of Humanity: A History of Humanitarianism*. Ithaca, NY: Cornell University Press.

Baudrillard, Jean. 1994. *Simulacra and Simulation*. Translated by Sheila Faria Glaser. Ann Arbor: University of Michigan Press.

Bauman, Zygmunt. 1976. *Socialism: The Active Utopia*. London: George Allen and Unwin.

———. 1993. "The Sweet Smell of Decomposition." In *Forget Baudrillard?*, edited by Chris Rojek and Bryan S. Turner, 22–46. New York: Routledge.

Bayat, Asef. 2013. *Life as Politics: How Ordinary People Change the Middle East*. 2nd ed. Stanford, CA: Stanford University Press.

Bayly, Susan. 2008. "Vietnamese Narratives of Tradition, Exchange and Friendship in the Worlds of the Global Socialist Ecumene." In *Enduring Socialism. Explorations of Revolution and Transformation, Restoration and Continuation*, edited by Harry West and Parvathi Raman, 125–47. Oxford: Berghahn Books.

Bélanger, Danièle, and Jianye Liu. 2004. "Social Policy Reforms and Daughters' Schooling in Vietnam." *International Journal of Educational Development* 24(1):23–38.

Bélanger, Danièle, Lisa B. Welch Drummond, and Van Nguyen-Marshall. 2012. "Introduction: Who Are the Urban Middle Class in Vietnam?" In *The Reinvention of Distinction: Modernity and the Middle Class in Urban Vietnam*, edited by Van Nguyen-Marshall, Lisa B. Welch Drummond, and Danièle Bélanger, 1–17. New York: Springer.

Benjamin, Walter. (1963) 2009. *The Origin of German Tragic Drama*. Translated by John Osborne. New York: Verso.

———. 1969a. *Charles Baudelaire: A Lyric Poet in the Era of High Capitalism.* Translated by Harry Zohn. New York: Verso.

———. 1969b. *Illuminations.* Edited by Hannah Arendt. Translated by Harry Zohn. New York: Schocken Books.

———. 1978. *Reflections: Essays, Aphorisms, Autobiographical Writings.* Translated by Peter Demetz. New York: Verso.

———. 1999. *The Arcades Project.* Translated by Howard Eiland and Kevin McLaughlin. Cambridge, MA: Harvard University Press.

Berdahl, Daphne. 1999. *Where the World Ended: Re-unification and Identity in the German Borderland.* Berkeley: University of California Press.

Berlant, Lauren. 2011. *Cruel Optimism.* Durham, NC: Duke University Press.

Betts, Paul. 2008. "Building Socialism at Home: The Case of East German Interiors." In *Socialist Modern: East German Everyday Culture and Politics*, edited by Katherine Pence and Paul Betts, 96–132. Ann Arbor: University of Michigan Press.

———. 2012. "Socialism, Social Rights, and Human Rights: The Case of East Germany." *Humanity: An International Journal of Human Rights, Humanitarianism, and Development* 3(3):407–26.

Bevan, Robert. 2006. *The Destruction of Memory: Architecture at War.* London: Reaktion.

Beyer, Elke. 2011. "Planning for Mobility: Designing City Centers and New Towns in the USSR and the GDR in the 1960s." In *The Socialist Car: Automobility in the Eastern Bloc*, edited by Louis Siegelbaum, 71–91. Ithaca, NY: Cornell University Press.

———. 2012. "Competitive Coexistence: Soviet Town Planning and Housing Projects in Kabul in the 1960s." *The Journal of Architecture* 17(3):309–32.

Bhabha, Homi K. 1994. *The Location of Culture.* New York: Routledge.

Biehl, João, and Peter Locke. 2010. "Deleuze and the Anthropology of Becoming." *Current Anthropology* 51(3):317–51.

Bittner, Stephen V. 1998. "Green Cities and Orderly Streets: Space and Culture in Moscow, 1928–1933." *Journal of Urban History* 25(1):22–56.

Bloch, Ernst. (1954) 1986. *The Principle of Hope.* Vol. 1. Translated by Neville Plaice, Stephen Plaice, and Paul Knight. Cambridge, MA: MIT Press.

Bockman, Johanna. 2015. "Socialist Globalization against Capitalist Neocolonialism: The Economic Ideas behind the New International Economic Order." *Humanity* 6(1):109–28.

Boltanski, Luc. 1999. *Distant Suffering: Morality, Media, and Politics.* Translated by Graham Burchell. Cambridge: Cambridge University Press.

Boudon, Philippe. 1972. *Lived-in Architecture: Le Corbusier's Pessac Revisited.* Translated by Gerald Onn. Cambridge, MA: MIT Press.

Bourdieu, Pierre. 1970. "The Berber House or the World Reversed." *Social Science Information* 9:151–70.

———. 1984. *Distinction: A Social Critique of the Judgment of Taste.* Translated by Richard Nice. Cambridge, MA: Harvard University Press.

Boyer, Dominic. 2006. "Ostalgie and the Politics of the Future in East Germany." *Public Culture* 18(2):361–81.

Boyer, M. Christine. 1983. *Dreaming the Rational City: The Myth of American City Planning*. Cambridge, MA: MIT Press.

Boym, Svetlana. 1994. *Common Places: Mythologies of Everyday Life in Russia*. Cambridge, MA: Harvard University Press.

———. 2008. *Architecture of the Off-Modern*. New York: Architectural Press.

Bradley, Mark Philip. 2004. "Becoming 'Van Minh': Civilizational Discourse and Visions of the Self in Twentieth-Century Vietnam." *Journal of World History* 15(1):65–83.

Bray, David. 2005. *Social Space and Governance in Urban China: The Danwei System from Origins to Urban Reform*. Stanford, CA: Stanford University Press.

Brody, David. 2010. *Visualizing American Empire: Orientalism and Imperialism in the Philippines*. Chicago: University of Chicago Press.

Browitt, Jeff. 2017. "The Garage as Vernacular Museum: Reading Contemporary Masculinity through 'Man Caves.'" In *Reimagining Home in the 21st Century*, edited by Justine Lloyd and Ellie Vasta, 207–23. Northampton, MA: Edward Elgar.

Brown, Kate. 2015. *Dispatches from Dystopia: Histories of Places Not Yet Forgotten*. Chicago: University of Chicago Press.

Buchli, Victor. 1999. *An Archaeology of Socialism*. New York: Berg.

———. 2013. *An Anthropology of Architecture*. New York: Bloomsbury.

Buck-Morss, Susan. 2000. *Dreamworld and Catastrophe: The Passing of Mass Utopia in East and West*. Cambridge, MA: MIT Press.

Bùi Thiết. 1984. *Vinh—Bến Thuỷ*. Hanoi: Văn hóa.

Bunnell, Tim, and Daniel P. S. Goh, eds. 2018. *Urban Asias: Essays on Futurity Past and Present*. Berlin: Jovis.

Bunnell, Tim, and Anant Maringanti. 2010. "Practising Urban and Regional Research beyond Metrocentricity." *International Journal of Urban and Regional Research* 34(2):415–20.

Butler, Judith. 2004. *Precarious Life: The Powers of Mourning and Violence*. New York: Verso.

———. 2009. *Frames of War: When Is Life Grievable?* New York: Verso.

———. 2015. *Notes toward a Performative Theory of Assembly*. Cambridge, MA: Harvard University Press.

Butter, Andreas. 2017. "Showcase and Window to the World: East German Architecture Abroad 1949–1990." *Planning Perspectives* 33(2):249–69.

Cairns, Stephen, and Jane M. Jacobs. 2014. *Buildings Must Die: A Perverse View of Architecture*. Cambridge, MA: MIT Press.

Caldeira, Teresa P. R. 2017. "Peripheral Urbanization: Autoconstruction, Transversal Logics, and Politics in Cities of the Global South." *Environment and Planning D: Society and Space* 35(1):3–20.

Cao, A. D. 1978. "Development Planning in Vietnam: A Problem of Postwar Transition." *Asia Quarterly* 4:263–76.

Carsten, Janet. 2019. *Blood Work: Life and Laboratories in Penang*. Durham, NC: Duke University Press.

Casey, Edward S. 2001. "Between Geography and Philosophy: What Does It Mean to Be in the Place-World?" *Annals of the Association of American Geographers* 91(4):683–93.

Castells, Manuel. 1977. *The Urban Question: A Marxist Approach*. Cambridge, MA: MIT Press.

Castillo, Greg. 2007. "Promoting Socialist Cities and Citizens: East Germany's National Building Program." In *Selling Modernity: Advertising in Twentieth-Century Germany*, edited by Pamela E. Swett, S. Jonathan Wiesen, and Jonathan R. Zatlin, 289–306. Durham, NC: Duke University Press.

———. 2010. *Cold War on the Home Front: The Soft Power of Midcentury Design*. Minneapolis: University of Minnesota Press.

Chalfin, Brenda. 2014. "Public Things, Excremental Politics, and the Infrastructure of Bare Life in Ghana's City of Tema." *American Ethnologist* 41(1):92–109.

Chen, Kuan-Hsing. 2010. *Asia as Method: Toward Deimperialization*. Durham, NC: Duke University Press.

Chin, Rita, and Heide Fehrenbach. 2009. "Social History, Popular Culture, and Politics." In *After the Nazi Racial State: Difference and Democracy in Germany and Europe*, edited by Rita Chin, Heide Fehrenbach, Geoff Eley, and Atina Grossmann, 102–36. Ann Arbor: University of Michigan Press.

Chow, Rey. 2006. *The Age of the World Target: Self-Referentiality in War, Theory, and Comparative Work*. Durham, NC: Duke University Press.

Chu, Julie. 2014. "When Infrastructures Attack: The Workings of Disrepair in China." *American Ethnologist* 14(2):351–67.

Chu Trọng Huyến. 1998. *Lịch sử thành phố Vinh, tập 1* [History of Vinh City, volume 1]. Vinh: Nghệ An.

———. 2004. *Tìm hiểu tính cách người Nghệ* [Understanding the character of Nghệ people]. Vinh: Nghệ An.

Clarke, Alison J. 2001. "The Aesthetics of Social Aspiration." In *Home Possessions: Material Culture behind Closed Doors*, edited by Daniel Miller, 23–45. Oxford: Berg.

Clodfelter, Mark. 2006. *The Limits of Air Power: The American Bombing of North Vietnam*. Lincoln: University of Nebraska Press.

Clodfelter, Micheal. 1995. *Vietnam in Military Statistics: A History of the Indochina Wars, 1772–1991*. Jefferson, NC: McFarland.

———. 2017. *Warfare and Armed Conflicts: A Statistical Encyclopedia of Casualty and Other Figures, 1492–2015*. Jefferson, NC: McFarland and Co.

Cohen, Jean-Louis. 1992. *Le Corbusier and the Mystique of the USSR: Theories and Projects for Moscow, 1928–1936*. Translated by Kenneth Hylton. Princeton, NJ: Princeton University Press.

Cooren, François. 2004. "Textual Agency: How Texts Do Things in Organizational Settings." *Organization* 11(3):373–93.

Corbain, Alain. 1986. *The Foul and the Fragrant: Odor and the French Social Imagination*. Cambridge, MA: Harvard University Press.

Cowan, Alexander, and Jill Steward, eds. 2007. *The City and the Senses: Urban Culture Since 1500*. Burlington, VT: Ashgate.

Coward, Martin. 2008. *Urbicide: The Politics of Urban Destruction*. New York: Routledge.

Crew, David. 2017. *Bodies and Ruins: Imagining the Bombing of Germany, 1945 to the Present*. Ann Arbor: University of Michigan Press.

Crowley, David, and Susan E. Reid. 2002. *Socialist Spaces: Sites of Everyday Life in the Eastern Bloc*. Oxford: Berg.

Dalakoglou, Dimitris. 2012. "'The Road from Capitalism to Capitalism': Infrastructures of (Post)Socialism in Albania." *Mobilities* 7(4):571–86.

Đàm Trung Phường. 2005. *Đô thị Việt Nam* [Urban Vietnam]. Hanoi: Xây dựng.

Đặng Phong. 2009. *Tư duy kinh tế Việt Nam 1975–1989: Nhật ký thời bao cấp* [Vietnamese economic thought, 1975–1989: Memoir of the subsidy era]. Hanoi: Tri thức.

Đặng Thái Hoàng. 1985. *Kiến trúc Hà Nội thế kỷ XIX và XX* [Hanoi architecture in the nineteenth and twentieth centuries]. Hanoi: Xây dựng.

———. 2009. *Kiến trúc nhà ở* [Architecture of housing]. Hanoi: Xây dựng.

Daniels, Inge. 2010. *The Japanese House: Material Culture in the Modern Home*. London: Bloomsbury.

Dao Van Tap. 1980. "On the Transformation and New Distribution of Population Centers in the Socialist Republic of Vietnam." *International Journal of Urban and Regional Research* 4(4):503–15.

Datta, Ayona. 2015. "New Urban Utopias of Postcolonial India: 'Entrepreneurial Urbanization' in Dholera Smart City, Gujarat." *Dialogues in Human Geography* 5(1):3–22.

Daughtry, J. Martin. 2015. *Listening to War: Sound, Music, Trauma, and Survival in Wartime Iraq*. New York: Oxford University Press.

Dawdy, Shannon Lee. 2010. "Clockpunk Anthropology and the Ruins of Modernity." *Current Anthropology* 51(6):761–93.

———. 2016. *Patina: A Profane Archaeology*. Chicago: Chicago University Press.

Day, Tony, and Maya H. T. Liem, eds. 2010. *Cultures at War: The Cold War and Cultural Expression in Southeast Asia*. Ithaca, NY: Cornell Southeast Asia Program Publications.

de Certeau, Michel. 1984. *The Practice of Everyday Life*. Translated by Steven Rendall. Berkeley: University of California Press.

de Graaf, Reinier. 2015. "Architecture Is Now a Tool of Capital, Complicit in a Purpose Antithetical to Its Social Mission." *Architectural Review*. Accessed February 24, 2019. www.architectural-review.com/8681564.

De Landa, Manuel. 1991. *War in the Age of Intelligent Machines*. New York: Zone Books.

Del Testa, David. 1999. "'Imperial Corridor': Association, Transportation and Power in French Colonial Indochina." *Science, Technology, Society* 4(2):319–54.

———. 2007. "Vinh, the Seed That Would Grow Red: Colonial Prelude, Revolutionary City." *Historical Reflections/Réflexions Historiques* 33(2):305–25.

———. 2011. "Vietnamese Railway Workers during the Revolutionary High Tide." *South East Asia Research* 19(4):787–816.

Derrida, Jacques. 1990. "A Letter to Peter Eisenman." *Assemblage* 12:7–13.

de Seversky, Alexander P. 1942. *Victory through Air Power*. New York: Simon and Schuster.

DeSilvey, Caitlin. 2006. "Observed Decay: Telling Stories with Mutable Things." *Journal of Material Culture* 11(3):318–38.

DeSilvey, Caitlin, and Tim Edensor. 2012. "Reckoning with Ruins." *Progress in Human Geography* 37(4):465–85.

Desmond, Jane C. 1999. *Staging Tourism: Bodies on Display from Waikiki to Sea World*. Chicago: University of Chicago Press.

District People's Committee. 2007. *Lịch sử khu Quang Trung, thành phố Vinh* [History of Quang Trung District, Vinh City]. Vinh: Nghệ An.

Douglas, Mary. 1966. *Purity and Danger: An Analysis of Concepts of Pollution and Taboo*. New York: Routledge.

Dovey, Kim. 2010. *Becoming Places: Urbanism/Architecture/Identity/Power*. New York: Routledge.

Drummond, Lisa. 2000. "Street Scenes: Practices of Public and Private Space in Urban Vietnam." *Urban Studies* 37(12):2377–91.

Dunn, Elizabeth C. 2004. *Privatizing Poland: Baby Food, Big Business, and the Remaking of Labor*. Ithaca, NY: Cornell University Press.

Dutton, George E. 2006. *The Tây Sơn Uprising: Society and Rebellion in Eighteenth-Century Vietnam*. Honolulu: University of Hawai'i Press.

Edensor, Tim. 2005. *Industrial Ruins: Spaces, Aesthetics and Materiality*. Oxford: Berg.

Edwards, Elizabeth. 1999. "Photographs as Objects of Memory." In *Material Memories*, edited by Marius Kwint, Christopher Breward, and Jeremy Aynsley, 221–36. Oxford: Berg.

Ehrenfeld, Daniel. 2004. "Foreign Aid Effectiveness, Political Rights and Bilateral Distribution." *Journal of Humanitarian Assistance*. Accessed April 15, 2018. https://sites.tufts.edu/jha/archives/75.

Elias, Norbert. (1969) 1994. *The Civilizing Process*. Oxford: Blackwell.

Endres, Kirsten W. 2014. "Making Law: Small-Scale Trade and Corrupt Exceptions at the Vietnam–China Border." *American Anthropologist* 116(3):611–25.

———. 2019. *Market Frictions. Trade and Urbanization at the Vietnam-China Border*. New York: Berghahn Books.

Engels, Frederick. (1872) 1979. *The Housing Question*. Moscow: Progress Publishers.

Errington, Shelly. 1990. "Recasting Sex, Gender, and Power: A Theoretical and Regional Overview." In *Power and Difference: Gender in Island Southeast Asia*, edited by Jane Atkinson and Shelly Errington, 1–58. Stanford, CA: Stanford University Press.

Espiritu, Yến Lê. 2014. *Body Counts: The Vietnam War and Militarized Refuge(es)*. Berkeley: University of California Press.

Fabian, Johannes. 1983. *Time and the Other: How Anthropology Makes Its Object*. New York: Columbia University Press.

Fassin, Didier. 2011. *Humanitarian Reason: A Moral History of the Present*. Berkeley: University of California Press.

Fehérváry, Krisztina. 2012. "From Socialist Modern to Super-Natural Organicism: Cosmological Transformations through Home Decor." *Cultural Anthropology* 27(4):615–41.

———. 2013. *Politics in Color and Concrete: Socialist Materialities and the Middle Class in Hungary*. Bloomington: Indiana University Press.

Feldman, Allen. 1991. *Formations of Violence: The Narrative of the Body and Political Terror in Northern Ireland*. Chicago: University of Chicago Press.

———. 2015. *Archives of the Insensible: Of War, Photopolitics and Dead Memory*. Chicago: University of Chicago Press.

Felski, Rita. 1989. *Beyond Feminist Aesthetics: Feminist Literature and Social Change*. Cambridge, MA: Harvard University Press.

Fennell, Catherine. 2012. "The Museum of Resilience: Raising a Sympathetic Public in Post-Welfare Chicago. *Cultural Anthropology* 27(4):641–66.

———. 2015. *Last Project Standing: Civics and Sympathy in Post-Welfare Chicago*. Minneapolis: University of Minnesota Press.

Ferguson, James. 1999. *Expectations of Modernity: Myths and Meanings of Urban Life on the Zambian Copperbelt*. Berkeley: University of California Press.

Fischer, Jack C. 1962. "Planning the City of Socialist Man." *Journal of the American Institute of Planners* 18(4):251–65.

Fischlin, Daniel, Ajay Heble, and George Lipsitz. 2013. *The Fierce Urgency of Now: Improvisation, Rights, and the Ethics of Cocreation*. Durham, NC: Duke University Press.

Fjelstad, Karen. 2006. "'We Have *Len Dong* Too': Transnational Aspects of Spirit Possession." In *Possessed by the Spirits: Mediumship in Contemporary Vietnamese Communities*, edited by Karen Fjelstad and Nguyen Thi Hien, 95–110. Ithaca, NY: Cornell Southeast Asia Program.

Flierl, Bruno. 1998. *Gebaute DDR: Über Stadtplaner, Architekten und die Macht. Kritische Reflexionen 1990–1997* [Built GDR: On city planners, architects and power. Critical reflections 1990–1997]. Berlin: Verlag für Bauwesen.

Foreign Languages Publishing House. 1958. *President Ho Chi Minh's Friendly Visit to the German Democratic Republic*. Hanoi.

Foster, Robert J. 2008. "Commodities, Brands, Love and Kula: Comparative Notes on Value Creation in Honor of Nancy Munn." *Anthropological Theory* 8(1):9–25.

Foucault, Michel. 1977. *Discipline and Punish: Birth of the Prison*. Translated by Alan Sheridan. New York: Vintage Books.

———. 1980. *Power/Knowledge: Selected Interviews and Other Writings 1972–1977*. Edited and translated by Colin Gordon. New York: Pantheon Books.

———. 1984. "Space, Knowledge, Power." In *The Foucault Reader*, edited by Paul Rabinow, 239–56. New York: Penguin.

———. 1986. "Of Other Spaces." *Diacritics* 16(1):22–27.

———. 2007. *Security, Territory, Population: Lectures at the Collège de France, 1977–78*. Translated by Graham Burchell. New York: Picador.

Fox, Diane Niblack. 2007. "One Significant Ghost: Agent Orange Narratives of Trauma, Survival, and Responsibility." PhD diss., University of Washington.

Fox, Thomas C. 2006. "East Germany and the Bombing War." In *Bombs Away! Representing the Air War over Europe and Japan*, edited by Wilfried Wilms and William Rasch, 113–30. Amsterdam: Rodopi.

Fredericks, Rosalind. 2014. "Vital Infrastructures of Trash in Dakar." *Comparative Studies of South Asia, Africa and the Middle East* 34(3):532–48.

Freeman, Carla. 2014. *Entrepreneurial Selves: Neoliberal Respectability and the Making of a Caribbean Middle Class*. Durham, NC: Duke University Press.

Freytag, Mirjam. 1998. *Die 'Moritzburger' in Vietnam: Lebenswege nach einem Schul- und Ausbildungsaufenthalt in der DDR—Vermitteln in interkulturellen Beziehungen* [The 'Moritzburger' in Vietnam: Life after schooling and education in the GDR—Mediation in intercultural relations]. Frankfurt: IKO Verlag.

Friedman, Sara L. 2006. *Intimate Politics: Marriage, the Market, and State Power in Southeastern China*. Cambridge, MA: Harvard University Press.

Friedmann, John. 2000. "The Good City: In Defense of Utopian Thinking." *International Journal of Urban and Regional Research* 24(2):460–72.

———. 2010. "Place and Place-Making in Cities: A Global Perspective." *Planning Theory and Practice* 11(2):149–65.

Fuerst, J. S. 2003. *When Public Housing Was Paradise: Building Community in Chicago*. Westport, CT: Praeger.

Gaiduk, Ilya V. 2003. *Confronting Vietnam: Soviet Policy toward the Indochina Conflict, 1954–1963*. Stanford, CA: Stanford University Press.

Gal, Susan, and Gail Kligman. 2000. *The Politics of Gender after Socialism*. Princeton, NJ: Princeton University Press.

Gandy, Matthew. 2004. "Rethinking Urban Metabolism: Water, Space and the Modern City." *City* 8(3):363–79.

———. 2006. "The Bacteriological City and Its Discontents." *Historical Geography* 34:14–25.

———. 2014. *The Fabric of Space: Water, Modernity, and the Urban Imagination*. Cambridge, MA: MIT Press.

Gell, Alfred. 1998. *Art and Agency: An Anthropological Theory*. Oxford: Clarendon Press.

Ghertner, D. Asher. 2015. *Rule by Aesthetics: World-Class City Making in Delhi*. Oxford: Oxford University Press.

Ghodsee, Kristen. 2005. *The Red Riviera: Gender, Tourism, and Postsocialism on the Black Sea*. Durham, NC: Duke University Press.

Gibson, James W. 1986. *The Perfect War: Technowar in Vietnam*. New York: Random House.

Gibson-Graham, J. K. 1996. *The End of Capitalism (As We Knew It): A Feminist Critique of Political Economy*. Cambridge, MA: Blackwell.

Gidwani, Vinay. 2010. "Remaindered Things and Remaindered Lives: Travelling with Delhi's Waste." In *Finding Delhi: Loss and Renewal in the Megacity*, edited by Bharati Chaturvedi, 37–54. New York: Viking.

Gidwani, Vinay, and Rajyashree N. Reddy. 2011. "The Afterlives of 'Waste': Notes from India for a Minor History of Capitalist Surplus." *Antipode* 43(5):1625–58.

Goodkind, Daniel M. 1995. "Vietnam's One-or-Two-Child Policy in Action." *Population and Development Review* 21(1):85–111.

Goodman, Steve. 2010. *Sonic Warfare: Sound, Affect, and the Ecology of Fear.* Cambridge, MA: MIT Press.

Gordillo, Gastón. 2014. *Rubble: The Afterlife of Destruction.* Durham, NC: Duke University Press.

Goscha, Christopher E. 2006. "Courting Diplomatic Disaster? The Difficult Integration of Vietnam into the Internationalist Communist Movement (1945–1950)." *Journal of Vietnamese Studies* 1(1–2):59–103.

Gough, Katherine V., and Hoai Anh Tran. 2009. "Changing Housing Policy in Vietnam: Emerging Inequalities in a Residential Area of Hanoi." *Cities* 26:175–86.

Graham, Stephen. 2005. "Switching Cities Off: Urban Infrastructure and US Air Power." *City* 9(2):169–93.

Graham, Stephen, and Nigel Thrift. 2007. "Out of Order: Understanding Repair and Maintenance." *Theory, Culture and Society* 24(3):1–25.

Gregory, Derek. 2013. "Lines of Descent." In *From Above: The Politics and Practice of the View from the Skies*, edited by Peter Adey, Mark Whitehead, and Alison J. Williams, 41–70. London: Hurst.

———. 2016. "The Natures of War." *Antipode* 48(1):3–56.

Grossheim, Martin. 2014. "Stasi Aid and the Modernization of the Vietnamese Secret Police." *Cold War International History Project, E-Dossier No. 51.* Wilson Center. Accessed July 28, 2017. www.wilsoncenter.org/publication/stasi-aid-and-the-modernization-the-vietnamese-secret-police.

Guattari, Felix. 1995. "On Machines." *Journal of Philosophy and the Visual Arts* 6:8–12.

Gupta, Akhil. 2012. *Red Tape: Bureaucracy, Structural Violence, and Poverty in India.* Durham, NC: Duke University Press.

Hải Ninh, dir. 1974. *Em bé Hà Nội* [Little girl of Hanoi]. Hãng phim truyện Việt Nam.

Hansen, Arve. 2016. "Driving Development? The Problems and Promises of the Car in Vietnam." *Journal of Contemporary Asia* 46(4):551–69.

Hansen, Miriam Bratu. 2008. "Benjamin's Aura." *Critical Inquiry* 34(2):336–75.

Haraway, Donna. 1988. "Situated Knowledges: The Science Question in Feminism as a Site of Discourse on the Privilege of Partial Perspective." *Feminist Studies* 14(3):575–99.

Harms, Erik. 2009. "Vietnam's Civilizing Process and the Retreat from the Street: A Turtle's Eye View from Ho Chi Minh City." *City and Society* 21(2):182–206.

———. 2011. *Saigon's Edge: On the Margins of Ho Chi Minh City.* Minneapolis: University of Minnesota Press.

———. 2012. "Beauty as Control in the New Saigon." *American Ethnologist* 39(4):735–50.

———. 2013. "Eviction Time in the New Saigon: Temporalities of Displacement in the Rubble of Development." *Cultural Anthropology* 28(2):344–68.

———. 2016. *Luxury and Rubble: Civility and Dispossession in the New Saigon.* Berkeley: University of California Press.

Harper, Krista. 2005. "'Wild Capitalism' and 'Ecocolonialism': A Tale of Two Rivers." *American Anthropologist* 107(2):221–33.

Harris, Steven. 2013. *Communism on Tomorrow Street: Mass Housing and Everyday Life under Stalin*. Baltimore: Johns Hopkins University Press.

Harrison, James P. 1993. "History's Heaviest Bombing." In *The Vietnam War: Vietnamese and American Perspectives*, edited by Jayne S. Werner and Luu Doan Huynh, 130–39. New York: Routledge.

Hart, Keith, and Horacio Ortiz. 2014. "The Anthropology of Money and Finance: Between Ethnography and World History." *Annual Review of Anthropology* 43(1):465–82.

Harvey, David. 2000. *Spaces of Hope*. Berkeley: University of California Press.

———. 2003. *The New Imperialism*. New York: Oxford University Press.

Harvey, Penny, and Hannah Knox. 2015. *Roads: An Anthropology of Infrastructure and Expertise*. Ithaca, NY: Cornell University Press.

Hatherley, Owen. 2015. *Landscapes of Communism: A History through Buildings*. New York: Penguin.

Hatzky, Christine. 2012. *Cubans in Angola: South-South Cooperation and Transfer of Knowledge, 1976–1991*. Madison: University of Wisconsin Press.

Hawkins, Gay. 2005. *The Ethics of Waste: How We Relate to Rubbish*. Lanham, MD: Rowman and Littlefield.

Hecht, Gabrielle, and Paul N. Edwards. 2010. "The Technopolitics of Cold War: Toward a Transregional Perspective." In *Essays on Twentieth-Century History*, edited by Michael Adas, 271–314. Philadelphia: Temple University Press.

Heidegger, Martin. 1993. "Building Dwelling Thinking." In *Basic Writings*, edited and translated by David Farrel Krell, 347–63. New York: HarperCollins.

Heins, Volker, and Andreas Langenohl. 2013. "A Fire That Doesn't Burn? The Allied Bombing of Germany and the Cultural Politics of Trauma." In *Narrating Trauma: On the Impact of Collective Suffering*, edited by Ron Eyerman, Jeffrey C. Alexander, and Elizabeth Butler Breese, 3–26. London: Paradigm Press.

Heise, David 1998. "Conditions for Empathic Solidarity." In *The Problems of Solidarity: Theories and Models*, edited by Patrick Doreian and Thomas J. Fararo, 199–211. Amsterdam: Gordon and Breach.

Herzfeld, Michael. 2015. "Anthropology and the Inchoate Intimacies of Power." *American Ethnologist* 42(1):18–32.

Hewitt, Kenneth. 1983. "Place Annihilation: Area Bombing and the Fate of Urban." *Annals of the Association of American Geographers* 73(2):257–84.

Heynowski, Walter, and Gerhard Scheumann, dirs. 1966. *400 c.c.* Studio H and S Berlin.

———. 1979. *Die fernen Freunde nah* [Faraway friends up close]. Studio H and S Berlin.

High, Holly, James R. Curran, and Gareth Robinson. 2014. "Electronic Records of the Air War over Southeast Asia: A Database Analysis." *Journal of Vietnamese Studies* 8(4):86–124.

Hirsch, Francine. 2005. *Empire of Nations: Ethnographic Knowledge and the Making of the Soviet Union*. Ithaca, NY: Cornell University Press.

Hirt, Sonia. 2013. "Whatever Happened to the (Post)Socialist City?" *Cities* 32(S1):S29–S38.

Ho, Cheuk-Yuet. 2015. *Neo-Socialist Property Rights: The Predicament of Housing Ownership in China*. New York: Lexington Books.

Hoan, Buu. 1991. "Soviet Economic Aid to Vietnam." *Contemporary Southeast Asia* 12(4):360–76.

Hoang Thi Lich. 1999. "Women's Access to Housing in Hanoi." In *Women's Rights to House and Land: China, Laos, Vietnam*, edited by Irene Tinker and Gale Summerfield, 77–93. Boulder, CO: Lynne Reinner.

Hoffman, Danny. 2017. *Monrovia Modern: Urban Form and Political Imagination in Liberia*. Durham, NC: Duke University Press.

Hội hữu nghị Việt–Đức tỉnh Nghệ An. 2011. *Những dấu ấn lịch sử về tình hữu nghị Việt-Đức thời kỳ đầu xây dựng lại thành phố Vinh 1973–1980* [Historical impressions of Vietnamese-German friendship during reconstruction of Vinh City, 1973–1980]. Vinh: Nghệ An.

Holston, James. 1989. *The Modernist City: An Anthropological Critique of Brasilia*. Chicago: Chicago University Press.

———. 1991. "Autoconstruction in Working-Class Brazil." *Cultural Anthropology* 6(4):447–65.

Hong, Young-Sun. 2015. *Cold War Germany, the Third World, and the Global Humanitarian Regime*. Cambridge: Cambridge University Press.

Horten, Gerd. 2013. "Sailing in the Shadow of the Vietnam War: The GDR Government and the 'Vietnam Bonus' of the Early 1970s." *German Studies Review* 36(3):557–78.

Hosek, Jennifer Ruth. 2011. *Sun, Sex and Socialism: Cuba in the German Imaginary*. Toronto: University of Toronto Press.

Howell, Jude. 1994. "The End of an Era: The Rise and Fall of G.D.R. Aid." *Journal of Modern African Studies* 32(2):305–28.

Hull, Matthew. 2011. "Communities of Place, Not Kind: American Technologies of Neighborhood in Postcolonial Delhi." *Comparative Studies in Society and History* 53(4):757–90.

———. 2012. "Documents and Bureaucracy." *Annual Review of Anthropology* 41:251–67.

Humphrey, Caroline. 1999. "Shamans in the City." *Anthropology Today* 15(3):3–10.

———. 2005. "Ideology in Infrastructure: Architecture in Soviet Imagination." *Journal of the Royal Anthropological Institute* 11(1):39–58.

Huntington, Samuel P. 1968. "The Bases of Accommodation." *Foreign Affairs* 46(4):642–56.

Huyssen, Andreas. 2003a. "Air War Legacies: From Dresden to Baghdad." *New German Critique* 90:163–76.

———. 2003b. *Present Pasts: Urban Palimpsests and the Politics of Memory*. Stanford, CA: Stanford University Press.

Igarashi, Yoshikuni. 2000. *Bodies of Memory: Narratives of War in Postwar Japanese Culture, 1945–1970*. Princeton, NJ: Princeton University Press.

Ingold, Tim. 2013. *Making: Anthropology, Archaeology, Art and Architecture*. New York: Routledge.

Iveson, Kurt. 2013. "Cities within the City: Do-It-Yourself Urbanism and the Right to the City." *International Journal of Urban and Regional Research* 37(3):941–56.

Jackson, Steven J. 2014. "Rethinking Repair." In *Media Technologies: Essays on Communication, Materiality, and Society*, edited by Tarleton Gillespie, Pablo Boczkowski, and Kirsten Foot, 221–39. Cambridge, MA: MIT Press.

Jacobs, Jane. 1961. *The Death and Life of Great American Cities*. New York: Vintage.

Jansen, Stef. 2015. *Yearnings in the Meantime: 'Normal Lives' and the State in a Sarajevo Apartment Complex*. New York: Berghahn Books.

Jerve, Alf Morten. 1999. *A Leap of Faith: A Story of Swedish Aid and Paper Production in Vietnam: The Bai Bang Project, 1969–1996*. Stockholm: Swedish International Development Cooperation Agency (SIDA).

Jones, Carla. 2010. "Materializing Piety: Gendered Anxieties about Faithful Consumption in Contemporary Urban Indonesia." *American Ethnologist* 37(4):617–37.

Joppke, Christian. 1995. *East German Dissidents and the Revolution of 1989: Social Movement in a Leninist Regime*. London: Macmillan.

Kaiser, Tim. 2016. "Transnational Impact on Urban Change: Modern Projects in Vinh, Vietnam." PhD diss., University of Passau. Rev. ed.

Kaminsky, Lauren. 2011. "Utopian Visions of Family Life in the Stalin-Era Soviet Union." *Central European History* 44(1):63–91.

Kaplan, Caren. 2018. *Aerial Aftermaths: Wartime from Above*. Durham, NC: Duke University Press.

Karvonen, Andrew, and Bas Van Heur. 2014. "Urban Laboratories: Experiments in Reworking Cities." *International Journal of Urban and Regional Research* 38(2):379–92.

Kelly, Elaine. 2010. "Imagining Richard Wagner: The Janus Head of a Divided Nation." In *Imagining the West in Eastern Europe and the Soviet Union*, edited by György Péteri, 131–52. Pittsburgh, PA: University of Pittsburgh Press.

Khoo, Nicholas. 2011. *Collateral Damage: Sino-Soviet Rivalry and the Termination of the Sino-Vietnamese Alliance*. New York: Columbia University Press.

Kim, Annette. 2015. *Sidewalk City: Remapping Public Space in Ho Chi Minh City*. Chicago: Chicago University Press.

Kocher, Matthew Adam, Thomas B. Pepinsky, and Stathis N. Kalyvas. 2011. "Aerial Bombing and Counterinsurgency in the Vietnam War." *American Journal of Political Science* 55(2):1–18.

Koh, David W. H. 2004. "Illegal Construction in Hanoi and Hanoi's Wards." *European Journal of East Asian Studies* 3(2):337–70.

———. 2006. *Wards of Hanoi*. Singapore: ISEAS Publications.

Kotkin, Stephen. 1995. *Magnetic Mountain: Stalinism as a Civilization*. Berkeley: University of California Press.

Kroiber, Andrew. 2017. "Coffee, East Germans, and the Cold War, 1945–1990." PhD diss., McMaster University.

Krüger, Joachim. 1991. "Die Anfänge der Beziehungen zwischen der DDR und der DR Vietnam" [The beginnings of the relationship between the GDR and the DR Vietnam]. *Asien, Afrika, Lateinamerika* 19(5):815–26.

Kulić, Vladimir. 2018. "Orientalizing Socialism: Architecture, Media, and the Representations of Eastern Europe." *Architectural Histories* 6(1). doi: http://doi.org/10.5334/ah.273.

Kumar, Prakash. 2012. *Indigo Plantations and Science in Colonial India*. Cambridge: Cambridge University Press.

Kunze, Thomas, and Thomas Vogel, eds. 2010. *Ostalgie international: Erinnerungen an die DDR von Nicaragua bis Vietnam* [Ostalgie international: Memories of the GDR from Nicaragua to Vietnam]. Berlin: Christoph Links Verlag.

Kusno, Abidin. 2000. *Beyond the Postcolonial: Architecture, Urban Space and Political Cultures in Indonesia*. New York: Routledge.

———. 2011. "The Green Governmentality in an Indonesian Metropolis." *Singapore Journal of Tropical Geography* 32(3):314–31.

Kwak, Nancy H. 2015. *A World of Homeowners: American Power and the Politics of Housing Aid*. Chicago: University of Chicago Press.

Kwiatkowski, Lynn. 2011. "Domestic Violence and the 'Happy Family' in Northern Vietnam." *Anthropology Now* 3(3):20–28.

Labbé, Danielle. 2014. *Land Politics and Livelihoods on the Margins of Hanoi, 1920–2010*. Vancouver: University of British Columbia Press.

Lampland, Martha. 2009. "Classifying Laborers: Instinct, Property, and the Psychology of Productivity in Hungary (1920–1956)." In *Standards and Their Stories: How Quantifying, Classifying, and Formalizing Practices Shape Everyday Life*, edited by Martha Lampland and Susan Leigh Star, 123–42. Ithaca, NY: Cornell University Press.

Laszczkowski, Mateusz. 2015a. "'Demo Version of a City': Buildings, Affects, and the State in Astana." *Journal of the Royal Anthropological Institute* 22(1):148–65.

———. 2015b. "Scraps, Neighbors, and Committees: Material Things, Place-Making, and the State in an Astana Apartment Block." *City and Society* 27(2):136–59.

Latour, Bruno. 2005. *Reassembling the Social: An Introduction to Actor-Network Theory*. New York: Oxford University Press.

Latour, Bruno, and Steve Woolgar. 1979. *Laboratory Life: The Construction of Scientific Facts*. New York: Sage.

Lê Duẩn. 1977a. *Báo cáo chính trị của ban chấp hành Trung ương Đảng tại đại hội đại biểu toàn quốc lần thứ IV* [Political report on the Fourth National Congress of the Central Party Committee]. Hanoi: Sự thật.

———. 1977b. *Nghị quyết đại hội đại biểu toàn quốc lần thứ IV* [Resolutions of the Fourth National Congress]. Hanoi: Sự thật.

Lê Minh Khuê. 1997. *The Stars, the Earth, the River: Short Fiction by Le Minh Khue*. Edited by Wayne Karlin, translated by Bac Hoai Tran and Dana Sachs. Willimantic, CT: Curbstone.

Lê Thanh Nghị. 1977. *Tư tưởng chỉ đạo: Kế hoạch 5 năm, 1976–1980* [Guiding ideology: Five-year plan, 1976–1980]. Hanoi: Sự thật.

Le Thi Hong Phuong, G. Robbert Biesbroek, and Arjen E. J. Wals. 2018. "Barriers and Enablers to Climate Change Adaptation in Hierarchical Governance Systems: The Case of Vietnam." *Journal of Environmental Policy and Planning*. doi: 10.1080/1523908X.2018.1447366.

Lea, Tess, and Paul Pholeros. 2010. "This Is Not a Pipe: The Treacheries of Indigenous Housing." *Public Culture* 22(1):187–209.

Lebow, Katherine. 2013. *Unfinished Utopia: Nowa Huta, Stalinism, and Polish Society, 1949–1956*. Ithaca, NY: Cornell University Press.

Lefebvre, Henri. 1961. "Utopie Expérimentale: Pour un Nouvel Urbanisme" [Experimental utopias: Toward a new urbanism]. *Revue Française Sociologie* 2(3):191–98.

———. 1991. *The Production of Space*. Translated by Donald Nicholson-Smith. Oxford: Blackwell.

Leheny, David. 2018. *Empire of Hope: The Sentimental Politics of Japanese Decline*. Ithaca, NY: Cornell University Press.

Leshkowich, Ann Marie. 2005. "Feminine Disorder: State Campaigns against Street Traders in Socialist and Late Socialist Viet Nam." In *Le Việt Nam au Féminin* [Việt Nam: Women's Realities], edited by Gisele Bousquet and Nora Taylor, 187–207. Paris: Les Indes Savantes.

———. 2011. "Making Class and Gender: (Market) Socialist Enframing of Traders in Ho Chi Minh City." *American Anthropologist* 113(2):277–90.

———. 2014. *Essential Trade: Vietnamese Women in a Changing Marketplace*. Honolulu: University of Hawai'i Press.

Levien, Michael. 2011. "Special Economic Zones and Accumulation by Dispossession in India." *Journal of Agrarian Change* 11(4):454–83.

Li Tana. 1998. *Nguyễn Cochinchina: Southern Vietnam in the Seventeenth and Eighteenth Centuries*. Ithaca, NY: Southeast Asian Publications (Cornell University Press).

Li, Xiaobing. 2010. *Voices from the Vietnam War: Stories from American, Asian and Russian Veterans*. Lexington: University of Kentucky Press.

Linfield, Susie. 2010. *The Cruel Radiance: Photography and Political Violence*. Chicago: University of Chicago Press.

Lipsky, Michael. 1980. *Street-Level Bureaucracy: Dilemmas of the Individual in Public Service*. New York: Russell Sage.

Litzinger, Ralph A. 2000. *Other Chinas: The Yao and the Politics of National Belonging*. Durham, NC: Duke University Press.

Löfgren, Orvar. 1984. "The Sweetness of Home: Class, Culture and Family Life in Sweden." *Ethnologia Europaea* 14(1):44–64.

Logan, William S. 1995. "Russians on the Red River: The Soviet Impact on Hanoi's Townscape, 1955–90." *Europe Asia Studies* 47(3):443–68.

———. 2000. *Hanoi: Biography of a City*. Seattle: University of Washington Press.

Lombard, Melanie. 2014. "Constructing Ordinary Places: Place-Making in Urban Informal Settlements in Mexico." *Progress in Planning* 94:1–53.

Lương Bá Quảng. n.d. "Thành phố Vinh: Xu hướng tổ chức và mở rộng không gian qua các thời kì" [Vinh City: Trends in the organization and expansion of space across time]. Unpublished manuscript, Institute of Design, Architecture and Construction, Nghệ An.

MacLean, Ken. 2013. *The Government of Mistrust: Illegibility and Bureaucratic Power in Socialist Vietnam*. Madison: University of Wisconsin Press.

Mains, Daniel. 2019. *Under Construction: Technologies of Development in Urban Ethiopia*. Durham, NC: Duke University Press.

Malarney, Shaun Kingsley. 1997. "Culture, Virtue, and Political Transformation in Contemporary Northern Viet Nam." *Journal of Asian Studies* 56(4):899–920.

Malkki, Liisa H. 1996. "Speechless Emissaries: Refugees, Humanitarianism, and Dehistoricization." *Cultural Anthropology* 11(3):377–404.

———. 2001. "Figures of the Future: Dystopia and Subjectivity in the Social Imagination of the Future." In *History in Person*, edited by Dorothy Holland and Jean Lave, 325–48. Santa Fe, NM: School of American Research Press.

———. 2010. "Children, Humanity, and the Infantilization of Peace." In *In the Name of Humanity: The Government of Threat and Care*, edited by Ilana Feldman and Miriam Ticktin, 58–85. Durham, NC: Duke University Press.

———. 2015. *The Need to Help: The Domestic Arts of International Humanitarianism*. Durham, NC: Duke University Press.

Mark, James, and Péter Apor. 2015. "Socialism Goes Global: Decolonization and the Making of a New Culture of Internationalism in Socialist Hungary, 1956–1989." *The Journal of Modern History* 87(4):852–91.

Mark, James, Péter Apor, Radina Vučetić, and Piotr Osęka. 2015. "'We Are with You, Vietnam': Transnational Solidarities in Socialist Hungary, Poland and Yugoslavia." *Journal of Contemporary History* 50(3):439–64.

Massey, Doreen. 1994. *Space, Place, and Gender*. Minneapolis: University of Minnesota Press.

Massumi, Brian, ed. 2015. *Politics of Affect*. Boston: Polity.

Mauss, Marcel. (1925) 2000. *The Gift: The Form and Reason for Exchange in Archaic Societies*. New York: W. W. Norton.

May, Ruth. 2003. "Planned City Stalinstadt: A Manifesto of the Early German Democratic Republic." *Planning Perspectives* 18(1):47–78.

McCoy, Alfred. 2012. "Foreword: Reflections on History's Largest Air War." In *Voices from the Plain of Jars: Life under an Air War*, edited by Fred Branfman, ix–xvi. Madison: University of Wisconsin Press.

McFarlane, Colin. 2011. "The City as Assemblage: Dwelling and Urban Space." *Environment and Planning D: Society and Space* 29(4):649–71.

McGee, Terry G. 2009. "Interrogating the Production of Urban Space in China and Vietnam under Market Socialism." *Asia Pacific Viewpoint* 50(2):228–46.

McGovern, Mike. 2017. *A Socialist Peace? Explaining the Absence of War in an African Country*. Chicago: University of Chicago Press.

McKittrick, Katherine. 2011. "On Plantations, Prisons, and a Black Sense of Place." *Social and Cultural Geography* 12(8):947–63.

Meeker, Lauren. 2013. *Sounding Out Heritage: Cultural Politics and the Social Practice of Quan Họ Folk Song in Northern Vietnam*. Honolulu: University of Hawai'i Press.

Miller, Daniel, ed. 2005. *Materiality*. Durham, NC: Duke University Press.

Miraftab, Faranak. 2009. "Insurgent Planning: Situating Radical Planning in the Global South." *Planning Theory* 8(1):32–50.

Mitchell, Timothy. 2002. *Rule of Experts: Egypt, Techno-Politics, Modernity*. Berkeley: University of California Press.

Moeller, Susan D. 1999. *Compassion Fatigue: How the Media Sell Disease, Famine, War and Death*. New York: Routledge.

Molnár, Virág. 2005. "Cultural Politics and Modernist Architecture: The Tulip Debate in Postwar Hungary." *American Sociological Review* 70(1):111–35.

———. 2010. "In Search of the Ideal Socialist Home in Post-Stalinist Hungary: Prefabricated Mass Housing or Do-It-Yourself Family Home?" *Journal of Design History* 23(1):61–81.

Morrison, Susan S. 2015. *The Literature of Waste: Material Ecopoetics and Ethical Matter*. New York: Palgrave.

Morton, Henry W. 1980. "Who Gets What, When and How? Housing in the Soviet Union." *Soviet Studies* 32(2):235–59.

Morton, Patricia A. 2006. "The Afterlife of Buildings: Architecture and Walter Benjamin's Theory of History." In *Rethinking Architectural Historiography*, edited by Dana Arnold, Elvan Altan Ergut, and Belgin Turan Özkaya, 215–28. New York: Routledge.

Mrázek, Rudolf. 2002. *Engineers of Happy Land: Technology and Nationalism in a Colony*. Princeton, NJ: Princeton University Press.

Mudry, Anna. 2017. *Vietnam: Gesichter und Schicksale* [Vietnam: Faces and fates]. Berlin: Pirmoni Press.

Muehlebach, Andrea. 2017. "The Body of Solidarity: Heritage, Memory, and Materiality in Post-Industrial Italy." *Comparative Studies in Society and History* 59(1):96–126.

Mumford, Eric. 2009. "CIAM and the Communist Bloc, 1928–59." *Journal of Architecture* 14(2):237–54.

Navaro-Yashin, Yael. 2007. "Make-Believe Papers, Legal Forms and the Counterfeit: Affective Interactions between Documents and People in Britain and Cyprus." *Anthropological Theory* 7(1):79–98.

———. 2009. "Affective Spaces, Melancholic Objects: Ruination and the Production of Anthropological Knowledge." *Journal of the Royal Anthropological Institute* 15(1):1–18.

Nelson, Diane M. 2015. *Who Counts: The Mathematics of Death and Life after Genocide*. Durham, NC: Duke University Press.

Ngô Huy Quỳnh. 2000. *Tìm hiểu lịch sử kiến trúc Việt Nam* [Understanding the history of Vietnamese architecture]. Hanoi: Xây dựng.

Ngô Văn Yêm. 2016. "Nhân triển lãm 'Thay hình đổi mặt' về các khu nhà tập thể ở Hà Nội: Suy nghĩ về khu nhà ở Quang Trung, Vinh" [Concerning the exhibit on Hanoi's collective housing, "Changing Façades": Thoughts about Quang Trung housing, Vinh]. *Kiến trúc quy hoạch* 12:8–11.

Nguyen, Cuong Viet, and Anh Tran. 2014. "Poverty Identification: Practice and Policy Implications in Vietnam." *Asian-Pacific Economic Literature* 28(1):116–36.

Nguyen Huu Dung. 1991. "Housing Development in Vietnam: The Role and Responsibility of the Architects." In *Planning and Building in the Tropics, Report*

No. 4 Vietnam, 95:56–73. Weimar: Schriften der Hochschule für Architektur und Bauwesen.

Nguyen, Lien-Hang T. 2012. *Hanoi's War: An International History of the War for Peace in Vietnam*. Chapel Hill, NC: University of North Carolina Press.

Nguyen, Minh T. N. 2016. "Trading in Broken Things: Gendered Performances and Spatial Practices in a Northern Vietnamese Rural-Urban Waste Economy." *American Ethnologist* 43(1):116–29.

Nguyễn Ngọc Ngoạn. 1966. "Ở nơi sơ tán chúng tôi nên làm gì thêm?" [What else should we do at evacuation sites?]. *Kiến trúc* 3–4:1–3.

Nguyễn Quang Hồng. 2005. *Lịch sử Mặt trận Tổ quốc Việt Nam thành phố Vinh, 1930–2005* [History of the Vietnamese fatherland front in Vinh City, 1930–2005]. Vinh: Nghệ An.

———. 2008. *Kinh tế Nghệ An từ năm 1885 đến năm 1945* [The economy of Nghệ An from 1885 to 1945]. Vinh: Lý luận Quốc gia.

Nguyen Quang Tuyen. 2010. "Land Law and Reforms in Vietnam: Past and Present." Asian Law Institute Working Paper, No. 015. Accessed Sept 25, 2018. www.law.nus.sg/asli/pub/wps. htm.

Nguyen Tuan Anh, Jonathan Rigg, Luong Thi Thu Huong, and Dinh Thi Dieu. 2012. "Becoming and Being Urban in Hanoi: Rural-Urban Migration and Relations in Viet Nam." *Journal of Peasant Studies* 39(5):1103–31.

Nguyen Van Phu, Phan Si Chau, Nguyen Son Thach, and Ngo Quang Trong. 1974. "Beiträge zur generellen und speziellen städtebaulichen Planung für den Wiederaufbau der Stadt Vinh in der SRV" [Contributions to general and specific urban planning for the reconstruction of Vinh City in the SRV]. Diploma thesis, Dresden Technical University.

Ninh Viết Giao. 2003. *Về văn hóa xứ Nghệ, tập I* [On Nghệ culture, volume 1]. Vinh: Nghệ An.

———. 2006. *Xứ Nghệ và tôi* [My land of Nghệ]. Vinh: Nghệ An.

———. 2008. *Về văn hóa xứ Nghệ, tập II* [On Nghệ culture, volume 2]. Vinh: Nghệ An.

Nixon, Rob. 2011. *Slow Violence and the Environmentalism of the Poor*. Cambridge, MA: Harvard University Press.

Norindr, Panivong. 1996. *Phantasmatic Indochina: French Colonial Ideology in Architecture, Film, and Literature*. Durham, NC: Duke University Press.

Norlund, Irene. 1984. "The Role of Industry in Vietnam's Development Strategy." *Journal of Contemporary Asia* 14(1):94–107.

Nye, David E., and Sarah Elkin, eds. 2014. *The Anti-Landscape*. Leiden, Neth.: Brill.

Olsen, Mari. 2006. *Soviet-Vietnam Relations and the Role of China 1949–64: Changing Alliances*. New York: Routledge.

Osborne, Peter. 2011. *The Politics of Time: Modernity and Avant-Garde*. New York: Verso.

Parreñas, Juno Salazar. 2018. *Decolonizing Extinction: The Work of Care in Orangutan Rehabilitation*. Durham, NC: Duke University Press.

Pence, Katherine, and Paul Betts. 2008. "Introduction." In *Socialist Modern: East German Everyday Culture and Politics*, edited by Katherine Pence and Paul Betts, 1–34. Ann Arbor: University of Michigan Press.

Pfaff, Steven. 2001. "The Limits of Coercive Surveillance: Social and Penal Control in the German Democratic Republic." *Punishment and Society* 3(3):381–407.

Phạm Văn Đồng. 1977. *Phương hướng, nhiệm vụ và mục tiêu chủ yếu của kế hoạch 5 năm 1976–1980* [Directions, tasks, and key objectives of the five-year plan, 1976–1980]. Hanoi: Sự thật.

Phạm Xuân Cẩn. 2008. *Văn hóa đô thị với thực tiễn thành phố Vinh* [Urban cultural practice in Vinh City]. Vinh: Nghệ An.

Phạm Xuân Cẩn and Bùi Đình Sâm. 2003. *Lịch sử thành phố Vinh, 1945–1975, tập 2* [History of Vinh City, 1945–1975, volume 2]. Vinh: Nghệ An.

Phan Thành Xuân. 2005. *Nhà lao Vinh* [Vinh prison]. Vinh: Nghệ An.

Phinney, Harriet M. 2006. "Asking for a Child: The Refashioning of Reproductive Space in Post-War Northern Vietnam." *The Asia Pacific Journal of Anthropology* 6(3):215–30.

Pike, Douglas. 1987. *Vietnam and the Soviet Union: Anatomy of an Alliance*. Boulder, CO: Westview.

Pile, Steve. 2005. *Real Cities: Modernity, Space and the Phantasmagorias of City Life*. London: Sage.

Pinder, David. 2015. "Reconstituting the Possible: Lefebvre, Utopia and the Urban Question." *International Journal of Urban and Regional Research* 39(1):28–45.

Piot, Charles. 2014. "Entangled Histories." HAU: *Journal of Ethnographic Theory* 4(1):369–70.

Pozniak, Kinga. 2014. *Nowa Huta: Generations of Change in a Model Socialist Town*. Pittsburgh, PA: University of Pittsburgh Press.

Prakash, Gyan. 2010. "Introduction: Imaging the Modern City, Darkly." In *Noir Urbanisms: Dystopic Images of the Modern City*, edited by Gyan Prakash, 1–13. Princeton, NJ: Princeton University Press.

Pred, Allan, and Michael J. Watts. 1992. *Reworking Modernity: Capitalisms and Symbolic Discontent*. New Brunswick, NJ: Rutgers University Press.

Provoost, Michelle. 2010. "New Towns for the 21st Century: The Planned vs. the Unplanned City." In *New Towns for the 21st Century: The Planned vs. the Unplanned City*, edited by Michelle Provoost, 8–27. Rotterdam: International New Town Institute.

Puar, Jasbir K. 2017. *The Right to Maim: Debility, Capacity, Disability*. Durham, NC: Duke University Press.

Purcell, Mark. 2013. "Possible Worlds: Henri Lefebvre and the Right to the City." *Journal of Urban Affairs* 36(1):141–54.

Purtak, Udo. 1982. "Voraussetzungen und Entwicklung des Wohnungsbaus unter humiden tropischen Bedingungen dargestellt am Beispiel des Aufbaus der Stadt Vinh in der Sozialistischen Republik Vietnam" [Prerequisites and development of housing under humid, tropical conditions using the example of the construction of Vinh City in the Socialist Republic of Vietnam]. PhD diss., Technical University of Dresden.

Qualls, Karl D. 2009. *From Ruins to Reconstruction: Urban Identity in Soviet Sevastopol after World War II*. Ithaca, NY: Cornell University Press.

Rabinow, Paul. 1989. *French Modern: Norms and Forms of the Social Environment*. Cambridge, MA: MIT Press.

Raffin, Anne. 2008. "Postcolonial Vietnam: Hybrid Modernity." *Postcolonial Studies* 11(3):329–44.

Rao, Ursula. 2013. "Tolerated Encroachment: Resettlement Policies and the Negotiation of the Licit/Illicit Divide in an Indian Metropolis." *Cultural Anthropology* 28(4):760–79.

Reid, Susan E. 2009. "Communist Comfort: Socialist Modernism and the Making of Cosy Homes in the Khrushchev Era." *Gender and History* 21(3):465–98.

Reinhardt, Mark, Holly Edwards, and Erina Duganne. 2007. *Beautiful Suffering: Photography and the Traffic in Pain*. Chicago: Chicago University Press.

Ringel, Felix. 2018. *Back to the Postindustrial Future: An Ethnography of Germany's Fastest-Shrinking City*. New York: Berghahn Books.

Robinson, Jennifer. 2006. *Ordinary Cities: Between Modernity and Development*. London: Routledge.

Rose, Jacqueline. 1996. *States of Fantasy*. Oxford: Oxford University Press.

Rose, Nikolas. 1999. *Power of Freedom: Reframing Political Thought*. Cambridge: Cambridge University Press.

Roskam, Cole. 2015. "Practicing Reform: Experiments in Post-Revolutionary Chinese Architectural Production, 1973–1989." *Journal of Architectural Education* 69(1):28–39.

Roy, Ananya. 2005. "Urban Informality: Toward an Epistemology of Planning." *Journal of the American Planning Association* 71(2):147–58.

———. 2011. "Slumdog Cities: Rethinking Subaltern Urbanism." *International Journal of Urban and Regional Research* 35(2):223–38.

Roy, Ananya, and Aihwa Ong, eds. 2011. *Worlding Cities: Asian Experiments and the Art of Being Global*. Oxford: Wiley-Blackwell.

Rubin, Eli. 2016. *Amnesiopolis: Modernity, Space, and Memory in East Germany*. Oxford: Oxford University Press.

Rupprecht, Tobias. 2015. *Soviet Internationalism after Stalin: Interaction and Exchange between the USSR and Latin America during the Cold War*. Cambridge: Cambridge University Press.

Rutherford, Danilyn. 2009. "Sympathy, State Building, and the Experience of Empire." *Cultural Anthropology* 24(1):1–32.

Said, Edward. 1978. *Orientalism*. New York: Pantheon Books.

———. 1993. *Culture and Imperialism*. New York: Vintage Books.

Saint-Amour, Paul K. 2003. "Modernist Reconnaissance." *Modernism/Modernity* 10(2):349–80.

Satia, Priya. 2014. "Drones: A History from the British Middle East." *Humanity* 5(1):1–31.

Schaefer, Bernd. 2015. "Socialist Modernization in Vietnam: The East German Approach, 1976–1989." In *Comrades of Color: East Germany in the Cold War World*, edited by Quinn Slobodian, 95–113. New York: Berghahn Books.

Schenck, Marcia C. 2018. "Constructing and Deconstructing the 'Black East': A Helpful Research Agenda?" *Wiener Zeitschrift für kritische Afrikastudien* 34(18):135–52.

Schleicher, Ilona, ed. 2011. *Die DDR und Vietnam: Berichte, Erinnerungen, Fakten. Teil 1 und 2* [The GDR and Vietnam: Reports, memories, facts. Parts 1 and 2]. Berlin: Verband für Internationale Politk und Völkerrecht e.V.
Schmidt, Hans, Rolf Linke, and Gerd Wessel. 1969. *Gestaltung und Umgestaltung der Stadt: Beiträge zum sozialistischen Städtebau* [Designing and redesigning the city: Contributions to socialist urban planning]. Berlin: Verlag für Bauwesen.
Schönle, Andreas. 2006. "Ruins and History: Observations on Russian Approaches to Destruction and Decay." *Slavic Review* 65(4):649–69.
Schumpeter, Joseph. 1942. *Capitalism, Socialism, and Democracy*. New York: Harper and Brothers.
Schwartz, Hillel. 2011. *Making Noise: From Babel to the Big Bang and Beyond*. Cambridge, MA: MIT Press.

Schwenkel, Christina. 2006. "Recombinant History: Transnational Practices of Memory and Knowledge Production in Contemporary Vietnam." *Cultural Anthropology* 21(1):3–30.
———. 2009a. *The American War in Contemporary Vietnam: Transnational Remembrance and Representation*. Bloomington: Indiana University Press.
———. 2009b. "'The Camera Was My Weapon': News Production and Representation of War in Vietnam." In *The Anthropology of News and Journalism: Global Perspectives*, edited by S. Elizabeth Bird, 86–99. Bloomington: Indiana University Press.
———. 2012. "Civilizing the City: Socialist Ruins and Urban Renewal in Central Vietnam." *positions: asia critique* 20(2):437–70.
———. 2013. "Post/Socialist Affect: Ruination and Reconstruction of the Nation in Urban Vietnam." *Cultural Anthropology* 28(2):252–77.
———. 2014a. "Imaging Humanity: Socialist Film and Transnational Memories of the War in Vietnam." In *Transnational Memory: Circulation, Articulation, Scales*, edited by Chiara De Cesari and Ann Rigney, 219–44. Berlin: De Gruyter Press.
———. 2014b. "Rethinking Asian Mobilities: Socialist Migration and Postsocialist Repatriation of Vietnamese Contract Workers in East Germany." *Critical Asian Studies* 46(2):235–58.
———. 2015a. "Affective Solidarities and East German Reconstruction of Vietnam." In *Comrades of Color: East Germany in the Cold War World*, edited by Quinn Slobodian, 267–92. New York: Berghahn Books.
———. 2015b. "The Other Veterans: Socialist Humanitarians Return to Vietnam." *History and Memory* 27(2):20–44.
———. 2015c. "Reclaiming Rights to the Socialist City: Bureaucratic Artefacts and the Affective Appeal of Petitions." *South East Asia Research* 23(2):205–25.
———. 2015d. "Socialist Mobilities: Crossing New Terrains in Vietnamese Migration Histories." *Central and Eastern European Migration Review* 4(1):13–25.
———. 2015e. "Socialist Palimpsests in Urban Vietnam." ABE *Journal: Architecture Beyond Europe* 6(2014):1–19.
———. 2015f. "Spectacular Infrastructure and Its Breakdown in Socialist Vietnam." *American Ethnologist* 42(3):520–34.

———. 2017a. "Eco-Socialism and Green City Making in Postwar Vietnam." In *Places of Nature in Ecologies of Urbanism*, edited by Anne M. Rademacher and K. Sivaramakrishnan, 45–66. Hong Kong: Hong Kong University Press.

———. 2017b. "Haunted Infrastructure: Religious Ruins and Urban Obstruction in Vietnam." *City and Society* 29(3):413–34.

———. 2017c. "War Tourism and Geographies of Memory in Vietnam." In *Monumental Conflicts? Twentieth Century Wars and the Evolution of Popular Memory*, edited by Derek Mallett, 130–45. New York: Routledge.

———. 2018. "The Current Never Stops: Intimacies of Energy Infrastructure in Vietnam." In *The Promise of Infrastructure*, edited by Nikhil Anand, Akhil Gupta, and Hannah Appel, 102–29. Durham, NC: Duke University Press.

Schwenkel, Christina, and Ann Marie Leshkowich. 2012. "How Is Neoliberalism Good to Think Vietnam? How Is Vietnam Good to Think Neoliberalism?" *positions: asia critique* 20(2):379–401.

Scott, James. 1998. *Seeing Like the State: How Certain Schemes to Improve the Human Condition Have Failed*. New Haven, CT: Yale University Press.

Sebald, W. G. 1999. *On the Natural History of Destruction*. Translated by Anthea Bell. New York: Modern Library.

Seremetakis, C. Nadia, ed. 1996. *Senses Still: Perception and Memory as Material Culture in Modernity*. Chicago: University of Chicago Press.

Shanks, Torrey. 2015. "Affect, Critique, and the Social Contract." *Theory and Event* 18(1). Accessed August 13, 2018. https://muse.jhu.edu/article/566087.

Shannon, Kelly, and André Loeckx. 2004. "Vinh: Rising from the Ashes." In *Urban Trialogues: Visions_Projects,_Co-Productions, Localizing Agenda 21*, edited by André Loeckx, Kelly Shannon, Rafael Tuts, and Han Verschure, 122–55. Leuven, Belg.: UN-Habitat.

Shermer, Michael, and Alex Grobman. 2009. *Denying History: Who Says the Holocaust Never Happened and Why Do They Say It?* 2nd ed. Berkeley: University of California Press.

Sherry, Michael S. 1987. *The Rise of American Air Power: The Creation of Armageddon*. New Haven, CT: Yale University Press.

Shohet, Merav. 2018. "Two Deaths and a Funeral: Ritual Inscriptions' Affordances for Mourning and Moral Personhood in Vietnam." *American Ethnologist* 45(1):60–73.

Siegelbaum, Lewis H. 1998. "'Dear Comrade, You Ask What We Need': Socialist Paternalism and Soviet Rural 'Notables' in the Mid-1930s." *Slavic Review* 57(1):107–32.

Simmel, Georg. (1903) 1950. "The Metropolis and Mental Life." In *The Sociology of Georg Simmel*, edited and translated by Kurt H. Wolff, 409–24. New York: Free Press.

———. (1911) 1965. "The Ruin." In *Essays on Sociology, Philosophy and Aesthetics*, edited by Kurt H. Wolff, translated by David Kettler, 259–66. New York: Harper and Row.

———. (1907) 1997. "Sociology of the Senses." In *Simmel on Culture*, edited by David Frisby and Mike Featherstone, 109–20. London: Sage.

———. (1907) 2004. *The Philosophy of Money*. Translated by Tom Bottomore and David Frisby. New York: Routledge.

Simone, AbdouMaliq. 2004. *For the City Yet to Come: Changing African Life in Four Cities*. Durham, NC: Duke University Press.

———. 2010. *City Life from Jakarta to Dakar: Movements at the Crossroads*. New York: Routledge.

Simone, AbdouMaliq, and Achmad Uzair Fauzan. 2012. "Making Security Work for the Majority: Reflections on Two Districts in Jakarta." *City and Society* 24(2):129–49.

Slessor, Catherine. 2017. "Reading the Ruins." *Architectural Review*. Accessed December 22, 2017. www.architectural-review.com/essays/reading-the-ruins/10026503.

Slobodian, Quinn. 2015a. "Socialist Chromatism: Race, Racism and the Racial Rainbow in East Germany." In *Comrades of Color: East Germany in the Cold War World*, edited by Quinn Slobodian, 23–39. New York: Berghahn Books.

———, ed. 2015b. *Comrades of Color: East Germany in the Cold War World*. New York: Berghahn Books.

Sloterdijk, Peter. 2009. *Terror from the Air*. Translated by Amy Patton and Steve Corcoran. Los Angeles: Semiotext(e).

Smith, David M. 1996. "The Socialist City." In *Cities after Socialism: Urban and Regional Change and Conflict in Post-Socialist Societies*, edited by Gregory Andrusz, Michael Harloe, and Ivan Szelenyi, 70–99. New York: Blackwell.

Smith, David W., and Joseph L. Scarpaci. 2000. "Urbanization in Transitional Societies: An Overview of Vietnam and Hanoi." *Urban Geography* 21(8):745–57.

Smith, Michael Peter. 2000. *Transnational Urbanism: Locating Globalization*. Boston: Blackwell.

Smith, Neil. 1996. *The New Urban Frontier: Gentrification and the Revanchist City*. New York: Routledge.

Sontag, Susan. 2003. *Regarding the Pain of Others*. New York: Farrar, Straus and Giroux.

Ssorin-Chaikov, Nikolai. 2006. "On Heterochrony: Birthday Gifts to Stalin, 1949." *Journal of the Royal Anthropological Institute* 12(2):355–75.

Stanek, Łukasz. 2012. "Introduction: The 'Second World's' Architecture and Planning in the 'Third World.'" *The Journal of Architecture* 17(3):299–307.

Star, Susan Leigh. 1999. "The Ethnography of Infrastructure." *American Behavioral Scientist* 43(3):377–91.

Star, Susan Leigh, and Martha Lampland. 2009. "Reckoning with Standards." In *Standards and Their Stories: How Quantifying, Classifying, and Formalizing Practices Shape Everyday Life*, edited by Martha Lampland and Susan Leigh Star, 3–24. Ithaca, NY: Cornell University Press.

Starostina, Natalia. 2009. "Engineering the Empire of Images: Constructing Railways in Asia before the Great War." *Southeast Review of Asian Studies* 31:181–206.

Stavrides, Stavros. 2007. "Heterotopias and the Experience of Porous Urban Space." In *Loose Space: Possibility and Diversity in Urban Life*, edited by Karen A. Franck and Quentin Stevens, 174–92. New York: Routledge.

Stoler, Ann Laura. 2004. "Affective States." In *A Companion to the Anthropology of Politics*, edited by David Nugent and Joan Vincent, 4–20. New York: Blackwell.

——. 2016. *Duress: Imperial Durabilities in Our Times*. Durham, NC: Duke University Press.

Storm, Servaas. 2018. "Financialization and Economic Development: A Debate on the Social Efficiency of Modern Finance." *Development and Change* 49(1):302–29.

Strassler, Karen. 2010. *Refracted Visions: Popular Photography and National Modernity in Java*. Durham, NC: Duke University Press.

Szelenyi, Ivan. 1983. *Urban Inequalities under Socialism*. Oxford: Oxford University Press.

Tambiah, Stanley Jeyaraja. 1984. *The Buddhist Saints of the Forest and the Cult of Amulets*. Cambridge: Cambridge University Press.

Thompson, E. P. 1967. "Time, Work-Discipline and Industrial Capitalism." *Past and Present* 38(1):56–97.

Thompson, W. Scott, and Donaldson D. Frizzell, eds. 1977. *The Lessons of Vietnam*. New York: Crane, Russak.

Thrift, Nigel. 2004. "Intensities of Feeling: Towards a Spatial Politics of Affect." *Geografiska Annaler: Series B, Human Geography* 86(1):57–78.

Thrift, Nigel, and Dean Forbes. 1986. *The Price of War: Urbanization in Vietnam, 1954–1985*. New York: Routledge.

Tilford, Earl H. Jr. 2009. *Crosswinds: The Air Force's Setup in Vietnam*. 2nd ed. College Station: Texas A&M University Press.

Tô Thị Minh Thông. 1985. "Chủ nghĩa Mác–Lênin về phát triển đô thị" [Marxism-Leninism on urban development]. *Kiến trúc* 2:53–5.

Todorov, Vladislav. 1995. *Red Square, Black Square: Organon for Revolutionary Imagination*. Albany: State University of New York Press.

Tonkiss, Fran. 2003. "The Ethics of Indifference: Community and Solitude in the City." *International Journal of Cultural Studies* 6(3):297–311.

——. 2013. "Austerity Urbanism and the Makeshift City." *City* 17(3):312–24.

Tran, Allen L. 2015. "Rich Sentiments and the Cultural Politics of Emotion in Postreform Ho Chi Minh City, Vietnam." *American Anthropologist* 117(3):480–92.

Tran, Hoai Anh, and Elisabeth Dalholm. 2005. "Favoured Owners, Neglected Tenants: Privatisation of State Owned Housing in Hanoi." *Housing Studies* 20(6):897–929.

Trinh Duy Luan and Nguyen Quang Vinh. 2001. *Socio-Economic Impacts of "Doi Moi" on Urban Housing in Vietnam*. Hanoi: Social Sciences Publishing House.

Trnka, Susanna, and Catherine Trundle. 2014. "Competing Responsibilities: Moving Beyond Neoliberal Responsibilisation." *Anthropological Forum* 24(2):136–53.

Truelove, Yaffa. 2011. "(Re-)Conceptualizing Water Inequality in Delhi, India through a Feminist Political Ecology Framework." *Geoforum* 42(2):143–52.

Truitt, Allison J. 2008. "On the Back of a Motorbike: Middle-Class Mobility in Ho Chi Minh City, Vietnam." *American Ethnologist* 36(1):3–19.

——. 2013. *Dreaming of Money in Ho Chi Minh City*. Seattle: University of Washington Press.

Trương Huy Chinh. 1985. "Phương pháp hiện thực trong quy hoạch thành phố Vinh" [Realist methods in the planning of Vinh City]. *Kiến trúc* 2:55–57.

Turley, William S. 1975. "Urbanization in War: Hanoi, 1946–1973." *Pacific Affairs* 48(3):370–97.

——. 1977. "Urban Transformation in South Vietnam." *Pacific Affairs* 49(4):607–24.

Turner, Karen Gottschang, with Phan Thanh Hao. 1998. *Even the Women Must Fight: Memories of War from North Vietnam*. New York: Wiley.

Turner, Sarah, and Laura Schoenberger. 2012. "Street Vendor Livelihoods and Everyday Politics in Hanoi, Vietnam: The Seeds of a Diverse Economy?" *Urban Studies* 49(5):1027–44.

Ulbrich, Peter, dir. 1965. *Denkt an Mein Land* [Remember my country]. DEFA-Studio für Dokumentarfilme (GDR).

——, dir. 1967. *Ihr Fragt, Wie Wir Leben* [You ask, how we live]. DEFA-Studio für Dokumentarfilme (GDR).

United States Senate, Committee on Armed Services. 1967. *Air War against North Vietnam: Hearings before the Preparedness Investigating Subcommittee*. 90th Cong., 1st Sess., Part 5, August 28 and 29. Washington, DC: U.S. Government Printing Office.

van der Hoorn, Mélanie. 2009. *Indispensible Eyesores: An Anthropology of Undesired Buildings*. New York: Berghahn.

Van Dyke, Jon M. 1970. "The Bombing of Vietnam." In *Ecocide in Indochina: The Ecology of War*, edited by Barry Weisberg, 207–21. San Francisco: Canfield Press.

Vann, Elizabeth F. 2012. "Afterword: Consumption and Middle-Class Subjectivity in Vietnam." In *The Reinvention of Distinction: Modernity and the Middle Class in Urban Vietnam*, edited by Van Nguyen-Marshall, Lisa B. Welch Drummond, and Danièle Bélanger, 157–70. New York: Springer.

Vann, Michael. 2003. "Of Rats, Rice and Race: The Great Hanoi Rat Massacre, an Episode in French Colonial History." *French Colonial History* 4(2003):191–204.

Vees-Gulani, Susanne. 2008. "The Politics of New Beginnings: The Continued Exclusion of the Nazi Past in Dresden's Cityscape." In *Beyond Berlin: Twelve German Cities Confront the Nazi Past*, edited by Gavriel D. Rosenfeld and Paul B. Jaskot, 25–47. Ann Arbor: University of Michigan Press.

Vellinga, Marcel. 2007. "Review Essay: Anthropology and the Materiality of Architecture." *American Ethnologist* 34(4):756–66.

Verbeek, Peter-Paul. 2005. *What Things Do: Philosophical Reflections on Technology, Agency, and Design*. Translated by Robert P. Crease. University Park: The Pennsylvania State University Press.

Verdery, Katherine. 1996. *What Was Socialism, and What Comes Next*? Princeton, NJ: Princeton University Press.

Vidler, Anthony. 2000. "Diagrams of Diagrams: Architectural Abstraction and Modern Representation." *Representations* 72:1–20.

Virilio, Paul. 1989. *War and Cinema: The Logistics of Perception*. Translated by Patrick Camiller. New York: Verso.

Võ Nguyên Giáp. 1975. *People's War against U.S. Aero-Naval War*. Hanoi: Foreign Languages Publishing House.

Vo Nhan Tri. 1990. *Vietnam's Economic Policy Since 1975*. Singapore: Institute of Southeast Asian Studies.

Volkov, Vadim. 1990. "The Concept of Kul'turnost: Notes on the Stalinist Civilizing Practice." In *Stalinism: New Directions*, edited by Sheila Fitzpatrick, 201–30. New York: Routledge.

von Schnitzler, Antina. 2016. *Democracy's Infrastructure: Techno-Politics and Protest after Apartheid*. Princeton, NJ: Princeton University Press.

Vonnegut, Kurt. 1969. *Slaughterhouse-Five: A Novel*. New York: Random House.

Vu, Tuong. 2005. "Workers and the Socialist State: North Vietnam's State-Labor Relations, 1945–1970." *Communist and Post-Communist Studies* 38(3):329–56.

———. 2008. "Dreams of Paradise: The Making of a Soviet Outpost in Vietnam." *Ab Imperio* 2:255–85.

Wacquant, Loïc. 2012."Three Steps to a Historical Anthropology of Actually Existing Neoliberalism." *Social Anthropology* 19(4):66–79.

Wajcman, Judy. 2014. *Pressed for Time: The Acceleration of Life in Digital Capitalism*. Chicago: Chicago University Press.

Wall, Tyler, and Torin Monahan. 2011. "Surveillance and Violence from Afar: The Politics of Drones and Liminal Security-Scapes." *Theoretical Criminology* 15(3):239–54.

Waterson, Roxana. 1990. *The Living House: An Anthropology of Architecture in South-East Asia*. Oxford: Oxford University Press.

Weber, Max. (1946) 1978. *Economy and Society*. Berkeley: University of California Press.

Weidauer, Walter. 1966. *Inferno Dresden: Über Lügen und Legenden um die Aktion "Donnerschlag"* [Inferno Dresden: On the lies and legends of Action "Thunderstorm"]. Berlin: Dietz Verlag.

Weinreb, Alice. 2017. *Modern Hungers: Food and Power in Twentieth-Century Germany*. New York: Oxford University Press.

Weis, Toni. 2011. "The Politics Machine: On the Concept of 'Solidarity' in East German Support for SWAPO." *Journal of Southern African Studies* 37(2):351–67.

Weizman, Eyal. 2017. *Forensic Architecture: Violence at the Threshold of Detectability*. New York: Zone Books.

Werner, Jayne. 2009. *Gender, Household and State in Post-Revolutionary Vietnam*. New York: Routledge.

Wernicke, Günter. 2001. "'Solidarität Hilft Siegen!' Zur Solidaritätsbewegung mit Vietnam in beiden deutschen Staaten Mitte der 60er bis Anfang der 70er Jahre" ["Solidarity supports victory!" On the solidarity movement with Vietnam in both German states in the middle '60s through the start of the '70s]. Berlin: Hefte zur DDR-Geschichte, Bk. 72.

———. 2003. "The World Peace Council and the Antiwar Movement in East Germany." In *America, the Vietnam War, and the World: Comparative and International Perspectives*, edited by Andreas W. Daum, Lloyd C. Gardner, and Wilfried Mausbach, 299–320. Cambridge: Cambridge University Press.

Wetherell, Margaret. 2012. *Affect and Emotion: A New Social Science Understanding*. London: Sage.

Wilke, Sabine. 2015. *German Culture and the Modern Environmental Imagination: Narrating and Depicting Nature*. Leiden, Neth.: Brill.

Williams, Brackette F. 1996. "Skinfolk, not Kinfolk: Comparative Reflections on the Identity of Participant-Observation in Two Field Situations." In *Feminist Dilemmas in Fieldwork*, edited by Diane L. Wolf, 72–95. New York: Routledge.

Williams, Raymond. 1975. *The Country and the City*. Oxford: Oxford University Press.

Williams, Rosalind. 2008. *Notes on the Underground: An Essay on Technology, Society, and the Imagination*. Boston: MIT Press.

Wimmelbücker, Ludger. 2012. "Architecture and City Planning Projects of the German Democratic Republic in Zanzibar." *Journal of Architecture* 17(3):407–32.

Wing Chung Ho. 2005. "Negotiating Subalternity in a Former Socialist 'Model Community' in Shanghai: From 'Model Proletarians' to 'Society People.'" *Asia Pacific Journal of Anthropology* 6(2):159–79.

Witkowski, Gregory R. 2015. "Between Fighters and Beggars: Socialist Philanthropy and the Imagery of Solidarity in East Germany." In *Comrades of Color: East Germany in the Cold War World*, edited by Quinn Slobodian, 73–94. New York: Berghahn Books.

Woodside, Alexander. 1970. "Decolonization and Agricultural Reform in Northern Vietnam." *Asian Survey* 10(8):705–23.

———. 1971. *Vietnam and the Chinese Model: A Comparative Study of Nguyen and Ch'ing Civil Government in the First Half of the Nineteenth Century*. Cambridge, MA: Harvard University Press.

Wright, Gwendolyn. 1991. *The Politics of Design in French Colonial Urbanism*. Chicago: University of Chicago Press.

Yan, Yunxiang. 2003. *Private Life under Socialism: Love, Intimacy, and Family Change in a Chinese Village 1949–1999*. Stanford, CA: Stanford University Press.

Yoo Sun-Young. 2001. "Embodiment of American Modernity in Colonial Korea." *Inter-Asia Cultural Studies* 2(3):423–41.

Yurchak, Alexei. 2006. *Everything Was Forever, until It Was No More: The Last Soviet Generation*. Princeton, NJ: Princeton University Press.

Zarecor, Kimberly Elman. 2011. *Manufacturing a Socialist Modernity: Housing in Czechoslovakia, 1945–1960*. Pittsburgh, PA: University of Pittsburgh Press.

———. 2018. "What Was So Socialist about the Socialist City? Second World Urbanity in Europe." *Journal of Urban History* 44(1):95–117.

Zatlin, Jonathan R. 2007. *The Currency of Socialism: Money and Political Culture in East Germany*. Cambridge: Cambridge University Press.

Zavisca, Jane. 2012. *Housing in the New Russia*. Ithaca, NY: Cornell University Press.

Zeiderman, Austin. 2016. *Endangered City: The Politics of Security and Risk in Bogotá*. Durham, NC: Duke University Press.

Zhai, Qiang. 2000. *China and the Vietnam Wars, 1950–1975*. Chapel Hill: University of North Carolina Press.

Zhang, Li. 2010. *In Search of Paradise: Middle-Class Living in a Chinese Metropolis*. Ithaca, NY: Cornell University Press.

INDEX

www.ingramcontent.com/pod-product-compliance
Lightning Source LLC
Chambersburg PA
CBHW050623280326
41932CB00015B/2502